KHALAF AHMAD AL HABTOOR

THE AUTOBIOGRAPHY

Published by Motivate Publishing

Dubai: PO Box 2331, Dubai, UAE
Tel: (+971 4) 282 4060, fax: (+971 4) 282 0428
e-mail: books@motivate.ae   www.booksarabia.com
Office 508, Building No 8, Dubai Media City, Dubai, UAE
Tel: (+971 4) 390 3550, fax: (+971 4) 390 4845

Abu Dhabi: PO Box 43072, Abu Dhabi, UAE
Tel: (+971 2) 677 2005, fax: (+971 2) 677 0124

London: Acre House, 11/15 William Road, London NW1 3ER
e-mail: motivateuk@motivate.ae

Directors:	Obaid Humaid Al Tayer
	Ian Fairservice
General Manager:	John Deykin
Senior Editor:	Simona Cassano
Editor:	Poonam M Ganglani
Editorial Assistant:	Aswathy Sathish
Art Director:	Anita Elena Manolache
Senior Designer:	Cithadel Francisco
Graphic Designer:	Noel de la Peña
Publishing Coordinator:	Zelda Pinto
Co-writer:	Linda S. Heard

© Khalaf Ahmad Al Habtoor 2012

The views expressed in this book are solely those of the author and do not necessarily reflect the views of the publisher.

British Library Cataloguing-in-Publication Data. A catalogue record for this book is available from the British Library.

ISBN: 978 1 86063 326 3

Printed by Emirates Printing Press, Dubai, UAE

KHALAF AHMAD AL HABTOOR

THE AUTOBIOGRAPHY

MOTIVATE
PUBLISHING

FOREWORD

It is my great pleasure to introduce this outstanding work illuminating the life and record of my distinguished brother and dear friend, Khalaf Al Habtoor. No doubt the growing prestige of the United Arab Emirates is enhanced by men of their word who are guided by their love for their homeland, their endeavour to improve it and their constant quest to contribute to its development and prosperity in general, without selfish motives or any shallow desire to keep up appearances.

Thus, I was delighted to write the foreword to the honest self-interpretation contained in this valuable book revealing the life's journey of Abu Rashid; a journey that is inextricably linked to that of the United Arab Emirates. It encapsulates what everyone close to my dear brother Khalaf Al Habtoor already knows.

Abu Rashid is one of the UAE's outstanding economic pioneers and a great example of a genuine patriot. Renowned for his business acumen, expertise and philanthropy, he has shown remarkable loyalty to the leaders and citizens of this country and is respected for his devotion to his work and his contributions to the growth of his homeland.

He is one of those distinguished citizens who make us proud for all their efforts, sacrifices, achievements and contributions. This valuable book proves that we are in the presence of a distinguished self-made man, who struggled and achieved his goals through hard work, fuelled by a patriotic spirit. Through his remarkable efforts, he has emerged not only as one of the UAE's economic leaders, but has also made an impact on our region and the world.

Aside from my admiration for Abu Rashid, there is a special reason why I am delighted to pen this foreword. I have a close and familiar relationship with Khalaf Al Habtoor and his family. His virtuous mother, Noura bint Ahmad (may she rest in peace) was the aunt of my late father Mubarak bin Muhammad Al Nahyan (may Allah be pleased with him). This strong familial tie that may not be known to everyone gives me great pride, as it has cemented my bond with Khalaf Al Habtoor; a relationship that since our first meeting many decades ago has never been broken. I have always considered Abu Rashid as a brother and a friend with whom I share my thoughts on many issues. I wanted through this brief note to renew my pledge to my brother and friend, Khalaf Al Habtoor, and most importantly to the strong kinship that has always brought us together under differing circumstances and conditions.

For almost half a century, Khalaf Al Habtoor's life has been one of continuous struggle to achieve his goals. It is a life full of experience in a wide array of areas, marked by successive achievements in the public domain and inspired by his concern for the UAE's national interests, which have always been his first priority. It is also a rich journey wherein he excels as a shrewd economist and businessman who is always in the first row among his counterparts. He enjoys a fine reputation not only in the UAE but also in the Gulf region and the world.

His experience and achievements that I closely followed are presented by the author in this important book, in a beautiful style that links the past with the present and explores the prospects for the future. It captures readers' attention by enriching their knowledge, but most importantly it is such a thoroughly enjoyable read that fatigue and boredom are temporarily banished.

Khalaf Al Habtoor is an open-minded man whose enlightenment began since early childhood. He opened his eyes and mind to everyone and everything around him, and soon understood that money is not everything. He learned early on that he needed to acquire expertise and knowledge and to show determination and persistence to achieve his ambitions.

Allow me, through this foreword, to express my deepest appreciation to my dear brother, whose friendship is a great source of joy for me. I would also like to note his distinguished intellectual and creative capabilities, as well as his sharp vision for the future and his ability to turn it into a concrete reality. As I said, Khalaf Al Habtoor stands in the first row of economists and businessmen, and is among those Emiratis who make us proud because they devotedly work for the development of their homeland in all areas.

Furthermore, Khalaf Al Habtoor's achievements are not only restricted to the economic sector. He has also made his mark through important achievements in education, the public domain and in the service of our society and homeland. We are very proud of the schools he established to nurture young minds with first-class education. We also express our gratitude and appreciation for his support and donations to universities and colleges. I would like to personally express my deepest respect to the obvious capabilities he shows as a member of the board of Zayed University, and his generous funding of a chair of professorship there, as well as the overwhelming success of his company in building the new campus of Abu Dhabi University, recognised today as a model for universities everywhere.

We Emiratis also remember with profound respect the great and effective role of Khalaf Al Habtoor as a former member of the Federal National Council, and of the Dubai Chamber of Commerce and Industry; and we appreciate his ongoing role as a member of the Council of Economic Affairs in Dubai. I would also like to highlight the awards and certificates of appreciation he has received from various countries, honouring his achievements and contributions in many domains.

I could elaborate more on this distinguished figure, but I must point out an important truth: I do not consider that there is any difference between a book and its author, the book being the story of a life journey and of a struggle worthy of praise and commendation. In this regard, I would like to share some of his ideas that deserve to be showcased as a rich and vibrant source of inspiration for our young generation. According to the author:

- *Thanks to the wise and forward-thinking leadership of our founding fathers, the late Sheikh Zayed and the late Sheikh Rashid (may Allah be pleased with them), we had the opportunity to establish a country of distinction that would merit the international community's respect and admiration. This was achieved, and thankfully, we now have a highly regarded state.*
- *One must respect himself first so that others would respect him.*
- *Men are an open book that teaches us about life.*
- *My father and I were two people in one body: we went together to the desert, we hunted, prayed and had fun – these moments are the most beautiful memories.*
- *Gaining experience is more important than money.*
- *Nothing is impossible, and we must show determination and take the right decision.*
- *I am Arab... I am Emirati. I do not turn a blind eye to errors, and this stems from my love for my country and government. If I say "I don't care", I don't deserve life.*
- *We who are privileged to live in the Emirates are one family.*

All the above and many other traits and qualities define the personality of Khalaf Al Habtoor in its multiple dimensions: the national, economic, social and educational dimensions. But, unfortunately, there is not enough space to elaborate on each one of them. These rare personal character traits have shaped his loyalty and devotion to the state leaders, the homeland goals and the march of the Arab nation. This is what makes his book a testimony to the greatness of the United Arab Emirates and its citizens, and to the state's identification with the goals and aspirations of Arabs everywhere.

The existence of such principled, high-achieving nationals like Khalaf Al Habtoor fills us with pride and optimism. That is why this autobiography will benefit a great number of people of different ages with differing interests. It also reminds us of our great love for the UAE and undoubtedly deepens our loyalty to our magnificent home country, thus reinforcing our passion to keep working for its advancement.

Lastly, I give thanks to God and to the sincere and judicious leadership of HH Sheikh Khalifa bin Zayed Al Nahyan, President of the UAE and Ruler of Abu Dhabi; and his brother, HH Sheikh Mohammed bin Rashid Al Maktoum, Prime Minister and Vice-President of the UAE and Ruler of Dubai (may Allah protect them). I also ask God to bless Their Highnesses and Excellencies the members of the Federal Supreme Council and all the UAE's rulers, without forgetting the Emirati people who make our nation unique.

May God bless us all!

Nahayan Mabarak Al Nahayan
Minister of Higher Education and Scientific Research
United Arab Emirates

A MAN OF IDEAS AND PRINCIPLES

Working for peace has been a motivating force in my life. These words could be said of me, just as easily as they could be said of my friend, Khalaf Al Habtoor.

We first met at his beautiful ranch in Khawaneej, Dubai, where we enjoyed a wonderful afternoon. My son Jack and his wife Elizabeth joined me in visiting with Mr Al Habtoor, his children, and grandchildren. As a farmer I enjoyed seeing the estate's free roaming animals alongside world-class facilities and polo fields. The time we spent with our gracious host was a highlight of our visit to the Emirates, with a good friend and family surrounded by natural beauty.

Since that time, Khalaf Al Habtoor has grown from a friend to a partner. In 1982, Rosalynn and I founded The Carter Center in the hopes that it would provide leadership in the areas of peace, human rights, and health. Over the past thirty years we have grown to an organisation that has worked in over ninety-three countries fighting disease, waging peace, and building hope. We are proud to count Khalaf Al Habtoor and the Al Habtoor Group as partners in our work.

Khalaf Al Habtoor has distinguished himself as a man of thought and action. Through his writing, he has promoted a platform of peace. For almost twenty years, his magazine *Al Shindagah* has served as a resource for those who care about the future of the Middle East and the United Arab Emirates. Mr Al Habtoor has been willing to take on all sides and expresses his strong views in a forward-looking manner.

As is well known, this courage to look forward has served Khalaf well in business. The cityscapes of the modern Arab world would not be the same without the many successful projects built under his direction. Dubai, in particular, has been blessed by his vision. But it is through his philanthropy and his writing that Khalaf Al Habtoor continues to build foundations that will last for generations. To read of his life is to take inspiration from his actions.

Jimmy Carter
President of the United States of America (1977–1981)

THE GENTLEMAN FROM DUBAI

During commencement exercises on 16 May 2010 on the campus of Illinois College, a venerable liberal arts school in mid-America, the college dean placed a doctorate hood for humane letters around the neck of Khalaf Al Habtoor, a leading businessman from the United Arab Emirates. He was unaware of the college until I came into his life twenty-five years ago. Because of my lifelong affiliation with the college and my friendship with him, I had the honour of handing him the honorary doctorate diploma a moment later, just before he addressed the graduating class. It was a thrilling moment for all concerned.

He is unique among the scores of people who have received honorary degrees during the 181 years since the college's founding. He is the first Muslim and the first Arab so honoured. He possessed the least formal education of all those previously recognised with an honorary doctorate. He had only six years of elementary classroom education, after which, at the age of thirteen, he entered the workforce full-time. Since then, he has been self-taught, mastering English, engineering, architecture, construction, human relations, personnel management, history and philosophy.

He can be strictly business and self-disciplined but the next minute as comfortable as an old shoe when he plays with grandchildren or joins arms and sings lustily with newly-found brothers as an honorary member of the college's Phi Alpha Literary Society.

Above all else, Mr Al Habtoor is a gentleman. He puts a good face on the words Arab, Islam and Muslim. During my long, eventful life, I have met many people of stellar attainment. Few can match Khalaf Al Habtoor. He is a billionaire, but he has not kept his earnings tied up in a counting house. He puts them to work in projects to benefit humanity. He is a builder of magnificent buildings, but his most impressive structure is the bridge of understanding he erects between cultures. They are sturdy spans that already reach halfway around the world. He despises war, brutality, oppression, racism. He is a strong voice for human rights and dignity. He is a proud Arab and Muslim, but he reaches for ways to make this a better world for all humankind, irrespective of race or religion.

At Illinois College, he provided graduates a unique, specific and enduring challenge. He recommended that all set high personal goals, stating, "I am living proof that you can be whatever you want to be". He encouraged students, present and future, to take part in building bridges of understanding between his East and their West. To that end, he announced an annual essay contest open to all Illinois College students with attractive prizes for the three best entries each year. Students can compete by writing an essay on the theme 'Bridging East and West'. The audience hung quietly on every word.

Each year, all Illinois College students, whether they compete or not, will surely give long thought to the essay theme and its expansive vision of a peaceful world.

In addition, Mr Al Habtoor endowed annual lectures by experts in interfaith and intercultural topics and funded the conversion of an historic campus building into a centre that focuses on heritage and leadership. These investments will enrich student appreciation of times past as well as challenges of today and tomorrow.

A human powerhouse, Mr Al Habtoor gained personal wealth by helping the United Arab Emirates grow from dusty desert infancy into today's strong, modern, progressive nation. Forty years ago when Habtoor Group began, the seven small, independent coastal nations had just settled into a successful federation. Now they are a thriving, progressive nation whose Dubai skyline of dramatic new buildings is unmatched anywhere in the world.

When I first met Mr Al Habtoor, he immediately impressed me as a disciplined man who has the right motivation and goals, knows what he wants to accomplish, assembles the right people and other resources, then sticks resolutely to a task until it is done – and done well. He celebrates forty years of progress but is not resting on laurels. He is already deep into future plans and missions. Through him, his children and the thousands of people he now employs, the missions continue.

I am confident about the ultimate triumph of justice in the Middle East because of leaders like Khalaf. He recognises the challenge and understands what must be done. Those who read this book, young or old, will, I believe, be inspired to seek their own personal heights of worthy endeavour.

Paul Findley
Member of the US Congress (1961–1983) from Jacksonville, Illinois

PREFACE

What an amazing journey it's been! Within a virtual blink of an eye, I was transported from a small fishing and trading port huddled along the mouth of Dubai Creek that was home to less than 20,000 inhabitants to one of the world's most stunning metropolises without having to travel anywhere.

When I was first encouraged to write my life story, I was hesitant. While the idea of writing my memoirs had often occurred to me, I had no idea how I would find the time in my packed schedule. Secondly, I have a natural tendency to look forward rather than back. I prefer to spend those rare solitary moments problem-solving, strategising, analysing geopolitical issues or simply winding-down from the stresses of the day.

After thinking long and hard, I came around to the idea of recording the extraordinary trajectory of my life that began when Dubai was a little-known sheikhdom in the British protectorate known as the Trucial States. I concluded that if my story could encourage even one person to follow their dreams, it was worth telling.

Initially, this book was destined to be a slim business-oriented volume, designed as a giveaway to mark the fortieth anniversary of my group of companies celebrated on 12 April 2010. But then I decided – 'in for a penny, in for a pound'. I felt that if my tale was to be recounted it should be told honestly from the heart. Hopefully, it will encourage young people battling to find their niche in an ever more challenging, complex and dangerous world and it is my hope that it will stand as a record of another era at a time when every trace of the past is disappearing. These are only two of the motivations that lead me towards penning this autobiographical work.

Firstly, it is important to me to make a small contribution towards better East–West understanding. We Arabs love to complain that we are misunderstood by Americans and Europeans. But unless we are prepared to open up, we will never be able to shake off false negative stereotypes. We're not used to baring our souls in public. We don't reveal all on talk shows. We're private people. But we do need to communicate to the rest of the world who we are and what we stand for.

Secondly, I am keen to share my views on a variety of topics close to my heart, including Arab nationalism, the external and internal threats that face the Arab world, the Afghanistan and Iraq wars, Lebanon's political instability, the Palestinians' quest for their own state, the 2011 'Arab Spring' – and the importance of interfaith understanding.

Tolerance and understanding are crucial during an era of increased Islamophobia in Europe and the US, sparked by the 11 September 2001 attacks on America's symbols of power.

In those dark post-9/11 days, I came to realise that ignorance is one of the world's great evils, which must be combatted with education and the dissemination of real knowledge. As Arabs, we must find ways to get our message across. We are a peaceful people with similar hopes and dreams to everyone else on the planet and we are just as distressed at the rise of extremist ideologies that threaten our region.

I wonder what my childhood hero, former Egyptian President Gamal Abdel Nasser, would have thought were he still alive to witness so many civil uprisings underway throughout the region and serious fractures between Arab states. It is clear that his pan-Arab vision of a unified Arab nation from the Atlantic Ocean to the Arabian Sea may be dead and buried. Perhaps his vision was naïve. Perhaps the only threads binding the various Arab countries are a shared religion and language. Perhaps we can never agree long enough to speak with one voice. I don't know!

Whether together or separately, it is time that Arab countries capitalised on their economic and geopolitical clout to stand as equals in the community of nations. The current generation of Arab presidents, emirs and kings failed to read the tea leaves and were unprepared for George W. Bush's 'New American Century' neoconservative foreign policy agenda as well as, in some instances, the frustrations over corruption and lack of freedom permeating their own streets.

The Arab League has also proved to be divided and ineffective. It is my fervent hope that coming generations will have learned lessons so that never again will another Arab country be bombed and plundered under democracy's standard. No one respects democracy as a concept more than I do. But it cannot be imposed. Democracy can only flourish in non-sectarian states where populations are educated. In principle, it is an excellent system of governance, but it has its faults. Democratic leaders with marginal majorities are often hamstrung by political opponents, while frequent changes of governments can translate to a lack of continuity.

That is far from the case in the UAE. Our own system of federal governance whereby the rulers of the seven emirates enjoy local autonomy is one that works exceptionally well. Our leaders have the well-being of the UAE at heart and are relatively accessible to their people, although I would like to see greater consultation and transparency between rulers and citizens in the way it was when our founding fathers were alive.

While nobody can deny that this region as a whole needs fixing, it should not be forcibly recreated as a mirror image of the West. Arabs need to take charge of their own destiny rather than relying on the West to solve our problems. We understand our own backyard and should be our own doctors.

Bringing a lasting peace to the Middle East is the main challenge we face but it's not the only one. We must find ways of tackling a cancerous, divisive ideology disseminated by the Islamic Republic of Iran that has infected Iraq, Lebanon, Syria and the Shiite minority in Bahrain. It threatens to destabilise the entire region if left unchecked. With the help of major powers, we must ensure that Iran will never become a nuclear-armed state, which would fuel Iran's territorial ambitions and alter the regional balance of power forever.

These challenges and many more will be thrashed out in these pages.

As I write, Dubai is well on the road to recovery from the effects of a global economic downturn that was triggered by greedy and irresponsible Western financial institutions and banks. For Dubai, in the great scheme of things, this was merely a storm in a teacup. I want to remind my compatriots where we came from and how fortunate we are today.

As a high-profile glamorous city, Dubai was victim to its own success. It became a target for the foreign media. Pundits were gleefully predicting that the emirate would disappear beneath a mountain of debt. Of course, it was all nonsense! Like every other place on earth, Dubai took a hit but it was unfairly singled out for attack. Is there any country on earth that doesn't have debts? In fact, compared to those of other countries, Dubai's were modest. I shrugged this off from day one as being a temporary setback. I was right. Within a short time, the emirate's expansion plans were back on track.

Dubai's rise from little more than a dusty village without roads to an acclaimed futuristic city where everyone wants to be is nothing short of a miracle. No other place in the region can compete in the near or distant future with the energy and drive that has made Dubai the business and tourist hub it is today. In my eyes, Dubai is much more than its fabulous resorts, world-beating architecture, megamalls and award-winning infrastructure – it's my home. I feel so privileged to have been born here. I still marvel at this gleaming metropolis and I'm grateful that my Group's companies – construction, automotive, hotels and schools – were given the opportunity to contribute towards Dubai's phenomenal growth.

In many ways, my own story mirrors that of my hometown. Each time I drive past one of the world's tallest hotels, the iconic Burj Al Arab, I feel a sense of pride that it was constructed by Al Habtoor Engineering that has come a long way since its very first project: a small private villa in Deira for which we received the princely reward of 60,000 Qatar-Dubai riyals. I still remember how in the evenings I would drive my car to the site and turn the headlights on so that work could proceed in the dark. I didn't make any profit but I was overjoyed that, at last, my fledgling company had success-fully reached the first rung of the ladder.

Thankfully, I was born in the right place at the right time and was lucky enough to cross paths with good people who helped me on my way. As a young boy, my biggest ambition was to one day own my own shop. Never in my wildest imagination did I ever envisage that I would one day be the Chairman of a respected international group of companies employing thousands; or that I would mingle with royalty, world leaders, politicians, tycoons, bankers and intellectuals.

I certainly didn't predict that not only would I be in a position to ensure my own family never wanted for anything, but that I would have the privi-lege of being able to offer a helping hand to those less fortunate at home and abroad. I find it shocking that in the twenty-first century children are still dying from preventable diseases, contaminated water and starvation, while millions are deprived of decent education. I believe we all have a duty to help eliminate such evils according to our means.

In the 1950s, along with most of Dubai's children, I knew what it was like to go hungry. But hunger pangs didn't bother me; I got used to such gnawing discomfort. I was still hungry as a teenager but not for food – I was hungry for new experiences and challenges. I refused to be limited by circumstance or to put a glass ceiling on my ambitions. They say that someone who knows what real hunger is like can never be truly full. Perhaps this is why I am constantly seeking out new personal and pro-fessional challenges.

The word 'retirement' isn't in my vocabulary and neither is 'holiday'. Wherever I am in the world, my mobile phone is always in use. I don't understand people who say family comes before work. My children and grandchildren are my oxygen, but a man needs to work for his own self-respect and to ensure the people who depend upon him are comfortable.

From the standpoint of physical hardship, my generation and previous generations had it tough; but in most other respects, young people today are faced with far greater challenges. They are bombarded with information as soon as they can talk. They are put under pressure to excel from the day they start school with constant tests and examinations. They are presented with choices that we never dreamt could exist in a world that is packed with the kind of temptations we never knew.

Today's youth face fierce global competition and are expected to battle their way to the top, armed with university degrees and a broad diversity of knowledge on a range of topics. They must wrap their minds around such subjects as financial markets, IT, international marketing, geopolitics, stem cell research and DNA. In their hands rests the planet's survival. They are the ones who must tackle global warming, dwindling natural resources, the problems of overpopulation, nuclear proliferation, ideological extremism and threats from rogue states.

Young people in my part of the world must also find a personal balance between their own time-honoured traditions and contemporary Western culture that consumes satellite television and the Internet. This is especially applicable to young Emiratis, whose traditions are increasingly being relegated to museums.

In a land where the indigenous population is the minority, they must find ways to embrace progress while preserving their unique identity. My own six children – three sons and three daughters – are modern-minded, technologically-savvy and well educated but, at home, many of the traditions we hold so dear are still kept alive. Others that don't suit this day and age, we've gradually rejected.

At the same time, our youth greatly benefits from a diversity of cultures and the opportunity to interact with people of all races, colours and creeds. I love that the UAE showcases what a peaceful world where everyone gets along can look like. If everyone on the planet had the chance to live in such a multicultural rainbow-coloured environment and gain an understanding that we are all brothers and sisters under one sky, racism would become a scourge of the past and there would be far fewer conflicts.

Some of my compatriots and a few members of my family are fondly nostalgic for the simple unhurried times of earlier decades and wish that the clock could be turned back. They miss the sense of community when everyone's door was open day or night and people had time to chat with one another. I call this the 'grass is greener' mentality except that sixty years ago there was hardly a blade of grass to be found.

The late British explorer and photographer Wilfred Thesiger preferred things as they were in the days when he crossed the forbidding Empty Quarter with his Bedouin companions. When he revisited Dubai in his eighties, he used to complain that it had become too fast, too modern. But I don't believe in getting stuck in a time warp. Unless some genius patents a time machine, life is a one-way ticket forward. The only moments we have are now and it is up to each individual to adapt and make the best of them.

Obsessing about the glorious past is somewhat of an Arab trait. We still talk about the Golden Age of Islam when Arab scholars, inventors and scientists laid the cornerstones of medicine, chemistry, mathematics, astronomy and philosophy. We rightly revere such names as Jabir Ibn Hayyan, Al Khwarizmi, Al Idrisi, Al Kindi, Ibn Al Nafis and Ibn Battuta, whose respective contributions to chemistry, algebra, philosophy, medicine and geography should not be understated. But where are their contemporary counterparts?

I believe that education is the key to this region's future and I am delighted that my own country, the United Arab Emirates, is investing heavily to produce a knowledge-based society. Whereas in the 1950s there were just a handful of schools offering a basic syllabus, today there are sixty colleges and universities where female students greatly outnumber males.

There is also a wealth of government-run and privately-owned secondary schools as well as schools for children with special needs. Moreover, the government of Dubai has pledged to create a knowledge-based society throughout the region with the re-establishment of the Bait al-Hikma or Arab House of Wisdom that was a well of learning during the Golden Age.

Throughout the Middle East and the Gulf is a rich pool of talent. In the Emirates, we capitalise on this human potential with job creation in just about every field. But it saddens me that certain countries within the region neglect to provide opportunities to bright youngsters who are often destined to waste their intelligence in inferior jobs or join the brain drain to the US or Europe, where Arab doctors, scientists, university professors and nuclear physicists have risen to great heights. These people are needed at home.

Thirdly, I consider this memoir to be a gift to my children and grandchildren, a chance for them to get to know Khalaf Al Habtoor the man, the human being, outside of my role as head of the family. I want them to be familiar with their roots, be proud of their Arab heritage and gain an understanding of the mountains I climbed – and the mistakes I've made. I would like them to know some of the fascinating people I've met, both the sad times and the fun times I've experienced as well as the principles on which my life has been based.

My story will, no doubt, represent different things to different people, but I would guess that most will see it as a rags-to-riches tale. It's true that I once rode camels and donkeys whereas now I drive a Bentley and fly in a private jet, but I know for sure that a person's wealth doesn't rest on how much disposable income they have. It lies in their physical and mental health, their strength of character, their kindness and generosity, the comfort of close family relationships, their ability to rise above adversity and their courage to grasp opportunities.

My knowledge and understanding has grown by leaps and bounds since the days I earned 250 rupees a month but, in essence, I'm the same person I was back then with the same personality, the same loves and hates, the same mannerisms – and the same way of walking. I consider material wealth to be the icing on the cake of my existence for which I thank God each day and pray He will guide me how best to use it to bring some light to those who endure deprivation quietly in the shadows.

With sixty years of yesterdays under my belt, there is still much to do. Each morning is an exciting new dawn. I have so many plans and projects still to be implemented. I have so many ambitions still unfulfilled. Sometimes I feel my life's only just beginning. But now it's time to take that promised journey back...

ACKNOWLEDGEMENTS

My heartfelt appreciation goes to those who inspired me to be a better person and provided support and comfort throughout my life's journey; and to everyone who assisted in bringing my idea of publishing my memoir into reality. My respect and thanks to:

My wise and gentle father, Ahmad bin Mohammed bin Khalifa Al Habtoor, who never left my side when I was a boy and made sure that I was properly educated on how to be a responsible man. He taught me how to swim, hunt and race camels. He introduced me to our country's greatest men and explained to me the benefits of listening to them and learning from their wisdom.

Sheikh Rashid bin Saeed Al Maktoum, the late Vice-President of the UAE and Ruler of Dubai. He was an exceptional leader who brought Dubai into the twentieth century and who never relinquished his dream of a Federation, despite many obstacles. He was my mentor and my role model. He taught me the value of patience, perseverance, calmness and hard work. With his guidance, I learned not to give in to stress and the importance of controlling negative emotions. He was a one-man school whose equal no longer exists. Being in his company helped shape my character towards becoming the man I am today.

Sheikh Zayed bin Sultan Al Nahyan, the late President of the UAE and Ruler of Abu Dhabi, a kind, generous and accessible leader who was close to his people and to his brother Arabs. His philanthropy is legendary. He gave without differentiating between people of different races, colours or religions. Being privileged to watch Sheikh Zayed's unique leadership skills up close opened my heart and also taught me that no matter how important the man, he is nothing without compassion and humility.

His Highness Sheikh Khalifa bin Zayed bin Sultan Al Nahyan, President of the UAE and Ruler of Abu Dhabi, and His Highness Sheikh Mohammed bin Rashid Al Maktoum, Prime Minister and Vice-President of the UAE and Ruler of Dubai, have gained my deepest respect and appreciation. Following in the footsteps of their fathers, our country's founders, they prioritise their people's well-being, security and prosperity while ensuring the UAE holds fast to its upward trajectory.

My mother, Noura bint Ahmad bin Khalaf bin Abdullah Al Otaiba, who loved me and cared for me. As a child, she watched over me and she continued to do so even after I married and became a parent myself. She taught me self-discipline; she kept me grounded; and it is thanks to her that I've never lost track of what is truly important in life.

My wife, Hamda, who has been the best life partner any man could ask for. Hamda took care of our six children and raised them to be fine young adults while I was busy carving out our future. She monitored their school work and their behaviour. She pushed them to reach their potential. In the early years, she was a hardworking housewife who never complained, even when things we wished to have, including basic necessities, were out of our reach. Hamda has devoted her life to me and our family; she has unstintingly given us all that she has to give. She has spent all her years thinking of others and in truth, she more than anyone else encourages me to help members of our extended family in need and to give to people less fortunate. Hamda deserves as much credit as I do for every good deed I've ever done.

My younger brother, Sultan, is the most loyal, trusted and supportive brother anyone could wish for and is also my best and closest friend.

Riad Sadik, my partner in my first venture, Al Habtoor Engineering, now Al Habtoor Leighton Group, and 'brother', who has always stood by me during good times and bad. Honest, strong and hardworking, he is a model of integrity. However hard the road ahead, he never gives up.

My children and my grandchildren, who have made me proud and given me so much happiness. Our carefree times together give me the greatest peace of mind and help me forget my worries.

Linda S. Heard, a great woman who gave life to my stories and helped me write this autobiography. Linda understands me very well and I wouldn't have trusted my life story to anyone else.

The members of my management team – Maan Halabi, Ala'a El Husseini, Saif Mazrooei and Noura Badawi. They helped me remember my stories and worked very closely with me on completing this book.

CONTENTS

INTRODUCTION

When Khalaf Al Habtoor asked me to work with him on his autobiography, I was slightly apprehensive but also excited. I've known him professionally for some years and felt privileged that he was willing to entrust me to help him with this task, so I didn't hesitate in accepting. It's been a long journey that began in early 2010, when I spent almost a month in Dubai familiarising myself with Mr Al Habtoor's daily routine, getting to know his family, friends and colleagues and gaining insights into what makes this self-made businessman, intellectual, political commentator and international philanthropist tick. The more I got to know him via his written memories, the more my admiration for him grew.

Khalaf Al Habtoor is super successful and charismatic. When he walks into a room, one immediately feels his presence. He's someone who knows what he wants and how to get it honestly and ethically. He possesses a complex personality, rich with empathy for those less fortunate. He knows what it's like to struggle against adversity and gnawing poverty. He fought and worked hard for everything he has and considers life to be a blessing. He was born with natural qualities of leadership, determination and business acumen that have driven him to great heights. But it is one thing to attain one's aspirations and quite another to understand how to create a contented, fulfilled existence that touches the lives of others.

Mr Al Habtoor understood the importance of balance early on. He puts every minute of his day to good use; he perfectively divides his time between his business commitments, charitable duties, his family, his personal fitness regime, his social life and travel. Time is one of his most precious commodities which he doesn't believe should be frittered away sleeping late in the morning. He is also a great believer in moderation in all things. It's a recipe for good living that clearly works.

He may have entered his sixties, but he has no intention of winding down. He's a hard man to keep up with; he walks fast, thinks fast and makes quick decisions when necessary. When it comes to the faults of others, he's tolerant with one exception – he doesn't appreciate people too lazy to fulfil their God-given potential. He doesn't lecture anyone but his very being is inspirational. He leads by example. Following a meeting with him in Cairo, I was driven to join a gym and eat healthily; I'm still working on becoming an early riser.

Despite being the recipient of many accolades – such as the prestigious Man of the Year Award from the American Biographical Institute, a Knighthood from the President of Lebanon, a World Forum Award from British Members of Parliament and the GCC Economic Power Award from the League of Arab States – he's a modest man. He selects friends from all levels of society according to their human qualities. As you read on, you will discover what a loyal and generous friend he can be. I communicated with a few of those lucky enough to be within his inner circle to find out their impressions.

Dr Imtihan Jawdat was the on-call physician when the author was admitted to an Abu Dhabi hospital in 1977 suffering from exhaustion, and ever since, they've been fast friends meeting up frequently in Dubai, Abu Dhabi, New York and Texas, where Dr Jawdat currently works.

"I admire Mr Al Habtoor for his hard work and unique vision in business," he told me. "I have also noticed over the years the philanthropic aspect of him in helping people in any way he can. My personal admiration for Mr Al Habtoor's character is his honesty, integrity, his ability to be a friend on an equal level and his unconditional love and care for his family."

The doctor recounted anecdotes that made a powerful impression on him during the earlier part of their acquaintance. "My father and I were invited to Mr Al Habtoor's home in the days when men and women were traditionally hosted separately. We were eating lamb together but when I had difficulty in extricating the brain (a Middle Eastern delicacy) from the lamb's head, I decided to place it in the centre of a plate and hit it with my fist. That did the trick, but all the contents splashed over Mr Al Habtoor and his clothes. He just smiled. He withdrew to change and returned to finish his lunch without any mention of the incident. When I was elected as President of the Arab American Medical Association of Houston, Texas, Mr Al Habtoor gave a generous donation to the association to establish an award that still exists today."

Former Republican US Representative from Illinois Paul Findley is not only one of Mr Al Habtoor's greatest friends, he has also won the author's greatest admiration for placing his devotion to the concept of a Palestinian state before his political career. He recalls his initial impressions of the author – "businesslike, punctual and sincere". Mr Findley and his wife have been the guests of Mr Al Habtoor on numerous occasions. "He's a gracious, cordial host, but not the back-slapping type," says Mr Findley, who was especially impressed by Mr Al Habtoor's concern for his wife, Lucille, when she fell ill with a liver infection during one of their stays in Dubai. "We will never forget Mr Al Habtoor's hospitality and concern for Lucille's health," he said.

Paul Rayner, a former Vice-Chairman of Credit Suisse (UK) Ltd, met Khalaf Al Habtoor several decades ago while he was working for Barclay's Bank. It was a business meeting that resulted in a lasting friendship. "We hit it off immediately," he said. "Khalaf has a warm, friendly and practical style and he has been an enormous influence on dealings within the region. I always had a love for and an interest in the Middle East, the Arab culture and Islam. My friendship with Khalaf is one of the strong elements that sustain this. During Ramadan, Khalaf always maintains a traditional majlis, which I've always enjoyed attending and having the opportunity to break the fast with him, his family and guests. He is always keen that the old ways and traditions are retained, despite maintaining a progressive and modern outlook. He's a kind, considerate and very far-thinking man, but he's always very much a family man and a true and loyal friend. In business, he is part of the success that is Dubai as well as being a fair and fearless political commentator. His views on the region, particularly the Palestinian and Lebanese situations, are insightful and centred. He has helped many causes with his generosity and I cite his input into Lebanon, both personally and financially, as a classic example. His opinions are sought by those in the highest of influential positions both at home and abroad."

His group's directors, executives and managers are proud of the opportunity to work with this rare individual. "He is a God-fearing man. He is the first to help others. You feel that you are in safe hands; he's not just an employer, he's a father for so many people," said the Al Habtoor Group's Director of Strategy and Business Development, Sanjeev Agarwala.

Chief Finance Officer, Arun Krishnan, appreciates Mr Al Habtoor's motivational skills. "He has a way of keeping the team together in the hardest of times. During the 2008 global financial crisis, some of our managers were nervous about the future and the continuity of the business. Mr Khalaf was the one who kept everyone together. He reminded them that we are a strong company, we have a solid base – and it was not just talk. When other companies were downsizing and cutting staff, not a single one of our employees were sacked and no one's salary was cut."

Group Managing Director, Maan Halabi, one of his right-hand men, describes his boss as "sharp and very far-sighted". "Sometimes we struggle to catch up with his long vision," he disclosed. "I might not agree with him and others might not agree with his business decisions, but later on those decisions are proved right. His instincts, combined with intelligence, vision and his willingness to take risks, are remarkable. Mr Al Habtoor believes that people are his company's primary capital and insists that without this fortune of people, his companies would not grow and develop."

Almost everyone in the Head Office told me of his ability to communicate on the same level with everyone, from the most junior office boy to employees in high positions. He is also known for his impatience as well as his forgiving nature. On those rare occasions he loses his temper, which he sometimes does when he feels he's being deliberately misled, he gets over it swiftly and doesn't hold a grudge.

Another of his trusted advisors, Ala'a Husseini, agrees that the author hones in on opportunities using his natural instincts. "He tells us never to delay what we are required to do today, saying just go ahead and do it. He keeps us on our toes with his enthusiasm. He believes so much in his businesses and hotel properties, that it cascades to the people around him who all share the same conviction."

All his colleagues admire his caring personality. "One minute he can say something and you know that he really cares; sometimes, he is really thoughtful and you think he doesn't have time to notice what's going on in your life, but then he surprises you by remembering every detail and checking that you're okay," said Liz, his long-time personal assistant. In fact, his caring extends way beyond his inner family, social and business circles.

Director of Projects and Real Estate, Yusef Shalabi, has known Mr Al Habtoor socially since the late 1960s and later helped supervise the construction of his very first hotel, the Dubai Metropolitan. Although the author's business decisions are usually logically thought through with his team of advisors, he can be an impulsive decision-maker, sometimes involving millions, Shalabi says, adding, "most of the time that works to his benefit". In this connection, he highlighted Mr Al Habtoor's investments in Lebanon, made largely to help a troubled country that he has grown to love.

Mr Shalabi spoke of the material support the author has given to individuals down on their luck. "He feels responsible for the livelihoods of his employees and reciprocates their efforts by giving them a decent life. There was a married Egyptian waiter who had a heart attack at a young age that resulted in partial paralysis. Because his movement was restricted, he would have never found another job, but Mr Khalaf didn't hesitate. Concerned about his family, he made him a timekeeper." Mr Shalabi also talked about Mr Al Habtoor's support for the Red Crescent and the Harvard Medical Centre in Dubai, and explained how he came to build a hospital in the poor and neglected north Lebanese town of Hrar. While watching television, Mr Al Habtoor saw the town's mayor complain about the lack of medical facilities in the area and promptly got in touch with the local mufti offering to construct a fifty-bed hospital, soon to be completed.

His biggest fans of all are his wife Hamda, their six children and their grandchildren. They describe him as a fastidious, disciplined man of action, who has set high standards for himself and the people he loves. "My father is very caring. He loves us and his grandchildren," said his youngest daughter, Meera. "Even when he's abroad, he calls to make sure we, his daughters, are in the house looking after our mum. He likes to see us smiling. He always notices if something is bothering us and wants to know the problem. He doesn't like secrets. My father is happy when we're all around him and he sees us happy and successful. But he gets angry when we're undisciplined. I'm married but I still can't do anything without telling him."

As the writer's memoir unfolds, you will discover his passion for the UAE, his pride at being an Arab and the astonishing frankness he displays about certain life-changing events and his innermost emotions. He honestly recounts his successes as well as his mistakes. He pulls no punches when it comes to his sometimes controversial political positions.

He invites the reader on a journey encompassing India, Egypt, Britain, the US, Eastern Europe and elsewhere. And most of all, he shows great sensitivity, warmth – and a self-deprecating sense of humour, unusual for a man of his stature. At its kernel, this may be a serious book with an important message for anyone with an interest in the Arab world or who would like to know how a boy from an impoverished desert town that hardly anyone in the West had even heard of could become one of the wealthiest men in the region, feted wherever he goes.

Most of all, it's a message of hope; a message that nothing is impossible, at times written in a style that will lift your spirits, as you're reminded that provided you have the will, our world is filled with endless possibilities.

Linda S. Heard
Political Columnist

CHAPTER 1

Roots

"For a tree to become tall it must grow tough roots among the rocks."

– Friedrich Nietzsche

Dubai's skyline has altered beyond recognition since the days we lived in a one-roomed *barasti* (palm frond) dwelling in the neighbourhood of Shindagha, then separated from Dubai town and Deira by the waters of the Creek. The only way we could cross to the other side was by *abra* (water taxi). Shindagha was also home to Dubai's ruling Maktoum family, although the main residential areas and souks were in Deira. The centre of government was the small town of Dubai where the ruler, Sheikh Saeed Al Maktoum, held an open majlis in Al Fahidi Fort that stands today as a repository of history and culture.

Apart from Sheikh Saeed's house – now a museum – my childhood environment has been erased like a lesson on a blackboard to make way for the twenty-first century. Only my memories remain intact... well, almost. The past was so dramatically different from the present in every respect that there are times when it seems like a dream.

It was 1949 when I emerged yelling into a world that no longer exists. I guess I was yelling because I'm not the kind of person that's forced to go anywhere quietly. I wish I could tell you the exact date of my birth, but back then records weren't kept. The only birthday that was celebrated was that of the Prophet (peace be upon him). Birthday parties, cake and cards are Western imports, now embraced by many throughout the Arab world. I'm not averse to blowing out a few candles myself nowadays.

A few years later, my younger brother Sultan was born. My grown-up brother Mohammed shared our home and contributed to the family's finances. I also had four elder sisters. One lived with her husband in Dubai. The other three had been married to men based in Saudi Arabia and Qatar. My parents were troubled that their daughters were so far away, but their main concern was to give them the opportunity of a better life. They must also have been relieved that there were now fewer mouths to feed. This was especially true during World War II, when there were shortages of food and everything else.

My mother and father acted out of the best intentions but, as it turned out, those marriages were strained and plagued with financial problems. Regretfully, I didn't get to meet my sisters until decades later, when I took them under my wing and made sure their children received the opportunities that were denied to them. Knowing the difficulties my sisters faced is perhaps one of the reasons I keep my own three daughters so close. They are mothers now, but their husbands know that they are still under my protection and always will be.

Our traditional *barasti* home seemed enormous to me as a toddler. In reality, it was tiny and cramped with three adults, a new baby and me, a small energetic boy who always wanted his own way. The only item of furniture was a bed which no one slept on. We preferred to stretch out on blankets or thin mattresses on the floor. These would be folded or rolled up each morning and neatly arranged on top of the bed where most of our meagre belongings were kept.

Furnishings consisted of a handmade woollen rug and cushions, on which we would lounge to chat or eat from a circular communal tray using our hands as was the custom. There were no windows and the gaps in the palm fronds meant our living space was open to the elements.

During chilly winter evenings, my father would burn charcoal inside a clay receptacle. On occasion, winds from the north would whip up huge waves that flooded our home, soaking our bedding. During sandstorms, we would wrap our *ghutrahs* (Arab headdresses) around our nose and mouth and watch helplessly as everything we owned became coated in layers of fine yellow particles. In the summer, there was little real escape from the humidity and heat. My parents did their best to keep us cool. They would make an opening in the roof of the *barasti* – known as a *barjil* – in an attempt to harness the breeze and funnel it downwards.

We had none of the modern conveniences that people take for granted today. Our toilet was basically a hole in the ground some way away from the *barasti*. Our drinking water was drawn from two-metre-deep wells that we dug ourselves. It was lukewarm, brackish and murky. It was also alive with worms and insects, which we would remove by using the cloth of our *ghutrahs* as a filter. It tasted terrible and couldn't have been very hygienic, but we didn't dwell on that as we carried it home in large cans or tins of ghee (clarified butter). We were just happy to find drinking water; any water. How spoilt we are now with our refrigerators packed with sparkling Perrier and Volvic supposedly drawn from lush green French volcanoes! It makes me laugh to think what a health nut I've become since.

The mosquito was another bane of our existence. Without nets or quinine tablets, many children and adults would develop fever and weakness without knowing they were suffering from malaria. Due to the absence of anaesthetics, antibiotics or pain medications, traditional healers often treated broken bones in sea water and would use searing red hot rods to cauterise tumours or serious wounds. It's little wonder that some people preferred to suffer their condition rather than submit to such painful treatments.

At that time, there were few doctors or clinics. It was common for women to die during childbirth and by some reports up to 50 per cent of all infants failed to survive. The sick rarely knew the medical name of their illness. When a diabetic was unable to recover from an injury, his sickness was given the name Jarrah or 'continuous bleeding'; those who suffered a heart attack or stroke were thought to have been possessed by jinn – supernatural beings with the ability to do good or evil, as mentioned in the Qur'an.

People then believed strongly in the power of evil spirits or the evil eye; some would throw salt to keep misfortune away; others would faithfully read the Holy Book for hours upon end or wear a talisman – a word that is derived from the Arabic word *talasim*. When a tragedy occurred that was beyond their understanding, the wicked *jinn* would usually get the blame. Very often amulets were pinned to babies and young children to ward off disease or to protect them from being kidnapped and sold as child soldiers or slaves, which were frequent occurrences during the first half of the twentieth century.

Dubai's Al Maktoum hospital was the town's first 'modern' medical facility. It opened its doors in 1951 under the directorship of a sergeant in the British Air Force called Dr MacKolly. But in the very early days, people preferred traditional Arab medicine that uses herbs, medicinal plants, molasses and berries to treat conditions such as rheumatism, asthma, allergies, infections and stomach upsets. Al Maktoum hospital was closed for business in 2009 and is slated to become a museum displaying old photographs and medical equipment.

Needless to say, we didn't have electricity. For that, we had to wait until the late 1950s when Dubai Electricity was up and running. As they say, necessity is the mother of invention. Our evenings were dimly lit by the glow of a candle or a lantern fuelled by cloth soaked in the oil of the date. The light produced was more atmospheric than illuminating. Sitting in a gloomy half-light, my parents would have been very surprised to learn that all around were oceans of oil and gas.

Although Abu Dhabi signed a concession agreement with Petroleum Development (Trucial States) Ltd – a consortium of British, French and American oil companies – in 1939, it wasn't until the 1950s that commercial quantities of oil were found; and it took until 1963 for Abu Dhabi to begin exporting. Dubai had to wait until 1966 before its own black gold was excavated, a find which initially drove the emirate's great transformation.

It seems hard to believe now, but we were happy with our simple uncomplicated existence. It was all we knew. We never thought of ourselves as being deprived because almost all of our neighbours were in the same boat. There were some exceptions.

The ruling sheikhs and a handful of foreign officials, wealthy pearl traders and Iranian merchants lived in imposing two-storey, multiroomed windtower houses, surrounded by courtyards and walls. These were constructed with coral and limestone, and often fitted with doors imported from India. Most boasted extensive women's quarters. Some contained more than one open majlis (meeting room), where visitors would be received according to their status.

The rich trading families of the day, such as Al Otaiba, bin Dalmouk, and bin Huraiz, would provide lunches and dinners for travellers and give food or money to the poor. Very few had the luxury of air conditioning or kerosene refrigerators. Even fewer drove an automobile. The 'Father of Dubai', Sheikh Rashid bin Saeed Al Maktoum, had imported a Ford from Bahrain during the late 1930s when he was Crown Prince, but it was only when his favourite horse died that he took to driving with any real enthusiasm.

Thankfully, there was no crime to speak of and most people happily left their doors unlocked and their windows open. Nevertheless, in 1956 Dubai got its own police force that was headquartered at Naif Fort, which is still in use as a police station. In the beginning, its recruits must have spent many a long hour twiddling their thumbs. Not so today, as crime has risen considerably in recent years and Dubai's police force has gained a reputation for being one of the most professional and sophisticated in the world for its forensic capabilities, intelligence gathering methods and use of cutting-edge technology.

We never felt that we were missing out. The smallest item was appreciated; the simplest meal of rice and fish was for us more delicious than any gourmet dinner served in a Michelin Star restaurant could ever be. A new *kandoura* (ankle-length tunic) worn for the first time at Eid was more valued than an Armani suit.

Each Eid, my cousin, Sheikha Sana'a bint Manee Al Maktoum, would always send new clothes for me and my little brother. I didn't know her well, but even so she was very kind to me. She noticed that I was a very active child and told my mother that I would be successful one day. When I was very small, Sheikha Sana'a bought me a bicycle, which was a great thrill, especially since no other child in the neighbourhood had one.

Suddenly I was 'the kid with the bike' surrounded by newfound friends keen to try it out. I rather enjoyed my celebrity status, but there was one slight drawback: I was too tiny to reach the pedals. To get the bike to move I had to straddle the bar and stretch my legs to their fullest extent. Onlookers must have been amused to see me wobbling over the sands. As I grew, that problem was solved.

Sheikha Sana'a was a great woman. Together with her husband, Sheikh Khalifa bin Saeed Al Maktoum – the brother of the Crown Prince, Sheikh Rashid bin Saeed Al Maktoum – she always saw to it that we never went without. Every three months, this caring couple would send us boxes filled with rice, coffee, sugar and ghee.

Sheikh Rashid used to send money to my father. But everyone had tight budgets, even the rulers, in those days. His cash contributions were, therefore, small but every little helped.

When I was five or six years old, I asked my father, "Do we have any money, *Abouya* ('my father' in Arabic)?"

"Of course we have money. We have a lot of money," he replied. He then fetched his special box and opened the lid to proudly show me the princely sum of 100 rupees, which was worth in the region of 100 dollars in today's terms. It seemed like an absolute fortune to me.

My father never judged anyone based on their monetary worth. A person had to earn his respect through honesty and good character. He would always tell me that I was as good as anyone else regardless of their wealth or position. By the same token, I reject being respected just because my name appears on a Forbes' List that ranks drug lords along with everyone else. As I evaluate others, I prefer to be held in esteem for my human qualities rather than my bank balance.

"Don't be intimidated by anyone!" Father would say. "When you meet someone, whoever they are, never cast your eyes downward. Look them in the eye!" All parents should say those words to their child. All children need to feel they are unique and all parents should bolster their child. There is so much wasted talent around all because people lack the confidence to chase their dreams.

My gentle father, Ahmad bin Mohammed Al Habtoor, was my rock from the day I could walk and talk. I don't think any child has been showered with more devotion than was lavished upon me throughout my young years. He usually called me *Al Sheiba* or 'old man'. You'll probably think that was an unusual pet name for a child. It actually derived from my having been named 'Khalaf' after my mother's paternal grandfather, Khalaf Al Otaiba. Moreover, I was unusually mature for my age.

Abouya adored all his children, but for some reason, he loved me more than my siblings. He would hardly let me out of his sight. Perhaps he thought of me as a mini-copy of himself or a 'chip off the old block' because we looked so much alike in terms of features and physique.

Characterwise we were very different. He was an uncomplicated, tranquil person who never strayed far from his tribal roots. There was nothing he enjoyed more than riding out into the desert to sit around a campfire with his Arab friends or to hunt dinner with his falcon perched on his arm. He also derived great pleasure from tending to his camels that provided us with nutritious milk.

The humble camel was the most valuable of beasts. From its hide, rugs, saddlebags and tenting were produced, while its hair was woven to make traditional *bishts* (men's winter cloaks). They were indispensable for those making long journeys due to their ability to negotiate sandy terrain and go without water for days. This loyal, proud – and occasionally bad-tempered – creature also provided young boys with the opportunity to prove their skill and stamina in the sport of camel racing. Racing camels are still prized in the UAE. Some enthusiastic owners hire special trainers as well as nutritionists from abroad and construct luxurious air-conditioned stables. There are even special camel swimming pools that are used as an aid to exercise. Our own camels were not nearly as pampered.

Together with fish, rice, dates, honey and cheese, camel milk was a main staple of our diet. Fruit was a real luxury that was mostly reserved for those recuperating from an illness or for joyous celebrations. Grapes, figs, oranges and lemons from Ra's al-Khaimah could sometimes be found in the local souk alongside imported fruit from Iran, but all fruit was very expensive. The very thought of a juicy orange or sweet lemon would make our mouths water and we never ceased to nag our parents to provide them. Tinned peaches, pineapples and apricots were occasionally available, but anyone who was fortunate enough to lay their hands on canned food usually hoarded it for special occasions.

Thanks to my father's expert hunting skills, staple foods were supplemented with desert game, such as houbara (bustard), *karawan* (stone curlew) and the *dhabi* (gazelle) whose meat was considered a real delicacy.

Locusts were another rare treat; we knew them as *jarad* (pronounced 'yarad'). When they swarmed over Dubai, it was fun to catch them in the air and when we had collected enough, they would be fried as a crunchy snack or stored in palm fronds. You'll probably find the idea of popping locusts less than appetising. In that case, you may be interested to learn that there are quite a few Biblical references to locust eating, while in New South Wales, Australia, government officers have published a book titled *Cooking with Sky Prawns* that is packed with twenty locust recipes, including locust dumplings and chocolate-covered locusts. I thought of asking my wife to try out a few... Just kidding!

Nowadays, when everyone worries about obesity and cholesterol, such a restricted diet would be considered healthy. Indeed, it may have been. Hardly anyone was overweight because food was so scarce that people would eat just enough to stave off hunger. Whenever one saw a person who, nowadays, might be considered fat, he or she was automatically assumed to be rich and healthy, while women with ample curves were looked upon as beautiful. Such perceptions of physical beauty have since altered in the Gulf along Western lines, but in parts of Africa, obesity is still thought of as a desirable female attribute while in Mauritania, girls are actually fattened up by their parents in order to enhance their marriage prospects.

Those who survived disease often lived well into old age. Both my father and paternal grandfather, whose diet was simple in their youth, lived well into their nineties. One of the main staples of their diet was the date, a miracle food rich in natural fibres, vitamins and minerals. We consumed them most days for breakfast, sometimes coated with flour and fried in ghee. We called this dish *Betheth*. Our camels thrived on them and father always went to great pains to ensure our stock was fairly split between the family and those graceful desert beasts.

Father never hankered after riches; not that I did but I was strong-willed and feisty like my mother and very ambitious; always yearning for more without really knowing what 'more' could be. My father didn't share my drive but he admired my spirit and rather than seek to diminish my enthusiasm, he quietly encouraged me towards my goals.

You could say I was a daddy's boy, but not in the sense that term is used today. I certainly wasn't showered with material goods. His gifts to me were far more precious. He took me with him on his travels abroad. He introduced me to everyone he knew, including the ruler, Sheikh Rashid, who became not only my role model and mentor but the man who, more than any other, changed my life.

Abouya also taught me to swim, ride, hunt and shoot. As a small trader of genuine pearls and gold, he schooled me in the basics of commerce. He was a businessman with the heart of a nomad and the soul of a poet. When he was a boy there were a few schools that had been established due to the generosity of well-heeled pearling merchants but, in those days, lessons were concentrated on Arab history, the Qur'an and basic mathematics needed for trading.

As befitting the son of Sheikh Mohammed bin Khalifa Al Habtoor, a religious sheikh (or, as we say in the UAE, a 'sheikh of knowledge') who was also a prominent citizen respected for his good deeds and wisdom, father was enrolled in a *Kuttab* (religious school) where he learned to read and write. The Holy Book was never far from his eyes but he would also spend many hours each week devouring poetry.

What a joy it was to sit in awe as he recited the lines of great Arab poets, stirring our imaginations and emotions. His favourites were Ahmad Shawki, Abu Firas Al Hamadani and the Nabati poet, Ibn Daher, who lived in Ra's al-Khaimah during the seventeenth century.

The verses of the tenth-century poet Abu at-Tayyib Ahmad ibn Huseyn Al Mutanabbi resonated with us more than any other. At dusk, when the sun's orange orb descended towards a purple-streaked horizon, Al Mutanabbi's poems served as a bridge between nature's extraordinary beauty unfolding before us and the noblest virtues of mankind.

I guess I must have poetry in my blood as I come from a long line of poets on both my mother's and father's sides of the family. Father was a talented poet himself. Oh, how I wish I had kept some of his verses. I do remember a few lines of just one, written in answer to a poem penned by Sheikh Rashid's brother, Sheikh Khalifa bin Saeed Al Maktoum, who was distraught after a falling out with his wife, Sheikha Sana'a. Father's response went a long way in putting the couple back together, or so I was told:

> I have received wonderful words, welcome as numerous as souls
> As numerous as all sunsets; and as numerous as pulling cause stillness
> From inner pouring he is infected, and in no sleep he will delight
> Complaining of love's abandonment; and from increasing delusions
> I say go towards the companion willingly, and give him the softest words.

My father adhered to the precepts of the Holy Qur'an by guiding me towards the beauty of Islam without resorting to compulsion. As a very young child, I was more interested in play than prayer, so he decided to lead me one step at a time. At first, he told me to stick to just the *Fardh* prayers, which are obligatory. Later on, I added the *Sunnahs* of my own accord.

I loved the togetherness of Ramadan but couldn't get used to fasting, so I'd sneakily gobble up everything I could lay my hands on when nobody was looking. He instinctively knew what I was doing, but instead of getting upset he would say to me, "Never mind my son! You can drink a little when you're thirsty and Allah the All-Merciful will forgive you." He was a great teacher!

Abouya also showed me by example the true meaning of manhood, which doesn't lie in muscle flexing or machismo, but rather in the ability to take responsibility for oneself and one's family.

My father had four siblings: two sisters, a brother and a half-brother. His brother, Abdullah, died when he was young. His half-brother was Sheikh Hasher bin Rashid Al Maktoum. One of his sisters was Hamda and the other, Madiya, was the mother of Sheikha Sana'a bint Manee Al Maktoum. Father was also a proud son of one of the biggest Arab tribes in the region, the Al Murrar, a sub-tribe of the Bani Yas that has its origins in the Arabian Peninsula. The only thing I know for sure is that my father's branch of the tribe has been traced back to the Oasis of Liwa that flanks the northern edge of the Rub' al-Khali or the 'Empty Quarter' – one of the harshest, driest and hottest deserts in the world stretching across 650,000 square kilometres from southern Saudi Arabia to Yemen, the United Arab Emirates and Oman.

Liwa consists of tiny villages, farms and date palms encircled by some of the highest sand dunes on the planet. It has gained prominence as being the ancestral home of both the Abu Dhabi and Dubai ruling families. Some of the most respected UAE families hail from the Liwa and still feel a strong emotional connection to the place.

The extended Al Habtoor family is comparatively small, but its members are spread throughout the United Arab Emirates and beyond. Through intermarriage, our clan forms part of a large family network that includes the Dubai and Abu Dhabi ruling families, Al Nahyan and Al Maktoum, as well as such prominent local names as Al Otaiba, Al Mijren, Al Shaafar, Al Ghaith, Al Mazrooie and Al Suwaidi.

The origin of our family name 'Al Habtoor' remains elusive. My friend the late Jack Briggs, who was Dubai's last expatriate police commander, stayed on after his retirement at the invitation of Sheikh Rashid. He had fallen in love with the place and its people and couldn't bear to leave it. He spent his twilight years looking after his sick wife, Cath, and translating books and papers from Arabic to English. One day, while we were chatting, he mentioned that Al Habtoor translated to 'Short Foxhunter'. Needless to say, I wasn't very pleased. I quite liked the 'foxhunter' part, but who on earth wants to go around with the label 'short'? It may be that the Al Habtoors of Yemen can help me out with this one. In truth, I've no idea whether they are distant relatives or not, but we do share the same surname.

In fact, I didn't know they existed until the day I met with the then Yemeni President, Ali Abdullah Saleh, some years ago in Lebanon. It happened that he booked the penthouse of one of my hotels in Beirut, the Metropolitan Palace. Before long, I was approached by his Head of Protocol, who said President Saleh would like to meet with me. He then accompanied me to the suite where I was warmly greeted by the President and his Foreign Minister.

Once the usual pleasantries were exchanged, President Saleh asked me about my roots.

"Khalaf, where do you come from originally?" he enquired.

"As the Americans put it, I was born and raised in the UAE."

To my surprise, he retorted with "No, no, you are a Yemeni".

"Well, what I know is that all Arabs historically originate from the Arabian Peninsula," I said.

"No, you *are* a Yemeni," he insisted. "We have a large Al Habtoor tribe in my country numbering around six thousand. They must be your relatives."

"Are they rich?"

"Not rich, but well educated."

"In that case, I think I'd better leave them to you. I don't have enough hotel rooms to host them all," I joked. It was a very pleasant encounter. I admired his efforts to deal with Iranian-backed Houthi insurgents who were making trouble in the north of his country, and his wisdom in rejecting offers from Western nations to send in troops. I was regretful that the Arab world hadn't been more financially and militarily supportive of this poor nation struggling to beat back a foreign-engendered cancer that, if left unchecked, could destabilise Saudi Arabia and beyond.

I hoped to see President Saleh again and invited him to Dubai; he had visited Abu Dhabi but had never seen my hometown. He was enthusiastic, but the turmoil in Yemen triggered by the so-called Arab Spring precluded his coming. Instead, his Minister of Foreign Affairs came to see me to pass his President's regards and to extend an invitation to me to visit Yemen. My encounter with the Yemeni leader had been brief and thereafter we had lost contact. Under pressure, he finally stepped down from office on 27 February 2012.

If my father was the shoulder on which we rested our heads, our mother, Noura bint Ahmad bin Khalaf bin Abdullah Al Otaiba, was our anchor. When I close my eyes, I can almost smell the bread she baked each morning that would be eaten for breakfast, sprinkled with sugar or spread with ghee. Could there ever be an aroma more comforting to a small child?

My mother's tribe was the Al Murar tribe. Three of her nephews were Sheikh Hamdan bin Mohammed, Mubarak bin Mohammed and Tahnoun bin Mohammed Al Nahyan. These were also brothers of Sheikha Hussa bint Mohammed bin Khalifa Al Nahyan – the mother of the UAE President and Ruler of Abu Dhabi, Sheikh Khalifa bin Zayed Al Nahyan.

Mother's father, Ahmad bin Khalaf Al Otaiba, hailed from a well-known pearling family that is one of the most prominent in the UAE today with multiple businesses in Abu Dhabi and Dubai. He knew my father well and liked him. When considering whether to give his daughter's hand in marriage to Ahmad Al Habtoor, he would have taken into account that the Al Habtoors were of a similar social standing to his own with shared historical roots going back to the Liwa.

She was a pretty woman of average build and height, but there was nothing average about her personality. She was a born leader, strong and determined with an inflexible sense of right and wrong. Those Westerners who believe the false stereotype of the downtrodden Arab woman would have quickly changed their views had they met my mother. I think many in the West fail to realise that Arab ladies are queens behind the doors of their own homes. Our own was kind, loving and hardworking with a moral fibre beyond reproach. She ruled our home with an iron will, dispensing affection and discipline in equal measures.

Everyone respected my mother for her wisdom, especially her elder brothers, who went on to hold important positions in the government of Abu Dhabi as well as the Federal UAE government, and who were known as strong advocates for the UAE's formation. They valued her advice and faithfully visited her every morning after *Salaat Al Fajr* (dawn prayer). She was also loved and admired by her daughters-in-law and everyone that was close to her.

Mother was always worrying about us children and what we might be getting up to. She would never sleep before I came home each evening. And I knew only too well that if I dared to return after the proscribed hour, she would shout at me and throw sand in my face.

I used to imagine that as soon as I had my own wife and children, I would be my own boss. Not so. When I became a young man, whenever she would tell me off, I would answer, "I'm a man now. I can do what I like," but that argument never worked. It didn't matter that I wore a business suit or a gold-trimmed *bisht* or carried a briefcase; as far as she was concerned, I was always a naughty youth who had to be kept on the straight and narrow.

Her relationship with my brother, Sultan, known for his calm temperament, was far less turbulent. Sultan was very close to his mother and was a lot better behaved than me. When he wasn't at home she knew he would be playing football or engaging in some other sport, whereas she had no idea where I was most of the time.

Much of my success in life is owed to my mother. She always believed in me and would tell me repeatedly that I would be 'someone' one day. She is also responsible for the self-discipline I exercise in my daily life that has served me well in business. She may be gone from this world, having lived till the age of sixty-four, but whenever I've been tempted to do anything I know she would disapprove of, I feel her presence and imagine her saying, "My son, be a man I can be proud of. I am watching you wherever you go!"

My mother was fifteen when my parents' wedding was arranged. Marrying early was the norm, the average age being sixteen or seventeen.

Nowadays that would be considered far too young, but in early twentieth-century Dubai teenagers were generally mature enough to take on responsibilities. These days, youngsters are more interested in spreading their wings and having fun before they settle down.

Arranged marriages were the way it was done at a time when young people were encouraged to put duty towards family before romance. In fact, the notion of romance was alien to the culture, but this doesn't mean that teenage boys were never seduced by a glimpse of flashing dark eyes or tormented by a romantic notion of love that was destined to be unrequited. It's a facet of human nature to find forbidden fruit more enticing than that which is freely available. Of course, even though the people of that era were hidebound by traditional conventions, there was the odd scandal that was usually hushed up.

Just about every civilisation has a Romeo and Juliet-type fable about star-crossed lovers, and the Middle East is no exception. Ours is the allegedly true story of Qays wa Layla. Qays ibn Al Mulawwah ibn Muzahim was a seventh-century Bedouin shepherd and poet who became obsessed with Layla bint Mahdi ibn Sa'd (popularly known as Layla Al Aamiriya), a childhood companion from the same tribe. When he was refused her hand in marriage only to be told that she was promised to another, he abandoned his tribe to wander the desert before eventually going mad and dying from a broken heart. He was found next to a grave on which he had written beautiful verses to his lady-love. As for Layla, who is believed to have suffered a painful longing for her rejected suitor, her husband carried her off to Iraq, where she became ill and died.

Everyone enjoys a tragic love story, but in the society in which I grew up there was little tolerance for stricken young men like poor Qays. Marriage then wasn't just a union of two individuals, but of two families which would negotiate the bride's dowry in terms of gold, silver, camels, silks, amber, essences perfumed with rose, jasmine and musk, and also fragrant woods, such as *oud* from the Agarwood tree, which is used to scent clothes.

The bride would bring to the marriage a large wooden chest decorated with brass studs containing linens, lingerie and household utensils. It was usual for relatives such as cousins to tie the knot, which ensured wealth remained within the clan and allowed a new bride to feel secure with people she already knew. Prospective marriage partners were appraised according to their lineage, social status and good character.

Families did their utmost to ensure the newly-weds were compatible. Love was an emotion that was supposed to develop after the ceremony. Mostly it did; sometimes it didn't. In that case, the best a couple could hope for was lifelong friendship and mutual respect. Mothers with sons of marriageable age would be on the lookout for modest girls from good families especially during weddings or celebrations when girls would engage in a rhythmical traditional dance performed in a circle called *al na'ashat*, involving the young dancers swinging their long hair from side to side.

Mothers would also get the opportunity to pick out a prospective bride when girls graduated from Qur'an class. For this colourful celebration we called *tawmina* the girls would be dressed in a new *thob* (kaftan) and draped in gold Arab jewellery from their elaborately-styled hair to their waists. The graduates would then visit each family in the area to ask for donations towards their Qur'an teacher's fees.

Girls would be seen playing with friends outside their houses until they were around seven years old. When they reached puberty, they were expected to cover their hair with a *shayla* (head covering). As soon as they were married, many would partially obscure their faces with a mask known as a burka; according to custom, however, covering the face is in no way a religious obligation. There is nothing in Islam that says women must cover their faces. It is a custom that pre-dates Islam in some countries and, in most cases, the wives of nomadic Arab tribes were free to leave their tents with their faces exposed to offer bowls of camel milk to thirsty travellers.

Naturally, prospective grooms hoped for a beautiful bride and, no doubt, there were quite a few disappointments on the day when those from very conservative families glimpsed their new wives unveiled for the first time. Whether they liked what they saw or not, they had to stick with them else shame the bride's family as well as their own. Even a woman who was divorced sometimes stayed with her children in an annex to her former husband's home. Others went back to their parents. Certainly no divorced woman was left to fend for herself on the street. Such disappointments are extremely rare now, when there is more intellectual and social interaction between the sexes, but it does happen.

I couldn't help but laugh when I recently read a report in our local English-language newspaper, *Gulf News*. It seems an unidentified ambassador and minister plenipotentiary from an unnamed Gulf state filed a case against his parents-in-law because the photograph of his bride that was shown to his mother turned out to be that of another of their daughters.

This was discovered following the wedding ceremony, when the shocked groom saw his new wife for the first time and found to his distress that she was "bearded and cross-eyed".

In the past it was also customary for men to marry two, three or even four wives, provided they could afford it. Islam permits a maximum of four wives with the caveat that they are treated equally without any distinction, which is virtually impossible to do. There have been numerous cases of men of advanced years travelling to places like India, Syria or Egypt, where they wed young girls only to abandon their foreign-born wives and children when they eventually return home.

Such multiple unions are also unworkable in a practical sense unless the man is wealthy enough to support more than one wife and is willing to divide his time and affection equally between his spouses. Even then, he could quickly find himself in the middle of a war zone if jealousy rears its ugly head. Admittedly, that doesn't always happen. Sometimes, wives develop a sisterly bond and help each other out with chores and child rearing, but heaven help their husband if they decide to gang up on him.

Life can be complicated enough with one wife, let alone two or more. I've never seriously considered this option myself, especially after witnessing how several of my close relatives fared. My brother Mohammed married several wives and couldn't cope. His wives didn't get along and his children didn't finish their education. As adults, most of them quarrelled and ended up disliking one another.

Likewise, I don't approve of marital unions whereby the groom is decades older than the bride, which were common during those times when poorer families sought to assure their daughter's financial future by wedding her to a comparatively wealthy man. This custom was also harmful to the children of such partnerships, because by the time they reached their teens their fathers were often too old to guide them or take care of them. Of course, there were – and are – many exceptions when kids with much older fathers turn out just fine.

My own parents were exceptionally lucky. Although their personalities were like fire and water, they were devoted to one another and to us.

CHAPTER 2
Childhood

"THERE IS ALWAYS ONE MOMENT IN CHILDHOOD WHEN THE DOOR OPENS
AND LETS THE FUTURE IN."

– GRAHAM GREENE

The skinny five-year-old child with skin burnt dark from the searing sun was too young to carry a gun or master a falcon, much to his annoyance. He was in such a hurry to be a man that one day he attached a morsel of fish to a hook, hoping it would attract a seabird that he could train as his very own.

He laid his trap on the ground and hid behind a sprawling desert plant to await his prey. Suddenly there was a deafening explosion that made him jump out of his skin. He thought his heart would beat out of his chest. He wanted to run, but his limbs wouldn't move. Transfixed with fear, he witnessed what no child ever should. From out of the sky dropped scattered body parts of a pilot whose plane had blown up in mid-air. One of the poor man's fingers twitched reflexively.

Terrified and trembling, the boy ran weeping to the sanctuary of his mother's arms. This incident was the stuff of childhood nightmares that plagued me for years to come, but there were no therapists in those days. Death was all around us and wasn't the sterile affair it is now. Most young children had paid their respects to a sibling, relative or neighbour who had passed away.

It wasn't the idea of death that upset me but rather the violence of the poor man's demise and the grotesqueness of the scene. It was some time before I plucked up enough courage to return to the same spot to retrieve my hook when, lo and behold, I discovered that it had worked its magic. Ironically, the day I caught my very own bird, a big metal bird fell out of the sky with tragic consequences; the horror of that incident remained with me for many years to follow.

I was told that the unfortunate airman was a British Royal Air Force (RAF) pilot. That was a logical assumption as at the time we were living in Al Layyah in the neighbouring sheikhdom of Sharjah that was home to a large RAF airbase. I've often wondered about his identity but have been unable to find any official record of that crash.

Like many other Gulf sheikhdoms including Dubai and Abu Dhabi, Sharjah had accepted British protection during the late nineteenth century to stave off the mighty Ottoman Empire and threats from Persia. In the 1950s, Sharjah was considered by major powers to be strategically important due to its territories that flanked both the Arabian Gulf and the Gulf of Oman. It had also been used as a convenient stopover point for European travellers to India since 1932, when Imperial Airways – the forerunner of British Airways – began operating the route.

The old fort-like structure that was used to control air traffic and also served as a guest house for transit passengers still exists as an aviation museum. The original airfield formed out of sand, soaked in oil and bounded by oil drums, has been replaced by major roads.

The relationship between locals and RAF personnel was basically a marriage of convenience. Most of the time, we didn't bother them and they left us alone. People did tend to get riled up, however, when they heard whispered accounts of the Bahrain-based British Political Resident, Bernard Alexander Brocas Burrows or later, Donald Hawley, the British Political Agent from 1958 to 1962, disrespecting the Trucial States' rulers by keeping them waiting.

Some of Her Majesty's representatives were diplomatic in their dealings with the rulers; others were pompous and harboured an inflated sense of their own importance, which I suppose was a leftover from the then disintegrating British Empire. On the whole, we never felt that we were living under occupation. There were even times when our British guests were useful. Traders who maintained a friendly relationship with them would often be assisted to obtain a British passport, which greatly eased business travel. Nevertheless, there was an air of resentment against the British that was exacerbated by the stirring anti-imperialist speeches of Egypt's former leader, Gamal Abdel Nasser, whose revolutionary ideas took the entire Arab world by storm.

* * *

My formative years from three to seven were spent in the small fishing village of Al Layyah, a port area of Sharjah that was virtually cut off from the mainland at high tide. We used to refer to it as a 'semi-island', as in order to reach the town we would often have to lead our camels through shallow seawater. Although it was devoid of trees or vegetation, Al Layyah possessed a stark beauty all of its own. It had an aura of tranquillity and friendliness, which offered its residents a sense of security.

Foreigners might have described it as 'picturesque', as all around were fishermen painstakingly mending their nets, drying and salting fish or sorting out their morning's catch that might consist of a species of grouper we call *hamour*, silvery sardines, tuna, wrasse, cutlassfish, barracuda and a particularly tasty fish we call *shere* (snapper) that is used in various dishes.

We loved living in this simple backwater. There wasn't much there apart from fishermen's huts and two takeaways that sold a dish we knew as *bajella* or Iranian-style hot beans, consisting of fava beans boiled in salty water with a squeeze of lemon and dried red peppers. This breakfast food was served with freshly-baked bread and dates. People went crazy for the tasty mixture. They would travel from all over to buy *bajella* from the speciality outlets near our home.

We were lucky that generous fisherfolk would turn up at the door almost daily, bearing their surplus catch as a gift. At least, I don't recall that father ever paid them. They must have felt sorry for us because we were the only people in Al Layyah who weren't in some way connected with harvesting the sea's bounty.

Obtaining drinking water was another story. For that we had to travel a few kilometres to the oasis town of Al Khan, shaded by towering date palms. During the hottest days of summer, we would sometimes stay there for easy access to sweet water that we had to frequently consume to prevent our bodies from dehydrating, especially when the thermometer threatened to hit forty-five degrees centigrade or more. We were used to high temperatures, but without water and shade we were always in danger of suffering heat exhaustion or heat stroke that could result in coma or death.

I have such wonderful memories of Al Layyah. It was there that I developed a passion for Pepsi Cola – which everyone agreed was the most delicious beverage in the history of mankind – as well as an enduring love of the sea. We children spent most of our time in the water diving for coins or swimming out to rocks over which we would clamber before gleefully pushing each other into the water. When tides turned treacherous, we would find ourselves carried out towards the horizon against our will or painfully battered against those giant formations.

There was great excitement each time a big ship was spotted anchored off the coast. We would whoop with joy and swim great distances just to catch a glimpse of its crew and passengers. Often, those people who seemed to us so exotic would point, smile and wave. If we were lucky, they would throw us oranges, bananas or other wonderful items that were such a delight to us small boys. Those grand travellers looked upon us as little better than performing monkeys, but we didn't care because we were so hungry.

We quickly learned to distinguish vessels owned by the British India Steam Navigation Company, whose main line was Britain to India, Ceylon (Sri Lanka), Singapore, Malaya (Malaysia), Thailand and Japan via the Arabian Gulf. In its heyday, the company owned more than 500 ships and managed over 100 more. It eventually merged with the P & O lines.

First class passengers on those impressive BI ships were particularly friendly. The gentlemen looked elegant in their shipboard whites, while the faces of the *memsahibs* (European women in colonial India) were often obscured by wide-brimmed straw hats used to protect their delicate fair complexions. Sometimes they would take out their Brownie cameras to take photographs of us, probably still affixed to yellowing albums forgotten in dusty attics. I promised myself that one day I would travel on one of those magnificent vessels to explore the mysterious world across the ocean. That day was to come sooner than I had imagined – but that's for another chapter.

How carefree we were bobbing about in crystal clear warm waters, consuming that heavenly fruit while trying to keep our heads above water to prevent salt from ruining the taste of these rare treats. It may be a trick of the memory, but it seems to me that the waters of the Arabian Gulf were bluer then. An artist might have painted them in shades of pale green and aquamarine that were streaked with silver glints when the sun's rays bounced off the tips of waves. But no artist would have been able to capture the water's silky warmth on our skin or our sense of being at one with nature in a vast universe without end.

We would dive so deep and swim so far out without considering the potential dangers. At times, the Sharjah coastline was visible only as a faint distant line. When the sea was exceptionally choppy, the land would be obscured by gigantic waves. On those occasions when we fleetingly feared that we might never reach home, we would surrender to the sea on our backs like flotsam allowing the tide to carry us to shore. I will never ever swim out this far again, I would tell myself and mean it… until the next morning when youthful bravado would once again kick in.

One of our more dangerous pursuits was to dive down deep without any breathing apparatus, to play inside the hulls of new wooden dhows that had been temporarily sunk by their makers. This was done so that the vessels could absorb water before they were eventually brought to the surface and put into service. Once inside, we would compete as to who would be the first to find their way out of these huge structures that could so easily have become our watery graves. I suppose it was akin to wreck diving without an oxygen bottle. We were young and reckless – and lucky to escape with our lives; in other words, typical boys who liked to imagine they were invincible superheroes. I still shudder to think how close I came to a horrible premature end.

My friends and I were all strong swimmers and accomplished breath-hold divers – skills that weren't unusual in those days. We were real water babies. The sea was in our blood as the coastal people of the Arabian Gulf had made a living from pearl diving for centuries.

The Moroccan Berber explorer Ibn Battuta, who spent thirty years travelling around the Islamic world, was one of the earliest travellers to give an account of this region's pearl diving methods as long ago as the fourteenth century. This excerpt from Ibn Battuta's *Travels in Asia and Africa, 1325–55* provides an insight into this honourable profession that was the region's lifeblood for centuries.

> Before diving, the diver puts on his face a sort of tortoiseshell mask and a tortoise-shell clip on his nose; then, he ties a rope around his waist and dives. They differ in their endurance under water… When he reaches the bottom of the sea, he finds the shells there stuck in the sand between small stones, and pulls them out by hand or cuts them loose with a knife which he has for the purpose, and puts them in a leather bag slung around his neck. When his breath becomes restricted, he pulls the rope and the man holding the rope on the shore feels the movement and pulls him up into the boat. The bag is taken from him and the shells are opened… The sultan takes his fifth and the remainder are bought by the merchants who are there in the boats. Most of them are the creditors of the divers and they take the pearls in quittance of their debtor so much of it as is their due.

Between Ibn Battuta's recorded impressions and the early twentieth century, nothing much had changed. Many families grew rich from the pearl industry but it certainly wasn't easy money. By some estimates, only one in 10,000 wild oysters will actually produce a natural pearl. It was even rarer to come across a valuable one with the desired colour, size and shape. Sometimes weeks would pass without a single pearl being found.

The bulk of the profits went to the pearl traders who sometimes owned their own vessels. The crew of the pearling boats and the divers were hardly able to eke out a living as not only were they paid a miniscule share of the profits, but once the season ended each September some would languish until the following April without work. Others would find temporary employment, such as fishing or camel herding or go back to their desert encampments.

Each year, those men put their lives on the line. They would grease their bodies and inside their ears before attaching themselves to ropes weighed with stones. Then they would draw a deep breath before swimming down to the pearl beds with wide net baskets hanging around their necks.

They used to dive down seventy metres or more on a single inhalation, aware that any delay in pulling them back up to the surface could result in brain damage or death. Many would return home suffering from exhaustion and malnutrition. Another peril facing the divers was infrequent yet deadly shark attacks. It may have been a harsh existence, but they managed to stay cheerful with on-board chants, songs and camaraderie.

The 1930s marked a turning point for everyone connected with pearling, as by then the Japanese had flooded the worldwide market with relatively inexpensive cultured pearls formed as a result of human intervention in a pearl farm. To the trained eye, their beauty was not comparable to that of natural pearls and they did not have the rarity value; but during the Great Depression of the 1930s and early 1940s, buyers in New York, Paris or London didn't have the luxury of being fussy.

The drop in demand for natural pearls severely hit local economies until such time the oil began to flow. The affluent pearling families were all badly affected by the new trend. Some became impoverished; others adapted and diversified into different businesses.

When I was a boy, just about everyone was connected to pearling merchants and divers. As I mentioned earlier, my mother's family, Al Otaiba, grew wealthy from the trade. My wife's father traded in pearls in Dubai and Qatar, and later became the owner of a small pearling boat from which he would dive himself. One day, upon his return from a pearling trip, he swam in the sea to get clean. That was the usual prelude to dousing himself with well water that was kept in a sheepskin container to remove the salt from his body, as was customary in the diving community. He was young and fit, but on this occasion, he failed to return home. The waters whose benefice he had relied on throughout his life ironically robbed him of it.

You may be interested to know that the United Arab Emirates is attempting to revive its pearl industry. The Dubai Multi Commodities Centre (DMCC) aims to return the country to its roots by marrying the spirit of traditional pearl diving with pearl farming's technological advances. With so many of our traditions being lost, it's a nice concept. But whether or not it will be commercially viable is yet to be seen.

* * *

Al Layyah was a favourite weekend spot for members of the British air force who came to picnic, swim and dive off the rocks. Mostly they were well behaved and we hardly noticed their presence. But at times they got drunk when they would shout abuse in our direction. My mother used to be so scared that she would lock us in our rooms and bolt the main door.

On one occasion, my brother Mohammed became so fed up of the antics of these intoxicated hoodlums that he enlisted the help of some of his burliest friends to drive them off. Within no time, their commander escorted the culprits to our home and ordered them to apologise, which they rather sheepishly did. Hospitality was so ingrained in our culture that they were no doubt pressed to enjoy a cup of Arabic coffee and dates.

You're probably wondering what possessed my parents to relocate the family to Sharjah in the first place. It was a most unusual decision on their part, especially since relations between Dubai and Sharjah were then less than cordial, partly due to border disputes and thugs and bandits who sometimes prevented camel caravans from travelling between the two sheikhdoms. Indeed, I believe our family was the only one to have moved from Dubai to set up home in Sharjah and I will always be grateful to Sharjah's ruling Qawasim tribe for welcoming us so warmly.

An interfamily dispute that threatened to get out of hand had necessitated the move. I must have been around three years old when we said our fond farewells to Shindagha. At first, we stayed in a house that belonged to my father's cousins, the sons of Sheikh Sultan bin Mijren, a relative of the Al Maktoums.

Most of the residents of Al Layyah belonged to tribes originating from the Abu Dhabi and Dubai branches of the Bani Yas, although they held strong allegiance to the Qawasim rulers of Sharjah. The alliance of tribes known as the Qawasim was once a formidable force to be reckoned with around the Trucial Coast. Indeed, they took on the British fleet during the eighteenth and early nineteenth century, with more than sixty large ships, 810 smaller vessels and 25,000 fighting men.

Well fortified with high walls and watchtowers, Ra's al-Khaimah was once their capital from where they ruled Sharjah, Ajman and Umm al-Qaiwain as well as several ports in southern Iran – including Lingah that was a vibrant centre of trade until 1898 when it was attacked and occupied by the Persians.

When Lingah's new rulers began imposing Persian customs duties, many of Lingah's ethnic Arab population headed to Dubai where Sheikh Saeed warmly received them as potential contributors to the city's economy. There, they mostly settled in an area called Bastakiya, where they constructed windtower houses with open courtyards along a network of narrow alleyways. During the 1980s, many of these beautiful homes were demolished. Those that still stand have been lovingly restored and largely been turned into galleries or cafés.

The Qawasim also had control of the islands of Abu Musa, Lesser and Greater Tunb in the Straits of Hormuz that were forcibly seized by Shah Mohammed Reza Pahlavi on 30 November 1971 and which to this day remain a major point of contention between Tehran and Abu Dhabi. This is a topic that merits further discussion in a future chapter as Iran's continuing possession of those islands has caused a diplomatic rift between the UAE and the Islamic Republic of Iran.

We greatly appreciated the bin Mijren's kind gesture and, admittedly, their house was a marginal improvement on the palm hut we had left behind. But cracked and partially derelict, it was no palace either. As the situation progressed from bad to worse, we feared the building might crumble on top of our heads while we slept.

It was then that the ruling family stepped in to offer us the use of a rent-free 'grand dwelling' owned by the wife of Sheikh Sultan bin Saqr Al Qasimi, Sheikha Meera. She was the mother of his sons, Sheikh Khaled and Sheikh Mohammed bin Sultan Al Qasimi, whose brother Sheikh Saqr bin Sultan bin Saqr Al Qasimi was then Sharjah's Ruler. They assured us that from now on we were their guests under their own care and protection.

What a posh place it was! It was the largest house in Al Layyah with solid walls constructed with imported stone slabs that outwardly resembled dried sponges but were, in fact, very strong. It consisted of two enormous rooms – or so they seemed to me – and an outside majlis flanking the boundary wall where my father received his male guests. I was thrilled to move in to that 'mansion' surrounded by a spacious courtyard large enough for our growing herd of around ten camels as well as our goats, four falcons and saluki hunting dogs.

The Arabian saluki is considered to be the oldest breed of hunting dog dating back to 5,000 BC by some accounts; their mummified bodies have been found in the tombs of Egyptian pharaohs, while their images appear in various ancient Egyptian wall paintings. Whereas Islam considers all other dogs to be unclean, the saluki is an exception. They have long been prized in the Gulf for their ability to track down gazelle and hare as well as for their intelligent and faithful nature. They have even inspired great poets to pen admiring odes. The ninth-century Basra-born poet Abu Nuwas wrote:

> I will sing the praise of a hound whose owner's good fortune is assured by his tremendous effort. All the good things they have come from him. His master is always like a slave to him; at night he brings him nearest his beds. If he is uncovered his master puts on him his own coat. What a fine hound you are, without equal.

In winter, when it was cold, wet or windy, we would tether the camels to the boundary wall and cover them before bringing the dogs, goats and hawks into the house. I became particularly fond of one of the female salukis called Karwa – a Farsi word meaning a type of 'clay jar', of the type in which her drinking water was kept. I usually insisted that she accompany me on our frequent hunting expeditions, although it's more usual for salukis to hunt in pairs.

A long-eared female goat prized for its abundance of milk was another of my childhood companions. She regularly gave birth to fluffy kids. Just observing their playful antics provided us children with hours of enjoyment.

When I wasn't swimming, hunting or helping my father take care of the animals, I would hang out with boys of a similar age. Al Layyah was really small, so all the children who lived there were pals. I was on a first-name basis with everyone under the age of ten, but spent most days in the company of Ahmad Bilaama, Sultan bin Tarish, Ahmad Al Moukarrab, Hamoud and Khamis bin Shamis, and the young sons of the bin Haddah family. I often think fondly of those carefree times and my fun-loving childhood buddies.

We had much in common. For one thing, we were all mad about football. We played barefooted without caring that our feet were often painful or bloody from sharp stones and broken glass. Soccer had been introduced to the area by Dubai's longest serving British resident, a man called George Chapman, who was appointed *wakil* (agent) to Gray Mackenzie & Co Ltd (now MMI) in 1951. Like his fellow Brit Jack Briggs, he had the ear of the sheikhs and was quite an influential character.

When the nights were especially dark, we would play a universal favourite with children everywhere, hide and seek. What fun it was to leap out of the shadows and scare one another, which always elicited a frightened yell! We had few toys, although some of the boys had marbles courtesy of the RAF; others, handmade wooden ships or home-made bats, which were used to play our own version of cricket. We sometimes also played with the RAF officers at their base in Sharjah.

The only blot on my wild and free existence was school. I didn't want to go and was unable to understand why I should. They say that schooldays are the happiest days of a child's life. They made me utterly miserable, which, by the way, is something I share with the great British bulldog, Winston Churchill, who didn't turn out too badly as you'll no doubt agree.

He has been quoted as saying, "Schools have not necessarily much to do with education… they are mainly institutions of control, where basic habits must be inculcated in the young. Education is quite different and has little place in school." As someone who had been put through the rigours of an inflexible British public school system, that was his view. Of course, these days, I don't agree with him, but at the same time, I fully empathise with the way he felt.

Likewise, America's sixteenth President, Abraham Lincoln, only received eighteen months of schooling and he went on to end slavery. On the importance of education he said "The philosophy of the schoolroom in one generation will be the philosophy of government in the next," a sentiment that is closer to my current thinking than Churchill's embittered standpoint.

It's just as well that I wasn't familiar with the lives of those great men then, else I would have been even more determined to escape the confines of the classroom.

I can't pretend to be a fan of Shakespeare, but these often-quoted lines from *As You Like It* sum up my feelings: "… and then the whining school-boy, with his satchel and shining morning face, creeping like snail unwillingly to school." There were days when I was so unwilling that I didn't bother going at all. When my parents got wise to the usual 'I'm sick' excuse, I decided to get creative and came up with all kinds of weird and wonderful reasons why I should stay home, but nothing would make them change their minds.

There was only one thing to do. I knew that the only way I could obtain my freedom was to get up early and dress in a pair of shorts and a T-shirt for school, which I believe was called Al Orouba. The fact that I'm unsure about the school's name speaks volumes about my utter disinterest. Off I would go looking like a model student each morning, but as soon as our home was out of sight, I would meet up with friends to head to the beach.

Naturally, it wasn't long before my father was alert to my tricks, when I would receive a hefty smack and a warning never to play hooky again. That didn't stop me. On one occasion, I persuaded a few schoolmates to help me capsize the *abra* that carried us to school. They were only too pleased to go along with the conspiracy.

We rocked the boat from side to side until it overturned. Just as I planned, we all ended up soaked through, so of course we were unable to proceed to class. Now, the whole day is mine to do as I please, went my thinking. But I wasn't such a clever young chap after all. Father wasn't so easily taken in. He only had to look me in the eyes to know when I was up to mischief. He walloped me even harder than usual for the twin sins of missing class and tipping over the water taxi.

My hostility towards school wasn't because I didn't love to learn new things. I've always sought knowledge and still do. It was simply that the lessons didn't seem to relate to anything in my life. Learning by rote subjects in which I had little interest, such as Arabic grammar, was a boring chore and I had to use every effort just to sit still.

To my mind, the school walls were like a prison preventing me from doing the things I loved most and, as I explained earlier, I wasn't one to submit easily to discipline from my own parents, let alone from foreign teachers who insisted that students stand up every time they came into the room. If someone had told me then that the day would come when I would own two schools of my own, I would have advised them to stay out of the sun.

Now if there had been a school for hunting, falconry or camel racing, I would have been beating down its doors, although when it came to those skills my father was a one-man academy. He was a master of such manly pursuits and owned quite a few airguns and shotguns. Practically every household kept a gun and often an extensive collection of weapons. These were primarily for hunting. But they were also an insurance policy against intertribal hostilities which had, indeed, broken out during earlier decades to do with competing territorial claims.

Now for a confession! When I was just six years old, I almost shot my mother. My memories of that unfortunate incident are fairly dim; maybe because my subconscious mind prefers not to remember something so terrifying. I recall grabbing one of my father's guns from its hook on the wall as a joke before waving it around in front of my mother and one of her friends, who were seated chatting. I can still picture the horrified expressions of the two women as I laughingly squeezed the trigger.

The resulting bang quickly wiped the grin off my face. It took a few moments for the awfulness of what I had done to sink in. I was more shocked than they were, as I hadn't realised the gun was loaded. I dropped it and ran. Luckily, the bullet whizzed past the women's heads and embedded itself in the wall so no one was harmed. I did learn a lesson that day. From then on, there was no one more cautious when handling a gun than me. Thanks to my tender age, I was comforted by everyone and easily forgiven.

The very thought disturbs me even now when I think what might have been and how an accident could have altered my life's path forever. How would I have been able to live with myself in the knowledge that my beloved mother had been injured or killed at my own hand?

Within a couple of years, I was proficient with both an airgun and a shotgun. I had plenty of practice as father would ask me to shoot rodents and smallish birds, with which he would feed his hawks and falcons. If he sent me out with an air rifle, he would say "Take these ten pellets and come back with ten birds".

Later, when he trusted me with a rifle, he would hand me ten 22-calibre bullets and expect me to bring home at least ten birds if not more, which I was sometimes able to do when a flock was tightly grouped together and a single bullet could take down two or three. By the time I was eight, I would help him train our birds of prey.

My father would first cover the bird's head with a hood-like piece of leather called *Al burgu* before asking me to hold the falcon tightly to ensure it didn't fly off. He would then walk some distance away and tell me to remove the cover from the hawk's eyes. Lastly, he would call the bird by name when it would fly in his direction and land on his arm.

Training falcons is not an easy task and requires great patience as well as time for trust to develop between the bird and its owner. They are not pets and it is rare for an affectionate bond to form between the *saqqar* (trainer) and his hawk. The *saqqar* needs his falcon to hunt and the bird relies on the man for its food and water.

One of my favourite pastimes from October to March was hunting houbara, whose meat is considered a great delicacy in my part of the world and is considered by some to be an aphrodisiac.

In 1984, when Queen Elizabeth's daughter, Princess Anne, was staying at my hotel the Metropolitan in Dubai, to participate in an equestrian event, my friend Sheikh Hasher bin Maktoum Al Maktoum, a nephew of Sheikh Rashid, engaged the princess in a lively conversation about falconry. But, unfortunately, he mispronounced the word 'bustard'. "We love hunting bastards here," he told her. That was one of the few times in my life when I felt embarrassed. I needn't have worried. Princess Anne was a great sport. She knew Sheikh Hasher was referring to the houbara and, thankfully, Her Highness laughed as loudly as the rest of us.

The houbara and the Saker falcon are facing extinction but in the 1950s, little thought was given to the preservation of wildlife. Humans were few in number while the sea teemed with fish and the air with migratory birds. With a hooded Saker or Peregrine on our gloved arms, we would head for the high dunes on camelback to follow the houbara.

Father was an expert bustard tracker. As soon as he recognised its tracks, we would get off our camels to inspect them. Amazingly, he could assess how old they were as well as in which direction the bird must have flown as long as three days earlier. He could even estimate its approximate landing point. "We'll enjoy a good lunch today!" he would say. I have no idea how he did it!

When the game bird was finally spotted, he would tell me to be quiet. We would then remove the hoods from our hawks' eyes. They would spend a few moments acclimatising to their new-found freedom when we would say "*Bismillah*" (in the name of Allah) and push them up into the air. Without hesitation they would soar high into the sky as fast as an F16 and streak after their target before plunging like a bullet to attack their powerful prey that can weigh as much as four kilograms. In every instance, the houbara had no chance. At times, it would succumb without putting up much of a fight, while at others, it would attempt an escape to no avail.

It was then our job to race towards the impact site, when our hawks would be encouraged to relinquish their grip on their prize. When visibility lessened before sunset, we would have difficulty in making out the silhouettes of our falcons.

Now it was Karwa's turn to earn her living. We would signal to her that she must chase the hawk before she bounded away with us hot on the chase. When she finally barked and wagged her tail, we would cast our gaze upwards when nine times out of ten, our falcon could be seen circling and swooping. We would also use the hawks to catch rabbits and hares but they weren't always as adept closer to the ground. So, as a last resort, we would set the salukis on them or pick up our guns.

For us, this 5,000-year-old noble pastime of kings and sheikhs wasn't so much a sport but a pleasant means of obtaining meat for the table as a welcome change from fish or crustaceans such as crab and *cigalis* (local sand lobsters).

The United Arab Emirates' late President and Ruler of Abu Dhabi Sheikh Zayed bin Sultan Al Nahyan was an avid falconer throughout his adult life. In 1976 he published a fascinating book titled *Hunting with Falcons* that is an acknowledged authority on the subject. Falconry is still popular among Emiratis; the difference is pedigree hawks can fetch over 100,000 dollars as opposed to around fifty dollars when I was a boy. Hunting with falcons is now banned in most areas of the UAE but it isn't unusual for keen practitioners of the sport to travel to places like Pakistan where the houbara is still plentiful, although nowadays, when conservation is a high-profile topic, they must first obtain a special permit.

In many respects, the falcon emblemises the UAE. It is pictured on dirham notes and on stamps, and since 1983 Dubai has boasted a falcon hospital that treats raptors without charge. In 2003, Dubai's municipality opened the National Falcon Centre which has its own raptor souk, training facility and museum. As a sign of the times, falcons are being used by a British-run company in Dubai to scare pigeons from the rooftops of five-star hotels, public grandstands and industrial warehouses.

A far less utilitarian activity is camel racing, which has evolved into a sophisticated sport in recent decades. Today, there are as many as 14,000 racing camels in the UAE, which compete on more than fifteen racetracks over four to ten kilometres. Races are beamed to television screens and every care is given to jockeys and camels. Ambulances, doctors and vets are always on standby. Not so in my day.

Because I was so slim and light at age ten and upwards, I was an ideal camel jockey. In those days, camel racing was a feature of Arab marriage celebrations and would take place way out in the desert. I've always loved to compete, so I would look forward to showing off my skill. There were times when I competed against Sheikh Rashid's sons, HH Sheikh Mohammed bin Rashid Al Maktoum, now the Vice-President and Prime Minister of the United Arab Emirates and Ruler of Dubai, and HH Sheikh Hamdan bin Rashid Al Maktoum, now Dubai's Deputy Ruler. Their uncle, Sheikh Khalifa bin Saeed Al Maktoum, would sometimes put up as much as five rupees as prize money. That was a small fortune to a boy who was allowed a mere quarter of a rupee each morning to take to school.

But there was one occasion when I strongly resisted entering a competition. I wasn't in the mood that day and in any case, my camel was weighed down by heavy metal pots and cookery utensils.

Unfortunately, one of my father's friends challenged us by saying he could easily beat me. That put me in an awkward position. I knew in my heart that I should say no, but I didn't want to let my father down or allow anyone to think I was afraid to lose. I am sure there are times in your life when you know deep inside that you shouldn't do something, yet you go ahead anyway against your better judgment. This was one of them.

As soon as the race began, I discovered that I couldn't control my beast. He was going too fast and the cookery stuff was banging against my legs. The longer we raced, the more I was in agony. In spite of the heavy load on his back, that camel flew. I did my best to bring him to a halt but nothing I said or did could slow him down.

By now, I had made up my mind to guide the camel towards a dune and jump off. But instead of concentrating on preserving my health – or even my life – I decided to hold on to the *khitam* (a camel's bridle) in an effort to save the animal. It was a mistake. When I leapt off into a dune, I was somehow tangled up in the reins. Screaming and crying, I was dragged across the sands until my father rushed to my rescue to find me battered and in pain. Worst of all was my bruised ego. I hated that my father's friends had seen me cry. Now, they would no longer think of me as a man but a baby.

This episode was just another lesson in the toughest university of all: the university of life. I learned to trust my instincts. I learned when to say no. I learned that life itself is the most precious commodity of all – lessons that served me well in the years to come.

CHAPTER 3

Adventure

"LIFE IS EITHER A GREAT ADVENTURE OR NOTHING."

– HELEN KELLER

"It's time to go home," announced my father, catching us by surprise. By now the family disagreement that drove us from Dubai had long been patched up and Sheikh Rashid had made it known that he wanted us to return to Shindagha. So in 1957, we packed up, thanked our hosts, said our goodbyes to our neighbours and headed back to Dubai.

I was always aware that our stay in Sharjah was temporary and was proud to be a child of Dubai. Nevertheless, Al Layyah felt like home to me as I had been little more than a toddler when we first arrived. I was sad to leave our lovely house and all my friends with whom I swore to keep in touch. I was also excited to turn a new page and within no time, I was able to forge new friendships. I couldn't escape school though. I enjoyed school a lot more because my friend, Saeed Saif, was in the same class. We were close, but we also fought daily when we would stop talking to one another. But no matter how angry we felt, we would always walk to my home together. Saeed would kiss my mother and get invited to lunch – regardless of whether I liked it or not.

My brother Sultan and I were swiftly enrolled in the new school, Al Shaab. It wasn't very far from home, but we had to wade through shallows there and back with rolled-up trousers, holding our shoes aloft. All our course books were printed with a picture of the Kuwaiti Ruler on the cover.

The teachers were mainly Palestinians, Jordanians and Egyptians who didn't stand any nonsense from wayward pupils. "We were scared to bump into one of them on the street," remembers Sultan. "If we neglected to do our homework, they would beat us. We could have never got away with putting our feet up on our desks or being rude to the teachers as some kids do today."

Now that Sultan was a little older, we were friends as well as brothers. We often played together, but as he recalls, like all little boys, we would occasionally get into fights. I was very protective of Sultan at school, a feeling that has always remained with me. I couldn't have wished for a more loyal and supportive brother. He has always stood by my side and until now he ranks high among the small circle of those who are closest and most dear to me. He is also one of my favourite travelling companions, partly because he is naturally blessed with a calm and steady personality.

Going back to the *barasti* was a bit of a come down after the comparative opulence and spaciousness we were used to. My elder brother was now married, so an extra room had to be constructed for Mohammed and his wife. In the beginning, I felt like Aesop's country mouse that visits his friend in the town and decides he prefers the peace and quiet of the countryside. But that feeling didn't last long. I quickly adjusted to my new life and was soon enjoying the buzz generated by Sheikh Rashid's ambitious designs.

The health of the seventy-five-year-old ruler, Sheikh Saeed bin Maktoum bin Saeed Al Maktoum, had been in decline for decades during which time Sheikh Rashid had informally taken over the leadership reins. Sheikh Saeed was now rarely seen out and about. By early 1958, he was no longer seen seated on one of the wooden benches of his simple majlis. Nevertheless, his death in the summer of that year came as a terrible shock to his people, who during Sheikh Saeed's forty-six-year-long rule, considered him as their beloved and respected patriarch.

When his passing was announced from minarets on the morning of 10 September, everyone rushed out of their homes to share their grief with friends and neighbours. Later that day, many thousands joined the funeral procession led by his sons, Sheikh Rashid and Sheikh Khalifa.

Thousands more lined its route to catch a last glimpse of the only ruler most of us had ever known. Wrapped in cloth, he was carried from his house in Shindagha on a simple wooden structure that was jostled by the crowds as men pushed forward, desperate to touch it. The heartfelt wailing of women and the haunting strains of muezzins' prayers pierced the warm humid air. Although I have no personal memories of Sheikh Saeed, I do remember how a cloud of sadness enveloped Shindagha for days following his burial, when everyone spoke of his warm heart and good deeds.

As recounted in the book *Rashid's Legacy* by Graeme Wilson, there is a well-known story that perfectly illustrates those qualities. One morning, he woke up before the rest of his household and came across a worker in the process of stealing a valuable Persian carpet from his majlis. "Put it back immediately else the guards will certainly catch you," he ordered. The thief quickly obeyed and was permitted to continue in his job for several years to come, as though the transgression had never occurred.

No one was more grief-stricken than Sheikh Rashid, who had been particularly close to his father. Throughout the ailing Ruler's long illness, he was never far from his side and always sought his father's advice on matters of state during his de facto rule as crown prince, when he had taken care of day-to-day concerns.

But duty called and on 4 October 1958, Sheikh Rashid embraced his destiny to become the ninth member of the Al Maktoum family to rule Dubai. Little did he know then that one day he would be appointed Vice-President and Prime Minister of a new federation of seven sheikhdoms under one flag – that of the United Arab Emirates.

There were few cameras around in those days, but both the funeral of Sheikh Saeed and the official accession of his son, Sheikh Rashid, were captured for future generations by a young photography enthusiast from Baluchistan, whose father had sent him to Dubai as a punishment for his lack of interest in the family business. It's hard to imagine now, but until the late 1970s, Dubai was considered a 'hardship posting' to which skilled expatriates were lured by fabulous salaries, accommodation, regular flights home and generous allowances.

Noor Ali Rashid enjoyed no such material advantages. Without qualifications he was left to fend for himself, but those precious photographs of Dubai's royals turned out to be his passport to an eventual appointment as the UAE's official Royal Photographer, allowing him an unprecedented access to almost all official and social events. When he was asked by a reporter why he attended the funeral when he was, after all, a foreign newcomer, he simply said, "Everyone else was going".

Noor Ali succumbed to a long illness in August 2010 at the age of eighty. During the holy month of Ramadan, just one day before he died, he visited me at my open majlis where friends, diplomats and politicians were gathered to wish me well.

He was pleased to learn that I was in the process of writing my autobiography and said, "I have lots of photographs in my library of your grandfather, your father and of you when you were young, which may be suitable for publication". For the first time ever, I saw that he wasn't burdened down with large cameras and equipment.

On this occasion, he carried a simple, small camera and asked if he could take my picture with his sons and grandsons whom he had brought along with him. He appeared very frail and ill, and much of what he said, in a voice pitched much louder than usual, didn't make any sense. It was as though there was a breakdown in the connection between his brain and his tongue. I wondered why he had made such an effort to see me, concluding that it was his way of saying his last farewell to an old friend. I had an uncomfortable feeling that I would never see him again.

Sadly, my assumption was correct. Two days later, while browsing the Arabic daily, *Al Khaleej*, I came across his obituary. I accepted his death as a blessing from God. At last, he could rest peacefully after years of battling a terminal illness. Whenever there is a major event he is greatly missed, but his rich legacy of almost 3 million photographs and several books will ensure he will never be forgotten as one of the pioneers who helped to make the United Arab Emirates the great country it is.

For the people of Dubai, Sheikh Rashid's transition from Crown Prince to Ruler was seamless. By the late 1950s, Dubai's population had swelled to around 30,000, when it was acknowledged to be the largest town on the Trucial Coast. It was now a bustling trading hub with an increasingly cosmopolitan flavour.

Dhows from East Africa and India were moored two or three abreast along the Creek. The souks were flourishing as never before, as traders from elsewhere in the Gulf and beyond flocked in. And new stores emerged to provide healthy competition to Spinneys supermarket that opened in 1942, and Jashanmal that had been selling menswear, household goods, newspapers, books and stationery since 1956.

In the years since we had been away, the town had experienced a major economic setback when its lifeline, the Creek, became strangled by a massive build-up of silt. As a result, boats were running aground or capsizing, while larger vessels were precluded from entering the mouth of the Creek. Worried traders pressed Sheikh Rashid to do something about the worsening situation, that was not only harming their businesses, but also Dubai's economy.

In 1954, Sheikh Rashid commissioned the British consultancy firm, Sir William Halcrow & Partners (now the Halcrow Group Limited), to come up with a solution. This entailed dredging the shallows, constructing breakwaters and building quays to facilitate the unloading and loading of cargoes. Sheikh Rashid was anxious to proceed, but the cost of the project, estimated to be in the region of 600,000 pounds (worth approximately 31 million pounds in today's terms), was prohibitive. The Emir of Kuwait came to the rescue with a massive 400,000-pound loan, but there was still 200,000 pounds to be found.

Not to be thwarted, Sheikh Rashid used the ingenious thinking which became his trademark. He began by setting up a Creek Dredging Fund and opened a customs office to ensure that 4 per cent custom duty was paid on all imported goods. This was headed by the Bahrain-born Mahdi Al Tajir who became one of Sheikh's Rashid's most trusted confidants and advisors. In later years, he took UAE nationality and was appointed Ambassador of the United Arab Emirates to the United Kingdom. I got to know him in the early seventies, when Habtoor Engineering was up-and-running. To me, he was always courteous and helpful.

Customs revenues permitted dredging work to commence in 1959 and, shortly thereafter, Sheikh Rashid was able to repay the Kuwaiti loan. By 1961, vessels with a maximum draft of 2.1 metres were able to negotiate the Creek without difficulty. In the 1960s and 1970s, the Creek was redredged to allow for the anchorage of larger craft up to 500 tons.

You could say that 1959 was a crucial turning point in terms of Dubai's status as a trading hub. With the Creek project now firmly underway, the Ruler tasked the British construction and civil engineering company, Costain, to construct Dubai Airport, which only took a year to complete. It consisted of a 1,800-metre-long compressed sand runway, a parking ramp and a small terminal.

In reality, it was little more than an airfield capable of handling small aircraft, but for us, its very existence as an entrée to the world was a source of great pride. By 1969, an enlarged and enhanced airport was serving nine airlines flying to twenty destinations. But even then we hadn't the slightest inkling that it would be the seed of a vast international airport, that in 2010 was recognised as the fourth busiest airport in the world in terms of passenger traffic, handling 130 airlines collectively operating 6,000 flights weekly.

The late 1960s were exciting years for the family too. My brother Mohammed was now the owner of a British Petroleum diesel pump station that supplied fuel to fishermen. I used to help out by manning the pump each day after school when I became good friends with BP's General Manager, Ted Thomas, and his Bahraini right-hand man, Mohammed Shems. They were both very supportive as was BP's Commercial Manager, Salem El Midfa'a from Sharjah, who always encouraged me to pursue my ambitions.

Needless to say that income generated from the diesel station was very welcome. It was such a relief not to have to worry where the next meal was coming from or whether enough money could be scraped up to purchase new clothes. A steady inflow of cash meant the family was no longer reliant on the generosity of others. It was also my passport to new thrills and excitement at the cinema.

In 1958, Dubai's first movie house, Al Watan, was built in Gamal Abdel Nasser Square, providing an endless source of enjoyment to adults and children alike. At last, we were able to get an idea of what the world beyond our borders looked like! In today's terms it was a fleapit, but we didn't care about the hard seats or the stifling smoky atmosphere as we watched Hindi, British, American and Egyptian films with wide-eyed wonder.

The Egyptian cinema industry had flourished since the 1930s, but the 1950s and early 1960s were its 'Golden Age'. We laughed at the antics of the comedian, Ismail Yasin; dabbed our eyes during poignant tales featuring Layla Murad or Faten Hamama; and were riveted by the flirtatiousness of Nadia Lutfi, Souad Hosni and Hend Rostom. Most young boys wanted to grow up to be like the dashingly handsome Rushdy Abaza or Ahmad Mazhar, both handsome guys who usually got the girl.

Egyptian movies and music had spread like wildfire around the Arab world to establish Egypt's reputation as the region's cultural heart. And certainly, the soulful songs of Farid Al Atrash and Umm Kulthum could be heard belting out from the souks and open-air traditional coffee shops of Dubai, where men gathered to smoke, do deals, play dominoes or enjoy a respite from domestic surroundings with old friends.

It's no exaggeration to say that Umm Kulthum was the Arabs' diva of all divas. She wasn't exactly a classic beauty, but she had the voice of an angel and a rare ability to stir deep emotion in people of all ages. Egypt's deposed King Farouk had decorated her with the highest order reserved for members of the Royal Family. This accolade from Britain's puppet king prompted her shunning by the Musicians Guild subsequent to the July 1952 bloodless revolution, when for a short time, her voice was no longer heard on the radio.

Egypt's new President, Gamal Abdel Nasser, was not amused. When he found out that she had been banned by the Guild, he said, "What are they... crazy? Do they want to turn Egypt against us?" Her songs were soon aired again and she remained the region's most beloved singer until her funeral in 1975 which drew 4 million mourners, making hers the fourth largest funeral attendance in history. President Abdel Nasser awarded Umm Kulthum the honorary 'First Lady of Egypt', a title always reserved for the president's wife in every country. This rare honour illustrates Nasser's admiration and respect for this irreplaceable chanteuse who capti- vated generations of Arabs with her ability to bring strong men to tears.

Cowboy movies kept us boys on the edge of our seats and there was no one who didn't love the action-packed tales of *Robin Hood*, epics such as *Spartacus* or *The Magnificent Seven* and tearjerkers like *Lassie*. But it was Bombay-made films (we didn't know it as Bollywood in those days) that really captured my imagination with their strong heroes, graceful heroines, villainous deeds, adventure, romance, tragedy, dance and song.

Actors Raaj Kumar and Dilip Kumar were my childhood idols, while the south Indian actress and dancer Vyjayanthimala Bali was my first love long before she gained megafame starring with Raj Kapoor in the 1964 movie, *Sangam*. India seemed like a fantastical world of silk-clad maharajas, long- haired bearded mystics, ornate palaces, shimmering lakes and lush hills; at least on celluloid. I could hardly wait to see for myself.

Within no time, my wish came true.

My father was asked by some of his friends to join an informal consor- tium of small traders, who regularly carried merchandise from Dubai to sell in India and brought back Indian goods to sell in the local markets. I was above the moon when he decided to take me along with him on the first run, which entailed having to sneak on-board a cargo liner as we couldn't afford the fare.

I was excited but scared as to what would happen to us, were we to be discovered. Thankfully, my elder brother sought out the captain to tell him that we were on-board. I'm not sure how Mohammed persuaded the cap- tain to accept his unofficial passengers, although I suspect there was some bribery and bullying involved. Before he disembarked, Mohammed told us the captain had been informed in no uncertain terms that he was personally responsible for making sure we were fed and for ensuring our safe arrival. Mohammed was afraid of nothing and so he was well suited for the role of our family's protector.

Now I was the one on the boat looking down at the boys swimming in the water below, but I had no fruit to throw their way; just a large bag of pistachios and peanuts which I intended to hang onto, as I hoped to exchange the nuts for pocket money. Unfortunately, my very first entrepre- neurial endeavour was a failure. On the first day of the three-day voyage,

I carefully laid out this bounty on a mat and waited for customers, but nobody was buying. I ended up scoffing all my wares myself.

The sea voyage turned out to be a disappointment. As much as I loved being in the water, I disliked being on it. Sadly, I was no sailor. Nights on deck were uncomfortable because my father would tie a rope around me and attach it to his wrist to prevent me rolling off the ship in my sleep; I knew just how our tethered goat must feel. I was far from happy about this precaution which I thought was entirely unnecessary but I knew that he had nothing but good intentions. He wasn't going to take any chance of losing me to the Arabian Sea.

Most of the time I was either seasick or bored, as once the ship passed Oman, there was nothing to look at except seagulls and the occasional school of dolphins. So I decided to explore and found myself on the first-class upper deck, where some children were playing table tennis. One of the boys invited me for a game. I had never played ping-pong before, but I soon caught on and had fun, until an eagle-eyed steward noticed I didn't belong in his section and kicked me out. That was slightly humiliating but not enough to deter me from going back again and again, until the vessel finally dropped anchor in the port of Bombay.

I can't begin to describe the thrill of arriving in India as we struggled down the gangway with our load. It was a great feeling to escape the endless rolling of the ship and the nausea which had remained with me throughout. But we were ill-prepared for the sea of surging, mostly un-washed, humanity outside the port. I had never before seen so many people gathered together in my life except at funerals.

The noise was deafening. Rickshaw boys, taxi drivers and touts for guest houses encircled us; some attempted to pull us away from the oth-ers. Beggars, some with horrendous deformities, held out their palms or grabbed our clothing. Begging was then a well-organised industry and in some instances, children were deliberately blinded or even crippled to elicit sympathy.

This was not the India of the movies. There were no elegant sari-clad maidens like Vyjayanthimala peeping at us through branches of a tree. Nevertheless, the short ride to our hotel in the Mussafir Khana neighbour-hood was eye-popping, with cows – which I later discovered were sacred to Hindus – laying down in the middle of traffic. The air was thick with the odour of spices, incense and sweat, with a faint aroma of sewage that at times became overpowering.

On subsequent visits to Bombay, I was forced to hold my nose as soon as I drove away from the airport – the smell of sewage was so intense. It was completely intolerable along almost the entire route to the city, although the government must have done something about that by now. It was off-putting for visitors, but most of all, I felt sorry for residents unable to escape that choking odour.

All over the city we saw entire families camping out on the street. Women made tea on Primus stoves with sleeping infants sprawled on their laps. Men were shaving or having their beards trimmed. Young girls combed each other's long black hair. Entire lives were being lived in the open air and I was appalled to learn that the authorities sent employees to patrol the streets each morning when the dead were loaded into carts. Rows of slums cobbled together with corrugated iron and cardboard made our *barasti* hut look like a desirable residence. I promised myself never to let go of my father's hand. It would be so easy for a small boy to get lost in the crowd.

My father's friends had recommended a hotel. It turned out to be cheap but was far from cheerful. It was the filthiest place I had ever seen. Everything was covered with a layer of grime. Worst of all, the rooms were permeated with the horrible aroma of public toilets. Its main advantage was that it was close to various markets, including the 'Smugglers' Market', which has since been renamed. There, we would sell our gold chains and rings. We came across several shady characters and indeed, the whole area had an underworld feel about it.

Mussafir Khana was certainly a world away from the elegant art deco buildings on Marine Drive or the posh residences lining Malabar Hill favoured by the elite. Real estate in this area today ranks among the most expensive in the world.

As most first-time visitors to Bombay do, we stood under the arched Gateway of India in Colaba, but it wouldn't have occurred to us to try to enter the majestic Taj Mahal Hotel, which faces it. Even if we had been able to afford inflated prices for a pot of Darjeeling tea with a buttered scone, we would have felt out of place among the bejewelled matrons in fine silk saris and the khaki-suited Englishmen leisurely enjoying tiffin or shopping for batik wall hangings in the hotel's upmarket arcade.

There is an unsubstantiated rumour that Jamsetji Tata of the Tata Mills fame chose to construct this ornate hotel that opened in 1903, because he was furious that he had been stopped from entering another of Bombay's grand hotels, Watson's. It's ironic, but had we attempted to pass one of Mr Tata's exotically attired doormen, we would have been similarly turned back. Not so many years later, of course, Gulf Arabs were courted by five-star hotels in India and elsewhere, when there was an assumption that anyone in a Gulf-style *kandoura* must be fabulously wealthy.

One of the worst aspects of being poor is not having to do without, but rather, not being seen; not being recognised for one's human qualities. People are always saying "never judge a man by the cut of his cloth", but how many really follow that precept? It's a sad indictment on human nature that the poor are either discriminated against or treated as though they were invisible. I vowed that no matter how much money I made, I would endeavour never to do that.

Anyway, we definitely didn't feel poor and now that we had a little money in our pockets, we could begin to enjoy ourselves. The first thing we did was to search for somewhere inexpensive to eat. I remember gorging myself on chicken curry and rice, which I decided was the most delicious meal ever. We were amazed at how big the grilled chickens were, as those in Dubai were scrawny and virtually meatless.

Like the angler who always exaggerates the size of the fish that got away, I later regaled my friends in Dubai with tales of chickens as big as lambs. Everywhere were stalls selling freshly-squeezed fruit juice, which I sipped for the first time in my life savouring every drop.

There were no parks or green spaces in Dubai, so you can imagine how impressed we were strolling around Malabar Hill's famous Hanging Gardens that was redolent with multihued flowers and dotted with bushes sculpted to look like various animals. I was fascinated to learn that the original purpose of these gardens was to cover a sweet water reservoir so as to protect it from carrion dropped by vultures circling the nearby Parsee Towers of Silence.

The Parsees are India's largest Zoroastrian community, whose ancestors fled from persecution in Persia during the tenth century AD. They are known for their great contributions to the country in the fields of science, industry and the arts, and also for the unusual way they dispose of the dead. Burial and cremation are prohibited in their culture, as earth, fire and water are considered sacred. So following various rituals, bodies are left atop the Towers of Silence to be eaten by vultures.

Until India, I never imagined there existed so many religions and languages. Besides Muslims, Christians and Hindus, who were prevalent in

Dubai, I came across Buddhists, Jains and Sikhs for the first time and was fascinated to learn that in India there are at least twenty-two officially recognised languages and hundreds of dialects. My time there was far more of an education than a year in school.

The highlight of our short stay was an opportunity to watch classical dancers, although it's probably true to say that we were riveted more by the dancing girls than their intricate footwork and delicate hand movements. Discovering beautiful girls was almost like a jungle explorer coming across a new and potentially dangerous species. I knew that my mother wouldn't approve, which of course, made the experience all the more delightful.

During the ensuing years, I accompanied my father to India on several occasions and grew to love the energy of the place. Sultan recalls that he went once with both my parents and Mohammed, who draped him in gold chains before setting off.

"As soon as we arrived at the Orient Hotel, Mohammed took all the gold, which upset me because I thought it was mine," he says. But he quickly forgot the loss of his treasure when he was taken on a tour of the city. "For me it was like going to New York," he says. "I was amazed at the buildings, the roads, the food; even the weather. We used to take a horse-drawn carriage to parks and zoos. It was beautiful. I never saw things like this before. Bombay was something very special."

I didn't realise it at the time, but this was India still in its infancy as an independent state. Gandhi's political heir, Prime Minister Jawaharlal Nehru, had faced many challenges since the British relinquished power in 1947, especially in terms of economic development. Despite a well-thought-out five-year plan that included heavy investment in agriculture and industry, unemployment was high and poverty was rife throughout the country.

As a staunch nationalist who had been one of the main forces behind India's independence, Nehru promoted unity among Indians of all religions and sects, but sectarian conflicts still plagued the country. Economic migrants from southern India flocked to India's richest city, Bombay, hoping like Dick Whittington to find the streets paved with gold, but found instead abject misery. Cut off from their natural support system, the extended family, they were alone in a strange city without work or accommodation and were often resented by local people as a source of cheap labour threatening their jobs.

India has come a long way since those days. With a population of more than 1.2 billion (as per a 2012 official estimate), it is the most populous democracy in the world. In 2012, it was recognised as the fourth largest economy and one of the fastest-growing on the planet. There is no doubt that a succession of governments have worked miracles to make India a major world power in little more than half a century, without wielding an autocratic stick in the way China has done.

Of course, Bombay is no more. In 1995, its name was changed to Mumbai to reflect the nationalist sentiments of the Hindu Shiv Sena party. But for me – and many others – this vibrant city will always be Bombay. That was the place where my childhood was enriched by so many hospitable and generous people willing to part with their last crust and where my senses were bombarded with an explosion of unforgettable colours, sights and sounds.

By the age of ten, I was already quite a seasoned traveller. But there is one journey that stands out from the rest as I almost didn't make it back.

It is the greatest dream of every Muslim believer to make at least one pilgrimage to Mecca and my father was no exception. As always, he took me along with him. En route, we stopped in Dammam, which is the capital of eastern Saudi Arabia. It is also the site of one of the biggest oilfields in the world that now accounts for one-quarter of the planet's entire reserves.

Once there, we were invited to stay with Sheikh Rashid's uncle, Sheikh Juma Al Maktoum, who was living with his sons in Saudi after being temporarily exiled by the Ruler for political reasons. But as luck would have it, before we could continue our journey to Mecca and Medina, I came down with a raging fever. No one knew what caused it, but my temperature was so high that everyone was afraid I might slip away.

Many fervent prayers later, I began to recover. However, my father was so traumatised at how near I came to death, that he decided to postpone our pilgrimage and take me home without delay. When he was unable to find a vessel sailing directly to Dubai, he booked our passage on a boat to the island of Bahrain, then the most cosmopolitan place in the Gulf thanks primarily to Standard Oil of California that had discovered the island's reserves in 1932. By 1955, Bahrain benefited from almost 9 million dollars of annual oil revenue, which had wisely been spent on schools, hospitals, running water and also an effective police force.

As usual I was seasick, but it was a lot worse this time because I was also unwell. I vomited all the way to Bahrain and wasn't able to eat a thing. By the time we disembarked, I was several kilograms lighter and so weak that a gust of wind could have blown me over.

My father was a friend of Sheikh Salman – the grandfather of Bahrain's current ruler, King Hamad bin Isa Al Khalifa – who sent his chief of protocol to welcome us and take us to a hotel run by a Yemeni family called Funduq Al Aayan, which loosely translated means 'Hotel for the Elite' or 'Hotel for the Rich and Famous'. It was anything but. It was a real dump, but for two weary and hungry travellers like us, it was as magnificent as Dubai's famous landmark the seven-star Burj Al Arab.

The owner instinctively understood that we were not able to afford a good meal and instructed his cook to make us a hearty meat curry with white rice on the house, which we bolted down like starving animals. It was plentiful and tasty, and by the time I finished the last morsel I began to feel as though I'd died and gone to heaven.

The only thing left to be desired was a good night's rest. That was a problem due to the heat and humidity. We tried sleeping in our room, but even though we were exhausted, we just tossed and turned. When we couldn't bear the stifling atmosphere any longer, we asked the owner if we could take our mattresses onto the roof instead. It was a lot cooler up there, but we spent half the night worried about being electrocuted. The roof was a spaghetti junction criss-crossed with dangling electricity cables and telephone lines that swayed dangerously close to our heads each time there was the slightest breeze.

Early the next morning, we made ourselves as presentable as possible in readiness for a meeting with Sheikh Salman at his palace that had been arranged by his aide. I was a little intimidated at first, but he was a kindly person who quickly made us feel at ease with friendly conversation over coffee and dates. He was also very generous. Not only did he pay for our accommodation, he also took care of our passage to Dubai. As if that wasn't enough, his chief of protocol boarded our ship just before it sailed to hand my father an envelope containing 2,000 rupees. We could hardly believe our eyes.

Shortly afterwards, Sheikh Salman passed away. He was succeeded by his son, Sheikh Isa bin Salman Al Khalifa, who during his thirty-eight-year-long rule was responsible for guiding his tiny island state towards independence from the British and for laying the foundations of the modern state Bahrain is today. Like his grandfather, the Hakim Sheikh Hamed bin Issa Al Khalifah, whose right-hand man was an Englishman called Charles Dalrymple Belgrave, Sheikh Isa was very much an anglophile. He owned a private beach where Britons and other Westerners had an open invitation to enjoy complimentary tea and cake, served to them each afternoon while they lounged on their deckchairs. This custom, however, wasn't very popular with most Bahrainis who were barred access from that beach.

I will never forget Sheikh Salman's kindness towards us, two weary travellers looking for a place to rest their heads, but I should add that hospitality shown to strangers wasn't unusual in those days and existed throughout all levels of society. Together with hospitality, generosity is very much ingrained in the Arab psyche and I'm very proud of those traits. Until comparatively recently, anyone who admired, say, a watch on someone's wrist, a cigarette lighter or a tie might find the object pressed upon by its owner who wouldn't take no for an answer. We are still a hospitable and generous people, but the modern age has made us rather more cautious and wary than we used to be.

One thing is certain. I can never forget all the good people who offered me a helping hand when I needed it. Each one contributed to my faith in human nature which may have been slightly dented on occasion but was never shattered.

We didn't get to perform Hajj on that occasion but I returned home with the profound knowledge that somebody up there loved me anyway.

CHAPTER 4

The Last Arab

"WE'RE A SENTIMENTAL PEOPLE. WE LIKE A FEW KIND WORDS BETTER THAN MILLIONS OF DOLLARS GIVEN IN A HUMILIATING WAY."

– GAMAL ABDEL NASSER

The 1960s was arguably the most exciting decade of the twentieth century. It was a time of transformation, innovation and revolution, when young people tired of post-World War II austerity threw out the old to make way for the new. In Western minds, this intriguing historical benchmark opening the door to the modern era is associated with the Cuban missile crisis, the construction of the Berlin Wall, the launch of man into space, the assassination of President J. F. Kennedy and of course, the Beatles.

The fashions of London's King's Road or the geometric hairstyles of Vidal Sassoon were of little concern to the Arab world with the exception of Egypt and Lebanon, whose moneyed classes sought to be considered socially progressive by emulating their Western counterparts.

When people in my part of the world think of the 1960s, their thoughts inevitably turn to the one man who dominated the era: President of Egypt Gamal Abdel Nasser, who, since being a main player in his country's 1952 revolution, never stopped dreaming of a powerful and united Arab world that would never again be at the mercy of foreign powers.

Nasser was unlike any other Arab leader before or since. His speeches were powerful and motivational; his personal charisma was magnetic and his sincerity was inspirational. His warm and emotive language touched the heart of every Arab, who felt the Egyptian leader's every breath was dedicated to their well-being.

"I am Gamal Abdel Nasser of you and for you," he said, following an attempt on his life in the autumn of 1954. "I will live until I die for your sake, on behalf of you and on behalf of your freedom and your honour... If Gamal Abdel Nasser should die, I will not die, for each one of you is Gamal Abdel Nasser... "

Certainly, no account of my early life would be complete without mentioning the effect this extraordinary Arab leader had on my own political consciousness.

I think it's fair to say that on the streets of Morocco to Iraq and everywhere in between, he was universally admired. In the homes of most ordinary people, his photograph had pride of place. His statues were erected in public squares. Dubai named a square in his honour. People had a personal connection with this most unusual man. To them, he was a father, a saviour, a dear friend. They loved him so unconditionally, that they willingly forgave even those mistakes for which he was unable to forgive himself.

I must have been around eight years old when I first became aware of President Nasser from my schoolteachers. By then his reputation as a modern-day version of Salah El Din had grown, following his courageous 1956 nationalisation of the Suez Canal. That audacious takeover triggered an unsuccessful attempt by Britain, France and Israel to invade the newly-independent Egypt.

London and Paris were internationally condemned for their aggression, not least by the then US President, Dwight Eisenhower, a staunch anti-imperialist, although it must be said that he was no fan of the Egyptian leader. Nasser's weapons deals with the Soviet Union and his recognition of the Communist People's Republic of China didn't go down very well with the White House.

The man at the forefront of the invasion was the British Prime Minister, Sir Anthony Eden, who succumbed to domestic pressure to prove to the world that the Empire was far from dead. Prior to the Suez blunder, Eden was one of Britain's most popular prime ministers, but the fiasco ripped his reputation to shreds.

Egypt's success in the face of such big powers astonished everyone. It was viewed as a symbol of Britain's diminishing status as a superpower and cast a light on the Western world's post-war divisions and disputes.

Nasser's nationalisation of the Suez Canal was carried out in retaliation against Britain and America for reneging on their promise to fund the construction of the High Dam in Aswan. Their U-turn was in response to Nasser's friendly overtures to China at a time when Chinese–American tensions were high. It wasn't that Nasser harboured Communist sympathies. On the contrary, he worked hard to rout out Communists from both Egypt and Syria in the face of criticism from the USSR. But he was prepared to shake the hand of the Devil if that meant keeping his newly-independent country afloat in more ways than one.

There was a time whenever the waters of the Nile overflowed, they flooded Upper Egypt, reaching as far as the Sphinx in Cairo. Homes were swept away; lives were lost; and many of the nation's poorest were displaced or stricken with malaria. The Aswan Reservoir – or the Low Dam – was inaugurated by Britain in 1902 but was insufficient to stem the devastating annual overflow. Unfortunately, the Nubians were asked to pay a terrible price for the High Dam which left much of Lower Nubia under water, rendering up to 90,000 Nubians homeless and leaving several important historical monuments and sites submerged.

Nasser's determination to take over the high revenue-generating Suez Canal was primarily motivated by financial concerns. He urgently needed capital to build the Dam, which he saw as essential to prevent rivers over-flowing, to conserve water for irrigating crops and to generate electricity for a fast-growing population.

During a speech to the nation on 26 July 1956, delivered in Alexandria, Nasser spoke the name of the Frenchman who initially conceptualised the Canal, 'Ferdinand de Lesseps'. His name was a code for Egyptian forces to begin seizing control. Nasser subsequently froze the Suez Canal Company's assets but compensated shareholders. Such a bold move was hailed by ec-static crowds in Egypt and beyond.

By all accounts, Nasser predicted that there would be a heavy diplomatic price to pay, but he was unprepared for military conflict especially since the Canal's nationalisation had been virtually rubber stamped by the United Nations Security Council, provided foreign ships could continue to enjoy unimpeded passage.

When Israeli troops invaded the Egyptian-controlled Gaza Strip and crossed the Sinai desert on 29 October 1956, attacking Egyptian military posts en route to the Canal Zone, Nasser and his government were caught by surprise. A day later, Britain and France issued an ultimatum. Nasser promptly ignored it.

On 31 October, they rained their bombs down on Egypt, in the belief that its President would be forced to relinquish the Canal to the reins of international control. As Egypt suffered an onslaught from the skies, British and French paratroopers were parachuted down in the vicinity of Port Said, as commandoes clambered off an armada of vessels close to the shore.

Nasser might well have worried that all was about to be lost when he heard that British soldiers were just twenty-five miles away from Suez, but something unexpected occurred. Soviet threats to utilise "every kind of modern destructive weapon" to put an end to the invasion, combined with US anger that Britain and France had dared to spearhead a covert mission in the face of Washington's opposition, forced Britain to withdraw its military.

Nasser's bold stand-off against such sophisticated armies turned him into a living legend throughout the Middle East and the Gulf. Not only were the mighty Great Britain and France no longer seen as invincible, they had inadvertently opened a window for the Soviet Union to step through, which it did with alacrity in Egypt, Syria and Iraq.

The son of a humble postal clerk, with a little help from Moscow and Washington, had rendered those imperialist powers impotent and embarrassed. His was an amazing display of bravery that brought a sense of empowerment to every Arab under foreign occupation.

Dubai wasn't occupied in an official sense and most of the time we got along well with our British guests. But sometimes we felt as though we were not in control, and certainly we did not have the power to plan our own foreign policy. All peoples under the sky would ideally like the freedom to choose their own destiny without foreign interference and so it is little wonder that many Dubai nationals found Nasser's stirring speeches riveting. I know I did.

Whenever we learned that President Nasser was scheduled to speak, my entire family would be glued to our battery-operated radio to which we had attached an enormous aerial for optimum reception. We were so excited the night before one of his speeches, we could hardly sleep. On those occasions, the streets of Dubai were almost deserted in the way they are nowadays when a World Cup final is beamed.

In the minutes before a broadcast, we would gather around the radio with a sense of great expectancy, but were often disappointed as Britain would do its utmost to jam the transmission. We had to strain our hearing to catch Nasser's words, which often faded away into the ether. Oftentimes, his messages would be preceded by patriotic songs sung by Umm Kulthum or Abdel Halim Hafez, who became Nasser's close friend. Such rousing nationalist tunes as 'Ya Gamal, Ya Habib al-Malayin' (Gamal, beloved of millions) made our spirits soar.

The US, Britain and Europe were aware of Nasser's capability to inspire devotion and feared his ability to unite all Arabs behind the same cause: to free the Arab world from foreign occupation. From their perspective, they were right to be afraid. The last thing they wanted was to see 100 million Arabs unified behind one flag and one leader; a bloc that would have greatly cramped their ambitions in a strategically important and oil-rich region.

One can only imagine the West's trepidation when the man, considered the main force behind the 1952 bloodless toppling of the dissolute King Farouk, forged a political union with Syria on 1 February 1958 termed the United Arab Republic (UAR), with Nasser at its head. Palestinian journalist and author, Said Aburish, was there during Nasser's first visit to Damascus as the UAR President and captured the joyous ambience with his pen: "For a week, the atmosphere in Damascus resembled a carnival when crowds in the tens of thousands roamed the streets singing old songs and new ones written to welcome their President and the hero of Arabism." Shortly afterwards, North Yemen's King, Imam Ahmad bin Yahya, sent an envoy to Damascus requesting membership of the UAR. In the event, North Yemen's links with the UAR were cemented with a loose confederation called the United Arab States.

Some years later, Iraq applied to join the UAR, but by then the union was on its last legs as Syrians began to rail against being Egypt's junior partner. In 1970, the then Libyan leader, Colonel Muammar Gaddafi, who considered Nasser his mentor, initiated a union with Egypt and Sudan – but that plan was thwarted by Nasser's death in September that same year.

Following many of Nasser's speeches, my friends and I would rush outside to join a pro-Nasser/anti-British demonstration. These were mostly peaceful, but like most protests there were the occasional violent outbursts. All over the region, young boys and grown men alike calling themselves 'Nasserists' or 'Arab nationalists' were reacting to Nasser's call in the exact same way, spawning numerous Arab nationalist organisations in Syria, Lebanon, Jordan and Iraq.

Nasser's liberation of Egypt was also the inspiration behind Algeria's war of independence fought by the FLN (National Liberation Front) against the country's French occupier. Throughout the eight-year-long Algerian struggle, Nasser supplied the FLN with weapons, provided air cover and supported the people's quest for freedom on the diplomatic stage. It was President Charles de Gaulle who reluctantly came to terms with Algeria's eventual independence. He held talks with FLN leaders and signed the Evian Accords, liberating the North African country from French rule in March 1962.

Earlier, Nasser had promoted Tunisia and Morocco's independence from France, granted in 1956; he was an enthusiastic backer of a united Africa free of colonisation, the vision of Ghana's first President, Kwame Nkrumah, whom he considered a friend. He also joined hands with Yugoslavia's Marshall Tito and India's Jawaharlal Nehru to champion non-alignment.

When Nasser spoke to us, we were no longer simply nationals of Algeria, Morocco, Libya, Syria, Jordan, Yemen, Iraq or the British-designated Trucial States, such as Dubai and Abu Dhabi. Suddenly, we were members of the same proud brotherhood. It didn't matter that we spoke different dialects, ate different foods, wore different styles of dress or belonged to different tribes. For the first time, we were Arabs sharing the same common goals. We would no longer accept being subjugated and oppressed. Certain Arab monarchs were unimpressed. Envious of Nasser's popularity, they feared his influence on their own streets and collaborated with the West to plot against him.

After listening to so many of Nasser's emotional speeches, I felt compelled to write to him. I was just ten years old. Realising that my handwriting was poor, I dictated the letter to Hamda, the daughter of my cousin (who later became my wife), and sent it by post.

I don't remember much of the content, but I do recall addressing Nasser as 'Father' and 'Great Leader'. "We need you to teach us; we need you to show us the light" was the missive's main thrust. Of course the chances of it ever reaching his hands were negligible but that didn't occur to me. I possessed the faith of a young Western child who writes to Father Christmas with his wish list, never for a moment doubting its arrival.

In my heart I did not expect to receive a reply from such an important person who was certain to be too preoccupied with affairs of state to bother answering a letter from a school kid in Dubai scrawled in a childish hand. Even so, each time my father or elder brother went to check our post office box, I would be on tenterhooks. Just when I began to accept that I would never hear from him, an official-looking letter from Egypt arrived with my name on it.

I can't begin to describe my feelings as I carefully opened the envelope, taking care not to damage even a centimetre of the paper. When I found his personally signed photograph, to say I was elated is an understatement. I had a faint suspicion that the accompanying letter would probably consist of a formal typed acknowledgment of mine, signed by one of Nasser's aides.

I was stunned when I saw that it was written in the Egyptian President's own handwriting. And when I read the salutation "My son Khalaf," I could hardly contain my happiness. I must have read it a hundred times. My Palestinian and Egyptian teachers were equally thrilled.

For many years, that letter was my most treasured possession, but somehow it's been mislaid, which is one of my deepest regrets. I wish I could recall everything he wrote, but I can never forget that he wished me every success in life and invited me to meet with him the next time I was in Egypt. How I would have loved to jump on a boat or a plane that very instant, but I didn't have the wherewithal to visit my old friends in Sharjah let alone make the acquaintance of a world leader in Cairo.

In all honesty, I wasn't captivated by Nasser's deeds as much as by the dignified spirit he embodied. At such a young age, I hardly understood what nationalisation meant. But I did take to heart his promise to liberate Palestine and his calls for a strong united Arab world without colonialism or feudalism, where even the poorest would be afforded respect and given the tools to forge a better life. "He who cannot support himself cannot take his own decision," Nasser said – a sentiment with which I very strongly identify.

Unlike the majority of world leaders who step out of stretch limos to pay lip service to their concerns about the poorer members of society before sipping champagne in glittering receptions and promptly forgetting all about them, Gamal Abdel Nasser genuinely sought to lift his people out of poverty. He came from a poor family himself and was proud of his heritage as illustrated by his following declaration: "I am proud to belong to this small village of Beni Mur. And I am more proud to be a member of a poor family from that village. I am saying these words for history that Nasser was born in a poor family and I promise that he will live and die a poor man." As history affirms, he kept to his word.

Nasser's father was born in a one-room house in the impoverished village of Beni Mur near the city of Assyut in southern Egypt and is believed to have descended from an Arab tribe with its roots in the Hejaz. Nasser himself came into the world in a poor suburb of Alexandria called Baqus on 15 January 1918, but he considered that village as his real home. By all accounts, he adored his mother who died when he was young; it was a loss that scarred his soul for many years.

Apparently, he was never close to his father. Most of his childhood and teenage years were spent shuttling between the Alexandria home of his grandparents and that of an uncle who lived in Cairo. Because of that, his education was frequently interrupted. He compensated for the holes in his schooling by reading historical, political and philosophical books and was passionately appreciative of poetry.

Following an unsuccessful attempt to enter the Royal Military Academy, Nasser attended law school although his heart was set on a career in the military. He later reapplied to the Academy and that time his application was oiled with a good word from the Secretary of State, Ibrahim Kheiry Pasha. Anyone who didn't come from an influential or wealthy family needed *wasta* (connections) to get ahead, which is equally true in Egypt nowadays.

It was at the Academy that he forged solid friendships with two men who would become his co-revolutionary comrades: Abdel Hakim Amer and Anwar El Sadat. According to Sadat, Nasser was a shy man with a naturally quiet disposition, who "quickly turned into a ferocious lion the moment he felt that anyone even simply thought of insulting him or hurting him".

The former editor of Egypt's daily *Al Ahram*, Mohammed Hassanein Heikal, who was also Nasser's trusted friend, advisor and biographer, described him as a rebel who led a conservative personal life. "He was never interested in women or money or elaborate food," he wrote. "After he came to power, the cynical old politicians tried to corrupt him, but they failed miserably. His family life was impeccable."

In 1944, Nasser wed Tahia Kazim, the daughter of an Iranian tea merchant and his Egyptian wife. The couple immediately moved into a modest villa in the Cairo suburb of Manshiyat al-Bakri, where they lived for the remainder of their lives together with their two daughters and three sons. He could easily have installed his family in one of King Farouk's fabulous palaces, but his unpretentious home was his haven; the place where he could set aside the duties of government to relax in the company of his family.

He was also a modest man. Although he drove the 1952 revolution, he felt he was too young and too little-known to become his country's president or prime minister. He thought the Egyptian people would not accept him, so he relinquished both those posts to the older and more experienced Mohammed Naguib, a popular army general. Nasser was content to serve as Minister of the Interior, Sadat became Minister of State and Amer was appointed Chief of Staff.

Four years after the revolution, it became evident that Naguib's ideas on policy didn't gel with those of the younger officers who were in a hurry to make sweeping reforms and reluctant to hand over power to civilian authorities. He was forced out of office, placed under house arrest and was succeeded by Gamal Abdel Nasser on 23 June 1956. Few outside Egypt even know the name Mohammed Naguib. Whenever they remember the 1952 revolution, the name Nasser rightly springs to mind.

Now that he held the reins, his reforms were sweeping. Robin Hood would have been proud of him. His introduction of food subsidies ensured that nobody went hungry. But the main cornerstone of his social programme was his land reform that involved the state's expropriation of land from 2,000 wealthy landowners that was given to new agricultural cooperatives or redistributed to the *fellaheen* (peasant farmers). He further mandated a massive reduction of rents to benefit the poor and embarked on industrialising his nation when many large-scale modern industries came into being.

The monarchy was abolished along with civilian titles such as 'pasha' or 'bey', wearing the *tarbouche* (fez) was discouraged, and the gentry were stripped of their wealth. Some left with little more than the clothes they were wearing.

Jewish communities were also encouraged to leave Egypt. They, and various other communities with foreign roots, were cast under suspicion following Israel's 'Operation Susannah' – otherwise known as the Lavon Affair – whereby Egyptian-Jewish saboteurs were instructed to bomb movie theatres, a post office, a train station and US Information Agency offices.

Initially Nasser's wealth redistribution policies boosted the Egyptian economy, but over the following decades they slowly began to backfire. His banishment of the aristocracy, wealthy elite and captains of industry led to far fewer jobs in the private sector, placing a burden on the state to provide young people with employment for life. Fearing the state would resort to a similar wealth-stripping strategy in the future, the nouveau riche salted away their cash from the prying eyes of the government, resulting in a black economy. Egyptian investors were scarce while foreign investment virtually dried up.

As the new landowners died, their parcels were divided up among their heirs, eventually becoming smaller and smaller and therefore unfit to grow certain crops. Moreover, his fixing of rents on houses and apartments initially benefited the lower income sector but as the years passed, landlords were unable to afford necessary repairs to roofs, facades or elevators, which accounts for the derelict state of many once beautiful buildings throughout Egypt. Families whose rent was, say, ten Egyptian pounds a month in the 1950s are paying the same amount today.

Nasser, in his revolutionary zeal, wanted to give all his people the same opportunities and bring everyone to the same level. His goal was idealistic but far from realistic. His expulsion of the rich and expropriation of their property and businesses made no economic sense as these were generally highly educated people with management experience and entrepreneurial flair. When their farms, factories and stores were taken over, they often became inefficient and run-down; this is the case in Zimbabwe today.

The flaw in his ideology was this: people aren't all equal and were not created equal in every respect. God has given each one of us different gifts and different challenges to overcome, which Nasser failed to take into account. There will always be an elitist class in every country; in communist countries, politicians enjoy privilege; in military states, the generals are top dog. And there will always be workers and bosses everywhere. What's more to the point is that every citizen should equally benefit from educational opportunities, health care, civil liberties and human rights.

His failed goal of forging an Arab nation literally broke his heart. Syria's secession from the United Arab Republic in 1961, following a coup launched by disgruntled nationalist Syrian army officers resentful of being placed under Egyptian commanders, devastated Nasser's Arab unification ambitions. His first reaction was to send in Egyptian Special Forces, but within three days he accepted the inevitable. "It's time to know when to leave," he said before formally handing over power to an all-Syrian leadership. It is surely significant that Egypt retained the name UAR as a symbol of Nasser's greatest hope until his passing.

Nasser was so traumatised by the split with Damascus that, according to Mohammed Hassanein Heikal, his mental and physical health was negatively impacted. Suffering from a weak heart and diabetes, he became reliant on painkillers. In 1966, he survived a serious heart attack, a precursor of worse to come, but was not sufficiently alarmed to give up his chain smoking habit. Egypt's 'Six-Day War' with Israel that broke out on 5 June 1967 had an even bigger impact upon Nasser's health and frame of mind.

On 14 May 1948, the Jewish Agency announced the birth of the State of Israel and the next day the armies of Egypt, Syria, Lebanon and Iraq mobilised against the Zionists, resulting in a year-long conflict. Following a ceasefire, Jordan had taken control of East Jerusalem and the West Bank, while Egypt held the Gaza Strip.

When Nasser and his comrades calling themselves 'Free Officers' took power, they swore to return Palestinian dignity. On 8 March 1965, Nasser expressed his goal of restoring the rights of the Palestinian people in clear terms: "We shall not enter Palestine with its soil covered in sand. We shall enter it with its soil saturated in blood," he said. He was, however, in no hurry to keep that pledge, preferring to wait until Egypt's military was trained and equipped for the gargantuan task.

He was determined to strike when the time was right, but that time wasn't now. From 1962 until 1967, Egypt's armies had been embroiled in a civil war waged in Yemen between the Mutawakkilite Kingdom of Yemen, supported by Saudi Arabia, Jordan, Iran and Britain, and the Yemen Arab Republic. Nasser originally envisaged a quick victory secured with the help of his country's Special Forces and air power, but the enemy was resilient and the fighting dragged on.

During early 1967, Egypt had as many as 55,000 troops – including most of his crack units – in Yemen, which quashes the argument of those who believe the 1967 War with Israel was initiated by Cairo. Nasser was courageous but not stupid enough to think his military was capable of decisive wins on two separate fronts. The fact is that he was a reluctant warrior overtaken by a set of escalating circumstances outside his control.

The 1967 Six-Day War was triggered by an Israeli attack on the Jordanian-controlled West Bank city of As Samu in 1966, when fifteen Jordanian soldiers and three civilians were killed. Jordan's King Hussein sent retaliatory forces which were overwhelmed, and subsequently condemned Nasser for failing to come to Jordan's aid.

On 15 May 1967, Israel's Prime Minister, Levi Eshkol, announced that Israel "has no aggressive intentions whatsoever against any Arab state at all". That same month, Anwar El Sadat returned from Moscow with a warning from the Soviets that Israeli troops were massing on the Syrian border intending to attack Syria and overthrow its regime, which turned out to have no basis in truth. That could have been an innocent blunder on the part of the Soviet leadership, but there is also another explanation that exists.

An article in the *Middle East Review of International Affairs*, volume 7, number 3, titled 'How the USSR planned to destroy Israel in 1967' is illuminating. It suggests there is documentary and anecdotal evidence that the warning was "deliberate disinformation" to kick-start a war so that the USSR could join the fray on the side of the Arabs.

Unaware that the news from Russia was a hoax, Nasser closed the Straits of Tiran – a body of water separating the Jordanian coastal city of Aqaba from the Red Sea – to Israeli shipping before deploying 100,000 troops or more in Sinai close to the Israeli border. He also ordered the expulsion of the United Nations Emergency Force (UNEF) that was created to monitor the demilitarisation of Sinai in the aftermath of the Suez Crisis.

Tensions between Egypt and Israel were now at boiling point. Fearing that Egypt had chemical weapons and was prepared to use them, Israel ordered 20,000 US Army gas masks to be sent on a specially chartered plane. Tel Aviv also put out a call for its military reservists.

On 30 May, a mutual defence pact was signed between Egypt and Jordan that welcomed its powerful neighbour's protection. Once he had appended his signature, Nasser had this to say: "Today they will know that the Arabs are arranged for battle, the critical hour has arrived. We have reached the stage of serious action and not of more declarations."

Such gung-ho rhetoric was common and was usually taken with a pinch of salt, but by then tensions were so high that housewives in both Israel and Egypt began attacking grocery store shelves to stock their larders while their husbands and sons were donating to blood banks. Advertisements in Jewish newspapers around the world announced that Israel was in mortal danger surrounded by enemies with intent to destroy her, appeals that resulted in a flood of volunteers and a fat war chest.

Charles Douglas Home, a journalist of *The Times* in London, realised that something was about to give. "The Arab armies can certainly afford to mass their armies on Israel's border for longer than Israel can remain at a high state of readiness," he wrote. "There is a danger that pressure from within might oblige Israel to do something rather quickly rather than submit to the economic strangulation of a long period of unrelieved tension."

Mohammed Hassanein Heikal agreed with Home. He knew that Egypt's closure of the Straits of Tiran to Israeli ships would force Israel to strike back. "Israel cannot accept or remain indifferent to what has taken place. Israel has to reply now, it has to deal a blow," he wrote. "Then it will be our turn to deal a second blow, which we will deliver with the utmost possible effectiveness... Let Israel begin! Let our second blow then be ready! Let it be a knockout!"

On 2 June, the war's main architect, General Moshe Dayan, gave thousands of soldiers a day off, commanding them to maintain a high profile on beaches and in restaurants or cafés to give the impression that conflict was far from his mind. On 4 June, Israeli government ministers decided to launch a first strike.

War finally broke out on 5 June, when Israel destroyed most of Egypt's fighter planes on the ground in a surprise attack. But we didn't know that at the time. The radio was our sole source of information and was never turned off during those six days. The reception was very poor but we were nevertheless able to follow the war's progress.

Early on, we were led to believe that victory was in the bag. How wrong we were! Radio broadcasts were nothing more than propagandist fairy tales concocted by military commanders. We were told that Arab fighter planes were in the skies and our tanks were nearing Tel Aviv. Everywhere in the Arab world, people's mood was euphoric until the truth could no longer be hidden.

We had been duped by those we trusted the most. No airplane had left the runway and most Arab tanks had been abandoned to the desert. That was the first time in my life that I knew the bitter taste of betrayal. I would never be so gullible again. It was then that the citizens of the Arab world understood that messages from their leaders, especially during times of war, should not be accepted as gospel.

The rest is history. Six days later, the conflict ended with Israel having seized the Sinai Peninsula and the Gaza Strip from Egypt, East Jerusalem and the West Bank from Jordan, and the strategically crucial Golan Heights from Syria. It was perhaps the greatest catastrophe ever experienced by the Arab world and without doubt the greatest setback for Palestinian aspirations.

For the first time in my life, I felt ashamed to call myself an Arab. I've rarely been so shocked or so saddened before or since. The defeat was particularly mortifying. It was hard to accept that a population of just 2.4 million, with a fighting force of just 264,000 including civilian reservists, could outmanoeuvre the Arabs' strongest armies. It was the most shameful moment in Arab history; the most shameful moment ever.

The loss of East Jerusalem was a knife through the heart of every Muslim. This ancient and beautiful city is home to the Haram al-Sharif (Noble Sanctuary) comprising one-sixth of Jerusalem's walled city. It is famously the site of the Al Aqsa mosque and the Dome of the Rock from where the Prophet Mohammed (PBUH) ascended to heaven on a winged horse, where he led Ibrahim (Abraham), Moussa (Moses), Issa (Jesus) and other prophets before him in prayer.

Muslims feel a powerful historical, religious and emotional connection to Jerusalem, in which direction the earliest Muslims turned to pray before they received a holy instruction to pray facing Mecca. Al Aqsa and the Dome of the Rock are considered by most Muslims to constitute Islam's third holiest shrine.

Since 1967, believers have been prevented from making pilgrimages to Jerusalem and only Palestinians with Israeli-issued permits may pray at the Haram al-Sharif, which is a scandal. I've only seen it in photographs or films. I can but hope that Jerusalem is liberated during my lifetime so that I – and every other Muslim – can breathe the fragrant air, walk the cobblestones where prophets once trod, pray in Al Aqsa and come closer to God's presence in this city we call Al Quds. Jerusalem is holy to Muslims, Jews and Christians and all should be made equally welcome there to practise their respective faiths.

Losing Jerusalem was a severe blow, but I never for a second thought of blaming Nasser. However, with the benefit of hindsight, I realise that his greatest error was to underestimate Israel's cunning.

Heikal, who once worshipped the ground Nasser walked upon, was not so charitable. In his book, *For Egypt and not for Abdel Nasser*, he maintains his friend made three serious errors of judgment. The first was the blockade of the Straits of Tiran to Israel-bound shipping; the second was placing Amer in charge of the conflict when his reputation was already soiled by corruption and unwise judgment. The third mistake, according to Heikal, was Nasser's rejection of a warning from King Hussein that Israel was conspiring with big powers to drag Egypt into a war it couldn't win.

To this day, I believe that conflict was masterminded by Israel as an excuse for a massive land grab to suit its expansion plans. It wasn't something that was organised off the cuff; it was probably months, if not years, in the pipeline. Some historians take the view that Nasser's massing of Egyptian troops – largely inexperienced volunteers and conscripts – in Sinai was a bluff to put pressure on Israel. Others suggest that Nasser half-expected Washington to step in as it did during the Suez crisis to prevent tensions from escalating. If so, it was a dangerous game of poker.

We can never know what was in the Egyptian leader's mind, but for sure Nasser was badly let down by his own intelligence service and generals who failed to advise him that the military, already exhausted from fighting in Yemen, was in no state to take on a modern, well-trained and highly sophisticated military force with the benefit of state-of-the-art weaponry courtesy of the US. Indeed, almost half the Egyptian army were still in Yemen as the 1967 War raged. Israel's soldiers were not only better disciplined than their counterparts consisting of ill-trained and poorly-paid conscripts, they were also motivated by their country's very survival.

Israeli fighters took the war more personally. Whenever they thought of their mothers, wives and children at home, they knew that failure was not an option; for them the war was a matter of life and death. When Arab soldiers remembered their own families, their only thought was to stay alive so that they could go home to provide for them. They knew that there was no life insurance policy that would pay out in the event of their death and they knew that their governments wouldn't compensate their loved ones. Their loyalty was directed to those depending upon them for sustenance rather than to the governments that sent them into battle. Their priority was their own survival rather than giving the battle their all, with minds concentrated on winning at all costs.

With the entire Arab world in a state of disbelief and trauma during the aftermath, there was no one more shaken than Nasser. He felt a personal sense of humiliation and betrayal that was largely directed at the person who was once closest to him – Field Marshal Abdel Hakim Amer, the man tasked with the war's conduct. Such an overwhelming defeat that robbed 11,000 Egyptian lives and mutilated his country's military was a bitter pill that sent the Egyptian leader into a deep depression.

On 10 June, Nasser startled his Vice-President, Zakaria Mohieddin, with the news that he was about to resign, before announcing his resignation on television with these words:

> I have taken a decision with which I need your help. I have decided to withdraw totally and for good from any official post or political role, and to return to the ranks of the masses, performing my duty in their midst, like any other citizen... This is a time for action, not grief... My whole heart is with you and let your hearts be with me. May God be with us – hope, light and guidance in our hearts.

Almost before he had time to put down his microphone, adoring Egyptians started pouring onto the streets in their hundreds of thousands; some openly wept, chanting "We are your soldiers Gamal... We shall fight!".

Arabs and Muslims everywhere shared their grief. I can count the times in my life when I've cried on the fingers of one hand; that was definitely one of them. The thought of being without the protection of this great commander was like staring into a frightening void. For all his all-too-human faults, the knowledge that he was there taking care of our interests gave me – and millions of others – a comforting sense of security. The groundswell of sincere emotion showed Nasser that his people were not ready to let him go.

Umm Kulthum didn't want him to quit either. She supported him and raised more than a million Egyptian pounds to reconstruct the military.

Once he resigned himself to the thought of staying on, he ordered the arrest of several military officers, including Amer, who either committed suicide while in detention of his own volition or was encouraged to do so. It should be said that until she died Amer's second wife, former movie actress Berlanti Abdel Hamid, insisted that her husband was murdered. Whatever the truth, Nasser was visibly shaken by his friend's death.

During 1968, Nasser focused his concentration on matters at home. Of particular concern to him was the invigoration of the Muslim Brotherhood that the defeat had elicited. In 1954, the Brotherhood had been banned and during the ensuing years thousands of its members were imprisoned due to their willingness to use force to implement their revolutionary religious ideology.

Driven into the shadows, it nevertheless succeeded in getting its parliamentary candidates elected as independents. In later years, the movement's existence was grudgingly accepted by the government provided its followers maintained a low profile and refrained from incitement. Since the 25 January 2011 popular revolution in Egypt, when the Muslim Brotherhood was legitimised and formed a political party, it has not only dominated parliament, its presidential candidate was voted into the top job by a whisker.

In the early days, Nasser had envisioned an open and democratic Egypt with an independent judiciary and media. But with so many enemies of the state – Communists, Zionist saboteurs, CIA agents and the Muslim Brotherhood – plotting his government's overthrow, his country had gained an international reputation as being oppressive. That reputation was reinforced when Emergency Law was imposed as a response to the assassination of Anwar El Sadat in October 1981. In recent months, the use of the Law has been increasingly restricted.

Nasser's resignation from the world came on 28 September 1970 when he suffered a second heart attack at the age of fifty-two, following an Arab League Summit. He slipped away in his own bed surrounded by his wife; Mohammed Hassanein Heikal, then Minister of Information; and Anwar El Sadat, his closest colleague who was to succeed Nasser as Egypt's president.

When I first heard the appalling news, I refused to believe it. For a while the world seemed like a dark and lonely place without him. I wasn't alone. An estimated 5 to 7 million weeping Egyptians turned up to pay their last respects, as his flag-draped coffin made its journey through the streets of Cairo atop a gun carriage pulled by five horses on 1 October. "Nasser is God's beloved... each of us is Nasser," they cried.

Scores of mourners were crushed to death by the surging crowd in what is now considered one of the largest funeral processions in history. Almost all the leaders of the Arab world – even those who had plotted against him – travelled to Cairo to join the funeral procession. According to Aburish, King Hussein sobbed, Yasser Arafat wept silent tears as he prayed with trembling lips and Muammar Gaddafi fainted twice.

It's become fashionable for former admirers of Nasser to excuse their youthful Arab nationalist leanings as naïve or foolish. They conveniently forget the days when they placed him on a pedestal as the most important leader since Omar Ibn Al Khattab, the *Amir Al Mu'minin* or 'Prince of the Believers' who succeeded Abu Bakr as Caliph of the Rashidun Caliphate. They forget that Nasser lifted our heads higher and higher and sought to deliver us from a condition of despair. I am not one of those people who now think it's cool to debase Arab nationalism as an old-fashioned con-cept. Gamal Abdel Nasser was one of the greatest leaders in history, but unfortunately, we were not ready for him. If he had been born in the West, he would have been lauded and written about more than Eisenhower, Churchill or de Gaulle. The Arabs are to blame for his failure. They were unprepared to face the threats that were posed by Israel and imperialist powers, and in some cases they conspired against him with his enemies behind closed doors.

I hate to admit it, but the Israelis have played a far cleverer game all along. They've skilfully utilised carefully contrived diplomatic, public relations, economic and military strategies to get them where they are now. While our leaders were sleeping, they were using media propaganda to indoctrinate the Western world in their favour. They created powerful lobbying organisations in the US and the UK to influence lawmakers and churned out Hollywood movies depicting the Israeli narrative while painting the Palestinians as primitive at best and at worst terrorists.

The Arab world is in urgent need of Gamal Abdel Nasser – or someone with the same qualities – now. We need an honest leader, a strong leader with the ability to bring all our heads of state together to speak with one voice, especially when the Arab League has become nothing more than a debating society where handshakes and hugs far exceed meaningful resolutions.

We need to be glued together by someone who is proud of his Arab nation, culture and people, and who isn't motivated solely by clinging on to his seat, self-aggrandisement and self-interest. We need someone who understands that standing by while others rob us of our land is tantamount to stealing our dignity; someone who cares about leaving a proud legacy and will reject the defeatist attitudes that have plagued us since the passing of Omar Ibn Al Khattab.

How deluded we are to think our honour hangs solely on the behaviour of our women, when, in fact, it resides in our manhood and our willingness to protect them. When Britain was threatened with invasion in World War II, almost every able-bodied civilian armed themselves with hammers and pitchforks to fight the invaders on the beaches and vowed their children would never grow up speaking German. And in 1982, when Argentina invaded a British dependent territory, the Falkland Islands, the then British Prime Minister, the 'Iron Lady' Margaret Thatcher, didn't hesitate to send warplanes, ships, commandoes and soldiers to successfully defend a mere 3,000 or so island residents. That's what honour means!

If Nasser had lived until now, Israel could not have invaded Lebanon in 1978, 1982 and 2006; Gaza could not have been strangled under siege and bombed at Tel Aviv's whim; Iraq would not have been invaded and plundered in 2003; and, today, a state called Palestine would likely exist. Why? Because a united Arab world would have real political clout and stature in the way the European Union (EU) has today. With just about every country in the world seeking broad alliances to bolster their economies and national security, Arab states should be doing the same instead of squabbling with each other.

It's time we asked ourselves these important questions: as long as we remain separate and vulnerable, what will we do if a crazed Israeli leader decides to demolish Al Aqsa so that they can excavate the ground below in an attempt to prove that this was the site where the Jews' Second Temple once stood? And unless we stand together, how can Arab countries protect themselves from sharing the same fate as Iraq; how can small Gulf states be safe from the territorial ambitions of their neighbour Iran that may be on the point of becoming a nuclear-armed power? Gulf leaders need to be especially alert when their countries are riddled with spies and agitators waiting for instructions from foreign powers to foment revolution.

In conclusion, we Arabs were not worthy of the man that Aburish called "the last Arab". He sacrificed everything he possessed to return our lands and our dignity, including his life. He couldn't do it alone; he needed our help. The greatest tragedy is that we were not up to the task.

CHAPTER 5
Youth

"YOUTH WOULD BE AN IDEAL STATE IF IT CAME A LITTLE LATER IN LIFE."
– HERBERT ASQUITH

Being a teenager is never easy. There are so many decisions to be made; decisions which can affect a young person's entire life. Most teens haven't developed the skills or wisdom required to successfully tackle such life-altering choices. This is where good parents come in. Mine backed me up all the way. They gave me enough freedom to follow my dreams but made sure that I knew there were boundaries that must not be crossed.

It was a comforting feeling to know they would always be there to lift me up should I make a mistake. Bolstered with an inner sense of security and armed with boundless energy and optimism, I was flying high in a world of unlimited possibilities.

In those days, young boys were expected to contribute to the family income. Even while still at school I felt duty-bound to do my bit. I was around fourteen years old when I decided to apply to an American geological company that someone told me was seeking an Arabic–English translator. There was just one minor problem besides my age and lack of qualifications or experience: at that time, I only knew two or three words of English.

Obviously, I wasn't hired as a translator, but something about me must have impressed my future employers; my sheer audacity perhaps. I couldn't believe my luck when I was taken on as a helper for three months in the summer at a monthly salary of 250 rupees.

My boss was a dark-haired, slim middle-aged English geologist called David. He was always neatly dressed in a suit and a pencil-thin tie when he came to work in the laboratory each morning. But as soon as he hung up his jacket and donned his white overall, he could easily have found a job as an extra in a movie playing a stereotypical scientist. He wasn't much of a talker, preferring to concentrate on his writing and research; he spoke only when he had something to say.

David patiently taught me how to develop photographs in a darkroom, but first we had to wear gloves to avoid contaminating the films, as well as protective shoe coverings to prevent chemicals from splashing onto our feet. I learned how to soak the film for a few minutes in water before submerging it in developing chemicals, fixing and hanging the negative up to dry. He was a man who cared about order and cleanliness and he would frequently stress the importance of neatness and regular hand washing. I don't remember that he ever left the office without first tidying his desk.

I appreciated the opportunity to learn something different and my new skill gave me a sense of importance. Unfortunately, one of David's American colleagues of Arab origin would always burst my bubble with scathing comments. He looked down on me from day one because he thought I was too young to handle the job and made sure I knew it; an attitude that made me all the more determined to do well. The snooty fellow couldn't get to me. I wouldn't allow it. But something David asked me to do on the very first day of my employment brought me to the point of quitting. "Khalaf, would you mind sweeping the laboratory floor before you go home," he requested politely.

I certainly did mind. I was so offended that I didn't know how to respond at first. Me, sweep floors! Who does he think he's ordering around, I thought to myself. I'm a trainee, not a servant. Being told to do such a menial task was an affront to my dignity... or so I believed then. I quickly decided that my dignity was priceless. To hell with the 250 rupees! I then startled the poor man by refusing his instruction point blank.

"Sorry, Mr David. I won't do that. Not my job," I said, half expecting him to blow up.

"That's okay," he said with a smile, before collecting a broom and dustpan which he used to sweep the floor himself. It took a lot to rattle David. He was a quiet, calm man with a controlled temper for which English people are well known, and he wasn't about to lose it for something so insignificant.

I stood watching him work for a while, still seething inside. Then it hit me that if my boss was prepared to do domestic chores, why was I complaining? I learned the meaning of humility. There is nothing debasing or degrading about doing an honest day's work whatever its nature, and nobody should be too proud to clean up their own mess.

From then on, at the end of each working day we cleaned the lab together. He must have been pleased with me because he upped my wages to three hundred rupees. I was delighted even though I never actually handled any notes myself. He always insisted on calling upon my parents to hand over the cash into their safekeeping. I didn't mind as every rupee was theirs, but it would have been nice to present them with the rewards of my hard work myself.

Within a short time, I began to look upon David as a fatherly figure, and indeed it was evident that he cared about my well-being; he always made sure I got home safely after work to the extent of waiting to see me disappear through the front door.

The misunderstanding over cleaning the floor was mainly cultural. In many respects, Westerners are more status-conscious than people from the Middle East or the Gulf. In New York or London, executives climbing the ladder worry whether they will be handed a key to the executive bathroom or be assigned a designated parking space; all symbols of success. But very often those same ambitious men and women are happy to make coffee for their bosses, queue up to buy lunchtime sandwiches for their co-workers and polish their own desks. Britain's former Prime Minister Tony Blair used to make his own cup of tea while at Number 10 Downing Street, which isn't something most Arab leaders would do publicly even if they felt so inclined.

Traditionally, in my part of the world, there has been a clear demarcation of labour. Most secretaries in the West expect to be asked to make coffee or tea whereas an Arab secretary would call for the tea-boy. If it happened that he wasn't around, in some instances, bosses and their guests would just have to wait until he turned up or do without.

In Dubai, that demarcation has become somewhat fuzzy, largely due to the expatriate influence. Throughout the subcontinent, however, it is even more pronounced than in the Middle East. In India, where there is still a strong caste system – despite a constitution which bans discrimination based on caste – cleaning toilets, leather making, road sweeping and other 'dirty' jobs are the province of Dalits or *Harijans* – formerly known as 'Untouchables'. Successive Indian governments have attempted to rid the country of discriminatory class barriers; so far without much success.

In my youth, the roles of men and women were also sharply defined. There was men's work and women's work, which rarely overlapped. Men didn't clean houses, wash dishes, cook or sweep floors for fear of ridicule. Such things were not considered manly, just as they weren't in Britain during the first half of the twentieth century. When men came home from the coal mines, they expected to find their dinner on the table. No wife could say, "Sorry! I just came home from a business meeting or a yoga class. Make it yourself!". World War II blurred the respective roles of British men and women as when able-bodied boys and men were sent to the front, women stepped up to keep the country running, driving tractors and manning factory assembly lines.

Things have changed in the Middle East and the Gulf too, but at a far slower pace. Younger Arabs, especially those who have studied at universities abroad where they've had to look after themselves, are not averse to helping out with housework or making breakfast for their kids. It's a good trend in this day and age when so many wives are pursuing higher education or careers. I support this trend.

Female contributions to economy and society are important and should be encouraged; at the same time, wives and mothers who choose traditional roles over a demanding career deserve our respect for putting their families before their personal ambitions. I very much admire career women who compete with their male colleagues without losing their femininity. Call me old-fashioned if you like, but like most men from my part of the world I still like opening doors for the fairer sex.

All good things come to an end. My three months working with David were up and I was once again without an income. But now that I had the seeds of a work résumé under my belt, during the following summer I was easily accepted into Dubai Customs Office at the mouth of the Creek. Sheikh Rashid had an office on the top floor and although I saw him coming and going most days, ever-conscious of my youth and lowly position, I didn't dare strike up a conversation. I didn't know that Sheikh Rashid was accessible to all his people regardless of their age or station in life or that he would sometimes stop his car to chat with ordinary folk just to get a pulse on the public mood.

Officially, I was a tally clerk charged with receiving defective imported goods from a company called Gray MacKenzie (now a subsidiary of the Emirates Group called Maritime & Mercantile International, known as MMI), which had been appointed as Dubai's licensed shipping agent as far back as 1891. The goods were shipped to Dubai on barges; as soon as they were unloaded, it was my job to count the cartons and ensure their contents tallied with the bills of lading. That may sound simple enough, but, whenever there was an exceptionally big load or several barges docked at the same time, my task became overwhelmingly burdensome and time-consuming.

One day, when surrounded by stacks of cartons almost as far as the eye could see, I decided that there had to be a faster and more efficient way of doing things. I was also fed up listening to complaints from Gray MacKenzie representatives who wanted everything cleared double quick and could not understand that I wasn't some kind of robotic human calculator with x-ray vision. It was time for a plan.

When I was just about at the end of my tether, I approached one of the Gray MacKenzie guys with a rather unorthodox, but infinitely more workable strategy. "I'm ready to count every single item because that's my job," I told him. "But I must warn you that such an extensive and detailed count could take weeks, if not months".

I then offered him my solution. "To save time, I suggest that we estimate the defective, damaged and missing items to make up, say, 30 per cent of the total. We can then siphon off 30 per cent to be automatically transferred to the defective goods godown."

Following much-heated argument and debate, my practical solution was accepted. It was basically a win-win situation for Gray MacKenzie whose customers were all covered by insurance for losses, and for the Customs Office whose committee regularly auctioned off damaged or defective goods to local traders thereby increasing revenue. My managers patted me on the back for this initiative and my fellow employees benefited from perishable surpluses such as pasteurised milk, juices and fruit, which were still rare and expensive commodities in Dubai in the mid-1960s.

I could easily have risen through the ranks of the Customs Office at a fast pace. It did cross my mind to quit school and stay on. The work was hard and very tedious at times but I didn't mind rolling up my sleeves. It was the internal politics that I couldn't bear to put up with.

My direct superior was a fine man called Juma'a Al Baher, who originated from Bahrain. I got on with him really well and he put a lot of effort into showing me the ropes. But, unfortunately he was disliked by several of my fellow employees, who did everything they could to cause him problems in the hope he would eventually be shown the door.

I did my best to keep a distance from all the backbiting, but when the slurs against my boss reached the ears of his own chiefs, I was dragged into the dispute. I had no intention of getting caught in the middle or succumbing to pressure to say anything bad about my friend Juma'a. There was nothing for it but to hand in my notice.

To this day, I have little patience with anything that smacks of office politics or employees who conspire to get someone ousted from their job. Such vicious tactics have no place in any of my companies. As far as I'm concerned, gossiping and muck raking should be strictly consigned to out-of-office hours – or even better, should be avoided entirely. This is not only common decency, for Muslims it is a religious injunction expressed in the Holy Qur'an thus:

> O you, who have believed, avoid much [negative] assumption. Indeed, some as-sumption is sin. And do not spy or backbite each other. Would one of you like to eat the flesh of his brother when dead? You would detest it. And fear Allah; indeed, Allah is accepting of repentance and is merciful.
>
> – Sura Al Hujurat 49: 12

My self-confidence at an all-time high after my successes as a geolo-gist's assistant and a customs tally clerk, I rather fancied myself as a banker. The international banking giant First National City Bank (now part of Citigroup) had opened its first branch in Dubai during 1964 and I was keen to get my foot in the door in any capacity.

This was an opportunity to make something of myself; a real career with prestige that could set me up for life. I didn't picture myself as a teller exchanging cash for cheques or taking in deposits. I envisioned myself in a dark pinstriped suit puffing a Cuban cigar with my feet on the desk, chatting with millionaire customers on the phone in the way that bank managers are often portrayed in movies. I soon came down to earth with a bump.

I discussed this career move with some of my female cousins who all had a fair grasp of the English language. This was a good chance to practise English before I headed off to the bank. They listened intently as I showed off my knowledge of basic expressions, such as "How are you?" "Where are you from?" "What's your name?", but before I could finish my limited repertoire, one of the girls interrupted me in full flow.

"Khalaf, that's enough," she said. "Keep the English you know, the little you know, for your interview. If you say everything now, it will be all used up and by the time you get to the bank you'll be empty." I couldn't quite follow her reasoning, but the practice session was abruptly terminated.

The very next day, I strolled to the First National City Bank (the precursor of Citibank) that was housed in a posh building in Bur Dubai and couldn't help marvelling at the sheer opulence of the place. Those Americans do everything bigger and better than everyone else, I mused. I lodged my application with the help of a cousin who was working there at the time and was certain he would put in a good word with the hierarchy.

My heart sank when I was presented with a questionnaire which I was expected to complete there and then. I gazed longingly at the exit, but short of embarrassing myself by running away, there was no escape. I struggled to fill in the form with my almost illegible handwriting and poor spelling, and knew it would take some deciphering. Still, for some odd reason, I was fairly sure I would, at the very least, be offered a two or three-month summer job.

Once the interview was over, it was a case of 'don't call us, we'll call you'. A few days later, I received an apologetic letter informing me there were no vacancies. I wasn't used to rejection and felt quite down for an hour or two. Like most young people, I was overly sensitive to anything implying that I wasn't good enough, and certainly my ego took a small dent.

But the Creator works in mysterious ways. Years later, when I was running my own successful businesses, I remembered that terrible job interview and laughed. Much later on, I invited the Chairman of Citigroup's Wealth Management division to the Habtoor Grand Hotel. In the course of conversation, I told him the story of how I had been turned down by his bank.

"Just imagine, if I hadn't been rebuffed, I might be the Chairman of Citigroup today; maybe even the Chairman of Wealth Management instead of you," I joked.

"Thank God, you weren't accepted," he said with a resounding laugh.

"No, it's me who should be thanking God," I answered. "If they'd given me that job, I might have ended up pen pushing in some awful office making money for you guys."

I hope I haven't given you the impression that my teenage years were all work and no play. I used to have fun going on picnics after school, driving used four-wheel-drive vehicles that my father bought at British military auctions to re-sell at a profit. I learned to drive when I was fourteen or thereabouts. There were no driving schools or Highway Code. Driving was a skill one picked up from observation or after a few casual lessons from friends or family members. It was much easier than now because there were few roads, no traffic lights, roundabouts or stop signs, and very little traffic.

The most important aspect of driving in Dubai during the 1960s was how to avoid getting stuck in sand, and if that happened – as it frequently did – how to get the car rolling again once the tyres began to sink deeper in. There's a technique to freeing vehicles from the grip of desert terrain, partly involving letting out some air from the tyres, with which every Dubai national was familiar as a matter of necessity.

Being able to drive was freeing in that I was now able to get around. It was pleasurable to cruise along virtually empty roads, but for me driving has always represented a means of getting from A to B rather than a leisure activity in itself. Nowadays, I actively dislike driving and rarely drive myself anywhere. With so many traffic jams, speed maniacs and normally mild people who turn into fire-breathing dragons once they get behind the wheel, driving can be stressful.

I also enjoyed many summer vacations in Al Ain, an oasis town belonging to Abu Dhabi around 130 kilometres south of Dubai that has always attracted visitors due to its lush greenery and low humidity. Al Ain is also the birthplace of Sheikh Zayed bin Sultan Al Nahyan, the late Ruler of Abu Dhabi, who was the United Arab Emirates' first President.

It was during one of those summer visits with the family that I first met my cousin Sheikh Mubarak bin Mohammed Al Nahyan and his sisters. I was very young, but I still recall being pleasantly surprised at the warmth with which they greeted my mother. Sheikh Mubarak was an emotional man who was very close to his family. He said my mother reminded him of his own. In those days, our income was limited. Out of pride, we would rather go without than ask anyone for financial assistance. Sheikh Mubarak didn't treat us like his poorer relatives; he's not that kind of person.

When I grew older and became a regular visitor to the Emirate of Abu Dhabi, both Sheikh Mubarak and his brother, Sheikh Hamdan bin Mohammed Al Nahyan, would invite me to their home, saying *beitna beitak* (our house is yours) and making me feel like their younger brother.

Sheikh Mubarak's son, Sheikh Nahayan Mabarak Al Nahayan, has inherited his father's good character. He is one of the most generous and welcoming hosts I know. He's always inviting people to his house for meals and he goes out of his way to make them feel at home, smiling and talking to everyone. He's also one of the most caring and energetic people I've ever met. He faithfully visits the sick to ensure they're being well taken care of and he often helps those afflicted with illness to get treatment abroad.

He genuinely loves and respects his friends and family. He never misses a wedding or a funeral. In fact, when his beloved aunt, my mother, passed away, he and his father, Sheikh Mubarak, were the first to arrive at her funeral; the Rulers of the other emirates came too. He is also a devoted son. When his father was ill, Sheikh Nahayan stayed with him all the time to attend to his needs, such as shaving and personal grooming. I consider myself a hard worker but I couldn't do one-tenth of what he does. I love to visit Sheikh Nahayan when I can. We're in close communication and every so often he sends me honey from his farm as well as deer and game birds each time he returns from a hunting trip. Like his father, I consider Sheikh Nahayan to be an extraordinary man; I only wish there were more like him in the world. God give him health, power and energy. May God bless him!

On other occasions, we would holiday in the Buraimi Oasis, straddling the UAE and Oman, where my family owned a cluster of palm huts. The oasis thrived and was continuously inhabited for 4,000 years thanks to an ancient irrigation system we call *falaj* that distributes underground springs via a network of natural canals to date palms. It was so peaceful to wander along palm-shaded narrow lanes listening to birdsong and a perpetual chorus of crickets and frogs.

Sultan, my brother, is particularly nostalgic for those lazy summer days. "The countryside was clean, the air was pure and the food fresh and delicious," he remembers. One year, we rented a date farm. We gathered the dates ourselves and carried home sacks of them. "The springs used to gush and flow like small rivers," Sultan recalls, "but now many of them have dried up."

It should be mentioned that most of the Buraimi Oasis is now in Oman, with a smaller section having been subsumed into Al Ain. Until 2006, there was an open border, but now expatriates require passports and visas to cross; Gulf Cooperation Council (GCC) nationals just require their identity cards. This is typical of the way the world is going. Security concerns have led to people everywhere being fenced in.

Al Ain, which is dubbed the 'Garden City', is now the UAE's fourth largest in terms of population and one of the most beautiful, although it no more resembles the serene, small town that will always remain etched in our memories.

As always, I spent a lot of my spare time with my father, who now that I was almost grown, was proud to introduce me to his trader friends and involve me in his business discussions. There were three or four that we visited regularly at their homes. Two of them were Mohammed Al Mulla and Obeid Al Mulla, wise and prominent businessmen who invited us both to dinner at their houses. The fare was very simple, such as bread, cheese and *foul* (mashed fava beans); we thought it was wonderful.

Whenever father was due to visit an important person's majlis, he would always ask me to go with him. One way or another, I gained a lot of free education just listening quietly to the discussions of others and found that I preferred the company of older people to hanging out with boys of my own age, who were often immature and silly.

There were plenty of bugs around then, as I've said before. By the age of fourteen or so, I had caught a particularly virulent variety that has stayed with me for life – the travel bug. I wanted to travel everywhere and taste everything good that life has to offer.

I must have been around fifteen or sixteen when I returned to Bombay, this time as a tourist. My friend Mohammed bin Dismal came with me. We ended up sharing a twin room in a small hotel to cut expenses. I still remember that the beds were separated by curtains, which we pulled for privacy before we slept and that the room cost five rupees a night. Mohammed's sons are now pals of my own but I lost touch with my old friend when he moved to Abu Dhabi. Our paths haven't crossed in years.

The one destination I longed to see was Cairo. I had heard so much about it, read so much about it, seen it in so many movies and, of course, it was home to my hero, Gamal Abdel Nasser – although the idea of knocking on his door brandishing his letter of invitation had disappeared along with my childish fantasies.

My brother Mohammed was aware that Cairo was at the top of my vacation wish list and when he heard that his best friend Saif Al Hathboor (affectionately known as Abu Abdullah or father of Abdullah) was going, he suggested that I joined him there. It was an opportunity because Abu Abdullah owned an apartment in the Egyptian capital and knew the city inside out. I couldn't have been more thrilled at the prospect.

Abu Abdullah was one of the greatest, biggest-hearted men I've ever met. Mohammed had contacted him before our flight to say, "Khalaf is coming. I'm relying on you to look after him". He met me at the airport and hugged me as enthusiastically as if I were his own son. It would be hard to find a more pleasant host. He was genuinely glad to see me.

Within no time I felt at home in his lovely, spacious flat on Abu Al Fida Street in Zamalek that had a fabulous view of the Nile and rather splendid houseboats (Egyptians call them *awamat*). Those were flanked by steep flower gardens where royalty and celebrities, such as King Farouk's mother, Queen Nazli, singer Farid Al Atrash and the actor Naguib Al Rehani used to throw private – and by all accounts often quite wild – parties.

The *awamat* also have a reputation for intrigue. German spies were found hiding on one in the Second World War, and later on some were used by political dissenters to plot revolution far away from prying eyes.

There were just the two of us staying in the flat plus an Egyptian house-keeper. She was quite a good cook, although her cleaning skills weren't up to much, as evidenced by the unhygienic state of the kitchen and bathroom. But I didn't concern myself with such trivial details; when compared to my home in Dubai, that flat was Buckingham Palace. I drove past it a few years ago and it doesn't look nearly as glamorous; either it's changed or my standards have – probably both.

Egypt's capital city didn't disappoint either. Its wide tree-lined boulevards, stately turn-of-the-century mansions and elegant Downtown shopping streets were quite spectacular to the eyes of someone from a small Gulf backwater, whose travel, until then, had been limited to Dammam, Bahrain and Bombay.

What really surprised me was how sophisticated some of the wealthier residential areas, such as Zamalek and Garden City were. In those fashionable, tree-lined places, the aristocracy had maintained their primary residences – palatial mansions which have mostly been turned into embassies, art galleries, libraries or museums.

The streets in the best areas of town were as clean as London or Paris. I know that anyone who has seen Cairo in recent decades might find that hard to believe. It's worth remembering that the city was home to just 6 million people in 1966, as opposed to 17 million today. Moreover, the Egyptian pound was then very strong; the currency was pegged to the dollar at the rate of two dollars and thirty cents. As I write, the exchange rate is a little over six Egyptian pounds to one dollar.

I couldn't help noticing that many of the passers-by were very stylish. In the evenings, it was usual to see men wearing bow ties, and all over, there were so many stunning young ladies dressed in the latest fashions, looking as though they had just stepped off the cover of *Vogue*. It was another world. No wonder I felt like a kid in a candy store! Actually, I thought I looked quite smart myself in my fine suit and tie. I wasn't as comfortable as I would have been in national dress, which is loose-fitting and cool, but as they say nowadays, 'no pain, no gain'.

For those of you who are unfamiliar with this region, I should explain that Gulf nationals of every strata of society are proud to wear national dress – consisting of a *kandoura* and a *ghutrah* (headscarf) held in place by an *egal* (thick black rope) – which we consider to be part of our heritage and traditions. Nowadays, we wear it as a prestigious nationalist symbol of who we are.

Naturally, I toured the pyramids at Giza, the Cairo Museum, the Citadel and the famous bustling Khan el-Khalili market. I enjoyed every minute of my sightseeing itinerary. But it was an upmarket tea shop in Downtown's Talaat Harb Square called Groppi's that imprinted itself most on my memory. There was nowhere quite like it in the Middle East, with the possible exception of Beirut.

Groppi's was the place to see and be seen, a cross between London's Fortnum & Mason and The Ritz. It was known for its impeccable service, but more especially for its delicious chocolates, croissants, gateaux, marrons glacés, jams and ice cream – all made in the tea shop's own factory with the best quality ingredients using recipes so secret they were written in French and kept in a locked safe. No single employee involved in the manufacturing process was allowed to know every ingredient in the final product.

This delightful marble-clad patisserie and tea shop was the favoured haunt of ambassadors, politicians, movie stars, intellectuals, poets and writers. Regular patrons would gravitate towards tables permanently reserved in their name. Before the 1952 revolution, it wasn't unusual to see King Farouk and his entourage enjoying a leisurely afternoon out there.

I was also told that in World War II it was a hotbed of foreign intelligence agents. Apparently, a British colonel was kind enough to treat two captured German spies to tea there before they were handed over for interrogation. How's that for an ingenious torture technique!

Groppi's chocolates had such a unique rich flavour that they were world renowned. King Farouk, who loved sweets attested by his burgeoning size, was their biggest fan. During World War II, he shipped 100 kilograms to King George for his daughters, Elizabeth and Margaret. Due to an ever-present menace from the Nazis, the precious cargo had to be freighted the long way round via West Africa, Spain, France, Belgium and Scotland, before they could be delivered to the young princesses.

I found the cosmopolitan ambience of Groppi's captivating and couldn't get over how pristine it was. The pavement outside was washed down daily and the bathroom was so clean you could almost eat off the floor; not that I was tempted to try.

Sadly, when I returned to Cairo in the mid-1970s, nothing was the same. I was excited to recapture the enjoyment of my earlier visit to Groppi's, but what remained was a faded neglected replica that looked in urgent need of a scrub down. On that occasion, I couldn't get to the toilet for all the filth strewn all over the bathroom floor. The Swiss pastry maker, Giacomo Groppi, who opened the tea shop more than a century ago, would be heartbroken to see what's become of his labour of love were he still alive.

Alright, I admit it. Besides being a health nut I'm also a clean freak, to use an Americanism. But don't worry! I've no plans to shut myself away in a darkened room like the millionaire American aviator and film producer-director Howard Hughes, whose fear of germs turned him into a recluse. In most of the world, soap is cheap and water plentiful so there's no excuse to allow filth to accumulate. I definitely can't understand why countries where unemployment is high and labour relatively inexpensive allow mountains of garbage to rot on the street, attracting vermin and disease.

Poverty is no excuse either. I'm not talking about absolute destitution when people's priority is finding something to eat or somewhere dry to rest their heads, but some of the simplest homes I've visited have also been some of the cleanest. It's all down to education and culture.

There was a time, not so long ago, when Hong Kong and Singapore were two of the dirtiest cities on earth; now they are among the cleanest. This is partly due to governmental intervention in the form of public announcements on television and fines. Ideally, parents should teach their children hygiene, but where that doesn't happen schools need to take more responsibility.

My first visit to Cairo would have been perfect, if I could have avoided upsetting my host. I won't reveal what I said or did to cause the upset, but it was nothing awful. At least, I didn't think so. The only reason I'm not being specific is that I don't really want my grandsons coming to me one day waving this book and saying, "Now we know that you did or said such-and-such in your youth, grandfather, why can't we?".

In fact, I had no idea that Abu Abdullah was angry with me until I showed up at his apartment building after a day out, intent on having a shower to remove the city grime. As soon as I walked towards the elevator to go up to the fourth floor, the usually friendly Sudanese *bawab* (doorman) rushed up to me looking uncharacteristically glum.

"How are you, my friend?" I said.

"Thanks be to God I'm well, but I'm sorry you can't go up."

"What do you mean I can't go up? I'm staying here. You know that. Are you crazy?"

"The Pasha told me to prevent you from going to his apartment," he answered, while staring at the ground and shuffling his feet. Obviously, this wasn't a role this normally affable man enjoyed.

"No, no, no! That's not possible," I protested. "You must have misunderstood what he told you. Abu Abdullah is like my father. What nonsense is this?"

"It's true, sir! He couldn't have been any clearer. I'm sorry to say this but he said he doesn't want to see your face ever again."

I could tell by the doorman's expression that this was no joke, so I just shrugged my shoulders and insisted that I must be allowed back into the apartment to pack my suitcase.

"Your suitcase is packed. It's here with me," he said. "I rescued it after the Pasha threw it out of the window onto the street."

Well, at least it wasn't squashed by a car – or worse still, stolen – even if it did look a little dented and dusty. Bag firmly in hand, I flagged down a taxi and told the driver to take me to the Nile Hilton. That was the first hotel that popped into my head. I remember feeling sad that Abu Abdullah thought I had let him down and regretted losing his friendship, but my main preoccupation was worrying how I was going to explain to my brother Mohammed why I was unceremoniously kicked out of his best friend's home. And God forbid the news would reach my parents.

I groaned when I thought of the stern lectures awaiting me back home. I was also hurt. Nobody appreciates being thrown out on their ear and especially in a strange land. Nevertheless, until now, I still have fond memories of Abu Abdullah, God rest his soul! He did what he thought was right.

Once I had recovered from the shock of being informed about the Nile Hilton's room rates – which, in reality, were very reasonable for a five-star hotel but way more expensive than the five rupees I was used to paying – my mood brightened considerably. Here I was, young and carefree, languishing in the lap of luxury in a city that never sleeps. Luckily for me, two of my cousins were in Egypt studying at the Police Academy, so I was fairly sure I wouldn't be entirely friendless during the rest of my stay.

As I sat on the balcony of my room smoking a cigarette (a disgusting habit I gave up decades ago) between taking sips from a cooling drink, I watched glittering river boats ferrying noisy revellers gliding past on the calm Nile waters below. I counted my blessings. Life was good. The night was young and so was I.

I really like this hotel, I thought, while wishing I could afford to stay a few extra weeks. Constructed in the late 1950s, when architects focused on functionality rather than creativity, its façade is dull and drab. However, it's perfectly located in the centre of town with fantastic views of the river and has spacious rooms. Most importantly, it has a rich history and a feel-good ambience which is something money can't buy. You might say, it's a hotel with a soul. It didn't for one instant cross my mind that there would come a day when I would be in a position to seriously consider buying it. I didn't go through with that purchase for various reasons, however. Today, the hotel is still owned by the Egyptian government and is undergoing a major overhaul. It is managed by the Ritz-Carlton and has been renamed The Nile Ritz-Carlton.

As I had hoped, the very next day, my two young cousins rallied around and took me out and about. What was a pleasant vacation then took a very exciting turn. While I was eating alone in the hotel's coffee shop, I noticed that the well-known Egyptian comedian George Sidhom, famous for his comedic shows, plays and movies, was sitting at a nearby table. I'd never met a real-life celebrity before, so I asked one of the waiters to introduce me.

To my great surprise, Mr Sidhom immediately smiled over at me and then got up from his table to join me. We hit it off straight away. I found him to be a simple, down-to-earth man with no airs and graces at all. We sat there chatting for ages about everything imaginable like two old friends.

Soon after, while I was walking from my cousin's apartment on Kasr el-Nile Street on my way to the Nile Hilton, I was astonished to see Fahd Ballan, a famous Syrian singer-actor, who was then at the height of his fame, strolling along beside me accompanied by the stunning blonde Egyptian movie star Nadia Lutfi, who had inherited her fair skin and hair from her Polish mother.

To say I was star-struck is an understatement. To put this scene into a Western context, it was like bumping into Clark Gable with Brigitte Bardot. Ballan was extremely popular in the Gulf because of his strong singing voice and manly appearance. Ms Lutfi had gained fame throughout the Arab region in the late 1950s after starring with the reigning king and queen of Egyptian cinema, Omar Sharif and his actress wife, Faten Hamama, in the movie *La Anam* (Sleepless).

She went on to act in fifty-three films; she took serious parts in a few, such as *Cairo Station*, also known as *Iron Gate*, directed by Youssef Chahine, and *Naser Salah El-Din* (Saladin and the Great Crusades) shown on US television; but mostly she played the female love interest in light dramas.

I don't know how I struck up the courage to approach them and say hello, but I was glad I did. Fahd Ballan didn't hesitate to shake my hand. He asked my name and where I came from and appeared just as fascinated to meet a young man from Dubai as I was to meet a celebrity. I tentatively invited him to join me for coffee and a snack and he accepted. After a friendly chat, we agreed to meet up again the following day when he promised to introduce me to his ex-wife, the beautiful Egyptian, half-Hungarian screen legend Mariam Fakhr Eddine, considered one of the most respectable actresses of the time.

I could hardly believe my luck to be in the presence of such a glamorous diva and tried my best not to stare too much. She was the perfect charming lady. I was so overawed by her looks and intelligence that I could hardly taste the pastries and Egyptian sweets she offered. I was intimidated by the fact that she kept switching between languages – she was fluent in six – but because she made me feel such a welcome guest, I soon relaxed and began to enjoy every minute.

From that day onwards, we got together every day. I told Fahd about my encounter with George Sidhom and he suggested we get in touch with the comedian to invite him to join us, which he did on several occasions. I had an amazing time in their company. This was the Cairo I had dreamt of seeing as a mesmerised child in the cinema; I almost felt like I had stepped into a movie, everything was so unreal and so far removed from my simple life at home. It felt so good to be accepted by such people. I had no money, no status, no fame and no influence. They liked me just for myself. What a good feeling and confidence boost that was!

A chance meeting with Fahd Ballan opened my eyes to an enchanting world where everything was possible. Now that I had tasted how life could be, I was determined, one day, to create such a world for myself. Abu Abdullah didn't know it, but when he threw me out of his home, he did me a great favour. Now that the barriers of possibility had been smashed, life would have never been the same again. On the flight back to Dubai, I was on cloud nine; my level of confidence had soared as high as the plane.

Once back on terra firma, reality beckoned. I knew I had to steel myself for whatever it might throw at me.

CHAPTER 6
Transformations

"WHEN YOU'RE FINISHED CHANGING, YOU'RE FINISHED."
– BENJAMIN FRANKLIN

6 June 1966 (6/6/66) was not only unusual in numerological terms; it heralded a dramatic change in Dubai's fortunes. On that day, oil was found offshore in commercial quantities by the Dubai Petroleum Company. The field which Sheikh Rashid named 'Fateh' or 'Good Fortune' took almost thirty years of excavation, but couldn't have come at a more opportune time, when the Ruler was poised to turn his visions into reality.

Three years later, Dubai exported its first-ever shipment, and within a few years the South-West Fateh, Falah and Rashid fields were discovered. Compared to Abu Dhabi's reserves, Dubai's were relatively modest. Sheikh Rashid was aware that oil revenue couldn't be relied upon forever and he knew that the emirate's economic future must be forged around commerce, banking, trade and tourism.

Most of Sheikh Rashid's projects, such as Dubai Dry Dock, Port Rashid, the expansion of the airport and the thirty-nine-storey World Trade Centre implemented in the 1970s – and thought fantastical by some of the established, conservative pearling families – were devised to establish Dubai as the Gulf's most important trading hub, with an open policy geared towards attracting investments from all over the world.

The sceptics were soon silenced when foreign entrepreneurs, international conglomerates, construction companies and banks were magnetised to set up new businesses in Dubai.

Referring to Sheikh Rashid as 'forward-thinking' has become somewhat of a cliché, but in truth, for someone who was brought up in a virtual village locked into earlier centuries, he was an exceptional visionary. Without Sheikh Rashid's innovative approaches, my hometown wouldn't be the thriving, high-profile, modern wonder it is acknowledged to be today.

Some of Dubai's neighbours were less fortunate. For instance, the Sultan of Muscat and Oman (now the Sultanate of Oman), Saeed bin Taimur, ruled a country that enjoyed independence from Britain – although with a very close relationship – and was flush with oil wealth. But he was unable to adapt to the twentieth century due to his ultra-conservative, old-fashioned mentality combined with restraints imposed upon him by an influential Imam Ghalib bin Ali Al Hinai, who sought to oust him in order to turn Oman into an imamate.

Oman under the reign of Saeed bin Taimur has been described as "medieval and isolationist". However, to his credit, the Sultan did succeed in preserving his country's independence as well as bringing tribes together and unifying Muscat and Oman. But as someone who was unable to trust banks, preferring to keep his money under his mattress, he was unable to adjust his thinking in accordance with contemporary socio-economic demands.

"I have watched with growing dismay and increasing anger the inability of my father to use the new-found wealth of this country for the needs of its people," his only son, Sultan Qaboos bin Saeed Al Saeed, Oman's current Ruler, was once quoted as saying. His dissatisfaction was duly noted and for that Sultan Qaboos was placed under house arrest for six years in one of the royal palaces.

After surviving an assassination attempt, Sultan Saeed became increasingly paranoid. With the backing of Britain and with Omani forces loyal to his son, he was persuaded to abdicate in July 1970, leaving Sultan Qaboos to manage a country neglected and underdeveloped with antiquated laws. He lived out the rest of his life quietly in England, where he passed away on 19 October 1972.

Sultan Qaboos, an educated man who studied at a private school in England and later graduated from the Sandhurst military academy, soon set to work to build schools, hospitals and highways before opening up his country to tourism and broadening international relations in a way that wouldn't threaten his people's cultural or social mores.

Abu Dhabi's then ruler, Sheikh Shakhbut bin Sultan Al Nahyan, was also unable to adjust to tomorrow's world, although not nearly to the same degree as Sultan Saeed. Abu Dhabi's oil had first been discovered in Umm Shaif in 1958, but the Ruler feared it would soon run out and felt he should conserve the proceeds, an approach which slowed up Abu Dhabi's growth. On 4 August 1966, the British government was advised by members of the

Al Nahyan family that Sheikh Shakhbut was about to step aside for his younger and more progressive brother, Sheikh Zayed, who had served as the Ruler's Representative in Abu Dhabi's Eastern Region since 1946. Just days later, Sheikh Shakhbut left quietly for Bahrain.

Within no time, Sheikh Zayed began implementing his plans to construct new roads, schools, hospitals and affordable housing, and soon developed a reputation for tolerance. There was nothing authoritarian about his ruling style. He kept an open majlis where he would listen to the opinions of others in order to reach consensus. Thanks to his long de facto governance of the Eastern Region around the garden city of Al Ain, he was able to relate to the concerns of desert tribes and felt just as home in a tent as he did in a palace.

Sheikh Rashid quickly warmed to Abu Dhabi's new ruler Sheikh Zayed as an honourable man of like mind with a similar visionary outlook. Together they spearheaded the United Arab Emirates and closely cooperated to ensure the flourishing of the new federation comprising seven emirates, with Abu Dhabi as its capital.

Sheikh Zayed, who garnered the honorific 'Hakim Al Arab' due to his wise leadership, was a truly remarkable man who believed his emirate's natural resources should be devoted to benefiting his people. Throughout his rule until his death in 2004, he was respected at home and abroad for his sincere faith, kindly spirit, moderation, philanthropy and altruism.

From the mid-1960s onwards, the region was like a giant awakening from centuries of hibernation. Change came fast and furious and was unstoppable. As Dubai and the entire Gulf were transitioning to meet the challenges of the future, so was I.

Those carefree days without responsibilities came to an abrupt end when I was just sixteen years old. My mother in her infinite wisdom decided it was time for me to settle down with a wife.

I wasn't at all happy about the 'suggestion'. I still felt like an emotionally immature kid; besides, I didn't have a steady income. And of course, like most young men everywhere in the world, I feared that marriage would diminish my personal freedom or hamper my ambitions. I was in no hurry to tie the knot but I've always been one to pick my battles. Taking on my mother wasn't one I could easily win, so I gave in without much of a struggle. Seeing their sons married is an obsession for most mothers in the Arab world. It's their life's greatest mission – as I'm sure most Arabs would agree – seconded only by their eagerness for grandchildren.

The fact that I knew and liked my future bride softened the blow. Hamda was not only our neighbour, she was also my second cousin. We had ridden our bicycles together when we were very young and on occasion she had helped me with my studies.

Most importantly, my mother was fond of Hamda and wanted to invite her into our home as a new daughter who would keep her company and help with housework and cooking. I wasn't exactly enthusiastic at the prospect of becoming a married man so young, but in those days marriage was inevitable sooner or later. Society expected it. The few men who held out until their mid-twenties or thirties – or very occasionally even later – were looked upon as odd. So when the date was set, I just shrugged my shoulders and said "No problem!".

Ours was a very simple wedding compared to today's lavish extravaganzas in five-star hotels, where the bill can often exceed 25,000 dollars. We didn't make use of wedding planners, hairdressers, beauticians, fashion designers, florists and confectioners. All we had was a pickup full of Pepsi and 7Up – courtesy of Sheikh Rashid's brother, Sheikh Khalifa – and a few roasted sheep. I felt a bit like a lamb to the slaughter myself.

At first, I didn't know what to make of my newly-wed status, especially when some of my friends treated it as a huge joke. I didn't blame them. When I looked in the mirror, a skinny kid looking much younger than his years stared back rather than a responsible married man. You could say that I grew into the role over time, making quite a few mistakes on the way.

At first, we felt awkward being married. We had only very recently left childhood behind and we had been friends since we were little more than infants, so it was difficult to adjust our feelings in one day and one night. We had only been wed for a few hours when I woke up my father in the early hours of the morning to explain that we were buddies, not suited to being man and wife. He was very upset for both of us; his first reaction was to get the marriage annulled. I was his priority because he loved me and couldn't bear to see me unhappy.

Our home was in an uproar when Hamda's mother, Osha, who is also my mother's niece, arrived on the scene. She is a woman with an exceptionally strong personality who never lowered her head for anyone. She had no intention of agreeing to any annulment, which would have reflected badly on her daughter who was entirely innocent of any mistake.

Osha sat with my mother for a long time discussing the problem with a cool mind. The two wise older women counselled Hamda and I to be patient and give our new relationship a chance to develop naturally. A few days later, my uncle Saeed Al Otaiba got involved to bring us back together. Within no time, everything was fine between us. All we needed was a little time to see each other in a different light, away from our families' spotlight. As it happened, our long friendship strengthened the foundations of our marriage. It became the thread that has bound us together for the past forty-seven years.

My preoccupation with being successful meant I wasn't around a lot of the time and my efforts to switch from a boy to 'the man', the head of the household, didn't leave room for the kind of attention expected by most young brides. It's worth pointing out that during that era young men were sometimes reluctant to show their softer sides for fear such displays of affection would be received as weakness.

In retrospect, being married to me couldn't have been easy for Hamda in those early days, but she was always incredibly loyal and encouraging and I don't recall that she was ever openly critical. However, my wife says that she was happy being married to a self-disciplined, ambitious man with a strong personality as she felt well-cared for and secure. Thankfully, she adored my mother and took her advice on everything. On those rare occasions my mother was upset with her over some minor disagreement, Hamda would kiss her head and ask to be forgiven.

Fatherless since she was two years old, Hamda had been brought up by a very strict mother, the well-known Abu Dhabi-born poet Osha Al Suwaidi, who has also been a successful businesswoman. My wife's mother had been loving but tough. When Hamda was just four years old, she was expected to wake up in the early hours of the morning for the *Fajr* prayer and to do household chores. She credits her mother's discipline as character building and believes that without it she wouldn't be the woman of strong character she is today.

Like my brother Sultan, my wife thinks about the old days with fond nostalgia. "We were happy. Everything was simple," she says. "We didn't have much money but we were all very close. I enjoyed caring for my first two children without nannies or maids and never minded cooking, cleaning or washing clothes by hand."

"I think people were happier in those days than they are now. Families didn't compete with each other; they stood by one another. Everyone's home was permanently open so anyone could just drop in at any time. Nowadays, you have to make an appointment to see friends who sometimes say they're busy – then, nobody was too busy." She is right, but as I've said nothing's perfect; some aspects of life were better then, but most weren't.

Although she was my mother's choice, I couldn't have asked for a better life partner or mother for my children, who all love her dearly for her gentle personality, patience, big heart and great wisdom. Whenever they have a problem, they rush to her for advice and a hug.

She's been by my side throughout the bad times and the good and she is one of the few who knows me and can relate to the past. She's never longed for great wealth or a glamorous, jet-setting, pampered lifestyle, like the trophy wives seen on so many rich men's arms who rarely stick around when the money runs out. She has her priorities right. Caring about her children and grandchildren and being a good wife to me come first. She keeps me grounded.

Now that I had a wife to care for, I was infused with renewed energy to find a reasonable source of income, so at the very least we could move to a nice house that wasn't put together with palm fronds and ensure our children never had to face the kind of hardships that poverty heaped upon us. As much as I hated being employed, I was resigned to finding a job; preferably one that would arm me with enough experience to make it on my own at a future date.

As luck would have it, I ran into Mohammed Saeed Al Mulla, a prominent Dubai businessman who was my father's and elder brother's friend. At the time, he was looking for someone to represent the interests of his construction company in Abu Dhabi. He seemed to think that I was an ideal candidate because he knew that many of my maternal relatives were from Abu Dhabi and that I was related to the Al Nahyan royals via the line of my mother's father, Ahmad Khalaf Al Otaiba.

In those days, business was run on the lines of who you knew rather than what you did, and in some respects it's the same today, which is why one sees so many ex-world leaders on the boards of international companies. A case in point is the Carlyle Group, a private equity firm whose list of board members, advisors and former employees reads like a global 'Who's Who', packed with former presidents and politicians. Of course, I wasn't in their league. I was just an eighteen-year-old kid with hardly a few Bahrain dinars (the currency used in the day) in my pocket, but the principle behind my hiring was the same.

I wasn't exactly sure whether I would have any sway over my relatives at all, as apart from my cousins – Sheikh Mubarak bin Mohammed, Sheikh

Hamdan bin Mohammed, Ahmad Khalifa Al Suwaidi and Khalaf Ahmad Al Otaiba – I didn't really know them. As I explained in the previous chapter, I got to know Sheikh Mubarak and his brother, Sheikh Hamdan, during childhood visits to Al Ain. Ahmad Khalifa Al Suwaidi on the other hand was a regular visitor to our home, as his mother 'Meera' bint Khalaf Al Otaiba was my mother's aunt and his sister was my wife's mother. Sheikh Mubarak, Sheikh Hamdan and Ahmad Khalifa are all cousins of the Father of the UAE, Sheikh Zayed bin Sultan Al Nahyan; together they played a major role in laying the foundations of the UAE along with Sheikh Rashid.

Mr Al Mulla was very encouraging, which boosted my confidence greatly and so, before long, I was leaving my home every morning at 4 a.m. for the three-hour-long drive to Abu Dhabi in a Land Rover over bumpy roads peppered with potholes, and returning each evening at 6 p.m. or thereabouts, anxious to see my bed.

The job itself was very demanding. I may have been employed as a white-collar representative of the owner in Abu Dhabi, but regardless of my official capacity in the company I was expected to muck in and do whatever was asked of me. I didn't really mind because most of my colleagues were just as flexible.

I drove pickups and sometimes trucks when materials needed to be transported from Dubai to Abu Dhabi, then I would help the labourers offload the consignment. In general, I was responsible for checking estimates and prices for steel, bending steel, sand and even water needed to manufacture one cubic metre of concrete.

I was also charged with ensuring various aspects of a given project were running to plan, which involved checking that the labourers would be transported to site on time, making certain that the pouring of concrete was on schedule and payments to subcontractors were timely. Almost every day-to-day task requiring follow-up and control was placed in my lap.

Most of the time, I just did whatever needed doing. Both fresh water and salt water used in construction had to be transported to the Al Mulla camp. We were continually opening taps and sighing to find them dry. One day, I was so frustrated at waiting around for water that I drove a mammoth water tanker to the sea's edge and started the pumps to ensure work could proceed without delay.

One of the most memorable days of my life was accompanying Mohammed Saeed Al Mulla and his friend Sultan Al Owais, a well-known businessman, poet and philanthropist, to visit Sheikh Zayed in an old palace where his brother, the former ruler Sheikh Shakhbut, used to reside.

We turned up at the front gate and told the police guard that we were there to see Sheikh Zayed. "Who are you guys?" he asked, while looking us up and down. He didn't seem very impressed. "What are your names and what do you do?" he shouted.

"Listen! Our friends Khalaf Al Otaiba and Ahmad Al Suwaidi are with His Highness right now. Just tell them that we are here to see Sheikh Zayed on business," said Al Mulla.

"What kind of business?"

Al Mulla had already ascertained that the guard wasn't too bright, so instead of elaborating and stressing our credentials as businessmen he simply answered "We are buyers and sellers". For such a highly-looked-up to, well-known personage, I thought this approach rather strange. We could have been selling fish, for all the policeman knew. But it did the trick.

Once Khalaf Al Otaiba, who is my uncle, learned of our presence he welcomed us to the palace. While we waited for an audience with His Highness, we took coffee with Khalaf and my cousin Ahmad Al Suwaidi, which was a great opportunity to know them better. Of course, I was thrilled to meet with the great man himself, Sheikh Zayed, and was even more delighted to be invited to drop in at any time.

From that day, I needed no formal invitation or high-flying companions to gain access to Sheikh Zayed and became a fairly frequent visitor to his majlis. It wasn't long before I was put in touch with the foremost Abu Dhabi families, including several of my mother's influential relatives.

Sheikh Zayed was always kind to me and generous with his time, but there was one occasion when I could easily have permanently fallen out of favour. Al Mulla had been commissioned to construct a palace in Abu Dhabi for the Crown Prince, Sheikh Khalifa bin Zayed. The consultant wanted to make his own variations to the agreed project, but I insisted that any changes, however minor, required pre-approval from the client, the Ruler's Office. I asked the consultant to get the necessary okay as well as a down payment for the job.

When my requests reached Sheikh Zayed's ears, he sent a messenger who told me the Ruler wanted to see me in his palace. But before I went I made sure that Ahmad Khalifa Al Suwaidi and Khalaf Al Otaiba – both members of the Ruler's inner circle – would be waiting for me in the Sheikh's majlis just in case I needed their moral support. This time, we were ushered into Sheikh Zayed's private majlis where he was deep in conversation with the British Chief Political Agent.

I had no idea concerning royal protocol; I had only ever been instructed to go by the book when dealing with clients. I must admit that I did feel a sense of foreboding when I noticed a slight frown appear on the forehead of one of the Ruler's aides, when the advance payment came up for discussion.

After some time, Sheikh Zayed politely asked Khalaf and Ahmad to leave, saying he wanted to talk privately with the visiting British Political Agent. I assumed that was the signal for me to leave too and headed towards the door feeling somewhat relieved that I wasn't going to be questioned about the project or, more particularly, on Al Mulla's terms and conditions. My relief was premature.

"Khalaf, wait! You stay!" said Sheikh Zayed, upon noticing my retreating figure. I was like a rabbit caught in the headlights. I could tell by the tone of his voice that something displeased him. My heart raced. *Now he will ask me questions I may not be able to answer*, I thought.

"But, Your Highness... I can see how busy you are. I can come back another time," I said, while trying to regain my composure. That ploy didn't work. Instead, he gestured for me to sit down and wait until he had finished talking to his British visitor.

I felt like a schoolboy who had been placed in a corner by his teacher for misbehaving. Only this was much worse. I had obviously unwittingly upset Abu Dhabi's Ruler, but I had no idea what I had done wrong. As soon as Sheikh Zayed was free, he asked me to sit near him.

As I had vaguely suspected, he was offended that I had not only asked for a written confirmation before work on the palace could start, but also for a down payment when it was common knowledge that Sheikh Zayed's word was his bond.

"Tell me Khalaf! Have I ever delayed any payments to your company in the past? You must know that I want to encourage you and everyone in this country to work and profit to improve the lives of their families. I want all my people to enjoy a decent lifestyle. I don't expect you to work for nothing, to work for free. I have chosen Al Mulla to build my son's palace, and never fear, you will be paid for the job... and probably a lot more than you're asking for as well."

There was no hint of anger in his voice, only kindness. I felt so small. I was small in age and physical stature. Now I was also small in character. All

I could do was hang my head in shame. This was the hardest lesson on how to behave I'd ever received.

In retrospect, Sheikh Zayed was perfectly right to feel slighted. Would anyone even dream of approaching, say, Queen Elizabeth II, demanding "Before we start work, you must sign on the dotted line and pay up"? Firms that supply Buckingham Palace would soon lose their royal warrants if they treated the sovereign with such disrespect.

"Your Highness, please accept my apologies for this misunderstanding. I should never have asked you to sign anything," I said. "If you will only find it in your heart to forgive me, I am at your disposal to work day and night to make sure this work is completed to your satisfaction. I'm ready to do anything you ask of me to make up for my mistake."

Sheikh Zayed's face immediately softened. He knew I was truly sorry for offending him and understood that I was little more than an inexperienced boy who still had a lot to learn about life. He went out of his way to calm me down and assure me that all was forgiven.

When Sheikh Khalifa's palace was finally built, everyone was happy; and true to his word, Sheikh Zayed not only settled the invoice promptly, he also paid a large bonus to show his appreciation of a job well done.

It's not surprising that I became fed up with that exhausting daily commute, which, by the way, is easily doable nowadays because of the excellent highway that links Dubai with the capital of the UAE. Six months later, I chose to stay in Al Mulla's Abu Dhabi camp six days a week. It was a decision that took me away from my family, but I did get to spend quality time with them on Fridays.

Life in the camp took a bit of adjustment at first. I had to share a basic room and a bathroom with three young strangers. Two were Egyptians, Mohammed Hijazi, an architect, and an accountant called Farouk Mohammed. My third roommate was Riad Sadik, a brilliant Palestinian civil engineer from Deir el-Kasi, who had fled Zionist aggression in 1948 for the safety of Lebanon together with his parents, four brothers and three sisters. He began his career in Saudi Arabia working for the Ministry of Transportation and was promoted to Chief Engineer of the Eastern Province prior to being recruited by Al Mulla as Technical Manager in charge of road construction.

Together we formed a closely-knit group, even though I was quite a few years younger than the others and lacked their formal education. We all came from completely different backgrounds, but somehow we got along well.

Initially, I had more in common with Mohammed and Farouk, who had been brought up with a similar conservative mindset. Due to my extended stay in Cairo, I felt comfortable with Egyptians and enjoyed the brand of humour for which they are well known everywhere in the Arab world.

On first sight, I assumed that twenty-three-year-old Riad, with his light hair, very fair skin, liberal outlook and an unfamiliar air of sophistication gleaned from living in Beirut, must be a European. I remember how shocked we were when he stripped off in front of us to take his shower, which he was used to doing as a student at the American University of Beirut. He didn't seem to notice our presence or consider that he might be offending our ingrained sense of modesty. He was as nonchalant about nudity as a British rugby player, unselfconsciously washing alongside his teammates in a locker room.

On several occasions, I overheard the Egyptians expressing their disapproval behind his back, but refrained from getting involved as, by then, I had grown to appreciate Riad's fine character and free spirit, and instinctively felt that he was a person who wouldn't give a damn about such narrow-minded opinions. I was sure that he didn't mean to give offence and simply wrote his habit off as a cultural anomaly.

Naturally, the two Egyptians had much in common and formed an immediate clique, which didn't matter to me because although Riad and I were like chalk and cheese, our friendship was based on the old adage that 'opposites attract'.

Within no time we were as close as brothers, which reminded me never to judge a book by its cover. In particular, I admired his charm and strength of personality. His leadership skills were immediately evident and he showed himself to be diligent in work and one of the best negotiators I've ever met.

When people are thrown together, there are times when a certain chemistry between them kicks in, peeling away the trappings of culture or nationality. It's a pity that most of us rarely take the time to get to know the person. Our friendship developed into a special bond based on the ability to be absolutely frank with one another. We worked well together and would often spend evenings in each other's company, talking away about everything under the sun. I had always sympathised with the terrible plight of Palestinian refugees, but Riad's first-hand accounts of his family's flight and all they had lost were illuminating and disturbing.

Riad says his earliest impression of me was of a perfectionist who was "enthusiastic, ambitious, forthcoming and very genuine. I saw from day one that there were no limits to your career. You always said what you believed in, you were always honest about those beliefs and you were refreshingly transparent, never hiding anything."

There wasn't much to do in Abu Dhabi at the time, but people made up for that by holding social gatherings and parties at their homes. I was never lonely as I had made several friends and got to know many members of my mother's family; one of them being my first cousin, Sheikh Hamdan bin Mohammed Al Nahyan, then in charge of the Ministry of Public Works.

Sheikh Hamdan knew I was on my own without my family and often invited me out in the evenings or to his home for morning coffee. He was a lovable type of person with a very special character and a warm heart. Sheikh Zayed had a lot of respect for him and relied on him as his second in command. Following the UAE's formation, Sheikh Hamdan was the third Deputy Prime Minister to be appointed.

On the evenings when I wasn't working until midnight, we usually visited another camp to have dinner with our friend Rahma Al Masaood, the son of a prominent Abu Dhabi merchant family, who later became a member of the Federal National Council. Today, Rahma is a partner in the Al Masaood Group – a big name in the construction, engineering and oil and gas industry.

Often our gatherings would be joined by his elder brother, Ahmad Al Masaood, and his younger brother, Abdullah Al Masaood. Ahmad was very close to the Ruler of Abu Dhabi and following the UAE's formation, to the President and Vice-President. Sadly, he died during the 1980s. Abdullah went on to be appointed Speaker of the National Consultative Council of the Emirate of Abu Dhabi. They were some of the best men I've ever met to this day, real men. We used to laugh a lot. Just being in their company was a lot of fun, but sometimes we would get into in-depth debates about life, business or society, which I thoroughly enjoyed. Those were great times.

When Al Mulla opened a branch in Al Ain, my cousin Sultan Khalifa Al Habtoor was appointed to manage it. I saw him frequently from then on as I was tasked with supplying him with materials and engineering support. He would always invite me for a bite to eat. We would sit cross-legged on the floor and open a can of Kraft cheese. The smell was tempting. Every morsel eaten with home-made bread was a real treat. The simple things in life really are the best. I have been to more grand banquets than I can count, but no caviar, truffles or lobster has been able to trump the taste of that processed Kraft cheese, which wasn't easy to come by then.

While in Al Ain, I would occasionally pay a visit to Sheikh Hamdan's brother, Sheikh Tahnoun bin Mohammed Al Nahyan, en route to our old house where we used to spend our summers. Sheikh Tahnoun was variously appointed as the Ruler's Representative in Abu Dhabi's Eastern Region, Deputy Chairman of the Executive Council of Abu Dhabi, Chairman of the state-owned oil company, ADNOC and Deputy Chairman of the Supreme Petroleum Council.

It was a very challenging drive over sandy terrain in my used Land Rover. I always took a loaded gun with me. The journey wasn't particularly dangerous, but we were raised to ensure that we were armed whenever we went outside our home territory. Thankfully, I never had to pull the trigger. Sheikh Zayed had cleared the area of brigands a long time ago.

Most Thursday evenings, signifying the start of our precious weekend, I would call in to see Riad in Al Mulla's Dubai workshop camp, where he stayed in a small executive bungalow. There we would often dine with his friends, who were mostly foreign engineers. I relished the chance to meet new people from different parts of the world and especially enjoyed the company of Mr and Mrs Lofran, a lively British couple, now that my English language skills had greatly improved.

On occasion, we would share a meal in one of Dubai's very few eateries. The most popular was a Lebanese restaurant called the Sahara owned by Mohammed Nasser. As the only half-decent restaurant offering regular entertainment and music, it was the hub of Dubai's social life. We could easily tell who our fellow diners would be from their cars parked outside. We knew most of them and it wasn't unusual for what was intended to be a quiet meal to turn into an impromptu party.

Whenever we wanted a quick bite or a quiet evening, we would pop into one of the Indian restaurants, compared to which the Sahara was a temple of gastronomy. The food served in those cheap and cheerful places was cooked in full view of customers and was usually as basic as the furniture and decor. The crispy samosas and pakoras deep fried on the street outside tempted us inside. Sometimes, though, we would be put off eating our dinner by a chef's unhygienic practices. Delhi belly was a common affliction to be avoided at all costs. But because we were usually hungry, we would somehow gulp down our meal and hope for the best.

Over time, we trusted one another sufficiently to share our work-related and personal secrets. Sincere mutual trust is such a rare commodity and I am grateful to have found it with Riad, who, until now, has never let me down. He's the one friend who is always there when I need him. Fate works in mysterious ways. Because we met and learned to trust each other, we went on to found Al Habtoor Engineering on a prayer and a handshake.

Today, Riad Sadik is Chairman of the Al Habtoor Leighton Group, a UAE national, a father of five and my good friend. Our lives are so hectic with work and family commitments that we can't get together as much as we did in the old days, but there is hardly a day that passes when we don't talk on the phone or meet in a business capacity.

All my old roommates reached the pinnacle of their respective fields. It was as if someone had sprinkled fairy dust over the cramped space we shared for three years. More likely, they were successful because they were talented, determined, unafraid to work hard and in the right place at the right time. Farouk Mohammed has long audited all the Al Habtoor Group's accounts – and still does – as President of the audit firm Grant Thornton UAE. Mohammed Hijazi was one of the very first architects to make his name in the country. Sheikh Rashid trusted him and charged Mohammed and his partner, Moaz, with several important residential projects.

Mohammed's business partner passed away some years ago, but Mohammed is still going strong. He's a real gentleman who is well respected in the UAE and his homeland Egypt as being a man of his word. Nowadays he spends most of his time in Cairo, either managing his office there or relaxing at his farm in the countryside. He still visits the Emirates now and again when we get the opportunity to reminisce about the good old days.

Towards the end of 1968 or the beginning of 1969, Sheikh Zayed asked me if I would be willing to join the Board of the Abu Dhabi Water and Electricity Authority, chaired by one of Sheikh Zayed's nephews, Sheikh Khalifa bin Mohammed Al Nahyan, the brother of Sheikh Hamdan bin Mohammed Al Nahyan. It was a great honour, which I was more than pleased to accept.

I took my new position very seriously – too seriously for some of the other board members. Anxious to prove myself and make a real differ-ence, I got together with one of my closest friends and relative, Faraj bin Hamouda, to delve into the nitty-gritty of problems needed to be solved.

Much to my surprise, each time we came up with what we believed to be an excellent proposal, Sheikh Khalifa would go into a rage. He wouldn't entertain any of our ideas. What's more, he would threaten to complain to Sheikh Zayed, his uncle, about my non-stop interference.

He must have thought I was a bossy upstart who didn't understand my place in the hierarchy. It wasn't that at all. I just wanted to fulfil my post sincerely and honestly. I wasn't the slightest bit interested in just going around showing off my new title without doing anything at all to deserve it. I didn't understand the ways of the world. I didn't know that, very often, little is expected of board members other than to turn up at meetings, keep quiet and lodge their vote now and again. I was by nature a hands-on person; I still am.

Admittedly, Sheikh Khalifa's threat to complain about me, albeit entirely unjustified, bothered me greatly. I had so much respect for Sheikh Zayed and dreaded that his faith in me would be diminished should Sheikh Khalifa go to the palace with his criticisms. I would explain to Sheikh Hamdan bin Mohammed what was going on when he would discuss the matter with Sheikh Zayed. Each time, Sheikh Hamdan would reassure me. "Just do your job. Don't worry about my brother. Let him say what he likes. Sheikh Zayed backs you all the way." I tendered my resignation to the Board just prior to my return to Dubai. Being so far away meant it was no longer practical to continue.

The decision to join Al Mulla was one of the best I ever made. Over the three years I stayed with the company, I gained training, good experience, self-confidence, important contacts, and was promoted to overall Manager of the Abu Dhabi branch. Most importantly, I made some wonderful friendships and linked with the best business partner ever. I can never forget the wonderful people I met in Abu Dhabi and I'm thankful to Sheikh Zayed for encouraging me to work and learn as much as possible. I credit my time there for providing me with a solid life education.

In all honesty, if Mohammed Saeed Al Mulla hadn't offered me the chance to show him what I could do, my life may have turned out very differently. I owe him a lot. He put me on the right track and pointed me in the right direction. He put his faith in a mere boy and three years later waved goodbye to a man.

"Never give up!" he would always say. And no matter how hard or twisted the road has sometimes become, with hand on heart, I can truthfully say that giving up is one option I've never even considered... and never will.

CHAPTER 7
Try, Try Again

"ONE SECRET OF SUCCESS IN LIFE IS FOR A MAN TO BE READY FOR HIS OPPORTUNITY WHEN IT COMES."

– BENJAMIN DISRAELI

Dubai was fast gaining a reputation as a boom town and the landscape was changing accordingly. In 1970, many of the *barasti* were being torn down to make way for new private and government construction. Sheikh Rashid had embarked on a policy of creating low-cost housing in Karama, Satwa and Al Qusais for poorer nationals, settled Bedu and the families of expatriate labourers.

On the Jumeirah Beach Road, lined with fishing hamlets where camels, donkeys, goats and chickens roamed freely, the Ruler authorised the building of 100 low-cost identical single-storey villas (known as 'the 100 villas') that were highly sought after due to their uninterrupted views of the beach and inexpensive rents, even though they were some distance from the centre of town. They were fitted with noisy air conditioning units and plagued by sewers that frequently backed up attracting mosquitoes; nevertheless, families topping the rental queue were considered extremely lucky.

Jumeirah went upmarket some years later, when an exclusive beachside gated community, Chicago Beach Village (CBV), boasting over 600 California-style single and double-storey villas with central air conditioning, was built primarily for expatriates connected with the oil, gas and aluminium industries. Close to where the magnificent Burj Al Arab stands today, it had its own private beach and a pier used by residents for fishing and very quickly emerged as *the* place to live.

The project was a joint venture between the Government of Dubai that leased the land and a tall, blonde American from Louisiana called Nick Popich who was responsible for CBV's construction, rental and maintenance. Popich also owned an offshore supply company called International

Marine Services (IMS) situated next door to CBV and was well known in expatriate circles for lavish parties held on his yacht.

Dubai was still a 'hardship posting', but Western expats would entrance friends and family back home with tales of a champagne lifestyle, swimming in warm Gulf waters under the stars, barbecues on the beach, dune driving, wadi bashing, sailing and fishing. They were beginning to enjoy the kind of good life reserved for the rich in their own countries. They had housemaids to clean and iron, cooks to prepare meals and nannies to care for their children, leaving couples with plenty of free time for sunbathing and socialising at the Dubai Exiles Rugby Club or around the bar in the Dubai Country Club that had its own popular all-sand golf course.

Comparatively grand stores were opening up in Deira; new companies were mushrooming; roads, bridges and tunnels were being constructed; and new faces began to arrive. Craggy-faced American oil men, togged out in white shoes, seersucker suits or checked shirts and jeans, flocked to the gold souk where dazzling chains, bangles and earrings were on display in hole-in-the-wall outlets without security windows, owned by Iranians and Indians.

Some street traders had mobile wooden cabinets stuffed with jewellery worth tens of thousands of dollars, which they wheeled from their homes each morning. The visitors would usually comment that they had never seen as much gold in one place in their lives and were amazed at how unprotected it appeared to be. They were unable to grasp the fact that theft was so rare, to the extent that shopkeepers hardly concerned themselves with the possibility.

The Creek was a hive of activity. Dhows were packed with agricultural produce, televisions, refrigerators and all manner of trinkets arriving from India, Pakistan, Iran, Zanzibar, Yemen, East Africa and states hugging the Arabian Peninsula. Indians from the Malabar Coast clad in lungis (ankle-length garment wrapped around the waist) would cluster together holding glasses filled with milky Malabari tea sweetened with condensed milk in one hand, and beedis (leaf-wrapped cigarettes) in the other.

In places, the ground was stained with red patches resulting from the Indian/Pakistani practice of chewing paan (betel leaf filled with spices and tobacco), a mild stimulant that once chewed would be spat out. Paan was banned by Dubai's authorities in the 1980s for being an unhygienic, unhealthy carcinogen that left unsightly stains on the city's streets.

Pakistanis sporting topis (skull caps), turbaned Baluchis from Iran and Pakistan, Indian merchants and accountants in beige safari jackets, and smartly attired Lebanese entrepreneurs with gold key chains and Cartier lighters driving flashy American Lincolns, Cadillacs and Pontiacs were leaving the 'Paris of the Middle East' – as Beirut was known prior to the beginning of the 1975 civil war – to throng up-and-coming Dubai in search of a pot of gold.

There were no hotels of international standards; so well-heeled new-comers had to make do with an inferior room in the somewhat sleazy old Bustan hotel near the airport, the ramshackle Omar Khayyam on the Creek, or the slightly more salubrious Carlton Tower in Deira that rarely had a room to spare. Beds had to be booked six months in advance and there was such a shortage of accommodation that visitors would be forced to head for Sharjah, where, if they were lucky, they would be allowed to sleep under a mosquito net in one of the chalets around the swimming pool of the Sharjah Carlton.

Ever since my resignation from Al Mulla, every minute of my time had been dedicated to seeking a decent income. I quit my job for two reasons: firstly, I was set on branching out on my own and, secondly, a very un-pleasant manager from Scotland whose name was David Tees had been promoted over my head and was out to show me that he was the boss.

Mohammed Saeed Al Mulla was far from happy to see me go. "How can you quit when you don't have any money?" was his reaction.

That was a good question. There were moments when I reflected that my decision to leave had been hasty. My paltry savings were running out fast and I was now responsible for providing for my wife and two sons, three-year-old Rashid and one-year-old Mohammed. I regretted that living in Abu Dhabi meant I hadn't been around to see Rashid take his very first steps or utter his first words, but I knew that my father had lovingly watched over him as my surrogate and I was resolved to give both children every chance to get ahead.

I was pleased that I was no longer a 'weekend Dad' and each time I gave my beautiful boys a cuddle I couldn't help wondering what their future would look like. Responsibility weighed heavily upon me because I knew in my heart that their lives would in large part be shaped by my decisions. For their sake, failure wasn't an option. There was no time to waste.

I perceived that Dubai was in dire need of new hotels, villas and apart-ments to accommodate the newcomers, and was eager to establish a con-struction company or build a fine hotel. However, such grandiose projects were way beyond the reach of someone like me without access to land or capital. I had no choice but to cut my canvas according to my means, which I did literally.

Owning a hotel was out of the question, but after coming across a brochure advertising beautiful Scandinavian-manufactured tents, I thought they were the next best thing. I imagined myself as a major importer of tents with warehouses and shops.

Excited by the venture, I ordered a number of tents and scraped together the cash to pay for them. But what a terrible disappointment when the consignment finally arrived! They had appeared huge in the catalogue, but in reality they were one-person tents used by Western outdoor types for camping.

I had announced their imminent arrival with great fanfare and made the mistake of unveiling them to a few of my friends. They stared at them, touched them, held them up for inspection and then broke out in uncontrolled laughter. My humiliation wasn't over. Each time I got together with my friends, my tents were the butt of their jokes.

One day soon afterwards I attended a meeting called by the National Transport Company opposite my parents' home in Shindagha, when my father's friend, Matar bin Julaijel (pronounced 'Yeleiyel'), who was also one of Sheikh Rashid's companions, yelled "Hey, Khalaf!" in a loud voice in front of everyone. "You forgot something when you ordered those small, one-person tents. You forgot to bring hoses to attach to their backsides to let out air." I managed to smile along with everyone else but didn't appreciate his crude comment or the fact that he chose to make it in public. If ever I was tempted to bop someone on the nose, it was then. Matar was a real character, a one-off; he always said what he thought without caring who might be offended.

Once, during Ramadan, he came to my family's open Ramadan majlis while our friends Abdullah Al Allawi from Bahrain and Sheikh Hammam – a short and rather plump Egyptian sheikh from Al Azhar who was the Imam of Jumeirah mosque – were also present. We were discussing and drinking coffee when Abdullah asked Sheikh Hammam a question on a finer point of religion.

"Sheikh, tell me. Is make-up forbidden during Ramadan? And how about manicures and pedicures?"

Matar just couldn't resist interjecting. "What a stupid question, Abdullah, when Sheikh Hammam himself has his own manicure and pedicure parlour." Of course that wasn't true, but Matar loved to ridicule. "Shame on you, Matar!" the surprised Sheikh retorted.

Our friend's irreverence knew no bounds. On one occasion, he interrupted Sheikh Hammam's Friday sermon that was on the lines of how blessed the younger generation was. "These days you have golden spoons in your mouths," the Sheikh said. Matar interrupted him saying, "Hammam, have you lost your mind? We eat with the companions of (Sheikh) Rashid out of a big tin and there's hardly enough food to go round. So what are you talking about?"

Sheikh Hammam was a patient man. He took a deep breath before answering, "Oh my God! Matar, you don't allow us to speak uninterrupted in homes or in mosques. What should we do with you?"

Many years later, I discovered that age hadn't tempered Matar, who still didn't possess a single diplomatic cell in his body. The last time I saw him was in the lobby of the Metropolitan Hotel in Beirut. He was almost eighty-five years old, but he looked fit and well. He told me that he had just returned from the States where he had a successful eye operation.

"I couldn't see clearly before the operation," he said. "My vision was blurred. When I woke up from the anaesthetic, it was much sharper. I looked to my right and left and saw two old Arab women standing over me. I asked one of them, 'Aunt (a term of respect for older women), who are you?' 'Matar, don't you recognise me? I am the mother of your son. I'm your wife.' I kept silent and asked the other woman who she was. 'I'm also your wife, the mother of your kids,' she said. Do you know something, Khalaf... at that moment I almost wished that I'd stayed blind."

But I digress. Going back to my tents, there wasn't much call for such leisure items in late 1960s Dubai. I was unable to offload them and they were left to gather dust along with my fantasy. Al Habtoor Tenting was not to be. Thank goodness for that!

Undeterred, I borrowed 50,000 riyals from Mohammed, my brother, to import refrigerators from Europe. Finally I was on the right track. Just about everyone I knew wanted one. Within no time I had sold all of them to people I knew. Everyone was happy; everyone, that is, except me. They all loved their smart fridges but were unable to pay for them. I chased those payments for ages without success.

You're probably wondering why I didn't insist on getting paid up front. It was different in those days. People generally trusted each other. It wasn't that my friends had contrived to fleece me. They had every intention of honouring their word. It was just that most of them were still living from hand to mouth. When they were presented with the choice of putting food on the table for their families or paying me, there was no contest.

After all my efforts I was practically penniless, in debt to my brother and feeling slightly dejected. I thought it might be helpful to approach Mr Al Mulla to ask for his advice. He listened patiently to my tale of woe and seemed interested in my ideas until he finally said, "Why don't you come and work for me again? Your old job is waiting for you." That wasn't what I wanted to hear at all. "Thank you very much for your offer, Sir," I said, "but I want to be my own man."

It was time to gamble even if that meant going for broke. They say 'he who dares, wins', but I knew from experience that things didn't always turn out positively. This is it, I told myself... sink or swim time. I decided to aim high and set about establishing my own engineering company. I did it on a ridiculously low shoestring budget. My capital could hardly cover laces, never mind shoes.

Step one was to open an office; not an easy task when I didn't have enough cash for a week's rent. I approached landlords, who, as you might expect, were not amenable to handing me an apartment key without a substantial deposit and several months rental in advance. It looked like a hopeless quest, until Rashid Al Yateem saved the day. Rashid, who was working for a substantial local businessman and property landlord, Mohammed Abdullah Al Gaz, knew my brother Mohammed and was inclined to help me out.

Rashid was very encouraging and agreed to let me have a one-bedroom flat in Deira that happened to have a magnificent view of the Creek with its dhows and fishing craft. "Don't worry about paying rent until you land your first project," he said. I will always be grateful for his strong faith in my abilities.

Once I had spruced up my new place, the next step was to fill it with desks and chairs which were all bought second-hand. I converted the bedroom into an office for myself and designated the living room for employees. The result was far from being confidence-inspiring. The walls were beige, the doors brown and the cheap desks were all made of unfriendly cold steel. Within a short time, a telephone was installed, but I didn't have spare cash to buy a typewriter and telex until several months later. It took a year before I was able to purchase one of those old-fashioned messy roller printers.

The best thing about that office was the wonderful panorama. It was fascinating watching the seabirds skimming the shimmering water and the activity around the dhows. Unfortunately, the view, as soothing as it was, couldn't make up for the horrible fishy odour that most days wafted in through the open windows. Donald Trump would have turned his nose up at that office. I was proud of it.

Step three was to find engineers who would work with me for a time without receiving a salary. That seemed like an almost impossible task until two temporarily out-of-work ex-Al Mulla employees agreed to come on-board. The first was Mohammed Younes, a Palestinian, who was married to my friend Riad Sadik's sister. He had worked as a purchasing officer with my former company. He possessed minimal educational qualifications but I took him on because I was close to his family and thought that he would be loyal. That turned out to be a good decision.

The second, Michel Aziz, a serious, reliable Egyptian, was an architect by profession. He did, however, understand the basics of engineering through observation and practice.

"I can't promise you a salary immediately," I told them. "But I can under-take to pay you as soon as the work comes in."

From then on, I faithfully wrote down what was due to them on a note-pad and looked forward to the day that I could reward them for their trust. Mohammed passed away some years ago, while Michel now runs his own architectural firm.

While I was busy with the start-up, Riad Sadik was still employed by Al Mulla. As always, we met up most Thursday evenings when I kept him up to date with developments.

Much to my delight, when the company had been up and running for six months or so, he said "I am ready to leave Al Mulla. Let's work together." From that day, he has been my business partner. He didn't have much money either, but he came with expertise, technical know-how and experience, which, when added to my administrative know-how and business acumen, meant our small team was complete.

All we needed now was a project. That was easier said than done as the company didn't have a track record. We had nothing to show a prospective client in terms of design or quality. We sat around for two months trying to drum up business, until a very well-known and influential local business-man, Juma Al Majid, asked us to build a modest house for one of his rela-tives, Majid bin Khalfan. After negotiation the contract price was fixed at

60,000 Qatar-Dubai riyals. We were young, enthusiastic and ready to work day and night to impress our first client.

The home was finished on time and when we saw that Mr Khalfan was entirely happy with the finished result, we breathed a sigh of relief. We made hardly any profit from that venture but that didn't bother us at all. That simple construction was a turning point. Al Habtoor Engineering was no longer just a name on a sign. We were ready for anything now.

Our second project was to construct a road from Sharjah to Ra's al-Khaimah that was financed by the government of Saudi Arabia. The main contractor was the Saudi construction company Bin Laden, which was well-known throughout the Gulf. My old company Al Mulla was one of Bin Laden's subcontractors on that job via Azmi Haroun, the resident engineer of the project's Italian consultant, Saouti.

Our part of the overall job was to build box culverts on site – small bridges over narrow tunnels that allow waters to flow. That also turned out fine and was a welcome boost for our bank balance.

Little by little, our reputation grew until small to medium jobs began to come in slowly but steadily. That's not to say that there weren't problems. It was frustrating waiting for imported materials to arrive and occasionally we would be faced with a shortage of labour. Our main difficulty was getting paid for our work and, due to our lack of management experience, we didn't always know how to handle those situations in an effective way. As some of you will know only too well, there is nothing more disheartening than to put all your care and energy into a job well done and then have to struggle to get due recompense.

Long after, we had built an apartment building in Dubai for a Palestinian gentleman living in Sharjah. Now that it was fully tenanted, he began delaying payments. His never-ending excuses as to why he couldn't pay and promises that he would very soon that never manifested really got to me. We had assisted this man to come up with financing for the project, which, when completed, fully adhered to his specifications and quality demands and was delivered on time; yet, here he was giving us the runaround.

During yet another meeting with the guy to talk about payments, when he trotted out the same old excuses and pretexts, I could feel my anger bubbling up inside. I felt a terrible sense of injustice. My tension rose until I finally snapped. "Listen here," I said. "Either you pay us our money now or I will fetch one of our Caterpillar bulldozers and smash that building to the ground. So you had better warn your tenants to get out."

I was young and hot-tempered. I would never have carried out that threat, but I must have looked so fearsome that he certainly believed I meant it. I wouldn't advise anybody else to try this tactic on payment-shy customers. But in this case, at any rate, it worked like a dream. I don't get enraged about such matters these days. For one thing, I've got other priorities and, for another, I've learned to control my anger. Chronic defaulters are dealt with by my lawyers and sometimes have to answer to the courts.

With a healthy – but still fairly modest – bank account, I was able at last to move my family into a real house. What a fantastic feeling that was! In 1970, I built a house opposite the grand mosque in Jumeirah in partnership with my elder brother. We split all the costs fifty–fifty. The whole family – my wife and sons, my parents, my younger brother Sultan plus Mohammed and his two wives and children – moved in there together.

We divided it into sections. My wife and I had two self-contained rooms on the first floor for us and our children. As you might imagine, it was very crowded, but we were used to that. At least we were no longer victim to the elements and, as a plus, we were surrounded by good neighbours, including some of my father's Maktoum family relatives.

In those early years, I put my heart and soul into my company. There were daily obstacles to overcome. When I wasn't seated at my desk at the office, I was at meetings with architects and consultants, sorting out problems with the labour force, forging connections or trying to procure new business. My mind was constantly racing and I could hardly find an hour for myself or my family. Just when I began to believe that everything in the garden was rosy, stress took its toll. When the human mind is stretched to capacity for lengthy periods, the body usually comes up with a wake-up call.

I woke up in the middle of the night with excruciating pain in my stomach. Pain is too mild a word. It was like a series of explosions in my belly. I had never experienced anything like it before. I was terrified. I just wanted the pain to end. My whole family was in a state of panic, especially my mother and my wife. They didn't know what to do for me.

Somehow I managed to call my partner, Riad Sadik, and another of my closest friends, an engineer called Abdullah Al Mousa, a great guy from a good family. I woke them up. "Please, please, come as quickly as you can," I said between screams. "I'm in trouble."

Both my friends sounded very concerned. They were at my house within no time at all, but to me the wait seemed like an eternity. Anyone who has ever known gut-wrenching pain can attest that during those moments every minute seems like an hour. Hospitals aren't my favourite place, but on this occasion I couldn't wait to get there.

Riad and Abdullah propped me up and, with my arms resting on their shoulders, I stumbled to Abdullah's car that was parked outside my front door. Everything after that was somewhat of a blur. I do remember arriving at the entrance to the Emergency Department of the Al Maktoum Hospital, where I was transferred to a hospital trolley. I was told to lie down, but each time I tried I was in absolute agony. My screams were so loud that people as far away as Sharjah may have heard them. Abdullah would hold me up every so often when the pain would become just about bearable.

Within minutes of my arrival, all the family – my parents, my wife, and my brothers Mohammed and Sultan – arrived looking very worried. Every time I looked at their concerned faces, and especially the terrified eyes of the women welling with tears, I started to imagine that the Grim Reaper might be lurking down the hallway.

Up popped an Indian doctor instead asking "Where is the patient?". He was youthful but very confident for his years and appeared very proud of his abilities. He introduced himself as Dr Chinshinwala. "I know that's a bit of a mouthful so you are welcome to call me Dr Chin," he said. In the state I was in, I didn't care what his name was. All I could do was pray that he knew how to fix me.

Dr Chin signalled to Dr Abdul Nabi Habib, a young intern from the UAE, to take a look at his patient. I thought he looked vaguely familiar. "I know you," he said. "You're Khalaf Al Habtoor." Any relief I felt at seeing a familiar face was quickly dispelled when Dr Chin told the intern, "Put your ear on the patient's stomach and tell me what you hear!".

The young fellow did as he was told. He bent down and pressed his ear where the pain was for several minutes, as though he was listening to a concerto. "Well, what can you hear?" Dr Chin asked him. "Er... I don't know," he said. "I'm hearing some very weird sounds."

"Aha! I know what's the matter with him," said Dr Chin with a sweep of his arm. "Take him to the theatre."

Theatre! 'Theatre' was one of the words in my enlarged English language vocabulary. I knew what it meant. A theatre was where an audience watched a play or a show. I wondered fleetingly whether the pain had made me crazy.

When my family realised that I was about to be operated upon, they freaked out. They didn't want to let Dr Chin anywhere near me; they wanted to put me on the next plane to the UK, so that I could be treated at one of the old-established London hospitals or private Harley Street clinics.

"No, no, no," I said. I was in no fit state to travel to Deira, let alone London, and for some reason I can't quite fathom, I felt comfortable putting my life in the hands of Dr Chin. They all argued with my decision until the doctor warned them. "It's up to you. Either he has the surgery now, or he will die." As it turned out, he was telling the truth.

As porters rushed me into the operating room, Dr Chin ran alongside, waved a consent form in front of my face and handed me a pen. "Sign there," he said. I didn't have a clue what I was getting myself into or what was wrong with me. I scrawled my signature and hoped for the best. Minutes later I was out for the count.

I was still in pain when the anaesthetic wore off. I found myself in a hospital bed with tubes in my nose and mouth, watching an Iranian orderly tidying my room. It took me some minutes to realise what had happened and where I was. I was still feeling lousy when Dr Chin turned up.

"You had a perforated duodenal ulcer," he told me. "The operation went well, but you won't feel 100 per cent for a while because food has penetrated the lining of the stomach and has poisoned your system." I was disturbed to hear that news. I was so worried that I began to feel sick. Thank God, within a week I was fully back to normal and raring to get back to my desk.

Dr Chin certainly had an unorthodox approach to diagnostics. Not many doctors would have operated without first taking an X-ray. He went with his instincts, and in my case his instincts were spot on. I thought he was a fantastic doctor. I still do even though I've come across many fine and highly reputable doctors since. I wasn't able to pay him much for saving my life, but he treated me with enormous care and respect.

As time passed, we became good friends. He often used to visit me at our home where he struck up a friendship with Mohammed, my brother. He remained my doctor for many years and was to operate on me again. I'll leave that story for another chapter.

My mother was also one of Dr Chin's fans. She was upset one day because one of our pregnant cows was ill. "I think there is a problem with the delivery," she told me. "Why don't you call your friend Dr Chin to help this poor creature?"

The funniest thing was that I actually called him and believe it or not, he came. "I'm not a veterinarian. I've never treated an animal before. But I'm ready to do my best." The cow survived and from then on, every time one of our animals was sick, we would pick up the phone to call Dr Chin. I can hardly believe we did that and when I look back I find it remarkable that he was always so nice and obliging. Most other surgeons would have taken great offence at being asked to tend to farm creatures.

Sadly, Dr Chin now suffers from Parkinson's disease, which is extremely debilitating for him. He had to give up surgery and no longer socialises much. Thankfully, he still derives pleasure from reading his beloved books.

Things were looking up. The family was enjoying a vastly improved lifestyle, the company was running reasonably smoothly, there were funds in the bank and we were paying our employees and creditors promptly. But somehow that wasn't enough. I had too many ideas for new business buzzing around in my head to sit back and relax. What bugged me most was my ambition to own a hotel, which was one that could not be fulfilled without a large plot of land on which to build.

At the time, Sheikh Rashid was making plots available to locals willing to invest in Dubai's future by building something useful. I didn't know the Ruler very well, but I hoped he would support my own endeavours. My father, a frequent visitor to his majlis, pushed me to go along with him.

Sheikh Rashid was usually deep in conversation with important people, so I would spend those early visits sipping cardamom-scented Arabic coffee in small cups constantly refilled by the Sheikh's old retainers from a tall Arabic coffee pot with a pelican spout. It's our tradition that tiny Arabic coffee cups will keep being refilled until the cup is wiggled, a signal that whoever's drinking doesn't want any more. I didn't always get to converse with the Ruler, but it was enjoyable meeting new people from Dubai and all over the Arab world.

In 1970, Sheikh Rashid was consumed with forming the Federation, together with its principal architect, Sheikh Zayed. What had once seemed like a nice idea had become essential and urgent as the British government could no longer meet the costs involved with overseeing British 'protectorates'. Britain announced its intention of terminating its treaty obligations in the area during 1968 and issued a confirmation in 1970 that 1 December 1971 would mark an end to the British presence.

Sheikh Zayed said that the first he had heard about Britain's withdrawal plans was on the BBC World Service, although he later received an official notification. For the people of our country, the news was disturbing. Some were only too pleased to know that the British would soon depart, while most worried that our land would be vulnerable to unwelcome attention from its powerful neighbour, Iran, which was keen to expand its military and regional influence.

As the British Ambassador to Tehran, Sir Denis Wright, who served from 1963 to 1971, admitted, "The British position in the Arabian Gulf would not have remained so intact for so long had not the Persian government been weak throughout the nineteenth century."

Our fears, largely based on Persia's earlier forcible takeover of the Port of Lingah, Qeshm, Hengam and Sirri Islands, and its sovereign claim on Bahrain, were well-founded. Just a couple of days before Britain's announced exit, on 30 November 1971, Tehran used its navy to seize three strategically-located small islands owned by Sharjah and Ra's al-Khaimah – Abu Musa, Greater Tunb and Lesser Tunb. London and Washington were heavily critical of the Iranian occupation, but made no move against oil-rich Iran, whose Shah Mohammed Reza Pahlavi was then considered a reliable ally of Britain and the US.

Almost everyone I knew was seething with anger at seeing those islands robbed from their rightful owners. And they were just as furious with Britain for standing back and doing nothing in response, when it had pledged to protect the Trucial States. It was believed that big Western powers were, in fact, glad that their strong ally had grabbed those islands to insert a military presence, when they were straining to keep Communism at bay. This was at a time when the Sultan of Oman's armed forces assisted by those of the UK, Iran, Jordan and India were fighting in the Dhofar region of Oman against the Popular Front for the Liberation of Oman and the Arab Gulf – a guerrilla organisation supported by the People's Democratic Republic of Yemen (South Yemen).

In reality, the Shah, who had declared himself 'King of Kings', 'Emperor', 'Light of the Aryans' and 'Head of the Warriors', had no intention of remaining in the pocket of Washington and London indefinitely. His navy was the largest in the region, his spies were all over the Gulf and his brutal 5,300-strong secret police force (SAVAK) was controlling the Iranian people with an iron fist. I wasn't surprised at all when the Shah's Atomic Energy Advisor, Akbar Etemad, revealed to the *New Statesman* in 2008 that his former boss had harboured plans to create a nuclear weapon.

Power had gone to the Shah's head as evidenced by his over-the-top celebrations of the 2,500[th] anniversary of the Persian Empire that were held during October 1971 under tents in Persepolis. A banquet attended by foreign royalty, presidents, prime ministers and celebrities cost over 100 million dollars and was registered in the Guinness Book of Records as being the most lavish in modern history.

Chefs from Maxim's in Paris were flown in. Guests were served breast of peacock and quail eggs stuffed with Imperial caviar on Limoges porcelain plates, and drank from Baccarat crystal glasses. Such wild extravagance and displays of megalomania made Washington and London nervous. American politicians such as Secretary of State Henry Kissinger and Senator Edward Kennedy would subsequently launch an anti-Shah campaign in Washington, characterising Mohammed Reza as a despot, an oppressor and a tyrant.

The Rulers of the seven emirates – Abu Dhabi, Dubai, Sharjah, Ra's al-Khaimah, Ajman, Umm al-Qaiwain and Fujairah – as well as those of Bahrain and Qatar, had been discussing some type of Arab union involving common defence and economic benefit for many years. However, it wasn't easy to bring so many different tribes together under one flag or fix long-disputed borders, while the emirs and sheikhs were concerned with losing their autonomy. Bahrain and Qatar, both under British protection, opted for complete independence, and by mid-1970 even a seven-emirate federation looked like it would never come into fruition.

With the 150-year-long British mandate shortly ending, time was now of the essence. Sheikh Zayed and Sheikh Rashid sat down at the table to negotiate a federation of their two sheikhdoms and jointly prepare a constitution prior to inviting the Rulers of the other five to join them. By 1 December 1971, when the Trucial States were officially no more, the Rulers of Sharjah, Ajman, Umm al-Qaiwain and Fujairah had been persuaded that membership of the new federation was in their best interests, following assurances that they would be able to retain their autonomy, financial control and unique identity.

On 2 December 1971, the United Arab Emirates was born, with six member states (Abu Dhabi, Dubai, Sharjah, Ajman, Umm al-Qaiwain and Fujairah) under the presidency of Sheikh Zayed bin Sultan Al Nayhan, elected by the Supreme Council. Sheikh Rashid bin Saeed Al Maktoum was appointed Vice-President and Prime Minister. Ra's al-Khaimah eventually joined on 11 February 1972, thereby completing the seven.

Our joy at witnessing the UAE's green, white, black and red flag – respectively symbolising fertility, neutrality, oil wealth and unity – unfurled and hoisted high for the first time was tempered by our trepidation. Together we were stronger, but without 'Big Brother' Britain we had no warships or fighter jets with which to defend ourselves from our enemies and were aware that there were many countries in the neighbourhood and beyond that coveted our oil.

I didn't waste too much energy pondering on the unknown or worrying about possible eventualities that were out of my hands. My primary concern was my fledgling company. We had tendered to construct the Plaza Cinema in Bur Dubai, projected to be the area's largest, but, as we couldn't provide either a bank guarantee or a substantial deposit, our chances of being selected were slim. I decided to test the waters with the owner of the project, Abdul Wahab Galadari, one of the three well-known Galadari brothers. He told me that my former boss, Mohammed Saeed Al Mulla, had also tendered.

"Are you in a position to compete with him?" he asked. "Yes, definitely," was my firm response. Amazingly, he agreed to provide me with the down payment from his own pocket and to actively support our bid.

The wealthy Galadaris together were an economic powerhouse in Dubai. They owned engineering, trucking, heavy machinery, automobile, ice cream, air conditioning and refrigeration businesses; and went on to open Dubai's first five-star hotel, The InterContinental, Dubai Bank and Dubai's first English-language newspaper, *Khaleej Times*.

Abdul Wahab Galadari built a vast commercial empire of commodity companies, residential complexes and the Hyatt Regency in Dubai, attached to the Galadari Galleria of shops built around Dubai's first ice rink. An ice rink in a country where temperatures have been known to hit fifty degrees centigrade caused a similar stir when it was unveiled in 1980, in the same way that Ski Dubai – the region's first indoor ski slopes – does today. I don't know why he took the decision to promote my company above such worthy competitors, but I'll always be grateful that he did and that we didn't disappoint him.

Our successful completion of the Dubai Plaza Cinema was our entrée to the beautiful days that followed. We considered ourselves privileged to work closely with highly professional people whose honesty was above reproach, such as the architect John R. Harris, and the resident partner of the quantity surveyors Widnell & Trollope, John Fulcher.

John Harris was known to be extremely trustworthy. He first arrived in Dubai in 1959 following a fortuitous meeting with the British Political Agent, Donald Hawley, who was vacationing in London. After meeting with Sheikh Rashid, Harris was appointed Dubai's first town planner.

An advisory committee, consisting of the Ruler's financial advisor, Bill Duff, Neville Allen of Halcrow and John Harris himself, was formed to implement the Harris plan. His first task was the expansion of the Al Maktoum Hospital from 38 to 106 beds.

As part of his strategy, John Harris later commissioned Al Habtoor Engineering to extend Sheikh Rashid Hospital and build the new Dubai Hospital. For us, those hospital commissions were a learning curve. Hospitals are technically challenging as they require all kinds of built-in services, such as under floor cables for sophisticated medical equipment, and we had to order special materials from abroad. They were complex jobs requiring specialist expertise. With our necks on the chopping block, we knew we had to rise to the challenge and we did.

Sheikh Rashid trusted Harris to the extent of authorising him to sign payment certificates, and instructed banks and contractors to accept Harris' signature as though it was his own.

There was no such thing as waiting around to get paid in those days. Those were golden times for contractors, when invoices were approved within forty-eight hours and cheques were instantly issued. Whenever disputes or misunderstandings arose over amounts due, John Harris and John Fulcher would immediately get involved to fairly sort them out. In my experience, those two men were always just. They represented fair ideals even when those ideals clashed with the interests of the persons who had appointed them to supervise the job.

Nowadays, unfortunately, architects or project management companies are far less ethical. They haven't the slightest interest in the right or wrong of a contractor's claims. Instead, they search for loopholes or excuses not to pay on the orders of their sometimes penny-pinching clients.

Whenever I'm faced with that kind of unscrupulous behaviour, I remember John Harris and John Fulcher, God rest their souls. They were a very different – and fast disappearing – breed of men who placed personal honour above lining their own pockets or buttering up their employers.

I've always demanded a sense of fairness from my own managers when dealing with clients. Islam treats profits derived from cheating others out of their rights as *haraam* (forbidden). Any fool can make money – or land in jail – if they're prepared to cheat, con, embezzle, steal or deal in weapons or drugs. Even those who manage to escape the long hand of the law can never hope to erase the scars on their souls. A man without principles and values is not a man. On the Day of Judgement, we will all receive what we deserve.

* * *

Throughout the first half of the 1970s, as the leaders of the United Arab Emirates worked as one to replace tribal loyalties with loyalty to the nation and create a united and peaceful society, the Middle East was torn by civil wars and conflicts.

The first was 'Black September', an armed conflict between the Hashemite Kingdom of Jordan and Palestinian groups, that broke out in September 1970. That was followed in 1973 by a full-blown war waged between Israel and Egypt aided by a coalition of Arab states that shook our region, and also had serious implications for the industrialised First World.

The architect of the conflict was the Egyptian President, Anwar El Sadat, who wanted to reclaim his country's dignity snatched during the botched 1967 War as well as Egyptian territory occupied by Israeli forces since. Egypt and Syria initiated a surprise attack on Yom Kippur, Judaism's holiest day, when the entire country was brought to a virtual halt.

When the Soviet Union threatened direct intervention on the part of Egypt and its allies, the United Nations imposed a ceasefire on 24 October. Both sides claimed victory, but the Israeli claims sounded hollow; its military superiority had been successfully challenged; its people were feeling traumatised, vulnerable and angry with Defence Minister Moshe Dayan for his troops' unpreparedness. Most of the world never knew how close two nuclear armed states, the USSR and the US, came to dangerous direct confrontation.

A side effect of that war was the Oil Crisis, which resulted in Gulf oil-exporting states enjoying greater wealth. The embargo was triggered by a decision taken by Sheikh Zayed who said, "Arab oil is not dearer than Arab blood." The UAE was the first country to impose a total oil boycott, targeting America and its allies in retaliation for Washington's decision to supply the Israeli military during the 1973 October War, which was adopted by the Organisation of Arab Petroleum Exporting Countries (OAPEC) – consisting of OPEC's Arab members plus Egypt, Syria and also Tunisia.

The embargo remained in place until March 1974, by which time oil prices had quadrupled; but even after the embargo was lifted, oil was never again an inexpensive commodity. Arab oil-producing companies had for the first time ever used their oil as a 'weapon' – or, at the very least, as political leverage.

The policy worked to a degree for a limited time as the Nixon administration 'encouraged' Israel to pull back from parts of Sinai and behind 1967 borders on the Golan Heights. However, using oil as a weapon wasn't a desirable long-term strategy because it had the effect of pushing consumer countries towards alternative fuels. Moreover, some countries including the US sought non-Arab suppliers and hoarded massive stockpiles.

For me, the biggest tragedy of that era was the civil war in Lebanon that began in the spring of 1975 and continued on and off to varying degrees until 1990, when according to official figures quoted in the *Time* magazine under the heading 'Lebanon: the terrible tally of death', 144,240 Lebanese had been slain, 197,506 had been wounded and 17,415 were missing, most presumed dead. During that dreadful period, many civilians were displaced while others joined the mass exodus out of the country. That hurt me deeply in a very personal way, as you will come to understand when you turn these pages.

CHAPTER 8

Challenges

"OPPORTUNITIES TO FIND DEEPER POWERS WITHIN OURSELVES COME
WHEN LIFE SEEMS MOST CHALLENGING."

— JOSEPH CAMPBELL

The first time I visited London was in 1970. It was a real eye-opener. It was altogether another world, another culture begging to be explored. I'd heard so much about it from my British friends in Dubai, but nothing they said prepared me for the real thing. I stayed in a small hotel with outside toilets on Bayswater Road, near Queensway and Hyde Park. My room was so small that there was no way to walk around the bed. I had to dive onto it from just inside the door. At just three pounds a night with breakfast, I couldn't really complain.

I had to get used to all the shops closing at 5 p.m. each evening as well as on Thursday afternoons, Saturday afternoons and Sundays, whereas in the Middle East and the Gulf they stay open from morning until late evening every day. At around 11 p.m. buses and tube trains were no longer available, and finding a black cab after 1 o'clock in the morning or when it rained, which was often, was next to impossible. The endearments of shopkeepers who referred to their customers, most of them complete strangers, as 'love', 'dearie' or 'mate', also took a bit of getting used to.

English people are generally very polite. They have a reputation overseas of being cold and aloof. I didn't find them so at all. They don't open up as quickly as some Middle Easterners or southern Europeans. It takes time before they will let you into their world. But once an Englishman takes someone as a friend, he'll be a friend for life.

The French, I've found, are similarly reserved. On first and second meeting, they tend to be formal. They're generous hosts. They're always inviting acquaintances to restaurants, but usually they will only invite intimate friends for a meal at their home. The Italians, especially the southerners, are more like us. Almost before you've had time to say "Pleased to meet you",

you're whisked off to Mama and the kids for a bowl of the best linguini with clam sauce in the world.

There were very few Arabs around in London those days apart from a handful of Iraqis, Yemenis and Palestinians, or so I was told. I don't think I came across any myself. Most Gulf Arabs didn't travel to Britain for holidays until after the 1973 so-called Oil Crisis when, because oil prices had rocketed, they had money to spare for leisure trips.

Their arrival en masse provoked a boom in the British capital. Major stores and boutiques in the West End, Knightsbridge and Kensington increased their prices and a room in a hotel became a lot more expensive. Lebanese restaurants, nightclubs featuring Arab singers and belly dancers, shawarma (roasted slices of chicken or meat wrapped in Arabic bread) and falafel (a deep-fried patty made from chickpeas and/or fava beans) stands, and cafés serving narghile (a Middle Eastern water pipe for smoking tobacco) opened up to cater to Arab visitors.

Along Bayswater's Queensway were newsagents selling a full array of Arabic language dailies, several bureaux de changes carrying Arab currencies, a takeaway with baby lamb roasting on a spit, and a small 24-hour supermarket selling things like henna, spices used in Arab kitchens and mineral water bottled in the Gulf.

Landlords in places like Edgware Road, Bayswater, Knightsbridge Road, Sloane Square, Park Lane, Swiss Cottage and Hampstead Village were charging ridiculously inflated rents, and owners of small properties who sold to Arabs very often became multimillionaires overnight. Apartments were selling like sliced bread and doubling in value annually due to the sudden high demand. London embraced its Arab visitors with gusto and they embraced London right back, uncaring that in many instances they were being ripped off.

In 1970, however, London's facilities were far less cosmopolitan. There were no European-style open-air cafés with patrons sipping cappuccino and browsing newspapers under giant parasols. And tourists would be warned in advance that British cuisine had a reputation for being bland and stodgy. Visitors from the Middle East and Asia often carried raw chillies or bottles of hot sauce in their pockets when going to a restaurant. They also had to learn that if they didn't specify that they wanted their coffee or tea black, it would always be served with milk.

That was long before the British understood that the rest of the world isn't into milky brews, except with breakfast, and before their taste buds became attuned to curry, which nowadays has surpassed the traditional fish 'n' chips in popularity. According to surveys, Chicken Tikka Masala – morsels of chicken marinated in yoghurt and spices, baked in a clay oven – is now ranked as Britain's true national dish. Its origins may lie in the Punjab, but it's popularly believed that it was an adaptation of Chicken Tandoori to suit British tastes concocted by chefs in some of London's first Indian restaurants that sprang up during the 1970s in London's then red-light district, Soho – also known for its authentic Chinese restaurants with strange red ducks hanging in their windows. The Scots might not agree. In 2009, a Scottish Member of Parliament sought to give Chicken Tikka Masala EU protected status as a Scottish dish!

Real British people could then be found strolling down Oxford Street and Regent Street or shopping in Selfridges and Liberty. Men and women mostly seemed well-dressed and elegant. There were a lot of beautiful people around. I'm afraid I can't say the same now that so many among the younger generation have taken to hoods or dowdy anoraks or adorned themselves with tattoos down their arms and rings on their tongues, noses and goodness only knows where else. The fashions were so much more at-tractive then too and there was a lot more individuality in evidence. In the evenings on Park Lane, women in long evening gowns and fur stoles could be seen stepping out of their Jaguars or Bentleys to enter the Dorchester or the Hilton. People, generally, were more put together and glamorous.

Finding a Brit in the West End of London nowadays is akin to finding lions on the Masai Mara where they're getting scarcer every year. There were plenty of foreigners hurrying past laden with shopping bags too, from Cypriots to Indians, Iranians, West Indians, Nigerians, Australians and Americans, plus all manner of Europeans.

A walk from the Marble Arch end of Oxford Street to Tottenham Court Road was almost like traversing the globe. Along the way were Hasidic Jews in wide-brimmed hats trimmed with fur; young English men and women with shaven heads dressed respectively in orange robes and saris, asking for contributions to the Hare Krishna movement; and a long-haired, unkempt old man wearing a sandwich board with the words 'The End of the World is Nigh' meaning 'Watch out for the Apocalypse!'. He used to spend every day walking up and down and shouting out his doom-laden slogan. I haven't seen him in recent decades so he may have checked out before it happens.

Another fellow used to devote his Sundays to standing on a box of Pepsi Cola shouting "All women are prostitutes". When he was asked why he held such a jaundiced opinion of the fairer sex, he would answer, "Women will only be nice to you if you give them something or if you promise them something".

I was stunned by the imposing and sometimes quaint architecture that was so well-preserved, and amazed at so much lush greenery in Hyde Park, Green Park and Regent's Park, where the famous London Zoo is housed. The whole city is like a historical open-air museum. I felt I was in a time machine travelling back through history. Even the London Underground, which Londoners call 'the tube', has a history. During the Blitz of World War II, families would shelter from bombs in its subterranean tunnels and Winston Churchill kept a spare war room down there somewhere, I believe.

To me, coming from a place where there weren't any metros, it seemed very modern and high-tech. I must add here that in September 2009 Sheikh Mohammed bin Rashid Al Maktoum inaugurated a driverless, fully-automated metro network – the first on the Arabian Peninsula – that outclasses just about every metro in the world.

The British capital had everything for the visitor. However, with so much going on, I may have been at a bit of a loss as to what to see or do had not my friend Ahmad Al Masaood from Abu Dhabi contacted a German lady he knew called Lisa to take me on a tour. "She's been there a long time and knows the place inside out," he told me.

Lisa turned out to be a treasure trove of knowledge. She showed me all the usual tourist spots – Buckingham Palace, the Tower of London, Trafalgar Square, where, of course, I had my photograph taken with its ubiquitous pigeon residents, hoping they would refrain from leaving their legacy on my suit. I'm sure you've noticed that anyone who ever went to London before the mid-2000s has a photo of themselves with breadcrumbs on their outstretched palm looking oddly ecstatic to find themselves in the midst of a pigeon storm. The birds are no longer flying around Nelson's Column in any numbers because Ken Livingstone, a former Mayor of London, said they were a health hazard and banned the public from feeding them. Just think! There's a whole generation of youngsters visiting the Square who will never be able to show their grandchildren one of those once mandatory pigeon pictures.

Lisa also took me along to Speakers' Corner in Hyde Park where all kinds of passionate individuals were expounding their controversial political and religious opinions with no holds barred.

There was definitely nowhere like that in the Middle East; there still isn't. I could hardly believe my ears when I heard people slamming the then Prime Minister Harold Wilson in a most unflattering way. Wilson had billed himself as a man of the people. He walked around in a raincoat smoking a pipe when, really, he preferred cigars. The newspapers would mock his heavy northern working-class accent and his habit of deluging the plain food he liked best with brown HP sauce.

He might have been a man of the people, but the establishment hated him and put around false rumours that he was an agent of the KGB or an IRA sympathiser. A 2006 BBC documentary, *The Plot Against Harold Wilson*, alleges that Wilson knew of two MI5 plots during the 1960s and mid-1970s to organise a coup to replace him with Lord Mountbatten, an uncle of Prince Charles who was India's last Viceroy. Wilson also believed that the secret services had been fomenting strikes to bring down his government.

I kept thinking that the police would turn up and haul off Hyde Park's daring orators at any minute. It hit me then that Britain really was a free country that encouraged free speech and expression. Over time, I grew to admire the restraint showed by its police forces as well as the country's just and independent judicial system.

At some point during that trip, I got together socially with Robert (Bob) Gibbons and the late Richard Dunn – two partners with the English law firm Fox & Gibbons, that had been very active for years throughout the Trucial States. They were the go-to foreign lawyers in Dubai and did very well there.

Richard passed away a few years ago but I am still great friends with Bob, who is an extremely knowledgeable and instantly likeable Scot. Tall with broad shoulders, Bob's stature is commanding. He's a person who can be relied upon both personally and professionally. Besides being a good lawyer, he's also business savvy. He manages several hotels in the UK for Emirati businessmen and owns sprawling estates in his home country, Scotland, that are perfect for fishing and hunting. I always enjoy his company because he has a rare personality and a fine sense of humour. He's so much fun to have dinner with, always laughing and making jokes.

You could say that Richard, also tall but with a few extra pounds around the middle, was the archetypal English gentleman and a real lawyer's lawyer. His life revolved around the law and his clients. He was very precise and dedicated to his work, which he put way before interests or hobbies.

We used to meet in a place off Savile Row – known for its high quality bespoke gentlemen's tailor shops – which was close to their London offices.

I enthused about their wonderful country to such a degree that they suggested I should think about buying a house there. Bob Gibbons thought I might like one in the midst of the fabled English countryside rather than central London. The idea appealed to me somewhat and I allowed it to simmer away on the back-burner for several years to come.

To put it as simply as I can, I absolutely fell in love with London, hook, line and sinker. "When a man is tired of London, he is tired of life; for there is in London all that life can afford," said the eighteenth-century British author, poet, essayist and critic Dr Samuel Johnson. London was the wealthiest place in the world when he lived. It was also noisy, crowded, filthy and smog-ridden. I wonder if he would like it even more were he around today.

It's certain that I'm not "tired of life" – not by Johnson's criteria anyway. I've gone back to London more times than I can count and find it just as exhilarating as I did forty years ago. I enjoy the anonymity it offers. Nobody cares what anyone else does or how eccentrically they behave. They're all far too busy dashing around and doing their own thing.

This 'live and let live' attitude does have its downsides. If you're on your own in London, it can get a bit lonely, and through talking to people I've heard that most residents don't know who their neighbours are and might refrain from stopping to assist a sick passerby on the street, due to their inherent suspicion of the other and ingrained reluctance to 'interfere'.

It's just the opposite in Arab countries where everyone knows – or tries to know – everyone else's business. If someone falls down ill on a pavement in my part of the world, he is soon surrounded by people asking to help, and usually, when someone's car breaks down on the road, several drivers will stop to see if they can assist.

* * *

Whenever most people in the Arab world thought about the United States in those days, it was held high as the 'Land of the Free and the Brave' as well as a land of great opportunity. The American Dream as a concept had reached our shores. The idea that America was awash with money that was being splashed around liberally was the thinking behind my first visit to the US in the mid-1970s.

It was with great excitement that I flew to Los Angeles together with Riad to discuss a business opportunity. A big moustachioed American called Leslie Fradken, who was the Sales Manager of JD Marshall, a supplier of equipment to Al Habtoor Engineering, had told us that a company called Whiteman was in dire financial difficulties. Whiteman manufactured concrete pumps that we distributed in the UAE where they were very much in demand. Leslie suggested that we meet with Whiteman's owner with a view to buying the company and seemed to think that American banks would be amenable to providing us with loans for that purpose.

Our enthusiasm was somewhat dimmed when we were met by unsmiling immigration officers, who set about subjecting us both to lengthy interrogation. Once allowed to proceed, we had to face grim-faced, oversized male and female customs officers, who asked whether we were carrying food or plants. "I don't eat much, so why would I be travelling around with food?" I told them somewhat indignantly.

Getting through Los Angeles Airport had been a gruelling experience and I remember thinking that the airport building itself looked so much better in movies. In reality, it was fairly plain and functional in comparison to some of the European airports I'd seen.

Patiently waiting for us outside was Leslie, who drove us to the Beverley Wilshire Hotel, then considered one of the best in the world. If you're not personally familiar with this marble Italian renaissance-style hotel near the world's most exclusive shopping street, Rodeo Drive, you'll probably remember it as the prime location for the 1990 movie *Pretty Woman* starring Julia Roberts and Richard Gere.

I remember every second of that journey to the hotel. I was astonished how big everything was, especially flyovers, tunnels, highways and cars, although I couldn't help noticing that while vehicles were generally bigger than those I had seen in London, most weren't nearly as luxurious. Just as startling was how ethnically diverse the American people were. I could hardly wait to step out of the car into Hollywood movie land, which had always held so much fascination for me. I almost had to pinch myself to know this was no dream. I really was in the home of Lady Liberty, the United States of America.

American customs took some getting used to. After a sound night's sleep in the lap of luxury, we went down to breakfast. While we ate a modest morning meal of toast and croissants with jam, it was eye-popping to see our fellow guests tucking into steaks, fried eggs, bacon, sausages and waffles drenched in syrup, all piled high on one plate. No wonder most Americans are larger than us if they start each day with that feast, I concluded.

Upon leaving the breakfast room for the lobby, a tall, elegant, well-dressed and very beautiful young woman walked towards us. "Good morning, gentlemen. Have a nice day!" she said with a warm smile. We were dumb-founded. All we could mutter was "thank you" before she floated away.

We walked towards the hotel's exit in bemused silence until Riad finally said "How do you know that girl? When did you meet her? When we said good night last evening I went to my room and slept. Where did you go?".

I didn't say anything at first, I just smiled back knowingly. It was fun to keep him guessing. In any case, I was too busy racking my brain to re-member whether I had, in fact, met that vision of loveliness in the UAE or elsewhere. But as she was the type of woman that once seen wouldn't easily be forgotten, the reason behind her overt familiarity remained one of life's little mysteries. That is, until we later found out that she was a hotel employee, a guest relations manager, whose job was to be nice and friendly with all the hotel's guests. This is the American way, we were told. The mystery solved, I did feel a little miffed that we weren't singled out as being special after all.

In the end, we were unable to buy Whiteman as we couldn't agree terms with the owner. But because we liked Los Angeles and saw that it offered a myriad of business opportunities, in 1976 we formed our own US-based company there, which we named Gulf American. Leslie was persuaded to quit his post with JD Marshall to become the General Manager of our new company.

On a subsequent trip to Los Angeles, when I was accompanied by one of my Arab managers called Adel Sadik and my good friend Kazem Abu Ghazaleh, a judge, we got lost en route from San Diego to Los Angeles. We turned off from the main highway at the wrong exit and soon found ourselves on another planet. We drove endlessly without seeing a single sign pointing to LA. The landscape looked different, people looked dif-ferent and when we stopped to ask for directions, we couldn't find anyone who spoke English.

"We must have driven into Mexico by mistake," said Kazem, when we all started to panic. "This is a foreign land. We cannot be anywhere near Los Angeles."

"I think so too," said Adel, who was somewhat of an authority on the area, or so we believed, as he had spent several years in LA during his days as a student. "But how could we leave America without showing our passports?"

At last, we came across a man who spoke a few words of English. He gave us directions to Hollywood in broken English, which we couldn't follow. Finally, we offered him 200 dollars to guide us back to our hotel, which he seemed delighted to accept. For him, that was a good deal. We had wasted four or five hours trying to find our way when the hotel was a comparatively a short hop away. I can only imagine that we must have wandered into East Los Angeles where residents were primarily Hispanics living on the lowest end of the socio-economic scale in soulless tenement blocks or ramshackle wooden houses with chicken coops. It was a world away from the movie stars' mansions on Beverley Hills and a side of America that outsiders rarely glimpse.

* * *

In 1976, with my engineering firm going from strength to strength and large contracts coming in fairly regularly, I figured it was time to think about diversifying my business interests. I had been advised to avoid putting all my eggs in one basket, so when a great friend of mine, Colonel Mohammed Saeed Al Ghaith, Chief of Police and head of Dubai's intelligence services said "Let's open a soap factory", I was receptive to the idea.

With my penchant for cleanliness, the word 'soap' had an attractive ring to it. What's more, who in the world doesn't need to wash themselves? And my soap would be a lot cheaper than imported brands. I was sure my locally-made soap would take the UAE market by storm. My zeal must have rubbed off onto Riad, who was keen to partner with us in the venture.

Riad volunteered to fly to London so he could meet with the management of Unilever to ask if they would be willing to give us a franchise to manufacture Lux soap. Unilever's products – Bovril, Brooke Bond Tea, Persil and Pond's skin cream – were all household names in the 1970s. Riad tried his very best to secure that franchise, but, unfortunately, he came back empty-handed.

We discussed what other use we could make of our factory building, which was situated in a fairly undeveloped area of Dubai called Rashidiya. It was all dressed up, but we had nowhere to go with it. It was a really stupid mistake on our part to have built the factory before getting the franchise.

Then the man we had hired as factory manager spoke up, interrupting the gloomy atmosphere. His name was Walid Derbass, a chain-smoker with nervous tics, who at around forty-five kilograms weighed even less than me. He made us all more tense just looking at him.

"We can still make soap. We can easily find out how to make it. We can import our own equipment and ingredients. True, we can't call it Lux, but we can label it with the nearest thing. How about 'Luv'? Maybe shoppers won't be able to tell the difference."

We looked enquiringly at one another for a while until I said, "So be it. Luv it shall be". Very soon, Luv was in the air in more ways than one.

None of us had really given much thought to what goes into soap as we had anticipated learning the details from Unilever. When I understood that one of the ingredients of a bar of soap was tallow, which is rendered beef, lamb or horse fat also used to make candles, I did feel a slight sense of discomfort.

In the event, we imported machines from Italy and all the ingredients including the fat from Germany. We actually managed to manufacture and package four tons of soap daily in several sizes, which were initially snapped up by local shops and small supermarkets. When our brand began to fly off the shelves – on second thoughts, crawl would be more accurate – we felt a real sense of achievement. We'd done it without any assistance from Unilever or any similar manufacturer.

I took great quantities home to distribute to my parents, brothers, friends and neighbours, feeling most generous. I told my wife that she should never again even think of buying fancy foreign brands. "It's a matter of loyalty," I told her.

Sure enough, there was always lots of Luv on display in the bathroom. I was pleased until it became apparent that I was the only one in the house washing with it. Every time I picked up a bar, it was the same size as when I'd used it last. I didn't have to be Sherlock Holmes to deduce that either my wife and kids had decided to refrain from bathing, which was highly unlikely, or enemy soap was hiding out in a cupboard somewhere. It was. The illicit stash was found and the 'traitors' were duly given a ticking off, which was a bit unfair of me when I had to keep driving away the niggling conclusion that I could just about bear to use it myself.

Unfortunately, what began as Luv at first sight quickly turned sour. Orders were cancelled and retailers returned their stocks. We were inundated with complaints. Some consumers were breaking out in rashes and hives, including a few of my managers who, like my family members, had been instructed to wash with Luv, or else. Unfortunately for them, they had been more obedient than my wife and kids.

When one of my employees would come to me complaining of itchy lumps, bumps and pimples, I would hand him a packet of anti-histamine tablets along with a tube of anti-allergy cream.

Obviously we were doing something wrong. We struggled on for several years gathering losses when I decided to have another go at persuading Unilever to trust us with a franchise, hoping that my charm would be more persuasive than Riad's had been.

I made an appointment with one of Unilever's directors, put on my best suit and tie and met him at the Britannia Hotel opposite the American Embassy in Grosvenor Square where I was staying with my family.

"What can I do for you?" he asked very officiously.

"I own a soap manufacturing factory in Dubai together with two partners. It's been running for a number of years and we would like a franchise to produce bars of Lux. Unilever would, of course, be rewarded with a substantial percentage of the profits." From the expression on his face, he thought I was a Middle Eastern hillbilly; definitely someone not worth bothering with.

"Who are you?" he asked, not waiting for an answer. Then with the trace of a smirk he said, "You had better not use too much soap. You might vanish and disappear." I was unsure how to react to such rudeness. It crossed my mind that it might just be English-style friendly banter.

I forced a smile and tried again. "We have the premises and all necessary equipment. We have the money, we have managers and employees. All we need is a well-known brand name like yours, some training and know-how. Why don't we join hands?"

"Sorry friend. I don't think you understand. Unilever is one of the biggest international companies in the world. Quite frankly, we're unable to consider you and your partners as potential franchisees. I'm only sorry you've wasted your journey."

"And by the way," he added, "be warned that your factory will close down very soon. We are aggressively marketing Lux in your part of the world and we can hardly keep up with orders. Don't even imagine you've got any chance of surviving because, believe me, you haven't."

I had met hundreds of British people in Dubai, but none of them were nasty like him. He was a real piece of work! It was with great disappointment that I flew back to Dubai where my partners were anxious for my news. "The Unilever man said 'we're too big and you guys are no-bodies,'" I explained.

The residents of Rashidiya started to complain about the putrid smell of animal fat permeating their fresh air – and in truth, it was really nauseating. It was then that I had to admit to myself that our product was doomed. It could never compete with quality imported brands and was causing more hassle than anything else.

To make things worse, Unilever sued us for labelling our product 'Luv', which they said was a deliberate attempt to capitalise on the Lux name. We won the case because we hadn't done anything to contravene any laws in place at the time. I ended up selling the factory at a throwaway price to an Iranian man who, I believe, shipped his product to Iran.

We made a big mistake entering into a partnership with Mohammed Saeed Al Ghaith because we didn't think his idea through well enough. Instead of doing a proper feasibility study and then finding a well-known personal care company willing to give us a franchise, we simply rushed forward because... well... we liked and trusted Mohammed. No wonder we lost all our money! That is not the way to go about starting up a new business, as we learned at our cost. Riad was the clever one. He only took a 20 per cent share; my own was 40 per cent. Sometimes I think I should ask him to pay me the difference.

There is a saying in Arabic 'You learn from your own pocket', which in my case was so true. I always advise people now to concentrate on businesses or careers that they know inside out or in which they have a natural interest. I wish someone had told me before I learned that lesson the hard way.

A couple of friends visited me at home in the mid-1970s and one of them said, "You know, people are making a lot of money from film production nowadays," before going on to elaborate enthusiastically.

"Is that so?" I said. "Why are you telling me this?"

"Well, I think now is a good time to capitalise on that trend," he said. "Why don't you open a film production company? We'll be with you all the way."

The idea was completely foreign to me. I knew nothing at all about film-making, so my first instinct was to say a firm "thanks, but no thanks". But they weren't going to give up that easily. They continued arguing their case and pushing their points with such vigour that I was persuaded against my better judgement to go ahead.

My three new partners and I allocated a large amount of money to the new venture, registered a company, rented office space and appointed a manager. The company produced three programmes that aired on television, but none of them were well-received. The day came when we realised that this company wasn't working out, so we called a meeting with the manager to discuss whether there was a way for the business to recover or whether we should withdraw our investment and place it in something more profitable.

It was then that we found out there was no money left; virtually nothing at all. Less than half had been spent on programme-making. The bulk had gone on hosting people in the movie business to lunch, dinner and parties. The manager had also been spending our money on his own late-night drinking, partying and womanising. My partners were disappointed but undeterred. They asked me to consider investing even more in the company under a new manager, but I refused and walked away, regretful that we had wasted our hard-earned cash on something none of us had any clue about.

I may have placed my fingers close to the fire, but I obviously didn't feel they had been burned, because around the same time I invested in a jewellery shop. Two Lebanese friends of Riad and myself, who had been based somewhere in Africa working with diamonds, came to Dubai saying they wanted to go into the jewellery business and needed a local partner and investor.

They were very charming and persuasive so, you've guessed it – I took the bait and so did Riad. My new partners may have been very likeable but I couldn't shake a nagging feeling that they were not trustworthy. A few things occurred to make me worried on that score. A year later, I decided I wanted nothing more to do with them or their possibly dodgy doings. It was around midnight when my feelings of uncertainty overpowered me to the extent that I called Riad to say: "Tomorrow morning, I want you to go to the shop, divide the merchandise into four and close it down".

He did just that. He divided the imported Italian gold equally before placing it in four bags. He kept one for himself, gave the other two to the Lebanese and came to my home bearing my share. I gave it to my wife and other female family members, but they took one look at it and deduced it wasn't pure gold. When I checked, I found out they were right and it wasn't too long before some of it began turning rusty.

Sometime after the jewellery store fiasco, I opened a luxury goods shop with another guy. We imported watches from Switzerland and silk cloth from various countries. A year later, most of the original stock was still waiting to be bought. I took it and distributed it among my friends. That was it! I'd finally had enough of partnerships. "Please don't propose any new partnerships with anyone else ever again," I told Riad, who was just as disenchanted as I was.

* * *

On 24 November 1977, our youngest son Ahmad was born. Unfortunately, he arrived two months prematurely and so had to begin his life in an incubator where he stayed for two months. I would visit him four times a day and whenever I looked at Ahmad's tiny fingers and toes and saw how he was struggling to breathe, I wondered whether this little person who had inherited my own flesh and blood would survive. He was the only premature baby on that ward who had to remain inside the incubator for such a long time.

To tell you the truth, I was gripped with fear. I had good reason. I had already lost a baby ten years before in 1967. He was my second son. We named him Khalid. Almost before he opened his eyes, we took him and our eldest boy Rashid to Qatar at the invitation of Sultan Abdullah Al Otaiba, who lived in the capital Doha near the homes of two of my cousins, Khalifa bin Mohammed Al Otaiba and Otaiba Abdullah Al Otaiba.

Then much to our great distress, Khalid became very ill. We immediately rushed him to Al Rumaillah hospital for treatment, which doctors said would take more than a month to complete. I was assured that all would be well. And as I was caught up with getting a new business off the ground, I reluctantly tore myself away to return to Dubai, leaving baby Khalid and Rashid in the excellent care of their mother.

Some weeks later, my wife and sons flew home. I took one look at Hamda's stricken face and my heart sank. I braced myself for bad news. "They say there's no cure," she said.

All we could do was to try and put the inevitable aside. We took each day as it came, trying to enjoy every moment with our precious son to the maximum. Six months later, Khalid drew his last breath. Hamda was inconsolable. Spiritually, I understood that his brief time on earth was God's will, God's plan if you like. But I couldn't help thinking this wasn't how it was supposed to be. Children aren't supposed to go before their parents.

Little Khalid was washed and wrapped in cloth. I held him tightly before placing his small, frail body into a hole in the earth and covering it over myself. Every parent who loses a child will tell you that the emotional pain is indescribable. There is nothing else quite like it. Only the fragrant scent of his hair remained with me for a long time to come. You keep asking yourself whether you could have done anything more and imagining an entire life that would never be. In the end, the only way to go forward is to appreciate the time you had with your special gift from God and that from now on he will always be at peace and safe from harm.

The thought of baby Ahmad joining his brother Khalid so soon was more than I could bear. I prayed to God that in His wisdom He would allow me to keep this child. Thank God my prayers were answered.

Even when Ahmad was a child attending primary school, he would often come to see me in my office when he would ask to check the accounts and discuss debits, credits and profits. He was fascinated by business and was always interested and involved in everything that was going on at the time. I was so proud of him when he graduated from the California State University of Long Beach with a degree in finance. Today, Ahmad is the CEO of one of my biggest companies, Al Habtoor Motors, working closely with my younger brother Sultan, who is that highly-successful company's President.

My sons Rashid and Mohammed are similarly bright and business-minded. Rashid is courageous, very intelligent and values his independence. Like me, he has a strong personality and likes his own way. A natural-born diplomat, he's well-liked and has developed great personal connections. As soon as he graduated from George Washington University with a degree in Industrial Engineering, he joined my company, but he was always keen to branch out on his own. I wasn't very pleased about that at the time, because I believed he would be more secure and his future brighter if he stayed with me.

Rashid isn't by nature a cautious person. I suppose I was the same at his age, but unlike me he was once very extravagant spending large sums on entertaining people far wealthier than he was. We all make mistakes when we're young and I put much effort into guiding him in the right direction. He started up his own company, Al Habtoor Trading Enterprises, and, with my backing and advice, he is doing well. He knows I'll always be there for him.

Mohammed, who has proved to be fearless in business, has worked closest with me. He has a likeable personality and is very socially adept, able to get on well with colleagues, friends and associates, both local and foreign. Since he completed his hotel and restaurant management studies in Washington DC, and catering management at the University of Slough, England, I've tried to mould him in a positive way. From time to time, we disagree on things related to work, but in the office I don't treat him as a son. Our relationship within those walls is purely professional. I interact with him in the exact same way that I relate to my directors.

When Mohammed first returned from the United States, he thought he would be given a big office and ten secretaries. Instead, he says, I handed him an apron and told him to work in my hotel as a waiter and later as a porter. I did that because I wanted him to realise the value of hard work and to ensure he didn't adopt an 'easy come, easy go' attitude to money. He appreciates my strategy now.

"I learned a great deal" during those early years, he told an interviewer, "particularly about consulting other people. I may like to put gold windows on a building, but if four managers say silver is better, then silver it is." Through working alongside employees as one of them, he is able to communicate with them and inspire them.

"I visit the staff accommodation and speak to those people," he said. "What good is it if they feel scared and start shaking when I enter a room? I don't want them to tell me that everything is perfect when I talk to them informally. I want them to tell me what is wrong. These people are the front line... I want them to feel empowered."

In the professional sense, I consider Mohammed to be a reliable and responsible pair of safe hands. He's not just my son; he's my right-hand man. In 2010, I promoted him to Vice-Chairman and CEO of the Al Habtoor Group because he's proved over and over again that he's the right man to handle that kind of responsibility.

I would like to think I've always been a good father to them. Whatever I did was always motivated by my desire for their happiness and well-being. Admittedly, I made one mistake when Mohammed and Rashid were eight and nine years old respectively.

Several wealthy friends of mine had sent their young sons to a private school in Switzerland in hopes they would return as sophisticated and polished young men. I thought to do the same with mine. So I packed off poor Rashid and Mohammed (Ahmad was too young to join them) along with their cousin, Ahmad Mohammed Al Habtoor, to the same expensive school, thinking I was doing the right thing. Mohammed didn't mind being there, but Rashid never stopped missing his family and friends at home and cried all the time. Their mother wasn't very pleased that her sons were so far away either. The whole family was against me and, in truth, the house wasn't the same without them. So I brought them all back again.

No one was more pleased to have them back than my father, who wanted to continue training them to hunt, shoot, ride horses and camels and how to drive through the desert in a four-wheel drive vehicle. To his mind, those skills were far more important for young Emirati boys than learning European languages and etiquette. He wanted his grandsons to be men, not mannequins.

Thank God my three sons are healthy, successful and happily married with great children of their own.

* * *

In the late half of the 1970s, I was still dreaming about owning my own hotel and hoping that I could find a suitable plot of land on which to build it, when Sheikh Rashid called my home. The call came at around 5.30 in the morning when I was still fast asleep. I soon opened my eyes when my wife yelled "Khalaf! Come quickly! Sheikh Rashid is on the phone".

It took me some minutes to pick up the receiver because I first needed to clear my throat and my mind of sleep. As soon as I told him "Good morning," he said, "Ah! So you were sleeping," accusingly, as though I had committed a mortal sin. "Why do you wake up so late?"

Before I could answer, he said, "Get dressed quickly. I want to see you right away. Come to Zabeel (his town palace). I want to show you some-thing." I don't think I've ever showered so quickly in my life. When I ar-rived at the palace, there was just time to gulp down a cup of coffee before he said "*Yallah!* Let's go".

With Sheikh Rashid sitting in the front seat of his Mercedes 230 long wheelbase next to the driver, I got in the back next to someone else whose name I can't recall. We drove in the direction of Abu Dhabi along what was then a one-lane road with traffic in both directions called the Abu Dhabi Road (now Sheikh Zayed Road). He wouldn't tell me where we were going until the vehicle turned off the road into the desert some way up and said, "Come on. Let's get out here." At that point, I had no idea what was in his mind.

I was staring at some white desert rats and wondering what on earth we were doing in the middle of nowhere, when he suddenly said, "This is yours," pointing at a vast expanse of desert all around us, as far as the eye could see. For a second or two, I was speechless. All I could do was stand and stare as he tried to explain to me where the land in question began and ended. My mind was racing.

"I want you to build a hotel here for a reason. I'll tell you, but I don't want you to talk about this with anyone. There are plans in the pipeline to move Dubai Airport from the middle of town to Jebel Ali where there is plenty of land for expansion."

I understood his thinking perfectly. Jebel Ali is thirty-five kilometres from the city of Dubai, so any hotel constructed on this particular piece of land would be closer to the new airport than any other. Gulf nationals, even those from fairly remote areas, began to fly frequently when Bahrain, Qatar, Oman and Abu Dhabi bought Gulf Aviation and rebranded it as their joint flag carrier, Gulf Air, in 1973. The airline was based in Bahrain and had a reputation for luxury due to its double-decker 'Five-star Tri-Stars' with restaurant-style seating and a boutique selling designer items in First Class. There were quite a few first-time flyers around then; they were usually the ones hauling themselves up the aircraft stairs laden down with bed rolls, blankets, cooking pots and even small Primus stoves – which rumour had it they would occasionally try to light in the aircraft aisle to make coffee.

I was overjoyed. I couldn't thank him enough. At last, I would have what I always wanted, a hotel (what I didn't know at the time was that Dubai Airport would remain where it always was and that it would take more than thirty years for an airport – Al Maktoum International – to begin operations at Jebel Ali).

I was excited to tell my family the good news. But wait... I didn't have any money. Reality hit me. Where would I find the enormous sum of money required to build, furnish and staff a good-sized hotel with the kind of facilities demanded by international business travellers? "I can't thank you enough, Your Highness," I said, "but where will I get the money for a hotel?"

Sheikh Rashid made it known that he wouldn't entertain lending me any money for the project as all the capital he had was reserved for new infrastructure and for Dubai's running expenses. He was unstinting with his help when it came to providing local business people with land or op-portunities to work on governmental projects, but as far as I know he never handed anyone large amounts of cash.

"Talk to me about anything... anything at all. But don't talk to me about money," he said.

Soon afterwards, I got the chance to have a lengthy one-on-one chat with the Ruler at his majlis when we discussed my plans for the hotel and other ventures. Sheikh Rashid sat back fascinated. He loved to talk about anything that would enhance Dubai.

I was so engrossed in conversation that I failed to notice that my father, anxiously awaiting his turn to speak, was getting impatient. He was unable to relate to my new-fangled notions and highfaluting ambitions, all of which he had heard a thousand times before. He had other priorities.

"Khalaf! You've talked enough," he interjected, cutting me off in full flow and surprising Sheikh Rashid. "Listen Rashid," he said. "That tunnel that you built to join Al Shindagha with Deira is no good. Our camels need more than an hour to cross from one side to the other."

The Ruler laughed and turned to me, saying, "Your father is cleverer than you. His business is much more important than yours". My father had known Sheikh Rashid a long time and was on familiar terms with him.

On another occasion, Sheikh Rashid told me a story about the old days. "I once went hunting with your father and Al Murr bin Al Sheikh bin Moujrin, his cousin. I told them there was no problem should they like to sit next to me at the front of the vehicle. There was plenty of room up front for both of them because they were so skinny. They said they would prefer to sit in the back, which was fine with me." he continued "The problem was the road was so bumpy and they were so light that they kept being thrown from the back seats into the open trunk. They came back to their seats a few times, but each time they were thrown back again. In the end they gave up. They both sat on top of the spare tyre, which they insisted was softer and easier on their bodies than the steel floor of the trunk. It was so funny to see Ahmad Al Habtoor and his cousin balancing on the wheel."

Prior to Sheikh Rashid's accession, when he was less burdened with governmental affairs, father would often accompany him on hunting trips to Pakistan, Iran and the deserts around Dubai.

Later, while Sheikh Rashid became the UAE's Vice-President responsible for forming the government without emirate-specific quota restrictions, all of a sudden two of my relatives, high-ranking ministers from Abu Dhabi, who had never picked up the phone to call me before, began to behave as though they were my best buddies. They were ringing all the time to invite me to lunch or dinner. What's going on, I said to myself.

There must be a reason why I've suddenly become their favourite person. But what can they possibly want from me when they're both so close to the President?

Shortly afterwards, I saw Sheikh Rashid to ask him "Is anything happening with the federal government?"

"Yes, as a matter of fact, we're in the process of dissolving the government and forming a new one," he told me.

"Would you mind telling me who you plan to nominate from Abu Dhabi?"

"That's not your business," he said.

"True, it's not my business, but I am really interested to know."

"No, no, I'm not going to tell you that," he said. "Don't beat around the bush! Tell me honestly, what's on your mind?"

I then told him about my new-found popularity among the high and mighty, while explaining that I didn't think that they could be trying to use me for some kind of *wasta* (clout) because nobody was closer to Sheikh Zayed than they were. There was nothing I could do for them that they couldn't do for themselves.

"You might be wrong there," he said. "I am the man who will take the decision on who will be asked to join the new government. They know full well that I will make that decision from my mind and my heart and not because of any pressure from anyone else."

I was aware that Sheikh Zayed held those ministers in high esteem and was very friendly with both of them. I had a strong feeling that the President would be unhappy in the event they were not reassigned to the cabinet. I strongly advised Sheikh Rashid to consider all the angles before he made his decision and said everything I could to persuade him to give positions to my two new 'best friends'.

Sheikh Rashid appeared completely unmoved by my appeals, but at the end of the day they were reappointed as ministers; when lo and behold, I never heard from either of them again.

Sheikh Rashid respected my opinions and seemed to enjoy my company, and I appreciated spending time with him. From the late 1970s, I saw him almost every day. In the early mornings, I would go to Zabeel Palace where we would drink tea or coffee and talk about the events of the day. Just before lunch, I would meet him in his office at the Emiri Court and I spent many an evening with him in the Jumeirah 'round villa' – dubbed the 'foundation of the Federation villa' – because that's where many of the pre-UAE discussions took place. The atmosphere there was usually friendly, casual and devoid of protocol. There, he was surrounded by the people closest to him, whom he liked and trusted. It was more homely than his palaces, where the grand decor could be intimidating to some.

During one of our regular gatherings at the round villa, I noticed that Sheikh Rashid wasn't his usual self; something was clearly bothering him. It wasn't long before he asked me to join him on the terrace, together with Mohammed Al Moussa and Khalifa Al Naboodah, for a private conversation about two members of the cabinet who overstepped formalities by liaising directly with the President instead of reporting to Sheikh Rashid – Sheikh Hamdan bin Mohammed Al Nahyan, the Deputy Prime Minister, and Ahmad Khalifa Al Suwaidi, the Federation's main architect and Minister of Foreign Affairs.

"Your Highness, if you permit, I would like to go to Abu Dhabi and explain your concerns to Sheikh Hamdan and Ahmad, so this problem can be sorted out?" I said.

Sheikh Rashid accepted my suggestion as he knew I had family ties with the Al Nahyan royals and enjoyed a great relationship with most of them, including Sheikh Hamdan and Ahmad Khalifa Al Suwaidi, my relative.

I duly visited Sheikh Hamdan in Abu Dhabi and discovered that he was entirely unaware of Sheikh Rashid's feelings. He promised that in the future he would respect the political hierarchy and report to Sheikh Rashid. Ahmad Khalifa Al Suwaidi came to see me at my home in Al Shaabiya Al Thaniya (Al Shaabiya 2) and told me he was happy to do "whatever Sheikh Rashid wants me to do". From that time forward, their collaboration was excellent. I'm sure that neither of those cabinet members meant any disrespect; as men who were particularly close to Sheikh Zayed on a personal level, they were used to taking matters straight to the top without worrying about protocol. But as soon as they were made aware of Sheikh Rashid's valid sensitivities, they responded positively.

On the political front, Sheikh Rashid often consulted with me as well as with Mohammed Al Moussa, Khalifa Al Naboodah and a few other close friends, especially on misunderstandings between Dubai and Abu Dhabi. Whenever he had a new idea, he would put it before the unofficial parliament made up of trusted friends and advisors in his majlis, to gauge their reaction before it was implemented. He was no autocratic ruler who believed his country was his personal possession. Sheikh Rashid felt that the country belonged to all its citizens. He liked to have the views of the people closest to him, even if they weren't necessarily experts on the topic at hand.

He loved to listen to what everyone had to say. Once he had absorbed and analysed all the different opinions, he would then get up and leave.

There were many light moments at the Jumeirah majlis too.

Mohammed Al Moussa, a successful businessman, was the type of real old-fashioned gentleman that no longer exists. I remember he asked someone from the police or the army to give him some guard dogs. His request was approved and they arrived to let him know he should expect to receive three-month-old German Shepherd puppies "so they can get used to you before they grow up and become more aggressive". Someone remembered that there were puppies in his car parked outside Sheikh Rashid's Jumeirah villa. "Actually, you can have the puppies now," he said. "Have a look at them and take them with you."

Mohammed was pleased. He went to the car to check them out before quickly running back looking scared. "How old are those dogs?" he asked. "You said they're three months; they can't be three months old. How big will they be when they're six months? Their 'balls' are the size of footballs now. Oh my God, I can't take them."

In 1977, a Lufthansa passenger plane, a Boeing 737 that took off from Palma de Mallorca, was hijacked en route to Frankfurt by members of the PFLP (Popular Front for the Liberation of Palestine). The plane was allowed to land in Rome for refuelling and later touched down in Cyprus and Bahrain. Following an incident in Bahrain when one of the hijackers threatened to shoot the co-pilot, it took off for Dubai, which caused great excitement in what was then a very quiet backwater. With negotiations underway between the hijackers, UAE authorities represented by Sheikh Mohammed bin Rashid and German Special Forces, I waited for good news with Sheikh Rashid, Mohammed Al Moussa and other friends at the Sheikh's Jumeirah villa.

Mohammed Al Moussa had a question for Sheikh Rashid: "If we were the ones being held hostage in that aircraft, would you negotiate with the hijackers for our freedom?".

"No way would I pay any money to release you guys," Sheikh Rashid said. We all laughed as we knew he would go the extra mile to rescue not only his friends but also every one of Dubai's citizens.

The plane left Dubai with its hostages, who were rescued shortly afterwards in Mogadishu by German and Somali commandos who stormed the aircraft. Sadly, our friend Mohammed Al Moussa passed away shortly after that.

Sheikh Rashid would often call me whenever he went to the airport to welcome foreign leaders or dignitaries. One time, he was irritated because I wasn't wearing my *bisht* (a traditional cloak worn on prestigious occasions). I explained that I hadn't thought of bringing it because I didn't know we were going anywhere special that day. Actually, I don't like wearing a *bisht*, it's too cumbersome for my liking; but there were times when not doing so would have breached etiquette.

"Go find a *bisht* for Khalaf," he said to his driver. Once I was suitably robed, we drove to the airport to join various sheikhs and officials gathered together waiting to greet Prince Sultan bin Abdulaziz Al Saud, who was Saudi Arabia's Minister of Defence and Aviation and the Kingdom's Crown Prince until his death in 2011.

Ah! Those were the days! Life was spontaneous and informal. There was no red tape. Whoever had the will to do great things had an open door. Sheikh Rashid may be gone, but I still feel his energy and spirit swirling around his greatest loves – Dubai and its people. Not a day goes by when I don't think of him and miss him.

CHAPTER 9

The Hotel

"THE GREAT ADVANTAGE OF A HOTEL IS THAT IT IS A REFUGE FROM HOME LIFE."

– GEORGE BERNARD SHAW

My lifelong ambition to own a hotel was so close and yet so far. As usual, a shortage of money was the main obstacle. I was worried that, if building didn't start within a reasonable period of time, there was a faint possibility that Sheikh Rashid might consider giving it to someone who did have the available funds. Even though I knew deep in my heart that he would never do that and he had given me no indication at all that he would, I didn't want to take any chances.

There was no other option than to apply for a whopping bank loan that was granted by the Bank of Oman (now Mashreq Bank) once the way was smoothed by a very influential person and notable businessman, Abdullah Al Ghurair. As soon as funds were made available in 1978, Al Habtoor Engineering began construction under the supervision of the main consultant, John R. Harris, who also designed the hotel.

Our engineering team had been joined some years earlier by a very qualified, hardworking, capable and extremely outspoken engineer called Yusef Shalabi. Riad and Yusef went back a long time, ever since their student days at the American University of Beirut. Before joining us, Yusef had been working in the area since 1967, initially for Mothercat in Sharjah and thereafter as Chief Engineer for the Lebanese catering company Albert Abela. Riad had introduced his friend to me socially during the Sahara restaurant days – when Yusef says I was "thin, eager, hungry and ambitious" – and, as I had heard lots of good reports about his work capabilities, I was happy to take him on.

Yusef is a real character who doesn't stand on ceremony. While building houses for the hotel's foreign management, he discovered that a Sudanese site engineer was continually delaying their progress. An absolute stickler for professionalism and deadlines, much to everyone's amusement Yusef picked up a big stick and ran after the engineer, threatening to beat him with it.

Another time, our Administration Manager, Farouq Sadik (Riad Sadik's nephew), came to me complaining that Yusef never shook hands with him or said good morning. I called Yusef to ask whether he had something against the man. "No, nothing at all," he answered. "He came to see me three days ago when I was very busy and didn't have any time to waste. I shook his hand and told him 'good morning' when I first met him. What more does he want?"

One of the features of the hotel was a genuine English pub, designed by the well-known architect/interior designer Thomas Saunders, that we named The Red Lion. To make it as authentic as possible, it required wooden beams made out of fibreglass – or, at least, Yusef thought so. That feature was horrendously expensive at 50,000 pounds, but he believed that without Tudor-style beams our pub would look like a poor imitation. Riad, who had his eye on the pennies, didn't agree.

"Where do you come up with such costly ideas, Yusef?" he told him. "Why don't you go see Khalaf and explain to him that there is no need for all this expense?"

When Riad finally came to me to share his point of view, I told him, "Let's be honest, Riad, you're not a night person. You're at home every evening with your wife. Yusef is out every night. He's an expert on all kinds of pubs so let's allow him some leeway on this." He was indeed. Yusef liked to think of himself as a bit of a Don Juan. He was certainly a ladies' man, which was the cause of regular rows with his first wife and he would land on friends at all times of the night, including me, to ask if he could sleep on their couch.

The actual construction was speedily carried out. It was made more efficient by our newly-acquired concrete pump – purchased from a bankrupt American company – and our decision to use 'tunnel-form construction', whereby concrete walls and slabs are cast simultaneously and poured into a steel framework to make floors and walls. It was a modern, safe, time-saving cellular type of construction that was rare in the UAE then.

While the foundations were still being laid, I contacted various international hotel chains and management companies to ask whether they might be interested in managing mine. Once I had reached a preliminary agreement with Grand Metropolitan, that successfully operated hotels and entertainment centres, I flew with my wife and children to London, where we stayed at the Britannia Hotel for a month, at the invitation of the company.

As I was fine-tuning the contractual details with Grand Metropolitan executives, such as their requirement for the hotel to have an Italian restaurant and a sophisticated Polo Bar in keeping with the Metropolitan brand, my wife and children were having a jolly time seeing the sights and shopping for clothes and items we couldn't get in Dubai.

London was as exhilarating as ever, but I kept wishing there were more taxis around. I had a very important meeting lined up on one occasion. I hurried back from a day trip with my kids, who had to be dragged out of a fun park, so that I wouldn't be late.

Our train arrived at Victoria Station on time. I was pleased that I had a whole hour to get back to the hotel where the meeting was to be held, but there wasn't an available cab to be found.

We were still standing in the street some thirty minutes later. I knew that British people are very punctual (we have something called 'British time' in the Middle East) and thought the man I had arranged to meet wouldn't wait long, so the only thing I could do was take off at a fast run in the direction of Grosvenor Square. I weighed fifty-five kilograms at the time – I must have lost five of them during that run. Worse, I arrived to my meeting late, exhausted and dishevelled. Thankfully, London no longer suffers from such an acute shortage of taxis.

Finally, the hotel was good to go with the exception of furniture and furnishings. When it came to interior design, I trusted Riad's taste. So he flew with his wife to Memphis, Tennessee, for the purpose of buying furniture from the same factory that supplied the Holiday Inn chain.

Once there, the couple met up with Yusef, who had been strolling around Memphis sporting a golden Rolex watch on his wrist until a cop tapped him on the shoulder and said, "Watch out! They'll cut your arm here for a lot less than that watch". I don't suppose the danger had occurred to him, as at that time you could forget any valuable on a restaurant table in Dubai and be certain it would still be there when you went back to retrieve it hours later.

Yusef had also been walking around with 4,000 dollars in 1,000-dollar bills that a money changer in Dubai had given him in exchange for UAE dirhams. Those high denomination bills caused him some problems. He landed in Memphis on a weekend when banks were shut and discovered that the hotel cashier and everyone else shrank back when they were asked to change those notes. They had never seen them before and thought they must be forgeries.

When he came across a bank that was open on Monday morning, the manager agreed they were legal tender while admitting that he'd never set eyes on one before either. Apparently, Yusef had to sign a form in the bank pledging never to use such high denomination notes in the future. The Federal Reserve had been phasing those bills out of circulation since 1969.

As it happens, Yusef should have hung on to them. They're collectors' items now, worth thousands of dollars each. Chances are you've never come across one of those bills either, issued when the US dropped the Gold Standard in US$1,000, US$5,000, US$10,000 and even US$100,000 denominations.

Buying furniture was new territory for both Riad and Yusef, although they were guided by a mock-up of the hotel's interior that they took along with them. In the event, they chose well. The furniture was bought and paid for, before being transported and shipped all the way from Elvis' hometown to the United Arab Emirates.

Before the grand opening, we were all very apprehensive. We were all hotel industry novices. Our main challenge was how to market it, how to fill our 200 rooms and eight suites. We could only hope that the incoming British manager knew what he was doing. For one thing, it was in the middle of nowhere and, for another, we had serious competition from the other hotels that had sprung up in recent years.

A five-star InterContinental had opened in 1975, followed by a Sheraton – both overlooking Dubai Creek – and the Chicago Beach Hotel in Jumeirah, later demolished to make way for the Jumeirah Beach Hotel, sited close to where the Burj Al Arab stands today. As my hotel was receiving its finishing touches, the Dubai Trade Centre opened at the beginning of the Abu Dhabi Road together with an adjacent hotel managed by the Hilton chain. Business visitors no longer had to book months in advance or find rooms in other emirates, and, unfortunately for us, Dubai's tourism industry was still some way off.

Then, just around the time the hotel was due to open, the Arabian Gulf countries, the Middle East and the world had to confront a new and disturbing reality. In January 1979, the unpopular Shah of Iran left a country that was beset by political unrest, anti-Shah protests and strikes for the last time.

Within hours of his leaving, public statues in his image were toppled by angry followers of the Ayatollah Khomeini, political prisoners were freed from jails and the dreaded SAVAK was disbanded. Whether or not Mohammed Reza planned to return once the dust had settled or not is uncertain, but, in any event, an opportunity failed to present itself. He initially announced that he was leaving for medical treatment. However, it was later to emerge that he had been encouraged by the US to go into exile.

Waiting in the wings in Paris along with his retinue of Iranian mullahs was the Ayatollah Khomeini. He had been preparing for the moment when he would arrive triumphantly in his home country for many years, inciting dissent and disseminating his tapes, sermons, poems and writings – some say they were smuggled in diplomatic pouches – throughout the poorer, less educated regions of the country.

On 1 February 1979, Khomeini landed in Tehran to be greeted by the ear-splitting cheers of up to 6 million of his followers. Khomeini wasted no time in nominating himself Supreme Leader, converting Iran to the Islamic Republic of Iran, closing down opposition newspapers and rewriting the constitution to allow a Council of Guardians to protect the country from anything deemed un-Islamic. By some accounts, not all his influential supporters knew about his radical and oppressive plans when they first welcomed him with open arms.

The wealthy elites were horrified to see their modern, pro-Western country thrust into the dark ages by glassy-eyed fanatics, who forced women to cover up and went around the cities chastising females when a single curl of their hair could be seen escaping from underneath their chadors.

By no stretch of the imagination was I ever an admirer of the Shah, but even so I was disgusted at the way he was treated by his 'friends' in the West. Not a single Western country would offer him sanctuary for fear of antagonising the Khomeini regime – that was demanding his extradition to face trial – which was utterly disgraceful when he had served American, British and European interests faithfully for decades.

It was only when the Shah required urgent cancer treatment that the Carter administration allowed him a temporary visa to be treated at New York's Cornell Medical Centre, which may have triggered the prolonged siege of the American Embassy in Tehran. Finally, the US authorities terminated his health care and told him that he had to leave the country.

The siege of the US embassy by 300 students calling themselves the 'Imam's disciples', who kept sixty-six American hostages prisoner – reduced to fifty-two when fourteen were released early on – was to last 444 days, during which Khomeini never ceased to demand that the Shah be handed over. The hostages were finally released and flown home on 20 January 1981, which was President Jimmy Carter's last day in office. Since that day, the Islamic Republic of Iran and the US have remained sworn enemies.

All I can say is bravo to the Egyptian President Anwar El Sadat for giving the Shah, his Empress Farah Diba and their children a permanent home. On 27 July 1980, Mohammed Reza died and was given a lavish state funeral. Today, his body lies in Cairo's Al Rifa'i Mosque, along with that of his former brother-in-law, King Farouk, who was Egypt's last reigning monarch.

A heavy cloud now hung over Iran's nearest neighbours. They rightly feared Khomeini's influence over their own Shiite minorities and were concerned about potential divisions that his persuasive preaching and extremist ideology might trigger. Something bad had happened, but we didn't know then just how bad things would get. In any case, all my focus was on the hotel; I didn't have time to worry about how current affairs might impact the Gulf region.

The Metropolitan Hotel was finally inaugurated in 1979 by Sheikh Rashid. When I asked him whether he was pleased with the finished result, he said, "It's lovely, but I can't help thinking it looks like a donkey tied up in a swamp." That wasn't very flattering; a 'princess tied up in a swamp' would have had a nicer ring to it as both the hotel's exterior and interior were very attractive. Still, it was indeed surrounded by rolling sand on all four sides as far as the eye could see, so I understood what he meant.

When I pondered on the hotel's isolation, I remembered that old joke about a thirsty man in the desert. Here it is, in case you've never heard of it:

A man's car breaks down in the middle of a desert. Without a phone or water he decides to set off, hoping to find a town. Dehydrated and very thirsty, the next day he comes across a man selling ties. "Water... water," he says. "No water," says the man. "Do you want to buy a tie?" The next day, the man is crawling across the sand with his tongue hanging out and what does he see but another man selling ties. "Water... water," he pleads. But again, the man asks him to buy a tie. On the third day, the man sees a five-star hotel in the distance. He hopes it isn't a mirage and is relieved to discover it's the real thing. As he drags himself up the steps to the entrance, crying "Water... water," the doorman bars his entrance. "Sorry, sir," he says, "you can't come in here without a tie."

It was quite a relief when *Gulf News* relocated under new management to a new building on the opposite side of the Abu Dhabi Road in 1986. We didn't feel quite so lonely. Some years later, the city had expanded to the extent that the Metropolitan was centrally located in the heart of Dubai's commercial centre, towered over by the tallest building in the world, the 828-metre-high Burj Khalifa, and flanked by showrooms, malls and high-rise residential and office developments.

In the beginning, we really struggled to find guests as, naturally, most visitors wanted to stay closer to the centre of town. Our only popular outlets were The Red Lion pub and another popular rendezvous called Lucifer's Disco, that was packed with British expats and the odd American, especially at weekends. Americans mostly met up at Pancho Villa's, where a tiny man dressed in a Mexican sombrero almost as wide as he was tall would welcome the offshore oil crowd in for burritos and margaritas.

The Red Lion and Lucifer's Disco were quickly elevated to some of Dubai's evening landmarks. The hotel wasn't doing nearly as well. To tell you the truth, I was uncertain about its long-term survival as I was under so much financial pressure. Then just when I thought that things couldn't get any worse, they did.

During one of my business trips to London, I received frantic calls from two of the Grand Metropolitan managers, Graham Colby and Majeed Khalil, who told me that there had been an order from the federal UAE government banning all sales of alcohol. Once the implications of the ban had sunk in, I cancelled all my London appointments, drove to the airport and managed to get a seat on the next British Airways flight to Dubai, a late evening flight which touched down in the early hours of the morning.

Without going home to see the family or change my clothes, I drove straight to Sheikh Rashid's morning majlis and found him talking to the Director of Dubai Municipality, Kamal Hamza, and the Owner and Founder of the Al Ghurair Group, Saif Al Ghurair, who was considered a pillar of Dubai society.

"*Bismillah Al Rahman Al Rahim!*" Sheikh Rashid said, registering his surprise at seeing me in a jacket and trousers rather than traditional dress. "Why are you dressed like that?"

I explained that I had just flown in from the UK. And then with a certain amount of dramatic emphasis I told him, "I've come straight from the airport to hand you the key to my hotel." Sheikh Rashid looked at me with a trace of confusion in his eyes.

"It's no use to me any longer," I went on. Everyone stared at me for a few moments, obviously thinking I'd forgotten my mind on the airplane luggage rack.

"What's this all about?" asked Sheikh Rashid.

"I've just found out about the liquor ban," I said. "If that continues, I might as well close the hotel doors right now. The only outlet earning any revenue at all is The Red Lion, which will lose all its customers. Besides, this prohibition is bound to harm business and investment. Any foreigner looking to start up a new company will think twice."

"Well, maybe this new rule is good for the country," interjected Saif Al Ghurair.

Faced with the possibility of all that I had worked so hard to create crashing down around me, I was in no mood for his interference. "I would respectfully request you to keep your opinion to yourself and allow His Highness to make his own decisions," I said as politely as I could muster.

The next thing I knew, Kamal Hamza, who was doing his best to give the impression he was a deeply religious man when I knew very well that he wasn't, piped up. "Khalaf, you shouldn't be against this decision," he said. "You should be patriotic, you should support it."

With that, I lost my temper. I had done my utmost to hold it in check, but it burst out like a volcano. "Don't involve yourself in something you don't understand and doesn't affect your pocket," I told him.

"This is my country. I love it. And there is nobody more patriotic than I am," I steamed ahead. "If that ban stays, the Americans and the Europeans, especially the British, will be gone. Alright, forget me; forget my hotel. The question we must ask ourselves is do we want an open country with a vibrant economy where foreign entrepreneurs and executives feel at home, or don't we? If any of the other emirates want to impose the ban, then that's up to them, but I was under the impression that it is up to each ruler to make his own decision on those kinds of matters," I said.

I told them that I had no objection at all to Muslims being barred from drinking, but asked why we should impose our own religious prohibitions on other people who are not bound by them. Having a glass of wine with a meal or a beer after a day's work is part of those people's culture, I told them. If we heap too many restrictions upon their lifestyle, the best qualified will seek new pastures and the others will expect to be paid double and triple before agreeing to remain. And don't think for one minute that we'll ever be able to get a tourism industry going; not now and not ever.

The Ruler saw that I was agitated and wisely pulled me aside. He told me that he was trying to clarify the matter and in the meantime I should stay quiet and carry on as normal. "Let this stay between me and you," he said. "Don't talk about it with anyone else."

As soon as I left the majlis, I headed straight for the hotel, where I found Graham and Majeed looking as though they were waiting for Armageddon. "Don't worry! Open the Polo Bar and The Red Lion. I've received a green light to ignore the ban for now." They were delighted but nervous at the same time because we had nothing official, nothing in writing. When they appeared hesitant to follow my instructions, I told them, "Either you open those outlets this minute or you're fired."

I couldn't reveal to them that I had received the go-ahead from Sheikh Rashid, which was worth a lot more than any official pieces of paper in triplicate covered with ministry stamps. As soon as the other hotels heard that The Red Lion was open for business, they wasted no time in following suit. A few weeks later, all hotels were officially informed that the ban had been lifted. But that wasn't to say that my problems in that regard were over.

The Red Lion became a magnet for policemen, poised to pounce like panthers in their squad cars waiting for patrons to leave the pub when they would be breathalysed or accused of having consumed alcohol in a public place, before being driven to a police station. As you might imagine, our regular customers were scared away.

This time, I called the then Minister of Defence, Sheikh Mohammed bin Rashid, who was also the overall responsible for Dubai's police force, to complain. He asked me to see him in his office.

"My hotel has only recently opened for business," I told him. "I've invested a lot of money. I'm up to my eyes in debt to the bank. Now it seems the police are on a mission to hassle my guests. It's beginning to feel very personal. I can only think that someone in the force is harbouring a vendetta against me." I had a good idea that the Chief of Police, Colonel Abdullah Abolhoul, was the man behind my problems as some years previously, in 1975, we had clashed over matters related to Al Ittihad School, which I had opened together with him and some friends. It turned out that I was right. Sheikh Mohammed is a fair and straightforward person. He told Colonel Abolhoul to ensure that I wasn't bothered again. I deeply respect him for that.

I was unhappy with the direction in which the hotel was going – or rather lack of direction – and took the decision to pull out of my contract with Grand Metropolitan a year after the opening. That was easily done. They were probably as glad to see the back of me as I was of them. But before the British management company packed up to leave, they insisted that we would now have to change the hotel's name. Luckily, when my lawyers checked the contract, they discovered that there was no such clause to that effect, so the name stayed.

Now it was down to me and my team to ensure the hotel's smooth running. The problem was that I didn't have a General Manager and didn't have enough time to interview and hire one abroad. I thought that a particular executive, who had been brought in by Grand Metropolitan, seemed like a capable fellow, so much to his surprise and everyone else's, he was appointed as the hotel's new GM.

The Grand Metropolitan people warned me against doing that. They told me that I had made the wrong choice, but I didn't listen to them. I probably thought that their attitudes amounted to nothing more than sour grapes over the parting of our ways.

They say that bad things happen in threes. That was certainly true in my case. With the hotel running at a loss, my finances weren't looking too healthy. It got to the point where I was paying all the day-to-day expenses out of my own pocket. I absolutely hated delaying payments. I had never defaulted on a payment to anyone in my life. But as the time to pay an instalment on my Bank of Oman loan approached, I feared that this time, barring a miracle, I wouldn't be able to meet it.

I wasn't too worried as I had a very good relationship with the Bank of Oman's Chairman, Saif Al Ghurair, and in those days most banks were flexible with nationals endeavouring to make the country a place that we could all be proud of. Nevertheless, to alleviate the pressure and avoid embarrassment, I went to see the CEO and Chairman of the National Bank of Dubai (NBD), Abdullah Saleh, in order to take out a second loan that would enable me to completely pay off my loan with the Bank of Oman.

When I received the okay on the new loan, I asked one of my friends, Khalifa Al Naboodah, then the Undersecretary of Defence, to lend his moral support by accompanying me to the Bank of Oman. Once there, we met with Abdullah Al Ghurair and his brother Saif to negotiate payment of outstanding interest and possible penalties on the original loan. They were both extremely helpful and understanding.

As it turned out, the NBD loan posed a far greater problem. I had come out of the frying pan, into the fire. My financial position was still precarious and I still faced difficulties in meeting instalments on time. Then, one day, a little bird told me that a person I had always considered as a mentor and father figure, who happened to be one of NBD's major shareholders, was actively attempting to convince the board to repossess my hotel. Apparently he wanted to buy it himself for conversion into a private hospital.

When I heard that, I was shocked and hurt. I wasn't sure whether to believe it or not. I couldn't figure out why an individual I had always held dear would plot against me behind my back with such ruthlessness – and especially when he, more than anyone, knew how hard my road had been. That was one of my first business encounters with the kind of dog-eat-dog mentality, normally associated with big financial centres like London or New York, that runs counter to our brotherly culture.

Thankfully, NBD's Chairman, Abdullah Saleh, a man who was highly respected for his ethics, hadn't been influenced by the plotter and was more than fair to me. He allowed me a grace period, rescheduled my loan payments and accepted post-dated cheques to secure future payments.

From then on, I pushed myself to the limit to make sure that every cheque was met on due date. When the ledger was finally closed completely, the bank was happy and I breathed a sigh of relief to be freed from a burden that had weighed so heavily on my shoulders.

Not everyone was happy, though. A few envious people who pretended to be my friends expected me to fail and were hoping that the property would be taken away from me. Thank God I proved them wrong. If I hadn't fought with such determination at that juncture, I think my future would have been irreparably damaged.

Around that time, Sheikh Rashid asked me if I would be willing to become a member of the Federal National Council. That was a big honour, but my time was already split between the engineering company and the hotel. More importantly, every time I opened my eyes in the morning there were new hurdles to overcome. I thanked the Ruler for his confidence in me while explaining that I was reluctant to involve myself with the affairs of the Federal National Council.

I knew that, if any criticism of Dubai or its Ruler were to reach my ears while I was there, I would get into arguments. Sheikh Rashid still insisted. I couldn't refuse the Ruler's request, but at the same time I couldn't scrape up either the time or the energy such an important post required. In the end, I turned up to the opening and closing sessions of Parliament, but as hard as I tried was unable to drum up much interest in debates and discussions that I suspected wouldn't bring any tangible results.

It was all too much for me. Following one meeting connected with the Federal National Council, I started to feel nauseous and dizzy. I was taken to a hospital in Abu Dhabi, where I was seen by Dr Imtihan Jawdat. He was a young Iraqi doctor, who later relocated to the United States, where he became a well-known cardiologist. After putting me through a series of tests, much to my relief, Dr Jawdat told me that there was nothing wrong with me that rest and relaxation couldn't cure. I didn't know then that we were destined to become great friends.

The pressure was on from all sides and I started to feel unwell with a grumbling pain in my abdomen. Before long, the pain developed into more than I could bear. Once again, I was screaming out in agony. I recognise that pain, I thought. I must have another perforated ulcer.

It was a Friday. This time, my family knew exactly what to do. They drove me to Rashid Hospital and asked for Dr Chin, only to be told that Friday was his day off. I refused to see any other doctor and asked my brother Mohammed to please go in search of him. Mohammed traced him to a party that was being held in a private club. Once Dr Chin learned of my plight, he was ready to leave the festivities immediately to come to my aid.

"Hello Khalaf, my dear friend Khalaf," he said with open arms. "Don't worry, I'm here now. You won't die while I'm here. I'll look after you." I knew at that moment that all would be well, but I couldn't help but notice that he wasn't his usual self. I looked at Mohammed quizzically as if to say what's up with Dr Chin? "He's drunk," said my brother. "He's too drunk to operate on you. We'll have to find another doctor."

"No way," I told him. "Nobody else is going to take a knife to me. There's no doctor I trust more than Dr Chin. Mohammed ganged up with my wife and kids who all did their best to persuade me to change my mind. I didn't listen to them. My mind was firmly made up. I begged my brother to step aside and allow me to have my own way.

Everyone trooped into the operating room behind me and I could hear them whispering that the doctor was drunk and had no idea what he was doing. By then I had a suspicion that they might be right because he was slurring his words. Somebody mentioned that I might have appendicitis.

"Yes, quite right," said Dr Chin. "I'll have to take out his appendix."

"No, no, it's not my appendix," I said. "It's the same pain I had before. It's my perforated ulcer."

Dr Chin didn't listen to me. He performed the operation to remove my appendix before he realised that there was actually nothing wrong with it. He then went in search of the real cause of my distress, which was just as I had predicted – a perforated ulcer.

At 6 a.m. the following morning he was at my bedside. "Khalaf my friend, I've come to apologise to you. You were right and I was wrong. You've been relieved of your appendix by mistake, but don't worry you don't need it anyway."

I didn't mind much. After all, what's an appendix between friends! At least he didn't walk off with a kidney. I still thought Dr Chin was the best surgeon in the world. "Whatever mistake you made, Dr Chin, I accept it," I told him with a smile. I wasn't sure whether I wanted to tell my wife and brother that I was now minus a healthy appendix. I didn't want to give them any excuse to say, "We told you so".

As time passed, I became more and more worried about that perforation. I still had painful twinges every now and again. When I would ask Dr Chin about them, he would answer, "Hurry, worry, curry." I couldn't argue with that diagnosis. I had the lot. I guess my belief in my friend's phenomenal medical skills had eroded somewhat by then. He wasn't exactly India's answer to Ibn Sina, that's for sure. I thought it best to get myself checked out by one of London's top surgeons, Dr Keith Reynolds, and flew there without informing Dr Chin that I wanted a second opinion.

Dr Reynolds opened me during an exploratory operation and said he was very impressed by Dr Chin's clean and tidy work. "That doctor has golden hands," he said. But as I was still suffering, he suggested doing an operation called a 'vagotomy' that entails cutting the vagus nerve to separate the stomach from the brain.

"If you choose to go ahead, I guarantee that there will be no more perforated ulcers," he said, "but I must warn you that there can be negative side effects," which he went on to list. They sounded pretty awful to me, especially delayed gastric emptying, which means digestion and elimination could take more than forty-eight hours, resulting in an unpleasant taste in the mouth or a bad odour. I told him to proceed immediately. Anything was better than endless pain. What he said would happen did happen. It took a few years for those side effects to go away completely.

In the meantime, my new General Manager appeared to have risen to the challenge. He was a public relations whiz and did everything that he possibly could to spread the hotel's name far and wide. At first, I was very impressed with his innovative ideas and the enthusiasm with which he carried them out.

For instance, he organised the very first Crufts-style dog show in the hotel grounds, which it goes without saying was appreciated by Dubai's British community. He also introduced an annual equestrian event that attracted world-renowned show jumpers, including Queen Elizabeth II's daughter, Princess Anne, as well as a very successful week-long Motor Show, signifying another first for Dubai.

On the prompting of my son Rashid, who like his brother Mohammed is mad about horses, I had opened a horse racecourse within the hotel's grounds. Children and novices came for horse riding lessons and adults wishing to ride into the desert or along the Jumeirah beach – an amazing experience at sunrise and sunset – would usually hire a steed on an hourly basis.

There was hardly a week when there wasn't something or the other going on. He came up with British Week, Turkish Week, Greek Week and a whole lot more – all novel and popular events with expatriates who enjoyed the opportunity to taste a variety of cuisines. When I saw that the hotel was constantly abuzz with one type of activity or another, I was convinced that I had been right to put my faith in my new General Manager.

However, I soon realised that there was a catch to all of this. My General Manager had been blessed with the gift of the gab, a vivid imagination and a flair for the hospitality industry, but the events he organised were rather lavish. And only when the auditors came in did I come to know to what extent they were weighing in on the budget. The wonderful events and shows, sure enough, also involved giving everyone connected with them a free stay in the hotel with permission to consume as much complimentary food and drink as they wished. Well, I liked my General Manager as a person and credit him for livening up the hotel's ambience, but I couldn't afford to keep him on any longer, as all of this was on the hotel's (and my) account.

But this wasn't the only thing that was affecting the hotel's profitability. We had signed a contract with Dubai Television to accommodate on a half-board basis Egyptian actors, actresses and directors who were working with our local television channel to make various drama series and soaps. Some were well known in the Arab world, such as Salah Sadani and Mustafa Fahmi; others were bit-part actors or unknowns.

I was delighted to get that contract not only from a financial perspective, but also because they were an interesting crowd and I liked having them around. Sadani and many of the others behaved in a very respectable fashion; but, unfortunately, the majority took advantage. Each time they had buffet breakfast or dinner, they would quietly walk off with masses of food in plastic bags for snacks or next day's lunch. We also learned that one prima donna was bathing each day using bottled mineral water. When we studied our profits and losses, we were disappointed that the loss column was far longer than the profit column.

My next General Manager, Mounir Tadros, was recruited in a far more orthodox fashion. He had extensive experience working for hotels in the Gulf and had previously been employed by Grand Metropolitan as a General Manager. We checked him out thoroughly before he was hired and were very impressed with him. He was a professional all-rounder. The first thing he did was introduce accounting systems and within a short time, everything was back on track. He was also a very likeable person with a friendly personality that was appreciated by the hotel's guests and staff alike.

Mounir had his quirks, however. One funny thing about him was his habit of closing the hotel's Italian restaurant, Don Corleone – named after a character in Mario Puzo's novel *The Godfather* – even when customers were queuing for tables. "That's enough now," he would say, turning them away. "It's almost time to close," as though our revenue had reached unacceptable sky-high limits, when in fact our profit margins were fairly low.

Don Corleone fast became one of Dubai's most popular eateries, but there was one person who objected vehemently to the restaurant's name. It had been opened by the Italian Consul General and had been covered extensively in the local press, so I was surprised when the Italian Ambassador drove all the way from Abu Dhabi to see me in my Ramadan majlis just to ask if I would consider changing its name.

He explained that he had come on the instructions of the Italian government, which wanted to disassociate itself from anything that smacked of the Italian mafia. As Don Corleone was a fictional character, I thought that the request was rather petty. It wasn't as though we were promoting the head of Sicily's criminal Cosa Nostra. It was just a bit of harmless fun.

"This is no problem, this is very easy," I said. "I am ready to change the name and close down the restaurant, if that's the only thing left to do."

He looked puzzled. "Sorry, but I don't quite understand what you mean by 'the only thing left to do'."

"If you can assure me Italy has solved all its problems and tackled every troublesome issue affecting the country, apart from getting my restaurant stripped of its name, I'm happy to help you out by closing it now, today."

"Of course my country has problems," he said. "Like any government we cannot solve all of them; there will always be something pending."

"Ah, in that case, renaming my restaurant is hardly an urgent priority. Why don't you come and see me again when it is." I never heard from the poor man again on that topic. Once again, the Italian authorities had been foiled in their attempts to bring down the mafia, only on this occasion there was nobody to blame but me.

We struggled hard to keep my hotel going in the early days, but it was all worth it. In the years that followed our guests included royalty, politicians, celebrities and Hollywood movie stars, including Omar Sharif, Bruce Willis, Wesley Snipes, Patrick Swayze, Jean-Claude Van Damme, Sylvester Stallone, super models Cindy Crawford and Naomi Campbell – and not forgetting Princess Anne and her first husband, Mark Phillips.

The old gal was given quite a few facelifts and extensions since the late 1970s in keeping with the exacting demands of today's travelling public. She aged beautifully, but unlike her glass and chrome high-rise competitors her walls were steeped in happy memories, fun times and never-to-be-revealed secrets from a soon-to-be-forgotten and wonderfully-exciting pioneering age.

It saddens me to write in the past tense, but in 2012 I reluctantly came to the realisation that as a businessman I couldn't allow sentimentality to trump change for the better. In the modern, futuristic city Dubai has become, old isn't necessarily gold. My 'princess in the desert' had to go to make way for a new 1.3 billion dollar complex we've named Habtoor Palace, to include three hotels, a theatre to stage Las Vegas and Macau-style shows, themed restaurants as well as a sports and tennis academy.

It was heartbreaking when the last guests checked out and to discover just how many of the Metropolitan Hotel's faithful patrons and long-serving staff members were saddened by its demise. For a time, the local newspapers were filled with nostalgic anecdotes. The day the demolition squad arrived was a particularly hard one for me, but the sands of time are ever-shifting and we must either move with them or be left behind.

CHAPTER 10

Peace

"Peace is not made at the council table or by treaties, but in the hearts of men."

– Herbert Hoover

With so much happening in my life, there were times when I longed for a bolt-hole, somewhere I could just hang out and tune out from the relentless pressures that had begun to adversely affect my health.

In 1978, during one of my regular visits to London, fate led me by the hand. While I was staying at the Carlton Tower Hotel in Sloane Street, I met up with a friend called Tarik Abou Samra. "You've never been to the heart of the English countryside," he said. "You don't know what you're missing. It's beautiful. Come on, let's go together now." I wasn't in the mood to go anywhere that day, but he kept insisting until I gave in.

We walked to where his Rolls-Royce was parked and as we got nearer, I was astonished to see a very attractive blonde girl behind the wheel. I was even more amazed to find Abou Samra standing alongside one of the back passenger doors patiently waiting for the young lady to get out of the car and open it for him. That isn't our custom. No Arab man would wait for a lady to open a door for him.

I moved to open the door of the front passenger seat when my friend said, "No, wait! She'll open it. That's her job." Then, before I could get in next to the driver he told me to sit with him in the back. "She's just my driver. You shouldn't sit with her," he said. I couldn't tell him that I preferred his driver's company to his.

As our journey took us further and further away from the mad metropolis, my eyes feasted on nature's amazing lush green panorama. We passed fields of grazing cattle, fast-flowing rivers, banks of wild flowers, whitewashed cottages and picturesque English villages, until we eventually stopped near the Compleat Angler Hotel that lies on a bank of the Thames in the small town of Marlow, Buckinghamshire.

We sat for a while listening to the sounds of water meandering past, when I was overcome by an unfamiliar peaceful sensation that all was well with the world. Moments like that can't be bought. They are fleeting and spontaneous. During those rare times of perfection, man cannot but help feel closer to God.

The American writer and psychologist Abraham Maslow named such intense feelings of happiness, well-being and integration with one's surroundings semi-mystical 'peak experiences'. I think I understand what he meant.

I expressed my appreciation of the calm and gentle environment to Abou Samra when he said, "I believe there is a house nearby that is up for auction. What do you think? Shall we take a look at it?"

It wasn't that near. We drove around for almost two hours looking for it and eventually we stopped for coffee at a riverside café in Maidenhead where we asked for directions. "It's easy," said one. "Just drive straight towards Cookham, then cross the bridge and you'll be in the village of Bourne End."

Bourne End, which is near to where the Rivers Thames and Wye meet and which boasts only 5,000 inhabitants, was tiny. Its high street was probably less than thirty metres long. When we saw a sign that read 'Flackwell Heath', we knew we were on the right track. We stopped to ask a passerby where Chapman Lane was and he said, "Here it is," while pointing to the entrance of the house.

It was raining heavily when we stepped out of the Rolls. I was sorry I'd forgotten my umbrella, an essential accessory which no English gentleman would leave home without. We quickly made our way up to the gate, which gaped open. By the time we walked up the drive to the front door of the house, our hair and clothes were soaking wet and our shoes muddy.

We were anxious to get out of the downpour when we rang the doorbell. A steaming hot cup of tea would have been nice. After a few minutes, the door was opened by an English housemaid.

"Yes? Can I help you?" she asked. When she was told that we had come for a preview of the house prior to the auction, she said, "Sorry, you can't come in here without an appointment."

"Can't you make an exception this time?" said Abou Samra. "We've driven here all the way from London. We just want to take a quick look round. We'll only be a few minutes." But the woman wouldn't budge.

"No, I can't let you in," she reiterated. "I can't allow you to tramp all over the carpets with shoes covered in mud."

Perhaps she was wary of us because we didn't look English. In those days very few foreigners found their way to Bourne End or Flackwell Heath. We were probably the first Arabs she had ever encountered in her entire life.

I was very disappointed that we couldn't see inside because not only had I fallen in love with the design of the house and its grounds, I thought the area around Maidenhead and Marlow was delightful in every way.

"Can you at least ask the owner of the house to call me?" I asked her. "I'm staying at the Carlton Tower Hotel in Knightsbridge. Here's my name and room number."

The owner, George Hotry, a local contractor who built most of the surrounding village houses, called at 4 p.m. on the day before I was booked to return to Dubai.

"I've seen your house at Flackwell Heath from the outside and I'm very interested in buying it. Are you selling?" I asked him.

"Yes, it's for sale," he said. "I'm happy to show it to you. Can we perhaps meet tomorrow?"

"Unfortunately, I'm travelling tomorrow," I said. But I was so determined not to let the opportunity slip from my hands that I found myself saying, "Let's have dinner at my hotel this evening. Oh, and, before I forget, please bring the title deed with you and anything else that proves ownership."

I was a man possessed. I couldn't stand the thought that someone else might snap up that house if I didn't act speedily. I called my friend and lawyer, Bob Gibbons, and told him what I was about to do.

"Bob, I need a favour. I've found my perfect house. Please come to the hotel this evening with your cheque book," I said. "I don't want to lose this house but I don't have enough money with me for a deposit."

When George arrived, Bob and Richard Dunn, another partner from the firm of Fox and Gibbons, were already with me. We all sat down for coffee and the deal was concluded without any fuss. Bob handed George a cheque in the sum of 10,000 pounds and George signed a receipt and gave us a copy of the deed and other documents. I was told exchange of contracts and completion would take between thirty to forty days.

I went back to Dubai on a Middle East Airlines (MEA) flight via Beirut, when MEA was considered to be one of the most prestigious airlines. I enjoyed flying with MEA because the airline's station manager, a great man, would usually meet me as I came off the flight and instead of having to wait around for my luggage to appear on the conveyor belt with all the other passengers, he would arrange collection of my bags and send them to my home. That act of kindness would always make my travelling experience so much easier. I looked out for him from the top of the aircraft stairs and, as usual, there he was standing below, smiling up at me.

The next morning, I could hardly wait to wolf down my breakfast and get to my office on the Creek to ask the accountant whether we could scrape up enough spare cash to transfer to Bob Gibbons. At that time, there was rarely any extra money in my Al Habtoor Engineering account. Nevertheless, we gathered together some from here and some from there and transferred it to Bob's account.

A month or so later, the house at Flackwell Heath was finally mine, but, like a bride whose husband has yet to look beneath the veil, the house's inner personality was still unknown and kept beckoning to me to be discovered.

That same year, I travelled to London with my family. We were booked to stay at the Britannia Hotel for a month, courtesy of Grand Metropolitan.

I had been looking forward to showing our new English home to my wife and kids and to moving in together, as I was certain they would love it as much as I did. They were all having a whale of a time in London when I asked them to pack their suitcases for our move to the countryside.

"I've bought a lovely house in the country," I said. "Let's check out of this hotel and move there. It's our new English home. It's amazing. You're going to love it."

I might as well have thrown a lead brick in their direction. Anyone would have imagined that I was carting them off to a shanty town or a rat-infested slum.

Instead of the happy, excited faces I had expected to see, I was met with glum expressions. Convincing them to leave London's stores, boutiques, restaurants, furniture galleries, beauty shops, Harrods, Hamleys and Selfridges for a tiny village surrounded by fields where no one knew us was the hardest sell of my life. They weren't buying.

They were happy with their luxurious hotel suites that overlooked the impressive US Embassy in fashionable Grosvenor Square. In a way, who could blame them? How could the promise of acres of fields compete with all that when they had never seen the place and, therefore, were unable to understand where all my enthusiasm was coming from?

They all lined up against me like troops on a battlefield. I dug in my heels and so did they, but against such uncharacteristic united resistance I decided to withdraw temporarily to fight again another day.

Mother Nature must have been enjoying a good chuckle when all that pushing and pulling was going on. That particular summer night was unbearably hot and humid, even for people like us coming from Dubai. And although the Britannia was a five-star hotel, there was no air conditioning in the rooms. We opened the windows wide and a few of the doors, but the suites were still so stuffy that none of us could get a good night's sleep. In the morning, they were waiting impatiently for me to finish taking my shower.

"Alright, you win, let's move to our new house," announced my wife. "Yes, let's go there," chorused my children.

"No, you were right, we should stay in London," I told them, feigning an air of indifference.

"But you don't understand, we want to go, we really do," someone said.

"Too late... subject closed," I answered.

I continued my pretend stubborn stance, until they were all begging me to change my mind. They didn't want another night of tossing and turning and neither did I. Of course, I was delighted that I had got my own way without having to lay down the law.

That same day we thanked the Grand Metropolitan people for their hospitality, thanked the hotel's Italian General Manager, Mr Kazaroto, for taking such good care of us, and checked out.

Once everyone was settled into our country abode, they were grateful that I'd taken the decision to buy that house. They were happy to see flowers, deer, foxes, squirrels, quail, fields of wheat and thousands of acres of green pastures, to feel the rain on their faces, breathe in fresh air and smell newly-mown grass. They all said in their own fashion, "Now we're in heaven."

One day, on a dark winter's morning, I woke up early for a meeting in London with executives from Grand Metropolitan. I showered, shaved, dressed, had breakfast and walked across icy ground to my car with two of my house guests, a young man called Ashley Lane and Ibrahim Juma'a from Dubai.

My brother Sultan and I have known Ibrahim since childhood and value his friendship. Ibrahim is a well-respected, talented composer. He is well-known in the UAE and throughout the Gulf for his haunting lyrics and music that even today are sought after by young singers. My late friend the poet Mohammed bin Hadher wrote a few poems inspired by some of my thoughts, and when Ibrahim transformed them into beautiful songs I was delighted.

He's a very honest and loyal person who loves to laugh. Well... he usually sees the funny side of things, but on this trip he must have forgotten to pack his sense of humour.

When I turned on the ignition, the car wouldn't budge an inch. It was stuck in a foot of snow. We tried everything to move it, but without success, so there was nothing left but to start digging it out. Everyone, including our housekeeper, came with shovels, garden spades and any implement they could lay their hands on. We tried pushing very hard, but the vehicle only moved a little.

By this time, we were all shivering and weary; everyone that is, except Ibrahim, who was standing around bored watching us do all the work because he didn't want to get his nice clothes dirty.

Ashley didn't think much of Ibrahim's unwillingness to muck in. Then he snapped. "Look around you, Ibrahim," he said. "Everything is white around here except your face." Ibrahim, who is naturally dark complexioned, became very angry. He yelled at Ashley and gave him a ferocious look as he made a move towards him.

The young guy wasn't going to hang around. He took off down the driveway, slipping and sliding all over the place with Ibrahim in hot pursuit. We laughed as we watched them falling down every now and then like Tom and Jerry. Ashley probably meant that Ibrahim's face should have been red with embarrassment for standing idly while everyone else was putting in so much effort, but, unfortunately, Ibrahim mistook his comment as a racist slur.

Apparently Ibrahim wasn't enjoying his vacation very much at all. Before I tell you the reason, I should explain that whenever I'm on a trip, I tend to stick to my usual routine, no matter where I am or what the weather. I normally wake up my guests or travelling companions at 5.30 a.m. for breakfast and then at 6 a.m. we all go out for an hour's brisk morning walk to get the blood flowing through my veins.

Anyway, one morning, soon after Ibrahim's contretemps with Ashley, I was ready for my walk when I noticed that my friend hadn't yet put on his shoes. "Ibrahim, why aren't you ready?" I asked. "It is time for our stroll now."

"I'm not going," he said. "You go. I'm on strike."

"Ibrahim, what are you talking about?"

"This is England. We are in a democracy. You cannot force me to do anything."

"When have I ever forced you to do anything? What do you mean? I would never force you to do anything you don't want to do," I said.

"Maybe not here, but if we were in another country, you probably would force me," he answered jokingly. "You're a dictator."

"Me? You think I'm a dictator?" I was incredulous.

"Yes, you *are* a dictator," he stressed. "This is supposed to be a holiday. Why do people normally go on holiday? They want to relax, sleep late and do their own thing. But on this holiday you make us wake up at 5.30 in the morning. You insist that we go for a walk in the freezing cold. This isn't a home, it's a military camp. So next time you're going on vacation, don't ask me to go with you." Ibrahim's surprising outburst was fairly light-hearted, but he meant every word.

My routine suits me but not everyone appreciates the same kind of lifestyle. I guess I introduced it to compensate for all the hard times I endured when I was young and for the long nights working with Al Mulla, and when I first opened my own company. Moreover, I value good health because I've been near death a few times during my younger years.

Eating well, getting plenty of fresh air, staying fit and making sure that I go to bed early for a sound sleep are important to me. I'll keep all the windows open even when it's freezing outside, although, admittedly, my house in Buckinghamshire has under-floor heating so my toes are always warm. I've always tended towards eating healthy foods. It's in my nature. Exercise is part of my nature too. My father was always very active and he raised me to be like him.

People often ask me how I can stay on the tennis courts for hours in summer when the temperature hits almost fifty degrees centigrade and the humidity reaches 100 per cent. My answer is simple. I just follow God's laws, have early nights and work during the day. I sometimes have to cool off by rubbing ice cubes over my face and neck, but usually my energy levels remain high.

I decided to forget about going out for late dinners at hotels, restaurants or friends' houses, where everyone is drinking or puffing away on cigarettes, decades ago. Or where friends' wives and girlfriends, often with faces plastered with layers of make-up, pretend they are best friends when all the time they are competing as to who is wearing the most expensive designer dress or the most valuable diamond bracelet. I've seen women greet one another with kisses and hugs, when I know for a fact that they hate the sight of each other.

Some people may enjoy that scene, but I find it fake and a total waste of time. I've no interest in running around with the so-called jet set. I'll leave that to the Silvio Berlusconis of this world. I like friends who are real, simple and down-to-earth like my neighbours in Bourne End, not those whose main goal in life is to show off and indulge their every whim.

True happiness cannot be found that way; instant self-gratification isn't the answer. Self-satisfaction by overindulgence in anything, be it food, drink, stimulants, gambling or an addiction to shopping, is nothing more than a quick fix, like a sugar high, that gets the adrenalin pumping only to leave the individual feeling more down than ever.

Genuine happiness or contentment comes from self-respect, self-discipline, right thinking, correct behaviour, moderation in all things and being willing to help others in need. Of course, happiness can't be bottled. It's a transient feeling that means different things to different people. Everyone has to find his or her own.

And it goes without saying that just when you think you've attained that elusive state, it flies away like a butterfly. You can't hold it for long. You have to constantly work towards attaining it. It's like trying to hold water in your hand. The more you close your fist, the quicker the water will trickle through your fingers. All you have to do is gently cup your palm and the water will remain. That's my recipe for inner peace and contentment, for what it's worth.

I saw through all the fakery when I was very young and decided all that wasn't for me. I much prefer spending time with my wife and children, my brother Sultan and my limited group of respectable friends who are decent, honest folk.

Most of the time, I feel great both physically and mentally, and when I focus on my work, my faculties are sharp and concentrated. However, there is one downside. I have lost a few of my closest friends who hate to wake up at dawn and sleep early. Even if I invite them to dinner at eight o' clock, they apologise and turn me down. This is because they've eaten lunch at 4 p.m. whereas I always have mine at 12.30 and I'm usually starving by 6 p.m. at a time when they are just finishing their lunchtime dessert or coffee.

I was sorry that Ibrahim felt as he did, but at the same time I understood his point of view.

Poor Ibrahim had a crush on Lady Diana and one morning, when we were driving from Bourne End to the charming old town of Windsor for coffee, he couldn't stop talking about her.

"I cannot understand how such a beautiful, elegant lady with such a fine personality would agree to marry Prince Charles," he said. "They're completely different people. They're so mismatched."

I didn't say anything. I was too busy thinking, yes, in your dreams, Ibrahim. I was sure he believed she would be much better off with someone like him before he said something that reaffirmed my thoughts. Obviously, he fancied himself as the perfect match for Lady Di.

He went on and on registering his disapproval until he realised I was maintaining a silence on the subject.

"Well... what do you think?" he said. "Why aren't you saying anything?"

"There's nothing to say."

"It appears that you don't agree with me then."

Then when he couldn't stand my silence any longer, he suddenly burst forth with "I'm the biggest idiot on earth".

"Why?"

"I'm an idiot to think she would prefer me to Prince Charles. He's a highly-educated blue-blooded royal. His ancestors go back over a thousand years. He's a future king, a huntsman, a polo player, a knight and he's respected all over the world. Look at me! I'm overweight and ugly. I've only got one eye. I can't ride horses, let alone play polo. She wouldn't look at me twice. What do you think now? Come on, say something."

"Ah, you've finally come to your senses," I said. "You took the words right out of my mouth."

I was happy to know that we had inherited a gardener called Fred Archer from the previous owner. It was such a vast garden that we couldn't do without someone to tend to the flower gardens and mow the lawn. Fred had lived in the village for most of his seventy years and cared for his flowers as though they were his children.

He was one of the most honest people I had ever met. The only problem was that each time I wanted him to plant a fruit tree, he would get very upset with me. "They'll ruin the landscaping and spoil the flowers," he would say. "Why do you want fruit trees? This is a garden, not an orchard."

I don't know how many times I explained to him that because we didn't grow fruit in my country, for me to have fruit trees in my garden and the ability to pluck apples or pears straight from the branch was an absolute thrill. I'm sure he must have thought to himself, that man's not short of a few bob, I don't know why he cannot buy his fruit in the greengrocer's like everyone else does.

When we first moved in, our neighbours were fairly reserved. Because we were the only foreigners around, they didn't know what to expect or how to treat us. It didn't take very long for them to warm up to us. They started visiting me at home and inviting me to theirs or to one of the local pubs for a meal. It took some time, but eventually they were able to look beyond my nationality and accept me as one of them.

The first neighbour I got to know well was an electrician called John Blend. We started off on the wrong foot because he complained about a renovation I intended to make to turn the house into a hotel, which he said blocked his view of the church in Marlow. Once he was placated, he did some work in my home. He later introduced me to his wife, Divinia, and his three children, John Jr, Earl and Emma. They've moved away now but we still keep in close touch.

Shortly afterwards, I had the pleasure of meeting the Reverend Herbert Heartley, the eccentric Vicar of Bourne End. He was such an interesting character, straight out of an English comedy series like the BBC's *Last of the Summer Wine*.

Poor Herbert Heartley had two weaknesses, women and whisky. It seems he had a soft spot for John's wife Divinia and didn't care who knew. Each time Divinia was on the scene, he would behave in a most inappropriate fashion. I was never sure whether the lady was amused, embarrassed or angry.

On several occasions, when we were hoping to enjoy a pub lunch together, various managers or owners would bar his entrance saying, "you can't come in here, Reverend. You know very well you've been banned". I was intrigued. Why would a man of the cloth be blacklisted from so many pubs?, I thought, not wishing to hurt his feelings by asking him outright.

In the end my curiosity got the better of me and I called one of those pubs to find out. I was told that when Reverend Heartley has a few too many, he becomes embarrassingly overfamiliar with the ladies. I could hardly believe my ears.

Early on, I used to try to convince pub owners to allow my friend Herbert in. "Don't worry, he's with me," I would tell them. A few reluctantly agreed, but each time he drank more than his limit, he was usually incapable of controlling his antisocial behaviour, and owners or managers would turn to me with frustration saying, "See!".

Once, a friend whose mother had just passed away called me to ask Herbert if he would conduct his mother's upcoming funeral ceremony. The

Reverend agreed and asked me to drive him there in my Aston Martin. I invited my friend Hassan Al Falasi to come with us.

All of a sudden, as we were passing a pub, Herbert shouted, "Stop! I have to go to the loo!" – a word that English people use for 'restroom'. That's just one of their quaint words or sayings on that topic. When foreigners hear Brits saying they 'need to spend a penny' or use 'the smallest room in the house', they are often confused.

Hassan was shocked to see Herbert exit the loo and head straight for the bar to order two shots of whisky, which he downed in one. "Now I'm all set to conduct that funeral service," he said. I later heard that a local Catholic church complained that the Vicar of Bourne End was a bad influence on one of their priests, who had become one of Herbert's regular drinking partners.

Nobody can deny that my friend Herbert didn't have his faults, but he had such a good heart and was so much fun that I couldn't help liking him in spite of them.

Another of my colourful Bourne End neighbours was a tall, broad guy whose name I don't wish to divulge for reasons you will come to understand – so I'll call him Richard. He was always nice and helpful. He made me laugh and was always really good company. Just to meet him for a few moments was enough to like him. We soon became good friends when he would frequently come over to the house, so frequently, in fact, that I gave him a room to sleep in, to save him driving home late at night.

Richard never had much money, so it gave me a great deal of pleasure to take him with me on my travels. It felt good to know he was getting the chance to see places he had never been able to afford to visit, such as South Africa, Turkey and Dubai.

Then some of my neighbours told me that Richard had been in trouble with the police on more than one occasion. I didn't want to believe them. I didn't tell him what I'd heard, choosing to carry on as normal until I could verify what people were saying about him.

All that changed when one of two beautiful, large and heavy statues dating back to the fifteenth or sixteenth centuries disappeared from outside the front of the house. I was unhappy when I heard that as they were a male–female pair and unique pieces of art.

The theft took place in broad daylight while we were all indoors except for my children, who were playing outside supervised by our maids. It's hard to believe, but some clever and extremely audacious thief drove a pick- up truck with an attached crane through the open front gates and lifted the statue, without being seen.

I never found out who drove away with that statue, but everyone around said it must have been Richard because no one else would dare to enter my grounds and steal something so valuable. I saw Richard a few times after that. He never admitted being the culprit, but from then on I could never regain my trust in him and could never rid our friendship of the cloud of suspicion that now polluted it.

It was never the same between us so I made the decision not to associate with him any longer. Without being able to prove his innocence or guilt, I knew that missing statue would always cast a shadow over our friendship.

Before I had remodelled and renovated the house, in the summer of 1984, I was contacted by my friend Danny Hamadeh who asked if he could stay in my country home with his wife Ann during their vacation. I told them that they were very welcome. It hadn't yet been done up but they both thought it was beautiful just as it was.

While they were there came news that a serial rapist and burglar dubbed 'the Fox', whose victims were both male and female, was on the loose in the area. They weren't that bothered until the security alarm went off in the house. Danny's immediate thought was that the Fox had come to get them. He was scared, but instead of checking out the situation himself, he asked his wife Ann to investigate.

"You are the man, you should be the one to find out what's going on," Ann told him... and quite right too!

"No, no, the Fox is English. You are English. This is your country," he said. "It's better that you deal with this." Ann was a brave girl. She went from room to room with Danny some way behind her. They rang my neighbour, John Blend, who soon turned up and switched off the alarm, which he said had been triggered by mistake.

"Don't be frightened! The Fox hasn't come here... at least not yet," he said with a laugh. Danny and Ann weren't laughing, though. They were so terrified that they packed and left early the next morning.

Much to our relief, the police nabbed the Fox that same year. He turned out to be a thirty-two-year-old labourer called Malcolm Fairley from a mining village in Sunderland. Thanks to a mass of forensic evidence, he admitted his crimes and was sentenced to eighty-two years in prison.

My father, God rest his soul, also enjoyed staying at the house, but he could never manage to get his bearings or work out directions. On one of his many visits, I put a small white car at his disposal, which for some reason we had named 'Barbara'.

Sometimes he would bring his driver Abou Saeed along with him. We gave Abou Saeed the nickname 'Shayboub', who was the brother of Antar, a legendary sixth century warrior and poet from Nejd, now in modern-day Saudi Arabia. Abou Saeed hated being called that, but we couldn't get out of the habit. Shayboub was an excellent driver, but like my father hardly spoke a word of English, which meant they were always getting lost and sometimes they would drive around in circles for hours before managing to find their way home.

Once I asked him, "Where do you go with my father on those long drives, Shayboub?"

"I don't know. I'm too caught up with driving. I get lost. I turn and turn and at last I find my way back." We all laughed. "But there is one thing I would like you to explain," he said.

"Yes, what's that?"

"If we drive down the M4 Motorway, we always end up in London. If we take the M40 Motorway, we end up in London. Is the city turning? How come whichever road we take, we find ourselves in London?" I laughed and told him, "To be very honest with you, Shayboub, that's a mystery I'm unable to explain."

Some years later, I was offered a huge amount of money for my place in Flackwell Heath, but when I casually mentioned the offer to my family they were distressed at the thought that I might let that house go. That never even crossed my mind.

I've never regretted that spontaneous decision. Being there gives me the kind of mental relaxation I can't find anywhere else. I'm glad I didn't buy a place in London. That isn't the kind of fast lifestyle I crave. I have no interest in late nights socialising with fickle friends in seedy nightclubs or casinos like so many others I know, who get caught up on that merry-go-round and don't know how to step off before they become old and tired before their time.

I loved the area so much that many years later I enthusiastically became the new owner of a historical English hotel, The Monkey Island Hotel, that has subsequently been renamed The Monkey Island Lodge. It was set on Monkey Island, a private island off Bray, two miles away from Maidenhead and accessible only by boat or across a footbridge. The island had been purchased in 1723 by Charles Spencer, the third Duke of

Marlborough, a keen angler, who built two structures characterised as a fishing lodge and fishing temple.

Made from wood blocks cut to resemble stone slabs, the Lodge contained a banqueting room with a ceiling painted by the French artist Andie de Clermont, depicting monkeys in various poses, although historically Monkey Island was probably a corruption of 'Monks Eyot', an archaic English word for island. As far back as 1120, during the time of King Henry I, the island had been home to an abbey. Monkey Island later became a favourite retreat of Queen Elizabeth I, who used to host French and Spanish ambassadors there, as the island was considered politically neutral ground.

I was captivated by the island's history, the quintessential English character of the hotel and its four and a half acres of landscaped gardens that included beds of sweet-scented lavender lining the pathway to the entrance. As it wasn't too far away from my Buckinghamshire home, I occasionally went there for dinner or high tea on the lawn with friends and family and we always had a jolly time.

One day, while in the company of my good friends John and Eva McGaw, I enthused about the hotel on Monkey Island and told them how much I'd love to own it. As it happened, they knew the proprietor because it was to be the venue of their upcoming wedding. They introduced me to the Iraqi owner, Basil Faidi, during their wedding celebrations, and I must have come up with an offer he couldn't refuse. Before I knew it, it was mine.

That acquisition was fairly capricious on my part. I gave no thought at all to whether or not the hotel would make money even as I was appending my signature to the contract. It was something that, to me, felt right at the time.

Although I thoroughly enjoyed owning Monkey Island and hosting so many of my friends there, it was no money-spinner. For one thing, a unique boutique with so much character demands its owner to be on the premises or, at the very least, should have an enthusiastic, committed manager with a big personality and society connections.

Besides the fact that I couldn't be around as much as I'd have liked, because the hotel's Temple and Pavilion were Grade I historically-listed buildings, it was virtually impossible to get necessary permissions for renovations and expansion. It was with a heavy heart that I put it up for sale.

Colin Perkins, a friend from Cookham, was upset with my decision. "You don't need to sell," he said. "Why don't you and I become partners, then we can look for a third partner and manage it together." It was a good idea as Colin loved the place almost as much as I did, but, unfortunately, the bad experiences with partners I'd had in the past prevented me from going ahead.

Monkey Island was sold to a Dr Andreas Papadakis, a cultured Greek-Cypriot-born publisher, in 2007. Some time afterwards, Colin came to Dubai and told me how disappointed he was that I had sold the hotel to someone else.

"Khalaf, I'm your friend. You should have allowed me first priority," he said.

I explained that the new owner didn't get the chance to enjoy his ownership either. Tragically, Dr Papadakis passed away just a few months after he took possession. When Colin heard the sad news, he was shocked and then relieved that he didn't buy it. This rather superstitious fellow grinned and said, "Ouf! Thank goodness I dodged the bullet."

To be honest, I still miss the place. Whenever I'm in the UK, I usually visit to have coffee with the owners and staff to wish them well – and to be reassured that the place is receiving the tender loving care it deserves.

* * *

Shortly after I first set eyes on the house which gave me the kind of inner peace for which my body had been crying out for some time, a seismic shift towards peace in the Middle East occurred.

On 17 September 1978, the Egyptian President Anwar El Sadat and the Israeli Prime Minister Menachem Begin signed the Camp David Accords, witnessed by President Jimmy Carter, who had brokered negotiations.

Anwar El Sadat, had been determined to pursue peace with Israel at all costs. The previous year, in 1977, he told parliamentarians "I am ready to go to the Israeli parliament itself and discuss it with them," a statement which all those present dismissed as nothing more than pleasant-sounding rhetoric.

That was until Sadat agreed to be interviewed by CBS anchorman Walter Cronkite, when the Egyptian leader said he was ready to fly to Jerusalem within days, subject to receiving an invitation from the Israeli Prime Minister Menachem Begin.

Soon afterwards, Cronkite interviewed Begin and asked him whether he was willing to receive his country's long-time enemy. "Any time, any day he is prepared to come, I will receive him cordially," came his answer.

Six days after the latter Cronkite interview on 20 November 1977, the Egyptian President boarded a plane at a military base close to the Suez Canal for the thirty-minute journey to Tel Aviv's Ben Gurion Airport.

Israelis were both dumbfounded at Sadat's sheer daring, and jubilant at the prospect of ending conflict. Many Israelis worried that the Egyptian plane heading their way might be delivering a bomb instead of Egypt's President, which was why the Israeli military was put on a state of high alert.

The Egyptian public was split. There were those who were relieved that they would no longer have to send their sons to war, while many others believed Sadat's visit was nothing less than treachery. The Palestinians and most other Arabs felt a deep sense of betrayal.

Personally, I was 100 per cent against Sadat's unilateral approach, which I believed had no chance of long-term success without the wholehearted support of Egypt's Arab allies.

The visit was so impromptu and extraordinary that Israeli diplomatic officials scratched their heads wondering how they were going to come up with Egyptian flags and brass bands who knew how to play the Egyptian national anthem.

On the day, Israeli newspapers had front page headlines welcoming their visitor, and Israeli radio stations broadcast Egyptian music and the songs of Umm Kulthum, who was well-known among Mizrahi Jews descending from the Middle East and North Africa.

On arrival, Sadat was greeted by Prime Minister Begin and his old foes from the 1973 War, Moshe Dayan and Golda Meir. He even surprised the latter with a kiss on the cheek amid the deafening sounds of a twenty-one gun salute.

His words before Israel's Knesset went a long way to allay Arab fears.

"First, I have not come here for a separate agreement between Egypt and Israel," he said. "This is not part of the policy of Egypt." Sadly, events didn't turn out as he had hoped. The rest of the Arab world declined to come to the table and were not sincerely encouraged to do so by either the US or Israel, which were not prepared to give way on the kind of concessions that would have been demanded by all Arab states.

Six months after Camp David, on 26 March 1979, the leaders of Egypt and Israel appended their signatures to a peace treaty, making Egypt the first Arab country to recognise the Jewish state. Normalisation of relations between the two countries began in 1980, but until today the peace between Egypt and Israel is a very cold peace indeed, especially at street level.

Whenever I think about Sadat's legacy nowadays I feel a sense of ambivalence. No doubt he proved to be a courageous statesman by flying into the heart of enemy territory bearing an olive branch. On the one hand, he regained Egypt's occupied territories without any loss of blood and improved his country's economy, but the negative repercussions of that treaty are still being felt.

In retaliation, the Arab League suspended Egypt's membership from 1979 until 1989. I think that was a mistake on the part of Arab League member countries, as without the leadership of the biggest Arab nation, Egypt – historically known by Arabs as the *Umm al-Dunya* or Mother of the World – the Arab world is fragile.

Egypt has never managed to regain the influence it once wielded over the region ever since. According to the terms of the peace treaty, it can no longer militarily defend the Palestinians and has had to cap the size of the Egyptian army.

Sadat could have been an even greater leader than his predecessor, Gamal Abdel Nasser, if he had only taken the time to persuade his fellow Arab leaders to join him at Camp David, even if that meant postponing negotiations for several years. His biggest error was to go it alone.

My opinion – and I am confident that history will confirm it – is that Sadat's policy of direct, face-to-face negotiation is the only one that can bring about a comprehensive Middle Eastern peace and a Palestinian state. But what is needed now are Arab leaders empowered to negotiate on behalf of all Arab states, not just their own.

The involvement of the US and the Quartet (the US, the EU, the UN and Russia) has pushed peace further away than ever before. Also to blame is the Arab world for hanging back, when Arabs should be at the forefront of the peace process rather than onlookers.

This isn't the West's problem, it's ours. The US and its Western allies don't care if the injury heals or not; they are only concerned with their own interests. All the blah-blah and endless peace conferences are nothing more than propaganda, to prove to the world – and especially the poorer third-world countries – that they're working hard to end Palestinian suffering.

It's no secret that every White House has been staunchly backing Israel with massive sums in aid, loan guarantees and fighter jets, helicopters and weapons. Moreover, US leaders, both Republican and Democrat, faithfully express their devotion to Israel during annual AIPAC meets. In this case, how can the US be expected or trusted to act as an impartial broker?

Palestinians have tried every means to obtain their rights, from armed militancy to heartfelt appeals to the international community, abidance by international law, cooperation with Washington's demands and calls to the United Nations for justice. On every front, the door has been barred.

There is no magical potion to instantaneously cure the Middle East's ills. But it seems to me that, as a first step, the Palestinian factions should settle their differences and come together to speak with one voice, which is no easy task when secular Fatah and Islamist Hamas are ideologically at opposite poles.

Secondly, the Palestinians should admit failure in spite of all their efforts due to their inherent lack of bargaining power, and hand an irrevocable power of attorney to a committee that includes prominent patriotic Palestinians and representatives of the GCC states, empowering such committee to negotiate with Israel on their behalf.

Thirdly, the Arab League should use all its clout to demand that America and the Quartet step aside to make way for direct Arab–Israeli discussions on the basis of the 2002 Arab Initiative, first unveiled during an Arab League summit held in Beirut.

That initiative promises full recognition of Israel by all twenty-two Arab League member countries as well as normalisation of relations, provided Israel withdraws behind 1967 lines; is also willing to negotiate a just solution to the Palestinian refugee problem and will agree to East Jerusalem being the capital of a new Palestinian state.

If all the above steps are taken, I strongly believe that a positive result will be achieved for all parties concerned.

Disappointed with the lack of any serious peace process due to the intransigence of Israel's Prime Minister Binyamin Netanyahu, in 2011 the Palestinian President Mahmoud Abbas applied to the United Nations for its recognition of Palestinian statehood, which requires a 'yes' vote from nine of the fifteen Security Council member countries. Unfortunately, this move was dead in the water from the get-go as the US announced it would wield its veto power.

While the US President Barack Obama has been a strong proponent of a Palestinian state formed loosely around pre-1967 borders, it appears he has succumbed to pressure from Israel, the pro-Israel lobby in the US and Congress – which has threatened to punish the Palestinians by cutting aid – to block the attempt. Cynics suggest that Mr Obama is more interested in firming up his re-election chances than genuinely pursuing peace. Whether we like it or not, the US is the key to a Palestinian state. As Israel's benefactor, it is the only country with the power to twist Tel Aviv's arm. It seems to me that it's beyond time that the Arab world did some arm-twisting of its own.

As George Bernard Shaw once said, "Peace is not only better than war, but infinitely more arduous." I can only hope that my generation bothers to do the work so that our grandchildren won't have to.

CHAPTER 11

Joy and Sorrow

"Keep me away from the wisdom which does not cry, the philosophy which does not laugh and the greatness which does not bow before children."

– Kahlil Gibran

The greatest sadness of my life was the death of my parents. I was comforted by the thought that they had enjoyed long, happy and productive lives and were greatly loved by their children. I knew that their passing was part of the natural cycle of life, but that didn't make their loss any less devastating. I was a man when they left me, yet I still felt like an orphaned child.

To lose a beloved parent is to feel the absence of the only people who will ever love you absolutely and unconditionally. Suddenly, too, one is faced with one's own mortality, as well as the realisation that the buck stops here.

My mother was the first to leave us. When she fell ill, we took her straight to London for treatment; but in spite of the best efforts of some of the finest specialists, she passed away a few months later. I was deeply saddened, but I believed that she was with God, which gave me some peace of mind.

The most difficult thing for me was how to tell my father she was no longer with us. Old age had made him frail, which was why he had been unable to be with my mother when she drew her last breath.

Father instinctively knew that there was something wrong and rightly believed that we were keeping a secret from him. When he was sitting peacefully, I leant over to gently kiss him on his head. He looked up at me, his eyes filled with questions, when I said, "May Allah give you patience and health... Our mother has gone from us." I tried my best to be strong for him. He had always been my source of strength and now it was my turn.

I didn't expect him to cry because, according to our belief, we should simply pray for the dead and ask Allah to forgive the deceased person's sins. I thought he would just sit in silence with his grief. Much to my surprise, he held out his arms to embrace me.

While holding me close to his chest, he said, "Son, we must thank Allah that she has moved to the place where He wanted her to go. That's the place where she is supposed to be, not here." He kept his own sadness inside him so as to calm everybody down when I had thought that I would have to calm him down. Even in that poignant, sorrow-filled moment, he was unselfish, wise and loving.

Father continued with his usual daily routine. He would wake up early to pray in the mosque, ensure his camels were being well-cared for and enjoy the company of his children and grandchildren. Then, one day, while in the midst of prayer, he fell down and hurt his hip. We took him to Rashid Hospital where it was operated upon by a local surgeon. It was a botched operation, resulting in my father's hip being badly repositioned and leaving it irreparably damaged.

My father went less than a year after my mother. The impaired hip had impacted upon his mobility, but, of course, it wasn't the cause of his death. He had put on a brave face but he never got over losing his beloved companion through life. They were more than husband and wife. They had been inseparable companions since they married as young teenagers. In all those years, their hearts and souls became intertwined. She was everything to him. She was his mother, sister, wife and best friend.

This is a well-known phenomenon. Death from a broken heart may not be scientific (although there is something called Broken Heart Syndrome), but it's real. When a couple is particularly close and one dies, the other often follows soon afterwards, perhaps because he or she can no longer muster the will to live.

* * *

It wasn't long after my parents went to God that Sheikh Rashid fell ill. He was sixty-nine years old. To all around him, he had always seemed invincible. His health had always been good and his energy boundless. Initially, his personal physician diagnosed that his weakened condition had been caused by a virus; but when he didn't fully recover, it was found that he had suffered a stroke.

His physical rehabilitation was slow despite being treated by the world's best-known heart doctors, but he retained his sharp mind. By 1982, Sheikh Rashid was almost back to his old self and in June that year he delighted his people by appearing in public after a long absence. They turned out in large numbers to watch his motorcade pass by and to cheer his recovery.

He seemed to improve by leaps and bounds from then on, although he would often travel to see his doctors in London, Chicago and Houston who were monitoring his progress. He soon became well enough to travel to Jebel Ali to inspect a new desalination plant and Dubai Aluminium Company.

Then, on 17 May 1983, his wife, Sheikha Latifa bint Hamdan Al Nahyan, suddenly died during a visit to London where she had gone for a routine medical check-up. Sheikh Rashid took the news badly; their partnership had been strong and true for forty-four years. Unlike most rulers of the day, he had only married once.

From the day he lost his wife, his public appearances were few and far between. He still took a close interest in Dubai's affairs and was the ultimate decision-maker, but because he was unable to fulfil most of his duties, they were divided between his sons, Sheikh Maktoum, Sheikh Hamdan and Sheikh Mohammed.

Throughout his long illness, Sheikh Rashid still met with family and friends almost daily at his majlis in Zabeel Palace. I used to go there most afternoons just to wish him well and to let him know how much he meant to me and everyone else. He was always eager to learn news of old friends and to know what was happening in Dubai. He could hardly hide his frustration that he could no longer get out and about to see for himself.

It was very painful to witness the most energetic person I had ever known in my entire life disintegrate before my eyes. His mane of newly-grey hair, gaunt cheeks and untrimmed beard made me compare this greatest of men to an injured lion. Each time I left his majlis, I could never stop my eyes welling up as I prepared to lose yet another person who was dear to me.

* * *

In 1980, I moved with my wife and children into the new house I had been building in Jumeirah, which is still home to me today. It is modern, spacious, light and airy with seven bedrooms, several large reception rooms and a large state-of-the-art kitchen. When the weather is nice, our raised veranda is where our extended family gathers to talk about the events of the day or to receive close family friends.

Later, I constructed a separate smaller house in the grounds to serve as my majlis, as well as two large villas for my sons, Mohammed and Ahmad.

My son Rashid, who likes his independence, declined to live inside the gated family compound, choosing instead to build his own house close by. The villas are surrounded by many kinds of bushes and fruit trees, such as date palms, mango trees and lemon trees, and at certain times of the year the air is fragrant with the scent of jasmine and other sweet-smelling flowers. Our years in the *barasti* or when we were cramped into two rooms in the Jumeirah 1 house soon faded into distant memory.

I was now the proud father of six children: sons Rashid, Mohammed and Ahmad, and daughters Noura, Amna and Meera. My three lovely daughters are my life's joy. They are closer to me than my sons and are as attached to me as I am to them. There is a saying that 'a daughter may outgrow your lap, but she will never outgrow your heart'. That's so true. My sons are much closer to their mother than to me.

Every morning at 7 a.m., I eat breakfast with Noura and Amna at home, except on Fridays, when I usually take them for buffet breakfast to my hotel on Jumeirah Beach, the Habtoor Grand Resort and Spa. My youngest daughter, Meera, has lived in Abu Dhabi ever since she married my cousin, Abdullah Khalaf Al Otaiba, who is the General Manager of the National Bank of Abu Dhabi 'Corporate'.

Meera never stays away for long, because she fears that I might forget her or prefer her sisters' company to hers. If ever she thinks I'm displaying any sort of favouritism, she shouts at me. When she comes to Dubai, she stays with her husband at their house in Arabian Ranches, but now they plan to build a new one next to mine. Before her marriage, she worked in my Group's head office as part of the Al Habtoor Research and Information team, under the guidance of Leslie Pope, a well-respected English academician who passed away some years ago.

She thrived in the workplace until she married Abdullah at the age of twenty-four. I think her time working in my company was well spent. Today, she is not only an excellent homemaker and mother, she is also a modern business-minded woman who works enthusiastically with her husband to build their future together.

Like those of all my children, her marriage was arranged. Meera says she prefers that way of doing things and congratulates me on making the right choice on her behalf. As she says, "If my father said 'yes' about a suitor, I could always refuse. But if he said 'no' I could not say 'yes'." That's true. I would never have forced any of my children to marry someone they objected to and, by the same token, I would not have agreed to them marrying someone I didn't feel was capable of making them happy.

Meera had only seen a photograph of her groom prior to their wedding day. She thanks God that she has a good husband, but, as the baby of the family who admits she was always fussed over and spoiled, she was very homesick in the beginning.

"I used to look at your picture and cry, and whenever I heard the songs of Umm Kulthum, I would feel sad remembering how we used to listen to her songs in the car," she told me. Meera is the most sensitive of my children and also the most volatile and outspoken. I think her sisters are a little afraid of her at times.

I make sure that I spend time with Noura and Amna each afternoon (and Meera when she's in Dubai), so that I know what's happening in their lives. They usually prepare a platter of fresh fruits for me and while I'm eating they tell me stories, make me laugh and take my mind far away from the pressure of work.

On the rare occasions that I don't feel very well, they hardly move from my bed, ensuring that I have everything I need and doing their best to lift my morale. If they are unusually quiet or preoccupied, I try to get to the bottom of what may be bothering them and do my best to cheer them up.

All three of my daughters are clever and intelligent. My eldest two, Noura and Amna, graduated in law from the Beirut Arab University but did not go on to practise law, preferring to devote their time to being wives and mothers.

Amna, a quiet and sensible young woman, is the Director of Al Habtoor Group's community schools – Emirates International School in Jumeirah and Emirates International School Meadows – a post she takes very seriously. Her sweet daughter Hamda, who was named after my wife, is called 'the Princess' as she is the most beautiful among all my granddaughters. During summer, I usually take Amna and her daughter Hamda with me on my travels.

Noura is very active and energetic. She does not like to sit around doing nothing. In many ways, her character is very similar to mine, but there is one major difference. No matter how much money she has in her budget, she cannot help herself from overspending. Her sisters love shopping, but at least they keep some cash in reserve for their savings accounts.

Noura is the mother of two boys and four girls; her youngest, Khalaf and Meera, are twins. Khalaf is crazy about football and sometimes brings his football with him to our daily family lunches. He's a real cheeky little chap. When I tell him off for shouting, he answers, "Grandfather, you are ugly!". I can't help but laugh at the way he says it. I tell him, "You and your father are ugly." He always says, "Give me money... I want to go to Spinneys" (a Middle East chain of supermarkets that has recently expanded operations to North Africa and Southeast Asia). He never dreams of saying "please", and if I don't fork out immediately, he gets cross and kicks my feet. He's a feisty little thing, a bit like me at his age. Perhaps that's why I love him so much.

A year after we moved to our new house, I took the whole family to Paris and brought along a Lebanese friend, who led me to understand that he knew French. It turned out that he knew only two words, "bonjour" and "oui". Noura was only around eleven years old at the time, but was able to speak basic French as she had learned the language in school. She did her best to translate for us. I was really proud of her.

On a subsequent trip to the French capital, I invited a young English couple, John and Sandra Anson, friends from Buckinghamshire, to join us. I remembered that Sandra had once told me that she understood some French. But as soon as we arrived in France, it became clear that her knowledge of French was almost non-existent. That didn't really matter, though, because they were both such pleasant travelling companions.

We checked into a wonderful old Art Déco hotel, the Prince de Galles, just off Champs-Elysées on the Avenue Georges V, and made our way to our rooms for a good night's sleep. No such luck!

I was woken just after midnight by ear-splitting rumbles and vibrations. What's this, an earthquake? Is it a war? For a while I thought I must be dreaming. After all, we were in Paris, not Beirut. I ran to the window, pulled back the curtains and was startled to see soldiers, officers, tanks and armoured personnel carriers on the streets outside as far as I could see. I don't think I've ever been so scared in my life. I didn't know whether this signified the start of World War III or a second French Revolution.

I remember swearing under my breath thinking, how could we have such bad luck? We come from the Arab world where there are revolutions and wars happening all the time, and in Dubai we've only watched them on TV. Now, here we are in democratic France and we find ourselves right in the middle of the action.

Within minutes, everyone in my party came knocking on the door of my suite. They were confused and worried. John and Sandra were sure we were caught up in a conflict and everyone else agreed. What else could it be?

"Okay. No one must look out of the window," I said, taking charge. "Turn all the lights off. Hide." But nobody was inclined to dive under the bed or leap into a closet. We were all frozen in a state of inaction wondering what to do next.

At first, we were so terrified that we were unable to muster up enough common sense to go down to the concierge to find out what was going on. When I realised that everyone was depending on me for leadership, I took control of my faculties and tried my best to lessen everyone's fears. "I'm going down to the lobby," I said. "You stay here."

I washed my face, quickly dressed and took the lift down to the hotel's reception area, expecting to see a big crowd of fearful guests in dressing gowns and slippers. To my great surprise, nobody was around. The lights had been dimmed and everything looked fairly normal. I found that scene so surreal under the circumstances that I was more fearful than before. How could we be the only ones in the hotel to have heard the noise and seen all that military apparatus?

I gingerly peered through a window and was horrified to see uniformed soldiers patrolling with heavy artillery less than five yards away. Oh, no! I'm not going out there, I thought, as I went in search of hotel staff.

There was nobody at the reception and to cap it all, the concierge was asleep. I assumed he had no idea his country was preparing for revolution or an invasion. He must be deaf not to have woken up with all that noise going on. I caught hold of his shoulder and he quickly jumped to his feet.

"Bonsoir Monsieur, how can I help you?"

"What's happening?" I asked. He looked at me with a blank expression. He had no idea what I was talking about and I was unable to explain as his English wasn't up to much. There was nothing for it but to grab hold of him and march him to the entrance door.

"Look... Look at all these soldiers!" I said. "What are they doing here?" He was more scared than me at the sight and any English he might have known was forgotten. As he babbled away incomprehensibly to himself, I dragged him outside by his sleeve and together we walked over to one of the officers. The temperature was around thirty degrees centigrade but my blood ran so cold it might as well have been below zero.

"Good evening, Sir. Would you mind telling me what's happening?" I asked. The officer didn't speak any English at all, but by then the concierge had woken up from his stupor sufficiently to be able to translate a few words. The officer's stern face broke out in a wide grin which turned into a hearty laugh. Why is he laughing? Is he mad?

"Don't you know that today is 14 July?" he said.

"Yes, I'm well aware of the date," I answered. "It's 14 July... so what?"

"Today is Bastille Day. It's the day we celebrate our Revolution. It's a national holiday. We are here to prepare for a big parade in the morning. Don't be concerned. There's nothing to worry about."

Once that was cleared up, the shaken concierge excused himself to dash to the toilet and I went back to my suite to tell the others that all was well. Even so, we were too hyped up to get much slept that night.

In the morning, we walked the short distance to the Avenue Champs-Elysées to watch the military parade that traditionally takes place in view of the President of the Republic who, at that time, was François Mitterrand. The atmosphere of gaiety and fun was a complete contrast from the night before. I can still picture John carrying my youngest son, Ahmad, on his shoulders so that the little fellow could enjoy the spectacle as much as we did and not get caught up in a sea of legs.

Later that same day, I had an appointment to visit an Egyptian family who lived nearby. I asked John and Sandra if they wouldn't mind taking my family out to lunch. "I'll be back soon," I told them.

Some hour and a half later, I found them on the corner of Champs-Elysées and the Avenue Georges V. They were sitting around a table outside Fouquet's – one of the most elegant and best-known café-restaurants in Paris and a once favourite haunt of such world-famous celebrities as Winston Churchill, Franklin D. Roosevelt, Jackie Kennedy-Onassis and Charlie Chaplin.

"I'm starving. Whatever you had, please order the same for me," I said to John.

"We haven't eaten anything yet. We haven't even ordered."

"Why is that?" I asked. "When did you arrive?"

"We've been here for ages. I keep calling the waiter 'Excuse me, *garçon, Monsieur... S'il vous plaît*'. He looks at me then purposely walks away."

"I see. Let's see if he's going to ignore me as well," I said. I caught his eye before calling out "Come here!" in a loud voice. I didn't feel that he deserved any courtesies.

He immediately came to our table.

"*Oui, Monsieur?*"

I asked him why he had left my friends and family waiting around for such a long time without being served. He made the excuse that he had been very busy and didn't hear them calling him.

"That's funny," John said. "Why did he ignore the Englishman and jump to the command of the Arab?"

"I don't know, my friend."

"I know why," he said. "This just goes to prove that the French really do hate the English." There may have been a grain of truth in John's conclusion. France and England may be neighbours separated only by a twenty-five-mile-wide strip of water, but throughout history the two countries have been foes and competitors.

Stereotypically, the French think the British are arrogant for expecting the whole world to speak English, and the British see the French as snobs who pretend they can't understand English even when they do. They even have uncomplimentary labels for each other. In England, the French are known as 'frogs' because they eat frog legs and, in France, the English are called '*les rosbifs*' (the roast beefs) for the same reason.

French people resent that so many English words, such as '*le shopping*', '*le weekend*', '*un leader*', '*le football*', '*airbag*' and '*e-mail*' have polluted their language. In 2010, an alliance of French groups calling themselves guardians of the French language characterised the invasion of English as "threatening the French language more than the Nazis did".

The following day, we hired two limousines and drove to the dazzling Palace of Versailles. We all wanted to see inside this former court of French kings and queens, but were deterred by hundreds of people queuing up to buy tickets. We were not used to queuing in Dubai and couldn't contemplate waiting in line for an hour or more; but at the same time, we were in Europe and were obliged to respect the rules of the country we were in. What to do?

I didn't want to disappoint the children, so I asked John and Sandra to take some money, walk to the front of the queue, speak to whomever was inside the ticket kiosk and try to get us in before everyone else. That was the way things were done in the Middle East in those days; not so much now, since the English queuing disease has hit our shores.

They looked at one another with disapproval, before John said they couldn't do such a thing. Anyone looking at their expressions might have thought I was handing them balaclavas and asking them to rob a bank.

Queue jumping in England is rare and when it occurs it is frowned upon. The English queue up patiently for however long it takes without much complaint; they accept it as one of life's unpleasant but necessary chores. I wasn't surprised when John and Sandra turned down my request. I knew them very well. They are straightforward, respectable people who like to go by the book. There was nothing for it but to go back to Paris. That was, until my daughter Noura piped up.

"Father, give me the money," she said.

"Why? What are you going to do?"

"Please father, just give me the money. I'll show you."

I can see her now with her curly brown hair and white schoolgirl socks running up towards the ticket window with all the confidence in the world, while all the adults, including myself, were cringing with embarrassment, hoping that nobody in the queue would realise what she was up to. We watched her approach a man near the front of the queue and saw her stretch out her hand to offer him the ticket money.

"Excuse me, please help us. We come from Dubai. We are so many," she said in perfect English. "Would you be kind enough to buy our tickets for us? In return, we would like to pay the entrance for you and your family," she told him. The man laughed, happy to oblige the charming little stranger. Her mission accomplished, Noura looked back towards us and whistled to get our attention, as we were about 100 metres far from her in the queue.

My little Noura saved the day. Because of her courage and quick wits, we all got to marvel at the grandeur of the palace, including its exquisite Louis furniture, rare artworks and stunning gardens. I'm sure that John and Sandra still didn't agree with our queue-jumping scheme on principle, but that didn't stop them enjoying the outcome too.

The next day we were booked First Class on the TGV high-speed train to Geneva from the Gare de Lyon. As we sat facing each other in a semi-private compartment, the atmosphere was light and jolly. The service and the food were great; the view from the windows even greater.

In those days, the food and service on European trains were superlative; unfortunately, both have gone downhill since. Our meal wasn't pre-ordered; it was a standard set lunch served to all First Class passengers. We noticed this particular meal included pork, which John was happily tucking into.

When we saw that Ahmad, who was sitting next to him, was about to eat the pork too, I called out "Ahmad, no, no! Don't eat that. Remember! We don't eat pork."

At just five years old, Ahmad had a mind of his own. He wasn't about to take orders from me as to what he should eat and shouldn't eat. He gobbled down the pork before I could stop him just to challenge me. From that day, John used to tease him, calling him 'Porky Ahmad'.

There was nothing called the EU or the Schengen Zone at that time. When we arrived in Geneva, we just showed our passports to immigration officers and that was that. Getting from country to country was so easy then.

It was as hot in Switzerland as it had been in Paris, if not hotter. There were no air conditioners in our hotel and we all had difficulty sleeping. We asked for fans, but instead, they provided mobile chillers. The following morning, I asked the reception to arrange for us to visit the highest mountain in the Alps Mont Blanc. Everyone had been talking about Mont Blanc as though it was the greatest place on earth. The way they went on about it, I was expecting something truly amazing and different.

Cars were organised to take us to the foot of the mountain at Chamonix, which, much to my surprise, was in France not Switzerland. Nobody had told me that when we set off, not that it would have made any difference. A French tour guide approached and told us to wait for the *téléférique* (cable car) that would take us up to the mountain's summit.

After a short wait, we clambered inside the cable car and up we went. At the top I breathed in a lungful of crisp, clean mountain air and looked around me... at nothing. I looked to the left, the right, behind me and in front of me, but there was only a great expanse of nothing. I looked at my family; I looked at the tour guide.

"Why did you bring us up here?" I asked him.

"To see the view... All our tourists love the view."

"What view? Look, I've no interest in being here for a moment longer. We need to go back down the mountain now, immediately, so we can find somewhere to have lunch."

The panorama, consisting of snow-tipped mountain tops and green valleys, was pleasant but didn't really do a lot for me or match my expectations. I didn't think it compared in any way to the view from the windows of my house in Flackwell Heath, which is far more diverse and interesting. As far as I'm concerned, one mountain is pretty much like all the others.

"Sorry, but the cable car is full up now. You will have to get in the queue and wait for thirty minutes until it returns." I started to feel like a prisoner on Alcatraz. I was annoyed that we had come all this way for nothing and worse, that we had to hang around just to get away from there. I took a deep breath and tried to make the best of things, which wasn't easy as I am by nature impatient.

My mood changed for the better after having a memorable lunch at a very nice mountainside restaurant where the most tender, juiciest meat imaginable was served. And those who had told me that Mont Blanc was something like the eighth Wonder of the World weren't strangled after all.

* * *

Travel is nice, but going home is always nicer. Everything was so easy in Dubai compared to Europe. It took only fifteen minutes or so for us to disembark from our plane, clear immigration, pick up our luggage and exit Dubai Airport. It was like walking into fairyland.

The whole place was lit up – the roads, the buildings, everything and everywhere. Dubai was no longer dry and dusty. The municipality had planted palm trees and an army of gardeners tended parks as well as grassy verges and flower beds lining the main roads.

The early to mid-1980s marked the beginning of an era when everything was available and so much was fresh and exciting. Nationals and expats had swelled to around 200,000 and were revelling in a life of ease and plenty.

Supermarket shelves were groaning with every kind of imported foodstuff, including Australian lamb, American beef, giant prawns from Thailand, and things most people take for granted like fresh milk and bottled mineral water. Tens of new restaurants had opened up and most of the hotels, including my own, were offering vast buffet breakfasts, lunches and dinners that outdid anything we saw in Paris or London.

The nice thing was that nobody was treated as just another number. You only had to eat once in a restaurant and the staff would remember your name months later – and would sometimes even recall how you liked your steak cooked or what you drank with your meal. Visitors were made to feel special; everyone was treated like a VIP.

There were boutiques selling the latest fashions from Paris and London in Satwa and Deira, and in our lone shopping mall, the Al Ghurair Centre, could be found every type of imported cloth and extensive ranges of leather shoes, sunglasses, watches and perfumes. Foreign newspapers were now available with newsagents, but at that time were heavily censored with black marker pen or, in some cases, were sold with entire pages ripped out.

The city came alive in the evenings now that there were so many places to go and so much to do. Residents were spoilt for choice when it came to deciding what to do during the weekend. People would often head to the simple Sandy Beach Hotel near the Hajar Mountain range in Khorfakkan, or to the nearby Hilton in Fujairah to dive in the warm waters of the Gulf of Oman that merges with the Arabian Sea.

Or they would drive past orange-coloured dunes to the mountainous area of Hatta that borders Oman, where they would be warmly greeted by the Hatta Fort Hotel's warm and effusive General Manager, Sergio Magnaldi, before their stay in one of the Hatta Fort Hotel's Alpine-style chalets. Magnaldi's professed love of Hatta wasn't just sales talk. He retired with his wife, Sandy, to the Isle of Man in 1997, only to return to his old job six years later.

First-time visitors to Dubai would be bowled over that such an idyllic place even existed. Dubai was like a best-kept secret as it didn't yet feature on the international map. The government now saw a massive potential in tourism, but it wanted to avoid mass tourism, preferring to retain Dubai's exclusive, upmarket ambience. It wasn't until the mid-1980s that Dubai began to be seriously marketed abroad as a new tourist destination for the well-heeled.

Instrumental in the promotion of Dubai far afield was Dubai Duty Free, that opened in 1983 as the first modern, Western-style duty free in the Gulf. It was set up by an Irish advisory team from Aer Rianta; two of the team's members, Colm McLoughlin and George Horan, stayed on as General Manager and Deputy General Manager respectively. They never returned to Ireland; they hold the same positions today.

Head of Marketing was Anita Mehra, a young American-Iranian woman whose father had set up the Iranian hospital in the 1970s. Not only was she responsible for marketing the Duty Free, she was also tasked with marketing Dubai as a hot new destination. Ms Mehra was an outstanding example of women power in what was then a man's world. She did an excellent job.

Dubai Duty Free soon gained a reputation as being the most value-for-money operation of its type; industry awards followed and the organisation began to sponsor international sporting events, such as the Dubai Masters, the first major snooker tournament in the Middle East. Dubai Duty Free is one of the Emirate's greatest success stories. From an initial annual turnover of just 70 million dirhams, its turnover in 2010 reached 4.66 billion dirhams.

Everyone benefited greatly from Dubai's new cosmopolitan, open spirit, which led to a sea change in the lives of local Emirati women. More young girls than ever were college or university-educated, most learned to drive at an early age and were now seen out with their female friends or husbands in restaurants and coffee shops.

In the years ahead, it wasn't uncommon to find Emirati girls working in the public sector and later in private businesses. I was pleased that my daughters were able to enjoy the same kind of freedoms they were used to in the UK and elsewhere in Europe. They were born at the right time, able to enjoy lifestyles that their mother's generation had been deprived of by custom and tradition.

Things were going well for me too. My hotel business was beginning to pick up, Al Habtoor Engineering was receiving substantial contracts and the real estate arm of my group was thriving as so many newcomers needed to rent apartments.

My biggest coup in the early 1980s was beating back strong competition to land the sought-after Mitsubishi sole distributorship for the entire United Arab Emirates.

Until that time, most agencies and distributorships were in the hands of non-UAE companies, so it hadn't really crossed my mind to pitch for that distributorship. That was, until I was approached by one of Mitsubishi's sales managers, Ghazi Shaker, and Aken Riknor, an American guy who had a very strong relationship with Mitsubishi's top executives in Tokyo and who was the current distributor's General Manager.

They told me that Mitsubishi wasn't happy with the way that A.A. Al Zayani & Sons from Bahrain was handling the distributorship. "They're not doing well at all; they're not selling enough," said Shaker.

"We heard about you and thought you might be interested in taking it because it isn't really functioning at present. Rather than allowing it to be handed to someone outside, we figured it's better for someone here in the UAE to take it."

To be fair to the Al Zayanis, the problems with their franchise wasn't so much due to a bad business plan, but rather a protracted interfamily dispute that led to boardroom wrangling.

That sounded like a good opportunity to me and, as I've never been one to walk away from a sound business opportunity, I got in touch with Mitsubishi's head office in Tokyo; and within no time the agreement was signed.

Until then, it had all been smooth sailing. We liked and trusted our Japanese partners, they had confidence that we could do a good job of marketing their product, so everything in the garden was rosy... Well, it would have been if the green-eyed monster hadn't popped out of nowhere to show its ugly face.

There were several influential people in the region pushing to take the franchise, with yet more influential individuals supporting their bids. Some of them approached me directly to ask whether I would be willing to pull out of my contract with Mitsubishi and I discovered that higher authorities had written to the manufacturer recommending other potential distributors.

Needless to say, I wasn't very happy with that cut-throat state of affairs. Full marks to Mitsubishi's management! All those demands, including a few from top UAE officials, were rejected or ignored. In fact, the Japanese made it clear that their decision was set in stone, and if I wasn't allowed to import their cars then they were not prepared to partner with anyone else from the UAE.

I can never forget their staunch moral support throughout those tense times. They were under enormous pressure, but not once did they consider bending to it; they even used to forward copies of those letters of recommendation, so that we knew exactly who was sending them.

As relieved as I was to receive Mitsubishi's support, there was still a major hurdle to overcome. Every distribution agency had to be registered with the Ministry of Economy and Commerce. Ours remained in the pending tray of the undersecretary, who, as we came to understand, favoured other interested parties.

After a lengthy and unusual wait, I called the undersecretary to ask him to expedite registration, but it soon became clear that under his watch that wasn't going to happen. He and whoever was pulling his strings clearly believed Mitsubishi would eventually get fed up with the delay and dump me.

However, when I discussed the matter with my Japanese partners, they said, "Don't worry, we're with you. We're prepared to be patient for as long as it takes". They knew that we were a young, energetic and enthusiastic team and saw how successful we had been in construction and in our other business ventures. We were in frequent communication and were always transparent with one another, which laid a solid foundation of trust.

When Sheikh Rashid formed a new cabinet, he appointed Saif Al Jarwan as the new Minister of Economy and Commerce. I think that Mr Al Jarwan already knew about the underhand attempts to cut me out of that contract. As soon as he moved to the Ministry, and without any prompting from me or my people, he instructed that my distributorship should be registered forthwith. Nobody asked him to do that. He did it because he was a man of principle who wasn't about to give envious bigwigs free rein to steal bread from the mouths of their fellow nationals.

That rocky start to our relationship with Mitsubishi in fact cemented our business relationship. They looked upon us more like partners than just another one of their distributors. I was happy to give them every support.

When we took over the Mitsubishi agency, the climate was just right. Japanese cars were relatively inexpensive, but had acquired a reputation for quality and reliability – and, importantly for the UAE, they came with good air conditioning systems that didn't overheat on a hot summer's day like some of their American and European competitors.

In earlier decades, Emiratis and some expats believed bigger was better when choosing an automobile, which was why American 'full size' brands with their plush interiors, cruise control and comfortable suspension were popular. But as petrol prices soared worldwide and parking spaces were at a premium, car manufacturers began downsizing according to the demands of the market. Those problems weren't yet noticeable in the Emirates, but smaller, more compact cars were viewed as more trendy and more fashionable than the American dance halls on wheels.

Consumers started realising that big might be beautiful but was no longer practical, which provided a perfect window for Japanese makers. In the UAE, Mercedes and BMW remained popular choices for men and women, but more and more families were looking for more economic second and third cars for their children while companies began buying utilitarian Japanese cars for their employees. In later years, of course, Japanese manufacturers successfully targeted the luxury car market.

With the Mitsubishi franchise, Al Habtoor Motors was born. In the years that followed, we added Bentley, Rolls Royce and Aston Martin to our stable and enjoyed a long and fruitful partnership with the manufacturers of the latter two, until we amicably parted ways some time ago. More recently, the Turkish coach and truck manufacturers Temsa, McLaren sports cars, and the crème de la crème of luxurious, high-speed cars Bugatti were great additions to our showrooms.

In 2009, the company emerged as the number one dealer of Bentley Motors Worldwide for the year 2008, which was an amazing achievement for my brother Sultan and my son Ahmad who take care of the motoring arm of my group.

* * *

On a regional level, the early 1980s were marred by conflict and instability, beginning with the Iran-Iraq War, that was triggered by disputes over borders, gaining control over the Shatt al-Arab waterway as well as ideological differences. Saddam Hussein was concerned at the effect Iran's Islamic Revolution was having on his country's Shiite population and the Ayatollah Khomeini believed Saddam was oppressing Iraqi Shiites.

The conflict began with border skirmishes in 1980, that led to Iraq's invasion of Iran in September, which eventually erupted into a full-scale war that was to last for eight years. The war left behind it a blood-soaked trail of an estimated half a million Iraqi and Iranian fatalities and achieved nothing in the way of tangible benefits for either side.

Khomeini sent untold thousands of his countrymen to their deaths by ordering 'human wave attacks' and Saddam used chemical weapons both on his Iranian foe and on Iraqi Kurds in Halabja, whom he believed were pro-Iranian traitors. Both countries were left with devastated infrastructure and economies. The only winners were the foreign weapons suppliers, who were laughing all the way to the bank.

In June 1981, Israel bombed Iraq's forty-megawatt nuclear-research reactor Osirak at Al Tuwaitha, near Baghdad, to "put the nuclear genii of Baghdad back in its bottle". The bombing was condemned by all members of the United Nations General Assembly, including the US, which supported a resolution censoring Israel. In reality, that attack had the opposite effect to that intended. Shaken, Saddam summoned his nuclear scientists to instruct them to begin work on building a nuclear weapon when he saw how vulnerable Iraq was to Israeli bombs.

Another shock was the assassination of the Egyptian President, Anwar El Sadat, on 6 October 1981. He was fatally shot while watching an annual Victory Parade. His assassins, led by an Egyptian Army Officer, Khalid Ahmad Al Islambouli, were in one of the trucks carrying troops. As the President watched an air display by the Egyptian Air Force, the killers leapt from their vehicle, lobbed grenades at the dignitaries and raked El Sadat and others seated nearby with automatic gunfire. Eleven others also lost their lives on that day and twenty-eight were wounded, including Egypt's Vice-President Hosni Mubarak, who then assumed the presidency on 14 October.

Al Islambouli, who was a member of the Egyptian Islamic Jihad movement, was tried in a military court, sentenced to death and executed along with three of his co-conspirators in April 1982. The murderers were lauded as martyrs in extremist circles. Tehran named a street after Al Islambouli, news which was not well received in Cairo and caused a diplomatic rift. Lamenting Sadat's death, the US President Ronald Reagan said, "America has lost a great friend, the world has lost a great statesman, and mankind has lost a champion of peace."

A year later, on 6 June 1982, Israeli forces invaded Lebanon for the purposes of destroying the Palestinian Liberation Organisation (PLO), in response to the assassination of an Israeli diplomat and the attempted assassination of another. In fact, the PLO was not involved in either incident and, according to the Syrian political analyst Sami Moubayed, the Israeli Chief of Staff knew this but was looking for pretexts to "screw the PLO". This was in response to Menachem Begin's call: "I want to see Arafat in his bunker".

In September 1982, the PLO withdrew from Lebanon after 1,500 of its fighters were killed and up to 8,000 had been captured. In the first two years of Israel's occupation, almost 18,000 Lebanese civilians were killed along with 1,200 Syrians and 1,800 other nationalities.

The Israelis didn't begin withdrawing from Lebanon until early 1985, when they had set up what Israel called a "security zone" in South Lebanon, that was patrolled by a small contingent of Israeli soldiers in partnership with a Lebanese militia called the South Lebanon Army (SLA), formed by Saad Haddad's 'Government of Free Lebanon' and financed and armed by Tel Aviv.

Major Saad Haddad shamefully defected from the Lebanese Army to shake hands with Israel and was rightly branded a traitor. There were eyewitness reports that members of his militia had cooperated with Lebanese Phalangists, who between 16 September and 18 September 1982 entered the Sabra and Shatila Palestinian refugee camps to massacre up to 3,500 Palestinian men, women and children.

That slaughter shocked the entire world, and in 1993 an Israeli commission found that the Israeli Defence Minister, Ariel Sharon, bore personal but indirect responsibility for the bloodshed.

So many lives wasted; so many hopes dashed; so many dreams unfulfilled... and for what?

Bob Dylan certainly knew what he was talking about when he wrote these lyrics:

> Come you masters of war,
> You that build all the guns,
> You that build the death planes,
> You that build the big bombs,
> You that hide behind walls,
> You that hide behind desks,
> I just want you to know I can see through your masks.

CHAPTER 12
Advocacy

"ANYONE WHO SAYS THEY ARE NOT INTERESTED IN POLITICS IS LIKE A
DROWNING MAN WHO INSISTS HE IS NOT INTERESTED IN WATER."

– ANONYMOUS

Throughout the 1980s and early 1990s, I was an active member of the Emirates Committee for Arab Solidarity, the brainchild of my good friend Taryam Omran Taryam. He founded the Arabic newspaper *Al Khaleej* and was the UAE's first ambassador to Egypt.

Among my co-members were the poets Sultan Al Owais and Mohammed bin Hadher; the writer Abdul Ghaffar Hussein; Faraj bin Hamoodah, Chairman of the Bin Hamoodah Group; Mohammed Abdul Jalil Al Fahim, Chairman of the Al Fahim Group; and Abdullah Saleh, the former Chairman of the National Bank of Dubai. All were loyal friends dedicated to the same mission. Our objective was to collect donations to help displaced and impoverished Palestinian families.

We chased everyone we knew to give something no matter how big or small; our efforts were very successful. We derived immense satisfaction from our activities, in the knowledge that to the cash-strapped Palestinians every dirham counted.

Our work was not just limited to helping Palestinians. In 1992, following a powerful earthquake in Egypt that toppled buildings in Cairo causing thousands of casualties, Abdul Ghaffar Hussein and I were very pleased to present a cheque for 2 million Egyptian pounds on the committee's behalf to Prime Minister Atef Sedki, in the presence of Dr Atef Ebeid (who was later appointed Prime Minister) to help earthquake victims.

I should mention that Abdul Ghaffar, then Deputy Director of Dubai Municipality, was an academic and thinker. He used to write different types of articles on a variety of topics that were mainly published in the *Al Khaleej* newspaper. He was a very funny character. He would get angry over something small, and all of a sudden he would see the funny side and laugh. The nice thing about him is that he was able to laugh at himself.

He told me that one morning, after noticing that the paper had published his picture alongside his article, he called Taryam to say, "Why did you publish such a bad photo of me? Why didn't you choose a better one?".

"This picture took forty-eight hours to prepare. After touch-up and retouch-up, I'm sorry but this was the best we could do," said Taryam.

There is another funny story recounted by Abdul Ghaffar. When one of his municipality colleagues, Obeid Al Marri, came to see him to follow up on some documents, he said "You know, Obeid, I must have an allergy; it started at around 10 a.m. this morning".

"Did you have breakfast?" Obeid asked him.

"Yes, I did."

"What did you eat?"

"*Khamir* (local bread and honey)."

Instead of being sympathetic, Obeid immediately responded with "Huh! I know why you have this allergy; your body isn't used to Arabic bread and honey, it's used to Iranian bread and *mihyawa* (a kind of rotten fish they eat in Iran)". Abdul Ghaffar was upset. "You're really arrogant," he said. But later he laughed and told us that Obeid was probably right.

I wasn't always in such good books with the Egyptian authorities, however. During President Anwar El Sadat's surprise visit to Jerusalem, I let it be known that I believed any peace treaty would be a mistake without the involvement of the Palestinian leadership and Arab states.

It seems that my reaction might have been duly noted by the powers that be in the Egyptian capital. As it happened, while the President was giving his famous speech to the Knesset, I was staying at the Sheraton Hotel in Cairo with a few of my friends. One of them was the famous Egyptian actor and director Hussein Fahmi, later appointed UNDP Goodwill Ambassador for the Arab States.

A Dubai TV representative came to my suite to see me. He said he had some unedited film which he wanted me to take back to Dubai for transmission to the then Director-General of Dubai Television, Riad Al Shuaibi, who owned a private production company. I was made aware of the film's contents and was more than happy to oblige.

On the day of my departure, I put the reel into my suitcase. On reaching the airport, much to my surprise, I was the only one among my fellow passengers who was stopped by a customs officer.

"Please open your suitcase, Sir," he said. I unlocked it and as soon as I opened the lid, his eyes scanned the contents. Almost immediately, he pounced on the film as though he already knew it was there.

"Ah, so you are carrying a movie. This is a crime. I'm sorry but you will have to be sent for investigation," he said. That was rather worrying, as there have been a number of people who were placed under investigation in Egypt who didn't show up again for months or even years.

The aircraft to Dubai took off without me and I was left waiting and wondering what was going to happen to me. One of the officers revealed that someone had alerted the authorities that I was flying off with a film and didn't have the necessary permissions. I told him that I had no idea that permission was required.

I was made to sit in a small, stuffy airport office, while airport security officials were discussing my case with the Egyptian intelligence services. I was apprehensive as to where this was going, so I contacted an influential friend to ask for help. He promptly got in touch with the PLO representatives at the organisation's Cairo office, to inform them that I was being detained at the airport for investigation. Thankfully, that did the trick. It wasn't too long afterwards that I was released.

Needing a shower and some rest, I went back to the Sheraton and returned to Dubai the next day without further mishap. I was unable to figure out the reasons behind the authorities' ill-treatment, until I remembered I had complained bitterly to Hussein Fahmi, comedian Mohammed Reda and actress Leila Hamadeh about President Sadat's unilateral peace efforts. I considered the possibility that I was targeted at the airport primarily because of my views. The fact that I was carrying a film may have been just a pretext to cause me discomfort.

Shortly after that unfortunate incident, I received a visit from an Egyptian official, who apologised to me on behalf of the Egyptian government. He said it had all been a mistake. It happened. I put it behind me and didn't allow it to sour my feelings towards Egypt, its government or its people.

At a later date, Prime Minster Ahmad Nazif came to Dubai with a few of his ministers and requested a meeting with me to discuss business opportunities in Egypt. I went to see him together with my sons Rashid and Ahmad at the hotel Al Qasr where he was staying. Our discussion was friendly and relaxed and we found his team's business proposals interesting. We tried to follow up on his suggestions on numerous occasions, but once again we hit a wall of bureaucracy when I decided to drop the idea.

As the largest Arab country that has long been our political and cultural heartland and which is the guardian of so many ancient historical sites, Egypt is very dear to me.

Around fifteen years ago, I can't recall exactly when, I was disappointed to find that the area around the Giza pyramids and Sphinx looked neglected and unattractive. Furthermore, despite the large numbers of visitors flocking to see the pyramids each year from all over the world, there were no facilities for them. All I saw was one or two men going around with a tray of lukewarm soft drinks and some camels and horses that looked like they could do with a drink themselves.

Anyone who wanted a bite, to sip something cool or use a restroom would have had to leave the enormous desert site to head for a café or restaurant on the main Al Ahram road, which was a long trek in the heat of summer. I couldn't understand why the Egyptian government didn't appear to treasure such an amazing site of the kind most other countries would capitalise on to the maximum. I could only deduce that the neglect was caused by lack of funds.

I found the situation so disturbing that I wrote a letter to the Egyptian Minister of Culture, which I copied to the Minister of Tourism, offering to commission a master plan for developing the area that would include a feasibility study, detailed sketches and mock-ups.

My vision included separate gated sections for camels, horses and donkeys, fountains and streams, public toilet facilities, as well as restaurants and international cafés. I also offered to gift the entire first phase of the project to the Egyptian people so that they could maintain and enjoy their unique legacy for centuries to come.

It sounds unbelievable, I know, but neither minister bothered to acknowledge receipt of my letter. They simply didn't respond at all. Months later when I hadn't heard a word from them, I wrote again, advising them to forget about my earlier offer. That communication was similarly ignored.

When I hadn't asked for anything at all for myself and was prepared to invest substantial sums of money into phase 1, their silence remains a mystery to this day. For some reason I'm unable to fathom, my efforts to help Egypt have always been frustrating.

To give you another example, years later I was introduced to the Egyptian Minister of Tourism and Civil Aviation, Dr Fouad Sultan. I found him to be a very knowledgeable gentleman who was obviously committed to the betterment of his country. He talked to me about his ideas to expand the tourist industry and said the government was considering the privatisation of all its hotels.

I told him that I might be interested in buying one or more, which would be renovated to international standards, provided he could agree to accept scheduled payments. He asked me to send him my proposals. I instructed my team to come up with ideas, which he appreciated. Once he had studied them, he told us that he was ready to give us the green light to go ahead.

In the meantime, he suggested that we met with the person responsible for hotels within the public portfolio. He then called the individual to let him know we were on our way to see properties available for purchase.

We headed straight to the man's office, whose name escapes me now. There was no one to receive us and nobody at the reception, so we stopped an employee to ask the way. Once there, his secretary asked us to wait. We waited for some time without being offered tea or coffee, which is customary everywhere in the Arab world at every level.

Eventually, she said, "You can go in now." I registered the fact that he wasn't courteous enough to step out of his office to greet us.

There he was, a large man sitting smugly behind a fat desk. He didn't stand up to welcome us and it was clear from his body language that he was out to show us that he was a big boss.

"Sit," he commanded, as though he was instructing his pet dog.

I explained that we had come to see him with a view to buying one or more hotels.

"Yes, I know that," he said. "A lot of people come to my office to discuss the same thing, but most of them are liars or crooks. All they do is waste our time. I don't like talking with thieves..." I cut him off in full flow before he could heap further insults upon us.

"Sir, are you talking to me?"

"Yes," he answered.

At that point my blood was starting to boil. "Come on, we're going," I told my people.

"Where are you going... wait!" he called out, as we swept out of the door in disgust.

Naturally, I called Dr Sultan to complain about the disrespectful way we had been treated and to register my surprise that anyone would behave that way to anyone at all, let alone to serious investors recommended by the Minister of Tourism himself.

"I'm so sorry, there's been a misunderstanding," Dr Sultan told me. "Let's put this right. Let's schedule another meeting."

"I think we have to forget about the idea," I said. "I came here as a good friend of Egypt with honest intent, but instead of being welcomed I was insulted and lumped together with thieves and liars." He kept on insisting that we should start afresh, but I was in no mood at all to be conciliatory.

That was one of the weirdest things I've ever experienced. I don't know whether the rude man was having a bad hair day or he had something against investors from the Gulf. Most probably he was just a jumped-up civil servant who knew he could behave as he liked because in a state bureaucracy like Egypt he had a job for life. Someone like that wouldn't last two minutes in one of my companies.

Anywhere else in the world, the foreign investor is king. He gets the red carpet treatment. But in Egypt, at least in my experience, he is treated carelessly. Actually, I've heard similar horror stories from other would-be investors, who are often asked to make under-the-table payments before they are allowed to proceed.

I found that curious, when Egypt's official policy is to encourage foreign investments by offering various incentives. It was as though there was a vast disconnect between the decision-makers at the top and the people required to implement policy.

As much as I love the Egyptian people for their warm hearts and humorous approach to life's difficulties, when it comes to business dealings we're not on the same wavelength.

In 2007, during one of my many visits to London, I went to see one of the Arab world's most internationally well-known billionaires, Mohammed Al Fayed, with a view to bringing the Harrods franchise to the UAE. I had never met him before, although I used to see him around Dubai when Sheikh Rashid was still alive.

Simply arranging to meet was problematic. Liz, my English PA, communicated with his office to set up an appointment and told me that Al Fayed couldn't meet with me before 6 or 7 p.m., which didn't suit me. I wanted to talk to him over lunch or just before lunch, which he wouldn't agree to. In the end, we compromised and fixed the discussion for 2 p.m. at his office on the fifth floor of Harrods. There, I was received in a very professional way by his English PA, who offered me coffee while I waited for him to arrive.

As soon as he arrived, he rushed over and greeted me warmly as though we were old buddies. "Khalaf, it is great to meet you," he said. I remember that he was wearing a Hawaiian shirt that didn't match at all with his conservative dark-coloured trousers held up by Larry King-type old-fashioned braces (the Americans call them suspenders).

I was in a hurry to get down to the business at hand, but he was more interested in trying to sell me a villa compound in Jumeirah adjacent to the Jumeirah Beach Hotel. He explained that it had been repossessed by the government, but tried to persuade me that as I was a local, I could easily sort out that 'little' problem.

"Look, Mohammed. I'm not here to talk about real estate," I told him. "I want to discuss acquiring a Harrods franchise."

Each time I tried to pin him down on that topic, he would deftly change the subject. It soon became clear that once he realised I wasn't foolish enough to consider buying villas in the possession of the Dubai government, he wasn't interested in talking business. Instead, he launched into an exposé of his personal life; things that I would never dream of discussing during a first meeting or any meeting for that matter; things that are too embarrassing to put down on paper.

I knew then that pursuing a Harrods franchise was a hopeless case and decided to relax, sit back and be entertained by this most unusual character. I was astonished when he called his right-hand man to come to his office in order to witness his bawdy conversation with an English club owner over the telephone's loudspeaker. There was nothing for it but to sit there and listen to his stories, so intimate they would make a barmaid blush.

We later received the mandatory Al Fayed tour around the store, including the Diana and Dodi memorial. He showed me various redesigned halls and made sure I learned how much each one had cost him. Naturally, he lingered at a bust of himself and was extremely proud of a grey-suited wax statue in his image.

Early on, I had felt some sympathy for Mr Al Fayed's struggle to get a British passport and his efforts to be accepted within his adopted home. But any sympathy I may have felt was then dispelled by his egotistical personality.

I don't blame the British government for refusing him citizenship. When anyone goes to a country that's not theirs, they should adjust to that country's way of doing things and respect its laws and regulations. Al Fayed, however, went out of his way to make vicious attacks against the government and the Royal Family before various courts, in newspapers and also during televised interviews. That isn't something he could have done in his own country, but in the UK he felt protected by its laws of free speech and free expression and he took full advantage of those pillars of democracy.

We have a saying in Arabic: '*Ya ghareeb koun adeeb*', which translates to 'You foreigner! Be polite!'.

* * *

Due to my fund-raising efforts on behalf of the Emirates Committee for Arab Solidarity and my private support for the Palestinian people, the Chairman of the Palestine Liberation Organisation, Yasser Arafat, would occasionally visit me during the 1980s to ask for my help.

The PLO had been admitted to the Arab League in 1974 and had been designated the "sole legitimate representative of the Palestinian people". When Arafat was given permission to address the United Nations General Assembly, his legitimacy opened the door for the PLO to forge relationships with world leaders. "Today, I have come bearing an olive branch and a freedom fighter's gun. Do not let the olive branch fall from my hand," he famously told UN delegates.

The first time I met Arafat was when I accompanied Sheikh Mohammed bin Rashid to receive the Palestinian leader at Dubai Airport. From then on, every time he came to the UAE to meet with Palestinian residents, he would call me or come to see me. My impression of Arafat was that he was basically an honest man with sincere intentions. He would usually grip my hand and rub it hard until I said "Abu Ammar, please! You are breaking my hand".

Arafat was one of the most persuasive negotiators I've ever met. He is often thought of as a warrior, but I got the impression that he was committed to a negotiated peace settlement. He always felt that the Americans were in Israel's pocket. Even so, he never gave up trying. At times he was under severe pressure to concede to American and Israeli pre-conditions, but he was strong minded; he never sold his people out for the sake of a quick and easy settlement.

Not everyone would agree with my characterisation of Arafat as 'honest' as subsequent to his death several billion dollars were discovered in his private bank accounts, primarily in Switzerland, but those closest to him maintained that was emergency money to be used for the cause.

I don't know for certain what was in his mind, but that does sound likely, as Arafat was known for his spartan lifestyle. By all accounts, during the Second Intifada (uprising), his bedroom in his Ramallah compound contained just a single bed, a lamp, a thread-bare rug, a television set and a small wardrobe where he kept his military uniforms. He didn't smoke and was known to eat very frugally. He wasn't at all the kind of person who needed money for his personal use. Unfortunately, the same can't be said for his wife, whom he married late in life.

The one point that I think everyone can agree upon is that he was the only Palestinian leader with the ability to unite all Palestinian factions and who was able to garner the support of just about all Palestinians.

During the first Palestinian Intifada that began in 1987 and ended in 1993, I met three times with one of Arafat's main rivals, the Co-Founder of the PLO and the Popular Front for the Liberation of Palestine (PFLP), George Habash (known to Arabs as *al Hakim* or 'the doctor'), in my capacity as member of the Emirates Committee for Arab Solidarity.

He was a great intellectual and a passionate believer in his cause. He was always exceptionally polite and possessed a powerful natural charisma. Condemned by Western powers, throughout the Arab world, George Habash was generally respected as a wise man and as someone who couldn't be bought.

During my time with the Committee, I kept a very close eye on Palestinian affairs with the help of others around the world, including a Jewish American called Ned Sherman who was a producer of documentary films.

I bumped into him in Manhattan while dining at the Pierre Hotel on East Sixty-first Street and Fifth Avenue. He was quite a character. He was over seventy years old, but age didn't deter him from making a play for the hotel's pianist, Catherine Landis. Every evening, he would buy a single red rose and place it reverently on the top of her piano.

Ned was very likeable and we quickly became friends. Although he was Jewish, he wasn't a Zionist; indeed, he had a lot of sympathy for the Palestinians and did not approve of the way Israel was treating them.

At that time, I was regularly invited to conferences organised by non-Zionist American Jews to discuss the Palestinian issue, but as I didn't have time to attend most of them, I asked Ned Sherman whether he would be willing to go as my representative and report back, which he said he would do. I would meet him whenever I was in New York, when he would usually invite me to dinner with friends and almost always had a beautiful woman on his arm.

The funny thing was, even though he was officially the host of those dinner parties, he would never fail to edge the bill across the table in my direction. I didn't mind. To use a Yiddish expression, the man certainly had *chutzpah*. I used to find it amusing to observe his technique and rather enjoyed the predictability of it. I invited both Ned and Catherine to the opening of the Metropolitan Hotel.

The word 'Zionist' has acquired negative connotations over time, so for those of you who are not familiar with the term, I should mention that it has come to mean people of any faith who support Israel's existence as a Jewish state. Whereas it is true to say that most Jews are also Zionists, there are also many Jewish activists, scholars and writers of all nationalities who advocate on behalf of Palestinians, including some Israelis.

Some of the most vehement critics of Israeli government policies are Jews. In 2008, when Israel was celebrating its sixtieth anniversary, a letter appeared in *The Guardian* signed by more than 100 British Jews, including writers, actors, academics and public figures. It read: "We cannot celebrate the birthday of a state founded on terrorism, massacres and the dispossession of another people from their land."

There have also been a number of American-Jewish activists organising flotillas and travelling on convoys to break Israel's siege of Gaza. Likewise, Jewish thinkers have bravely studied the influence of the pro-Israel lobby on Congress, such as the professors John Mearsheimer and Stephen Walt, whose essay 'The Israeli Lobby' was published in the *London Review of Books*. The article defines the pro-Israel lobby as a "loose collection of individuals and organisations who actively work to steer US foreign policy in a pro-Israel direction" with "unmatched power".

The largest and most powerful pro-Israel lobbying organisation is the American Israel Public Affairs Committee (AIPAC) which Walt and Mearsheimer characterised as a "de facto agent for a foreign government" with "a stranglehold on the US Congress" due to its "ability to reward legislator and congressional candidates who support its agenda and to punish those who challenge it".

I think it's fair to say congressional representatives are fearful of crossing swords with pro-Israel lobbying groups and AIPAC in particular. Even those with Arab roots rarely, if ever, dare to vote against Israel's interests in Congress. They know that doing so is the kiss of death for their careers.

It's unusual for any legislator to stand up and be counted among those ready to fight for a cause, regardless of the consequences. Former Republican US Representative, Paul Findley, Co-Founder of the Washington advocacy group, the Council for the National Interest and a board member of If Americans Knew, did just that.

The exceptional courage of Congressman Findley, who represented Illinois for twenty-two years, is evident in his 2002 article 'Liberating America from Israel' wherein he writes:

> Thanks to the suffocating influence of Israel's US lobby, open discussion of the Arab–Israeli conflict has been non-existent in our government all these years... For thirty-five years, not a word has been expressed in that committee or in either chamber of Congress that deserves to be called debate on Middle East policy. No restrictive or limiting amendments on aid to Israel has been offered for twenty years, and none of the few offered in previous years received more than a handful of votes. On Capitol Hill, criticism of Israel, even in private conversation, is all but forbidden, treated as downright unpatriotic, if not anti-Semitic. The continued absence of free speech was assured when those few who spoke out – Senators Adlai Stevenson and Charles Percy and Reps. Paul "Pete" McCloskey, Cynthia McKinney, Earl Hilliard and myself – were defeated at the polls by candidates heavily financed by pro-Israel forces.
>
> As a result, legislation dealing with the Middle East has been heavily biased in favour of Israel and against Palestinians and other Arabs year after year. Home constituencies, misled by news coverage equally lop-sided in Israel's favour, remain largely unaware that Congress behaves as if it were a subcommittee of the Israeli parliament.

Strong stuff indeed!

Paul Findley has written successful books on the lobby: *They Dare to Speak Out: People and Institutions Confront Israel's Lobby* and *Deliberate Deceptions: Facing the Facts about the US–Israeli Relationship*.

It was sometime in November 1989 that I was first introduced to Congressman Findley. At that time, Arab leaderships and influential Arabs were proactively assisting the Palestinians in their pursuit of peace. I decided to invite politicians, diplomats, prominent businessmen, writers and scholars sympathetic to the Palestinian cause to an event held in my hotel, the Dubai Metropolitan, co-organised by me together with Taryam and others.

My friend Riad Sadik was very interested in Mr Findley's views on the topic. It seems that they had crossed paths the year before over dinner at the home of long-time Dubai residents David and Melanie Stockwell. Riad suggested that I invited Paul Findley to speak during the meeting. He told me that the Congressman had defended Arab causes during his successive congressional terms in office out of a sense of fairness and true patriotism, many decades before he personally came into contact with any Arab people.

The conference and dinner, held in the hotel's new French restaurant, was well-attended by such VIPs as the UAE National Assembly Speaker, the US Consul-General, various diplomats, prominent Arab thinkers and businessmen concerned about the conflict, as well as a number of interested Britons and Americans.

At first meeting, I was very impressed with Mr Findley's public speaking, knowledge and the forthright way he expressed his opinions. His speech was well-researched, educative and based on facts. Whenever he speaks, he attracts large audiences. I felt there was much we could learn from him.

He stressed that Arabs should be fearless in demanding their legitimate rights. They should insist that their leaders be firm, honest and transparent when visiting the White House and take a true stand behind closed doors rather than trumpeting their thoughts to the media and spouting empty rhetoric for public consumption. On hearing that, I instantly became a Paul Findley fan. I was sorry that I had asked him to restrict his talk to no more than five minutes.

"This reminded me of my Massachusetts colleague, Silvio Conte, who told me he never spoke longer than fifteen minutes, adding that he never lost an election," Paul commented.

The following day, we happened to be on the same flight to London. That was opportune for me as I was able to say goodbye to him and assure him that if he ever needed anything to support his worthy endeavours, he could count on the committee's support.

On a personal level, we clicked immediately in spite of the twenty-eight-year age difference between us. Our chemistry gelled and our conversation flowed easily. He has visited the Emirates many times since and on several of those occasions I have invited various diplomats to meet with him. Most value the opportunity, but others, especially those from G8 countries, rarely apologise for not showing up when they have said that they would. Whether or not they were fearful of the lobby's retribution, only they can know.

In 2002, Paul came to Dubai to address a public session at the Zayed Centre in Abu Dhabi. That same evening, Paul and other intellectuals, including professors from UAE universities, were invited to a debate on the Palestinian cause held at the Metropolitan Hotel, which I moderated. I was also one of the speakers and didn't hold back my anger against the Bush administration for its damaging Middle East policies. I was intent on being as honest as I could, but not everyone appreciates honesty.

A professor at one of the UAE's colleges attacked my speech in a newspaper, especially my accusation that the US is biased in favour of Israel. I was surprised that there is anyone left in the world who would argue with that. Even most American officials would proudly acknowledge that their country supports Israel absolutely and unconditionally.

At Paul's request, in 2006, I hosted a luncheon at my residence to welcome representatives from the Council on American–Islamic Relations (CAIR), America's largest Muslim civil liberties advocacy organisation to which members of Dubai's business community were invited. I was happy to do that because I consider extremely worthwhile the work that CAIR does in highlighting discrimination and bigotry against Muslims in America, which increased to unacceptable levels following the 11 September 2001 attacks on US soil.

Today, Paul Findley is one of my dearest friends and a man who has all my admiration and respect to the extent that I occasionally ask him to cast an eye over my political newspaper columns.

We are both family men and we've got to know one another's wives, children and grandchildren socially. I also very much appreciate Paul's writings. I have sent copies of his books, *Silent No More* and *They Dare to Speak out* to selected prominent recipients in Britain and other European countries and have republished many of his articles in my group's bi-monthly magazine, *Al Shindagah*.

A few years ago, he asked me to consider making a contribution towards the restoration of Illinois College's Whipple Hall, constructed in 1882, with a view to its transformation into a leadership centre. Illinois College is where Paul himself studied and he has since been a member of its fraternity.

The centre – now known as the Khalaf Al Habtoor Leadership Center – is a venue for lectures as well as home to a library containing Lincoln papers, memorabilia, furniture and personal items that Paul has donated to the college. Six of the College's former students once tutored Abraham Lincoln and were considered to be his trusted friends. Lincoln was later made an honorary member of the two campus literary societies: Phi Alpha and Stigmatic.

The Centre also houses an office reserved for Paul in honour of his years in Congress and the worthwhile causes he has championed during his long service to the nation. I was pleased to be able to support this endeavour in recognition of my long friendship with Congressman Findley and also because Abraham Lincoln, who abolished slavery and was able to maintain the Union against all odds, is one of the historical figures that I most admire.

In May 2010, I flew to Jacksonville, Illinois, at the invitation of the college's President, Axel D. Steuer, to speak to graduating students. At the same time, I was awarded an honorary doctorate and was inducted by the college as a member of its Phi Alpha Literary Society.

This is a rare honour that I am proud to share with my friend Paul, former White House correspondent Helen Thomas, Pulitzer Prize recipient Professor David Herbert Donald, the Palestinian-Jordanian author Rami Khouri, and of course America's sixteenth president Abraham Lincoln. It was overwhelming to find myself in such illustrious company.

While there, Paul and his family were kind enough to show me around Abraham Lincoln's Presidential Library and Museum in Springfield, where visitors can take a virtual journey through the great man's life, from his early years in a log cabin all the way to the White House and the Ford Theatre in Washington, where he was assassinated. I found his story inspirational. Paul, who has authored the book *A. Lincoln: The Crucible of Congress*, is an expert on Lincoln and one of his most avid admirers.

* * *

In spite of my positive hatred of formal education when I was a boy, I have come to realise its importance. For decades, I have looked upon education as the number one priority for the future of our planet, which is why I am open to helping educational institutes improve their facilities. In 2010, I was pleased to inaugurate the American University of Cairo's Khalaf Ahmad Al Habtoor Football and Track Stadium, which is a world-class Olympic standard facility.

I was also one of the Co-Founders of Al Ittihad School in Dubai, which opened its doors in 1975. As a father, I wasn't happy with the standard of education in the government-run schools, so when Dubai's Chief of Police

Abdullah Abolhoul came up with the plan of building our own private school together with a few friends, I jumped at the idea.

Getting the necessary permits was easy, but we needed financial backing. So, accompanied by the former Chairman of the National Bank of Dubai Abdullah Saleh, a keen supporter of our efforts, I went to see Sheikh Rashid, who unhesitatingly pledged his assistance. The Ruler and his son, Sheikh Mohammed, made the largest donations to the project. The balance was made up by generous individuals, various banks and our own contributions.

I was appointed as Chairman of the school's Board of Governors, a position I took very seriously with an open heart until my friend Abdul Ghaffar Hussein called me to say the Board wasn't happy with my chairmanship for reasons he didn't explain. Perhaps that was because I didn't have as much time to devote to the post as I would have liked due to my business commitments. I was happy to comply. I wasted no time in penning my letter of resignation, in which I recommended Dubai's Director of Information, Sheikh Hasher Al Maktoum, one of the school's Founders, as the new Chairman. I knew that he had excellent connections with Dubai's Ruler and was a very capable and committed man.

I later telephoned Sheikh Hasher Al Maktoum to find out whether he was open to my suggestion. He instantly agreed and was accepted by the board as my replacement. After some time, the board members expressed their dissatisfaction with his management style too. He is a very clever man, but he was too laid-back for their liking. Several of them later called me to say that I had done a good job and to apologise for asking me to resign.

During the 1990s, I built my own schools. I asked John R. Harris to design the first, a primary school, which opened at the start of the academic year in 1991. It was very successful from the start, which prompted me to add a high school not long afterwards.

At this juncture, it's important to make a clarification. In spite of my criticism of US foreign policy, especially with regard to the Arab world as a whole, I admire the US probably more than any other country for its contribution to the world in terms of science, technology, human rights, personal freedoms and civil liberties.

In many ways, it's a model that should be emulated by other nations, which is why so many oppressed and disenfranchised people from the four corners of the globe are queuing up for citizenship or trying to smuggle themselves in through Mexico.

From the perspective of non-US citizens, America isn't perfect, because in its dealings with foreign countries it always puts its own interests first, which may be understandable, but leads some to contend that the US doesn't have friends, only interests. That said, the US is more a force for good than otherwise and it should be remembered that it donates more aid, medicines and food to third-world states and to countries dealing with natural disasters than any other. There is little doubt that the American taxpayer is the most generous of all.

Besides more than 3 billion dollars in economic and military aid the US donates annually to Israel, 1.3 billion dollars goes to the Egyptian military, along with 250 million dollars in political and economic assistance; 463 million dollars to Jordan; 3.5 billion dollars to Pakistan; and the West Bank/Gaza receives 400 million dollars (most of which goes to the West Bank). Other beneficiaries of substantial sums in US aid each year include India, Bangladesh, Ethiopia, Liberia, Indonesia, Haiti and Bosnia – and of course there are many others.

Overall, I think the American people are well-intentioned and fair-minded. I believe that if they knew the truth about the Israeli–Palestinian situation, which is incorrectly portrayed in the US media, they would demand a just settlement. Quite a few of my best friends are Americans and some of my happiest moments have been spent in the US.

I would also commend two American presidents for doing their best for the Palestinians. The first is President Bill Clinton, who attempted to mediate a final status settlement to the conflict in 2000 between the then Israeli Prime Minister Ehud Barak and Yasser Arafat. Kudos to Clinton for going the extra mile to come up with a solution at a Camp David Summit, when the Palestinians were offered 73 per cent of the West Bank (expanding over a ten to twenty-year period to 90 per cent) and 100 per cent of Gaza.

Compared to what is on the table nowadays, that was a good deal, but the main stumbling block was the final status of Jerusalem. Arafat, rightly in my opinion, would not accept anything less than Palestinian sovereignty over East Jerusalem and the Haram al-Sharif.

For a while there it looked like the outstanding issues were resolvable. People all over the Arab world were practically planning holidays to Jerusalem. It seemed inconceivable that the talks wouldn't have a happy ending. Tragically, time ran out on the process. Negotiators attending permanent status talks at the Taba Summit say they came closer than ever to an agreement. Israeli elections that brought Ariel Sharon to power interrupted that dialogue.

At the same time, President Clinton's second term in office was up. He was succeeded by President George W. Bush, who took a hands-off approach, saying it was up to the parties concerned to achieve peace.

Arafat suddenly found himself out in the cold. Whereas during the Clinton presidency he was one of the most frequent visitors to the White House, Bush labelled him a terrorist and refused to shake his hand. Bush's later efforts to secure Middle East peace were half hearted and insincere.

The other president who stands out from the rest is President Jimmy Carter. He brokered the Israel-Egypt peace treaty in 1978 and negotiated a framework for peace in the Middle East with President Anwar El Sadat that wasn't ultimately adopted, as Arab states weren't ready for it.

Since leaving office, he has devoted himself to such good works as observing elections abroad to ensure they are free and fair, building homes for the poor in places like Vietnam and working to improve global health. In 2002, he was awarded the Nobel Peace Prize for his efforts "to find peaceful solutions to international conflicts, to advance democracy and human rights, and to promote economic and social development".

President Carter and his team also helped draft the 2002–2003 Geneva Accord, a permanent status agreement to end the Israel-Palestine conflict. Latterly, he has become an outspoken critic of Israel's policies towards the Palestinians and in Lebanon.

In his book *Palestine: Peace not Apartheid*, Carter maintains that Israel's policies in the Palestinian territories constitute a system of apartheid and accuses the Israelis of depriving Palestinians of their human rights. The book received deserved praise from many quarters, but was slammed by many in Israel and friends of Israel in the US as being anti-Israeli.

President Carter was a person I had always wanted to meet, so imagine my delight when I learned that he was scheduled to visit me during an upcoming visit to the UAE in September 2009. I was staying at my farm at Khawaneej, not far from Dubai Airport, at the time. Admittedly, I was a little nervous concerning his impending arrival. How should I greet such a great statesman? How should I receive a man of his great calibre? What is the protocol?

I needn't have been concerned. When I learned that he was on his way, I walked to the main gate to wait for him. Before long, a fleet of cars drove up carrying the President, his son and daughter-in-law, as well as US and

UAE security details. He went out of his way to put me at ease from the first moment we shook hands.

We sat down together in the main farmhouse and engaged in a long conversation on a variety of subjects. He told me about his missions in Africa where he works to rescue people from starvation and eradicate such terrible diseases as polio and Guinea Worm.

Naturally, we talked about the Israel-Palestine conflict and how we could assist the Palestinians on a humanitarian level. We also spoke about the presidency of George W. Bush, when I couldn't help but vent that, in my opinion, he not only damaged the world politically and militarily, he created a chasm between Americans and Arabs and was largely responsible for the 2008 global financial crisis.

He told me that he and his family had been enthusiastic supporters of President Barack Obama in the run-up to the 2008 US elections. I asked him, "How many of you guys voted for Obama?" He explained that his was a small family with just twenty-three members, who all voted for Obama with the exception of one.

I agreed with his thoughts on President Obama, who is without doubt a good, honest person, but I couldn't help feeling a sense of disappointment that three years into his term of office many of his promises that held out so much hope for the Middle East had yet to materialise.

Our one-to-one dialogue over, I introduced the President to my children and grandchildren. He was amazed at how large my family is compared to his own. When I asked him if he would have like to see my horses and farm animals, his face lit up. He explained that he used to be a farmer himself and still enjoys the down-on-the-farm atmosphere. I told him he would find a big difference between the size of my farm and most American farms and ranches, which is relatively large in UAE terms, but not nearly as expansive as them.

It was a truly memorable day which I will always cherish. I was positively surprised at how intelligent, energetic, easy-going and down-to-earth President Carter is, but what impressed me most were his human qualities. He is a person with genuine concern for humanity's problems and is a good human being. God bless him and give him long life and continued good health.

Before saying goodbye, the President invited me to visit him in his hometown, which I promised to do during one of my future trips to the US. I consider his invitation not only a great honour, but also an opportunity to know more about his missions and views on the world.

"Let's keep in touch", he said, which we've done ever since. Whenever I come across something that might be of interest, I write to inform him.

I was thrilled to receive this kind appraisal from President Carter on our meeting:

> In October 2009, I had the opportunity to visit Mr Khalaf Al Habtoor at his ranch in Khawaneej, Dubai. Both of our families enjoyed a wonderful afternoon. My son Jack and his wife Elizabeth joined me in visiting with Mr Al Habtoor, his children and grandchildren. As a farmer, I enjoyed seeing the estate's free-roaming animals alongside world-class facilities and polo fields.
>
> The time we spent with our gracious host Sheikh Khalaf was the highlight of our visit to the Emirates and ended much too soon. To spend time with a good friend and family surrounded by natural beauty is one of life's greatest pleasures. I am grateful for the hospitality and friendship shown by Sheikh Khalaf and look forward to our next time together.

* * *

For as long as I can remember, I've made a conscious effort to keep my finger on the global political and financial pulse by reading as much as I can and talking to people in the know. Up until the 1990s, news disseminated in the UAE on television and in newspapers was focused on local topics while imported foreign paper would always arrive in newsagents a day or two late.

As I was keen to express my opinions on the Palestinian issue – an Arab view if you like – to the outside world, I launched the Al Habtoor Research and Information department that was tasked with delving into the annals of history as well as keeping me up-to-date with current events.

My main purpose was to focus on the way anti-Arab and anti-Islamic propaganda is churned out to indoctrinate Western publics with the carefully orchestrated Israeli narrative. I also felt that someone should defend Arabs and Muslims from the endless terrorism slurs thrown our way. To that end, in 1993 I published the first issue of the magazine *Al Shindagah* (named after the place where I was born), as a vehicle for my thoughts and ideas in the form of articles and columns, and also to carry news about my hotels and various companies.

Around the same time, I began writing opinion columns that were published in English and Arabic newspapers, on topics ranging from the

Lebanese political situation, the Israel–Palestine conflict, the preservation of Arab identity, Islamophobia, the death of Princess Diana, the importance of interreligious understanding and the wars in Afghanistan and Iraq.

Hundreds of my articles have been published and were republished in four books: *In My Own Words* (2002), *An Enemy Called Apathy* (2004), *Essays for Truth Seekers* (2007, 2010 and 2012) and *Thinking Clearly* (2002), a compilation of essays and research papers on regional and global issues affecting the Arab world by Al Habtoor Research and Information.

I am very outspoken in my articles and always receive positive feedback from readers, who appreciate honest views, even if they don't always agree with them. Articles on two issues that are closest to my heart can be found reprinted at the end of this book, as well as an article on a woman I greatly admire, Mother Teresa, that I commissioned Julia Wheeler to write for the magazine.

Mother Teresa was one of the greatest ladies in history and I wanted readers to be aware of her good works. I only wish there were more people in the Arab and Islamic world prepared to sacrifice for the well-being of the poor and disenfranchised in the way that she unstintingly did.

Some fifteen years ago, I commissioned Dr Mahmoud El Deek, who has a Ph.D. in Islamic History, to write a book on the commonalities between Islam and Christianity, titled *Final Mission*. It was penned in Arabic and translated into English by an American called Vincent White. I felt compelled to initiate this important project when it became clear to me that so many misunderstandings between Christians and Muslims are either manufactured by outside parties or derive from ignorance.

To this day, I am convinced that few non-Muslims realise that Islam reveres many of the same prophets as Judaism and Christianity. Islam considers Jews and Christians to be 'People of the Book', and like Muslims, are the spiritual sons and daughters of the Prophet Ibrahim (Abraham), the father of Ismail and Isaac.

Those who haven't read the Holy Qur'an are probably not aware that an entire Sura (chapter) is devoted to Maryam (Mary), the mother of Isa (Jesus) or that she is mentioned in the Qur'an more than she is mentioned in the New Testament.

Maryam is highly regarded in Islam as a chaste and virtuous woman selected by God to bear one of God's messengers, the Prophet Isa. Sura Maryam is the nineteenth Sura of the Qur'an, that besides the miraculous birth of Isa also narrates that of Yahya (John the Baptist), who was a gift from God to his elderly father, Zechariah, whose wife was barren. On a personal level, I consider Sura Maryam to be one of the most moving chapters; each time I read it is for me a deeply emotional experience.

Likewise, the Prophet Musa (Moses) is given honourable status in Sura Maryam as a prophet, messenger and lawgiver. His stories are recounted in thirty-six Suras of the Qur'an and include the story of how he was placed in a basket set adrift on the Nile by his Israelite mother from where he was plucked by the Pharaoh's wife, together with his long wanderings in the desert, his flight from Egypt and his receiving of the Ten Commandments.

When violent fanatics purporting to be Muslims are distorting Islam's tenets, I believe it is important for non-Muslims to distinguish between Islam as a religion and the misguided acts of a few. Islam is a peaceful, tolerant faith that champions the rights of women and enjoins its followers to seek knowledge and use their intellect.

In my opinion, which I have voiced on several occasions, man doesn't need an intermediary in the form of rabbis, priests or sheikhs to connect with the Creator. Every person has his or her hotline. Wise men schooled in religious doctrine and dogma hold an important place in every faith, but in the final analysis they are human beings like the rest of us and it is up to each one of us to listen, analyse, think and debate before reaching our own conclusions.

God has given us the biggest gift of all, the human brain, enabling us to judge between good and bad, black and white, night and day. No human being can grant divine forgiveness or blessings. For that, man must raise his head to the Almighty to ask quietly for whatever he needs. If his wish isn't immediately fulfilled, he must exercise patience, for only God in his wisdom knows what's best for his children. All we can do is open up our minds, raise our heads in prayer and believe from the depth of our hearts.

I grew up in a family bound together by shared religious convictions, which have always remained with me. The Holy Book was very dear to my father. My mother used her savings to build a mosque in Al Shabiya Al Thaniya (Shabiya 2), not far from the main Jumeirah Mosque, as soon as we moved from Shindagha to Jumeirah. We respectfully tore it down in 2005 and replaced it with a stronger and more modern structure, before reopening the mosque in my mother's name.

As soon as I was able, I made my own contribution to God by constructing a mosque in the 1980s, close to my home near Al Wasl Road. This service to worshippers is a blessing for any Muslim able to afford it, both in this life and the hereafter.

The mosque's Syrian Imam built up such a faithful following that each Friday it was usually full to overflowing, inspiring me to construct a much bigger one. I briefed the architect to design it on the lines of the Sultan Ahmed Mosque, also known as the Blue Mosque, in Istanbul, with a large dome and four minarets, although, of course, it isn't as lavish or anywhere near the same scale. I derive great peace of mind in the knowledge that I am actively doing something to thank God for all the goodness he has bestowed on me and also to provide a serene place of worship for my fellow Muslims.

It saddens me that so many non-Muslims have difficulty understanding the essence of the Islamic faith, which promotes peace, tolerance, charity, right thinking, self-discipline and a code of respectful behaviour. Many fail to realise that Islam is not simply a faith; it's also a way of life.

The Prophet Mohammed (PBUH) was a merchant who became God's messenger, after receiving divine revelations from the Creator, while reflecting alone in a cave. This was at a time when the people of Mecca were worshipping idols and warring against other tribes.

These words of God delivered to the Prophet by the Angel Jebril (Gabriel) enshrined in the Holy Qur'an are considered absolute and unchangeable. For us, the Qur'an is more than a religious text; it guides our every waking hour and brings comfort to our souls. It teaches us how to live our lives and inspires us to be better than we are, which is why every Muslim treats the Holy Book with such reverence.

Muslims down the ages, from calligraphers to bookbinders, have devoted their art to preserving the Qur'an's message. Qur'ans have been illuminated with gold leaf, their leather or metal bindings tooled with gold or studded with precious stones. There are Qur'ans so small they can rest in the palm of a hand or so large that one can take a calligraphist up to a decade to pen. However simple a Qur'an might be in appearance, its message is just as precious.

All Muslims would like to be able to memorise every word of the Qur'an and many do. UAE nationals who memorise the Holy Book are honoured in the UAE. And there are many stories of prisoners who have turned their lives around after spending their incarceration learning the Qur'an by heart.

Put simply, for believers, the Qur'an is more than a book; it must be kept in a high place and must never touch the ground; it should never be soiled, defaced, burned or handled with disrespect.

Anti-Islamic bigots know little about Islam, but they do know Muslim sensitivities and use those sensitivities to inflict pain on the devout. One such is the Florida pastor Terry Jones, who in 2010 heaped insult on the Islamic religion and threatened to publicly burn hundreds of Qur'ans. He was dissuaded from doing so by the US President Barack Obama, who feared a violent backlash against American troops in Afghanistan and Iraq and also against American citizens abroad.

However, Jones was determined to do the harmful deed, no matter what terrible repercussions might ensue. In March 2011, Jones put the Qur'an on trial and carried out his earlier threat, eliciting violent protests in the Afghan cities of Mazar-e-Sharif and Kandahar that resulted in deaths and injuries.

Unfortunately, US law is powerless to prevent this type of notoriety-seeking acts of blasphemy. Instead of being charged with inciting violence, Jones was given round-the-clock protection. It's a different story in Britain, where the Pastor Jones has been refused entry.

When a British National Party (BNP) candidate was caught on video burning a Qur'an in his garage, he was promptly arrested under the Public Order Act and tried. Likewise, many European countries have anti-bigotry laws on their statute books, as well as laws against anti-Semitism, under which, several people have been jailed or fined. It seems to me that US lawmakers should consider a bill to prevent such deliberate acts of incitement.

I do not in any way defend the mob violence that took place in Afghanistan, but it's worth remembering that the majority of those involved were uneducated and driven by raw emotion. What Terry Jones did was pre-planned and premeditated. It's important, too, to remember that a faith should not be judged by the actions of a minority of its followers, who, through ignorance, sometimes fail to comprehend what their religion requires of them.

As a matter of principle, however, I believe people who go out of their way to denigrate any faith do not deserve attention because that's their motivation. By shining a spotlight on their insults, we unwittingly fall right into their trap. The Qur'an is God's word and doesn't require human protection; its message is stronger than any one of us and all of us put together. This is why the fatwa issued by Iran's Supreme Leader, the Ayatollah Khomeini, on 14 February 1989, against the author Salman Rushdie was a mistake.

His novel, *The Satanic Verses*, was generally judged to be a yawn, until the fatwa elicited violent protests against him all over the Muslim world, when it naturally provoked curiosity and became a best-seller, making Rushdie richer and more famous than he could ever have hoped to be.

Down the ages, there have been zealots who have distorted their faith to justify cruelties. Examples are many, beginning with the European Crusaders, who ravished and slaughtered on their way to Jerusalem, to the Spanish Inquisitors who forced Muslims and Jews to convert to Christianity on pain of death, and the witch hunts in Europe and America, when up to 100,000 innocent people were killed or burnt at the stake accused of heresy.

In 1994, Baruch Goldstein, an American-born Israeli doctor and supporter of Israel's terrorist Kach party, shot dead twenty-nine Muslims worshipping inside a mosque in the Haram Al Ibrahimi (Cave of the Patriachs) in Al Khalil (Hebron). And Yigal Amir, the man who assassinated Israel's peacemaking Prime Minister Yitzhak Rabin, said he acted alone on orders from God. The nineteen 'Muslim' terrorists who attacked America on 11 September 2001 were of the same ilk.

Another high priority in Islam is charitable works. One of the five pillars of Islam is *Zakat* (alms giving) whereby every Muslim is obliged to give a percentage of his or her material wealth to the needy. Moreover, in some instances, authorities responsible for its collection fail to distribute it fairly.

Muslims are also encouraged to practice *Sadaqah*, which though not obligatory, is considered spiritually cleansing. *Sadaqah* is voluntary charity, which doesn't necessarily involve money. Spreading happiness, showing compassion, doing acts of kindness or helping to improve the environment are actions under *Sadaqah's* umbrella.

I've tried to hold an open discussion on this topic, but it is something that hardly anyone wants to talk about in this region. Unfortunately, whenever I raise this sensitive subject, I rarely receive any meaningful response.

Some time ago, I opened a discourse on philanthropy with prominent people from GCC countries. It was during a lunch attended by Sheikh Mohammed bin Rashid in honour of the Prime Minister of Qatar Sheikh Hamad bin Jassim bin Jabr Al Thani, and the then Qatari Deputy Prime Minister and Energy Minister Abdullah bin Hamad Al Atieh. I told some of the VIP guests that I had recently returned from a visit to New York and was astonished by the generosity of the Rockefeller family.

To illustrate my point, I recounted the following story:

"While strolling around Manhattan, I admired the impressive United Nations Headquarters, which a New Yorker friend told me had been donated to the City of New York by the American oil magnate John D. Rockefeller. 'There are many more buildings, including schools, universities and hospitals, all over the US that were gifted to the nation by the Rockefellers,' he told me."

Judging by their faces, my lunch companions were unimpressed. "Khalaf, don't be so naive," said one of them, Abdullah Al Attiyah. "Those kinds of donations are made so that they can be written off against taxes," he added. He may have put me down as gullible, but I'd rather be gullible than a hard-bitten cynic like him, who deserved the glare I threw his way.

It's shameful that educated people in high positions that enable them to do so much good in the world discredit others who are trying their best to make a difference. It's a pity that they mistake kindness as merely a ploy to evade taxes. Good deeds should be acknowledged and appreciated, not discredited. Some may call me naive, but I will never stop believing in the innate goodness of humankind, which is often discounted due to the actions of a few bad apples.

I was amazed when in 2010 some thirty-eight plus American billionaires pledged to commit half of their wealth to charity, to highlight the responsibility of those who have towards the have-nots. Warren Buffet, who started his career going door-to-door selling chewing gum, and Bill Gates, a computer nerd who founded Microsoft, launched The Giving Pledge to encourage rich Americans to help combat global disease, poverty and lack of education.

Buffet has promised 99 per cent of his fortune to those causes, saying 1 per cent is sufficient for the needs of himself and his family. "Neither our happiness nor our well-being would be enhanced by holding on to more", he said. Other American billionaires agree with the principle, but shy away from making a similar commitment, for fear of alienating their children.

George Soros, who once worked as a railway porter and waiter in London, hasn't signed up to the Pledge, but it is estimated that he has already given away over seven billion dollars to various charitable, anti-apartheid and pro-democracy endeavours in Eastern Europe and Africa.

I tell my fellow Arabs, when it comes to charity, we can learn a lot from the West, which is unknowingly implementing Islamic principles related to philanthropy more faithfully than parts of the Arab or Muslim world.

But by no means is it right to say that all wealthy Arabs are uncharitable. There are, of course, notable exceptions. One such was the late Sheikh Zayed, who built mosques, Islamic institutions, hospitals, orphanages, libraries, scientific institutes and even entire cities all over the world.

Sheikh Zayed's son, Sheikh Khalifa bin Zayed Al Nahyan, President of the UAE and Ruler of Abu Dhabi, is continuing his father's tradition. He has launched the Zayed Humanitarian Award in his father's memory, which recognises outstanding philanthropic works worldwide. Each year I pay a courtesy visit to Sheikh Khalifa and his brother Sheikh Mohammed bin Zayed, the Crown Prince of Abu Dhabi and the Deputy Supreme Commander of the UAE Armed Forces, to show my respect and my appreciation of the way they are taking care of the country and faithfully holding on to their father's generous spirit.

Likewise, I appreciate the way that Sheikh Mohammed bin Rashid continues in the spirit of his father, Sheikh Rashid, by encouraging people to work by giving them projects rather than cash handouts, while at the same time taking care of those who cannot care for themselves. Sheikh Mohammed's philanthropic efforts are wide-ranging and well-known. In 2007, he set up a ten billion dollar fund for a knowledge-based society to improve education in the Middle East, and a year later he launched the Arab Centre for Philanthropy to encourage charitable donors. His Dubai Cares and Noor Dubai initiatives respectively aim to educate one million children in poor countries and restore sight to one million suffering from treatable visual impairment.

I look upon my own secure financial state as a blessing from God, which should be utilised in a responsible way. My decisions to invest in good causes is done without differentiating between the beneficiaries' nationality, religion or skin colour. One of my greatest pleasures in life is being able to give back, for that is the way I thank God for his protection and benefice.

Whenever I am not sure about the worthiness of a certain cause, I nominate the Red Crescent to research the charity on my behalf and to make the ultimate decision on whether I should go ahead or not. I also have a department that screens pleas from individuals down on their luck, which is done on an almost daily basis. Such a screening process is crucial to ensure donations don't end up in the hands of crooks, or, even worse, extremist organisations.

One of the fundamental Islamic duties is for all Muslims who are able and can afford it to make pilgrimage or Hajj to Mecca, which is both a privilege and a penance. As I've recounted in an earlier chapter, my father and I were thwarted from performing the Hajj when I was a child, because I became very ill en route. I would have loved to have made that sacred journey with him, but it was not to be.

Since that setback, I have twice made a journey to the House of Allah we call Umrah and, in 2004, I performed the Hajj, an obligatory pilgrimage, which was one of the most fulfilling experiences of my life. I felt weak and powerless, but at the same time secure in the arms of the Almighty, whom I asked for forgiveness and blessings.

It's almost impossible to describe one's emotions while listening to recitations from the Qur'an or praying in the Masjid al-Haram next to Islam's most sacred site, the Kaaba, built by the Prophet Ibrahim and his son Ismail on the instructions of Allah and delivered by them to Mecca together with the Black Stone, that dates back to the time of Prophet Ibrahim. The emotion is so overwhelming that even those with the hardest of hearts will bend and weep.

During the annual Hajj, up to 3 million worshippers from all corners of the earth circle the Kaaba. All the believers are dressed alike and all are equal under God. In that place there is no differential between anyone due to their nationality, colour, social class or gender.

With so many people around, noise levels are invariably high. Sleep is almost impossible. But the strangest thing is that pilgrims rarely feel tired. Even without any rest, they feel they can go on worshipping forever. Nothing can exhaust them as they pray with a pure heart and a mind cleansed by good thoughts. I usually dislike noise, but the sounds of people praying or reading aloud didn't bother me at all. I returned to Dubai energised and at peace with the One who made me.

CHAPTER 13
Halcyon Days

"HAPPINESS ALWAYS LOOKS SMALL WHILE YOU HOLD IT IN YOUR HANDS, BUT LET IT GO AND YOU LEARN AT ONCE HOW BIG AND PRECIOUS IT IS."
– MAXIM GORKY

As we rang in a new decade, the 1990s, we were still reeling from the sudden collapse of the mighty Soviet Union. There was a feeling in the air that our planet had undergone a seismic shift for the better and anything was possible.

Dubai was as near to idyllic as any of its citizens could ever have dared to hope. The emirate now had its own airline, Emirates, which fast became the UAE's flagship. I was invited to be a passenger on the leased aircraft that flew guests around the Gulf marking the airline's inaugural flight, but unfortunately couldn't attend. It seemed inconceivable then that the fledgling carrier would emerge as one of the planet's fastest growing airlines, or that twenty plus years later its network would stretch to 120 destinations in around seventy countries, carrying over 34 million passengers in 2011.

Dubai's new eighteen-hole championship golf course, Emirates Golf Club, was a celebrated event. Locally and internationally, people enthused over its avant-garde clubhouse, designed by Karl Litten to represent a cluster of Bedouin tents, and its luxuriant greens where there were once only sand dunes. It was the very first all-grass course in the Gulf. The foreign press were terming it "the desert miracle". I attended the club's opening in 1988, a huge affair attended by the UAE's rulers, VIPs, dignitaries and famous international golfers.

When I learned just how much water was needed to irrigate the fairways' Bermuda grass and lakes daily, I couldn't help thinking back to the days when we had to dig wells and carry brackish water home. Water shortages were now a thing of the past. Most of Dubai's requirements were met by Dubai Aluminium Company's (DUBAL) desalination plant, inaugurated by Queen Elizabeth II in 1979.

I'm no golfer, I prefer more energetic sports, but I was just as delighted with the Club as any committed golfing aficionado, because its very existence meant that Dubai had finally arrived as an upmarket global tourist destination.

Dubai's biannual Air Show inaugurated in 1989 attended by 10,000 industry visitors not only cemented Dubai as an aviation hub, it thrilled nationals and expatriates alike. Even those who were unable to get tickets would gather around the site to watch daredevil aeronautic displays. For those of us who did, the show presented a wonderful opportunity to meet old friends and get to know new people while lunching and having coffee in the various company-sponsored hospitality chalets.

In the run-up to the show, everyone who thought they were anyone would wait on tenterhooks for their invitation to the most spectacular party in town and were most offended if theirs failed to arrive. Those parties were special; guests were almost faced with a marathon walking from one end of the international buffets – marked Italian, Indian, Chinese, Lebanese etc. – to the other.

It was surprising that even at the height of the global downturn, some 53,000 industry professionals and visitors attended the 2009 show where 100 civil and military aircraft were on display.

You might have thought that international luxury goods manufacturers had unearthed a gold mine the way they were gravitating towards Dubai to launch perfumes, watches, fashions and cars, each vying to make their launch events more memorable than their rivals with sumptuous buffets and firework displays.

More often than not, expensive gifts would be offered to guests on their way out. At one beach dinner hosted by a perfume company, perfume bottles were distributed by exotically-attired riders on white Arab steeds. Almost every other day there were invitations to grand occasions on my desk, most of which I had to turn down for lack of time.

I had been a member of Dubai's Chamber of Commerce for a few years during the early 1980s together with Saif Al Ghurair, Majid and Abdullah Al Futtaim, and Saeed Al Naboodah. I learned a lot from them, but as always I didn't feel comfortable sitting around a committee table, because by its very nature decision-making by a committee is always slow and cumbersome. Most of the important decisions were ultimately taken by the Ruler's office. My character is such that once a consensus is reached, I expect rapid action.

Although I've never worn an official hat with ease, I've always been at my country's disposal to offer advice and help out when asked to do so. Once I was invited to lunch by the Ruler of Sharjah, HH Dr Sheikh Sultan bin Mohammed Al Qasimi. It turned out to be a semi-formal affair attended by the Crown Prince of Abu Dhabi, Sheikh Khalifa bin Zayed Al Nahyan, now the President of the UAE; and by then Minister of Foreign Affairs Ahmad Khalifa Al Suwaidi.

As I scanned the room, the penny dropped. I was the only person from Dubai. That was unusual. I was pleased to have been invited and enjoyed everyone's company, but couldn't get rid of the thought that there was something wrong. Oh God, should I have come, I thought?

When the lunch was over and people were taking their leave, the reason for my invitation became apparent. Before I could take my leave of Sheikh Sultan at the door, he asked me to go with him to his house. As we drove, he expressed his trust in me and asked if I could consent to do him a favour.

"There is a border dispute between Dubai and Sharjah," he said. "I've asked Mohammed Saeed Al Mulla to mediate, but as yet I haven't heard back from him. I don't know whether he has passed on my message or not." Sheikh Sultan said he had every respect for Dubai's then Crown Prince Sheikh Maktoum bin Rashid Al Maktoum, who was the de facto in charge during the years when Sheikh Rashid was incapacitated by illness, and told me that he would have like the disagreement to be patched up as soon as possible.

He explained that while he had no objection to Dubai police crossing into Sharjah as after all "we were all one country", they should respectfully ask permission before doing so. The problem was that the border between Dubai and Sharjah en route to Hatta had never been properly delineated, which was causing confusion for everyone.

"What would you like me to do?"

"I want you to ask Sheikh Maktoum and Sheikh Mohammed to work with us in finalising that border, and once that's done, to order the Dubai Police Force not to enter our territory without taking permission," he said.

As soon as I was able, I requested a meeting with Sheikh Mohammed, then the Minister of Defence, to explain Sheikh Sultan's concerns. He listened attentively before advising me to bring this matter to the attention of Dubai's Crown Prince, Sheikh Maktoum.

I managed to see Sheikh Maktoum that same afternoon, who expressed his surprise that Sheikh Sultan hadn't approached him on the issue directly.

I explained that Sheikh Sultan had wanted to discuss it face to face, but couldn't get hold of him. "He says he has encountered difficulties finding you," I told him.

"Me! Am I difficult to find? What do you think?"

"Your Highness it's true," I said, after deciding that honesty was the best policy.

He was keen to sort things out without delay. The first thing he did was to ask me to drive with him along the Hatta Road to the disputed area around Merghim. Sheikh Maktoum brought a map of the area along with him and, once we had reached the disputed area, he pointed out where Dubai ended and Sharjah began. In doing so, he was guided by an agreement between the two neighbouring emirates that had been negotiated many years before.

Sheikh Maktoum subsequently instructed the police to cease infringing territory belonging to Sharjah. Both sides were satisfied with the outcome and I was gratified that I had helped in some small way to bring them together.

Everyone in Dubai worked long hours from Saturday to Thursday afternoon. Weekends, however, were made special with government-sponsored beach festivals open to all where young and old would go to picnic or watch world-famous Arab and Western entertainers.

At one point, Dubai strove to enter the *Guinness Book of Records* with the 'World's Largest Cake' that snaked along the Creek until it was either consumed in situ or carried away by the crowds in plastic bags. Around this time, the government regularly organised Friday festivals on Jumeirah Beach, when well-known international singers and dance troupes were flown in to entertain nationals and expats, who came with their children in huge numbers to enjoy all the fun of the day.

In later years, Dubai came in for unfair criticism in the foreign press for seeking to come first in everything, whereas excellence was the only tool the government had at its disposal to assist our tiny emirate in becoming known and being able to compete with far larger and more populated neighbours.

There was very little left of my childhood city. Residents started joking that every time they returned from vacation, they found a different landscape. Expats would say it takes longer to construct a garden shed at home than a high-rise building in Dubai.

Thankfully, however, in the mid-1980s the government began to appreciate the importance of retaining the last remnants of Dubai's history and heritage. There was nothing remaining of Shindagha apart from Sheikh Saeed's house and one other, but Bastakiya's windtower houses, once slated for demolishment, were renovated and preserved, and are today home to art galleries, museums and restaurants.

Rumour has it that Prince Charles, who has strong opinions when it comes to traditional architecture, had advised the government to preserve Bastakiya during one of his many visits, but I can't verify that.

Gone were the days when people I met on my travels would ask where I was from and then proceed to stare at me blankly when I told them. Europeans especially were fairly Dubai-savvy, thanks in part to the efforts of the Dubai Commerce and Tourism Promotion Board, set up in 1989 to transform Dubai's image abroad as the Hong Kong of the Middle East. Managed by ex-Hong Kong Tourist Board executives, the Board was instrumental in carving the emirate's tourism profile with the Arab world and beyond.

Even those who knew nothing about the emirate had usually heard of Emirates airline, Dubai Duty Free and the Gold Souk that still sold the most inexpensive gold on the planet, although its shops had gone posh with reinforced glass windows and air-conditioning. There was so much to do and see and so many entertainment venues that visitors were spoilt for choice.

Now that tourism was in full swing, it became apparent that most visitors were gravitating towards beach hotels, a trend that put my own at somewhat of a disadvantage. It was then I took the decision to build the Metropolitan Beach Resort in Jumeirah, so that hotel guests could have access to a private beach.

A few well-intentioned people tried to dissuade me from going ahead, arguing that the resort was too far away from the Metropolitan Hotel; but the question of distance was overcome with regular shuttle buses that ferried guests to and fro on a complimentary basis. I'm glad that I stuck to my guns because not only did the hotel's occupancy rates go up when the resort opened in 1988, its facilities and food outlets also attracted the paying public.

I spent many enjoyable times at the Metropolitan Beach Resort. It soon became the hub of my social life and it was thanks to the resort's Sri Lankan tennis coach, Sylvester, that I swung a racket for the first time.

"Sir, why don't you play tennis?" he asked me. "It's a fantastic sport and a great way to exercise."

"Oh no, I prefer walking and swimming. I enjoy horseback riding sometimes, but I'm no tennis player," I said.

"I can teach you, I can coach you," he insisted.

"Thanks Sylvester, but I have no interest at all in games like tennis."

From then on, he was like a dog with a bone. He was so determined to get me on the court that one day he handed me a bag. To my surprise, inside was a T-shirt, shorts, tennis shoes and a pair of white socks. I acknowledged his kind gesture and thought I had better give tennis a try just to get him off my case. I've never looked back since.

I admit it; I'm an incurable tennis addict nowadays. I make time for an hour's play every single day of my life. Even during the fasting month of Ramadan I try my best to find a partner willing to join me on the court in the afternoons.

Tennis is well and truly in my blood. Not only do I derive enjoyment from the physical activity demanded by the game that is the best stress-buster, I thrive on the challenge of beating my opponent. I always play hard to win, just as I do in life. Challenge is a real adrenalin rush for me and winning is an affirmation of the lynchpin of my life – a can-do philosophy that never accepts second best.

Over the years, I've partnered some of the world's top-ranked tennis players in doubles matches. There are too many to mention, but they include the Serbians' former World Number One players Novak Djokovic and Ana Ivanovic. Russian players Svetlana Kuznetsova, Vera Zvonareva and Maria Kirilenko, and Victoria Azarenka from Belarus, as well as the Australian Jelena Dokic are all well-known players that I've been lucky enough to team up with. And no, I'm not going to disclose whether or not I played against any of those professionals let alone whether I succeeded in beating any of them. That's for me to know and you to wonder.

Sylvester should get a medal for introducing me to this fine sport that has done wonders for my health, but my wife and daughters might not agree. It's not my fault that some of my opponents are not only talented, they also happen to be some of the most athletically beautiful young women in the world. At home, I'm outnumbered by women who are always teasing me on that score. Sometimes I just can't resist teasing them right back.

When we get together to watch a match on TV, they band together to launch an unflattering critique of the physical appearance of the best-looking female players, especially the ones I know personally. And, of course, being the chivalrous man that I am, I rush to the players' defence, which always brings the full weight of woman-power down on my head.

Tennis became such an indispensable part of my life that in 1998 I launched the first professional ladies' tennis event in the region, the Al Habtoor Tennis Challenge, an annual event that is held under the supervision of the International Tennis Federation (ITF). I wanted to encourage women to participate in the game while helping to boost Dubai's reputation at the same time. Today, it's a much anticipated event on the emirate's sporting calendar.

Whenever friends ask me why I brought a women's tournament to Dubai, I usually give a tongue-in-cheek answer just to enjoy the expressions on their faces. "I wanted to beautify my resort with sportive and attractive young women," I tell them.

I've also made a lot of friends of many different nationalities through tennis. One of my regular opponents on the court is Raya Dimashki, a hardworking Syrian businesswoman and mother of four. Her game isn't up to much – I always beat her and her partner, but she's great fun to be with. She's a really bad loser. Each time I win, she complains bitterly before later confessing that she just can't beat me. One time, she arrived with her partner announcing that they were the "Loser Team".

When Raya dresses like a junior player, I pull her leg, saying I'm going to tell my wife that her skirts are too short. She tells me off and threatens never to come again. She may not be one of the best players, but she is a great friend and a great woman.

Another of my regular opponents is Karim Alayli, a young professional player from Lebanon, who was his country's number one player for many years and represented Lebanon in international Davis Cup competitions. I really believe he's good enough to compete with the world's best players, but unfortunately, until now, he's been short on luck.

Karim has been trained by the same coach since he was six years old, a very nice man called Hassan Bader, whom I've got to know quite well. Aside from being an accomplished player, Hassan is a very genuine and refreshingly honest man. He isn't particularly worldly-wise, partly because he can't communicate in any other language besides Arabic and has never had the opportunity to travel much.

Whenever the ladies tournament comes around, I arrange it so that he gets a game with some of the competitors. I soon noticed that when he plays against attractive young women his game goes markedly downhill. He becomes confused and embarrassed hitting the ball all over the place like a novice.

Once I asked him why he always did so badly against the girls. He thought for a while before saying, "This is all a new atmosphere for me. In Lebanon, I coach fat old men who sometimes bring their fat cigars onto the court with them. I have never before played with stunning girls like these. Somehow I feel uncomfortable, especially when I think about my wife, Hala."

There aren't many men around with that kind of sensitivity, which is something I fully respect. He joined me on a trip to Brussels and Paris once. He was blown over by those European cities. He couldn't stop talking about the train journey from Belgium to France, the wide boulevards such as the Champs Elysées, the Galeries Lafayette and other glamorous stores, and French cuisine. He felt that he had been to paradise and back and still refers to that journey as "the best time of my life".

On the other hand, I don't think there's anything wrong with a man who appreciates female beauty, provided he keeps to his own values, stays within the confines of his religious beliefs and doesn't hurt anyone else. I recently invited Sir David Frost to lunch at my Buckinghamshire home, at a time when the antics of the former Italian Prime Minister Silvio Berlusconi were topping the news.

Like most people I spoke to in the UK, Sir David was highly critical of the red-blooded Italian's affairs concerning various young women. I think he was surprised when I came out in support of Berlusconi. "What's the big deal?" I told him. "I've never met Mr Berlusconi, but I admire his appetite for love and life." After all, he's a son of one of the world's most free-living, romantic countries and at least he's being transparent.

"Would you prefer it if I liked men?" Berlusconi is quoted as having asked an interviewer. As far as I'm concerned, Berlusconi and Bill Clinton, who was almost impeached over his liaison with Monica Lewinsky, have the edge on so-called devout leaders like George W. Bush and Tony Blair, who claim that God propelled them to wage wars, causing the death of untold numbers of innocent civilians. I've since suggested to a few of my friends that we fly to Italy with 'Viva Berlusconi' banners, although admittedly no one's taken me up on this offer.

It was thanks to tennis that I met Ghaffour Moundir, a Moroccan coach with French citizenship who lives with his wife and three children in

Zurich. He's crazy about the game and enjoys coaching children as much as adults. Whenever he gets a holiday, he flies to Dubai to play tennis with me. He goes out of his way to be helpful and I always look forward to his visits. Recently, however, something very strange occurred involving Ghaffour.

An anonymous SMS sent from abroad was sent to my mobile. The sender warned me about my tennis buddy in his message. The gist was that Ghaffour was badly behaved and had offended a mutual friend, a very respectable married Australian lady with kids called Karen Smith. I didn't believe the slur for one minute, but I thought I should make an effort to discover who was behind it. I sent an SMS back to the sender asking who he was. There was no answer.

When I next saw Karen, I told her what had happened and she revealed she and her husband had met a man the year before who was now stalking her and sending threatening messages. I asked Ghaffour if he knew who the person was and he said, "No, I've never met him. But I know who you're talking about. He's sending me nasty messages too. I have no idea why."

The extraordinary thing was that the mysterious man was aware of Karen's every movement as well as Ghaffour's. It was as though he owned a private surveillance satellite or had bugged their homes and hotel rooms. I began to be concerned when it became clear that the stalker knew that Karen was with my driver, Jawa, who was waiting for her outside a well-known mall in Dubai. He actually had the nerve to call Jawa's mobile phone, demanding to know Karen's exact whereabouts. How he found out the cell numbers of everyone who knew Karen, however remotely, is anyone's guess.

After that, this deranged person deigned to reply to my original SMS. He said he was in Dubai and offered to meet me in the afternoon, as soon as I finished playing tennis. I wrote him off as a nutcase and didn't reply.

The funny thing was Ghaffour and our friends Karim and Hassan were seriously scared of the menacing stranger. Whenever Ghaffour went for afternoon prayers, he would insist that Karim accompanied him to the mosque. On one occasion, I found Hassan hiding behind the sofa. I laughed for days at their paranoia.

Did they imagine that a knife-wielding masked man would jump out at them from behind a palm tree? There aren't too many of those types in Dubai. This happened years before Mossad assassins planning to kill a Hamas commander were going around Dubai in tennis gear and floppy hats, when my friends' phobias would at least have been understandable. At that time, they were entirely irrational.

I've been very blessed in life with decent friends and companions. I consider myself a good judge of character, but like most of us there have been times when I've badly misread someone.

A case in point is my encounter with a scruffy Egyptian bit-part actor called Samir Rayhan, who often came to stay in the Dubai Metropolitan Hotel with colleagues from the Egyptian cinema under contract from Dubai TV. I couldn't help noticing how poorly Samir was being treated by everyone, including the director and his assistant. He was so downtrodden and unselfconfident that he was going around bowing to everyone who glanced in his direction. He looked so ground down all the time that I began to feel sorry for him. I decided to ask his boss the director why he was so unkind and disrespectful to the poor man.

"Samir Rayhan? Oh, he's no one; don't worry about him," the director said. "If I treat him nicely, he'll get bigheaded and imagine he's somebody. He's lucky I'm helping him out with roles."

I was annoyed that this hard-hearted fellow thought it was okay to treat a fellow human being as a nonentity, unworthy of even basic courtesies. It crossed my mind that I should make an effort to sit down with Samir to see if he needed help. The next time I passed by the hotel, I sought him out for a chat. It was evident that his level of education was next to zero. It was clear too that his personal standard of hygiene was below zero. He owned one pair of soiled trousers, a pair of dirt-encrusted shoes and sandals that had seen better days. Worse in my book, he was a chain-smoker, spending the little money he earned on five packets of cigarettes each day.

On those grounds, he wasn't at all my type of person, but nevertheless I enjoyed his company. He had quite a sense of humour. He was light and funny; altogether a pleasure to be around. I'll give him a makeover, I thought. A clean-up, a new wardrobe and a few social graces could change his life.

So, in the beginning, I took him on as a sort of project, like the professor in the movie *My Fair Lady* who wagers that he can transform a girl selling flowers on the street into a fine lady accepted by high society. Although, in this case, there was no wager involved. My only motivation was to bring a sense of dignity to someone with little self-worth who had lost his way.

Some people are resistant to change. He wasn't. He was grateful that I had taken an interest in his welfare. I bought him a few smart suits, shirts and ties – and, of course, several pairs of shoes to suit a variety of occasions.

There was one point on which I was adamant. I told him that from now on he was expected to take regular daily showers. As someone who was used to bathing rarely, for special occasions, he complained that too much soap and water irritated his skin. I warned him that if he wanted my help showering wasn't negotiable. Very reluctantly, he agreed.

Outwardly, Samir's makeover was a great success. He started to walk tall. However, he still needed to learn how to interact with people of all levels. That was my next challenge. I advised him on conversation skills and table manners, before inviting him to a few dinners with friends. Sometime afterwards, I arranged visas for him to travel with me to Europe and the US, to broaden his outlook. He turned out to be an excellent travelling companion, easy-going and relaxed.

Instead of the small piece of luggage he had when I first met him, he now travelled around with three large expensive designer suitcases that would make Paris Hilton proud. The first time I spotted them, I asked some of the guys with me, "Whose bags are those?". They informed me they belonged to Samir. I asked him why he needed so many suitcases, while thinking to myself that his classy luggage was worth more than his entire wardrobe.

"One bag is filled with my shoes," he said. Bearing in mind this was someone who used to own only one pair of shoes, I thought I was hearing things. I only take two pairs of shoes with me when I go on a trip; one is packed and the other I wear. He was a new man in all manner of ways.

Some years later during Ramadan, Samir would come to the Metropolitan Beach Resort each afternoon with me to socialise, take a sauna and cheer me on during my game. I enjoyed his laid-back company and funny anecdotes as always, until our friendship was ruined by a horrible incident. But before I elaborate on this story, I must run through my daily afternoon routine.

I tried – and still try - to leave my office around 12.30 p.m. when I would enjoy an hour's siesta in my private beach bungalow before heading for the tennis court. While I slept, Samir would go off to the sauna or amuse himself somewhere else. Because I could never bring myself to completely trust him, I'm not quite sure why, I never left him alone in the bungalow.

Suddenly I started noticing there was money missing from my wallet. Every day, for up to two and a half weeks, 500 dirhams or 1,000 dirhams was gone by the evening. First I thought I must have miscounted, lost the missing money or forgotten where I'd spent it. Eventually, I had to face the unpleasant realisation that someone I probably knew was systematically stealing from me. I racked my brain as to who that could be; an impossible task when everyone around me was a tried and true employee or friend.

So one day I laid a trap to catch the thief. I carefully counted the notes in my wallet, which as always I left in the bungalow before heading off for my game. I then asked a Lebanese friend of mine called Sami (more about this character in a later chapter) to stand on the roof of a nearby restaurant, Munchi, so as to get a bird's-eye view of the scene. It wasn't too long before my spotter ran up to me, grinning from ear to ear.

"I saw him," he said. "It's Samir. He's the one. I saw him get into your bungalow." Sami didn't bother to hide his glee. He had always detested Samir and relished the thought that the Egyptian interloper might finally be excluded from my circle. In truth, I took Sami's 'evidence' with a large pinch of salt, as I was well aware of his antipathy towards Samir.

"It couldn't have been Samir. How could it be? He was with me all the time."

"He was with you most of the time, that's true, but not all the time. What happened was, he opened one of the windows of your bungalow earlier and left it slightly ajar. Then as soon as he made sure that you were really into the game and wouldn't notice his absence, he walked back and climbed in through the window."

I was still not sure what to believe. I had always been generous to Samir. We had shared many good times. Why would he steal from me when, if he was short of money, he only had to ask?

When Samir turned up shortly afterwards, I don't know how I managed to refrain from accusing him there and then. As soon as I was alone, I asked my security chief to install hidden cameras in the bungalow as part of a practical joke.

The very next day, the thief was caught on tape. I was told that it was, indeed, my friend Samir who climbed in through the window just as Sami had witnessed the day before.

Apparently, he was sweating buckets as he cautiously looked around to make sure that no one was inside. As he entered my bedroom, he wiped the perspiration from his face with a towel that he carried with him. He was only there for a few minutes, but that was ample time for him to locate my wallet, open it and then slide out a few large denomination dirham notes.

My security chief gave me the tape to watch, but I couldn't bring myself to do so. Knowing the truth was sufficient. When we strolled back to the bungalow, Samir had no idea he had been found out. While he was in the shower, I checked his wallet. It was literally bulging with some of the stolen dirhams and dollars. I confiscated the lot apart from a 100 dollar bill, which I threw on the floor to alert him.

I had just finished praying *al Asr* when I heard him yelling, "I've been robbed... I've been robbed! I'm calling the police!". I could hear Sami doing his best to calm him down.

"What happened?" I asked, pretending to be concerned.

"All my money's gone; all of it. A thief must have taken it while I was in the shower." I had never before seen him that angry.

"That's funny. I meant to tell you. The same thing has happened to me," I said, trying to keep a straight face. "But who would dare to sneak into my bungalow and walk away with our money?"

"I don't know. All I know is someone came here and took all my money," he said, becoming more agitated by the second. "We have to get the police."

"No, no police," I said. "We can't risk newspapers getting hold of the story and ruining the resort's reputation."

"How will I get my money back? What about my money? It's a lot!"

"Calm down, stay calm," I said. "We'll find a way to solve this problem without dragging in the police." If we had been competing for an Oscar, I'm not sure who would have walked off with the statue. Both of us were actors playing a role, but I had the advantage of knowing the whole script.

It soon became obvious that he wasn't about to be parted from his ill-gotten gains without a struggle. He kept on repeating the same refrain. "I want my money. We have to bring in the police."

"Fine, we'll do that," I said, walking towards the phone. "Actually, it's a good idea. The thief must be caught before he does it again."

His face brightened a little until I said, "Don't worry. We'll get our money. It's simple. All the police have to do is check the fingerprints on our wallets. There are bound to be fingerprints. Even if they're not very clear, they have advanced techniques these days."

"Oh yes, that's good." The poor man looked quite stricken. He instantly tried to backtrack.

"On second thoughts, you're right. We have to protect the reputation of the hotel like you said. That's more important than anything else. So let's not call the police. But look, I'm not like you. I can't afford to lose thousands. Please, you have to compensate me."

I almost felt sorry for him until I heard that he was set on stealing from me twice. He had no feelings of remorse whatsoever. He actually wanted me to replace the money he had filched from me in the first place.

"No problem! Let's go to the Metropolitan Hotel. We need to sit down and discuss what we can do to track down this rogue on our own," I said.

As soon as we arrived at the hotel, I asked my security guards to enter Samir's room to look for any money that might be hidden inside one of his suitcases or elsewhere, as not all the missing cash had yet been retrieved. In the event, they found a substantial stash, which they brought to me.

Shortly afterwards, I came across Samir and Sami engaged in a heated argument. Samir had apparently changed his mind again. He wanted to call the police there and then. As a pivotal party to my plot, Sami was trying to restrain him from dialling.

"We've already discussed this," I said. "The best thing to do is for you to come to my office tomorrow. I can promise you all will be clarified by then."

When he turned up at my office the next day, he knew that something was up as I was far from my usual welcoming self. "I want you to listen carefully to what I'm about to tell you without interrupting," I told him. "The person who has been stealing my money over the past two to three weeks is you. No! Don't say anything... I want you to go outside for ten minutes, think very carefully, and then come back when you are ready to admit what you've done. Don't worry! I have no intention of handing you over to the police, whatever you say. I want you to be honest and admit your mistake. There is only one punishment for you. From this day, we will no longer be friends. Now go!"

He was in shock. Sweat was trickling down his face. But before he could open his mouth, I told him, "Go and wait for me to call you back in."

The man who returned wasn't the same one who had left. This was the man I had met all those years ago, the obsequies man who put up with disrespect from his colleagues. His eyes reddened and glistening, he bent to kiss my hand, which I quickly withdrew. He even tried to kiss my feet. He was a broken person.

I couldn't bear his distress. I'm not a revengeful man. Some people are their own victims; they just can't help becoming their own worst enemy. "Enough! Stop! Samir, sit down. Now I'm going to tell you the story of what exactly happened," I said.

"What story?" he said, looking perplexed.

"You didn't steal anything."

"I didn't?"

"No. The real thief was a genie who got under your skin and controlled your mind for a time. Had you been in your right mind, you could have never done such a thing to a good friend. You were manipulated by a wicked spirit. That wasn't you. I know you too well. You couldn't help yourself."

I came up with this fanciful tale to cheer him up. It didn't occur to me he would actually believe it, but he did – or at least, he made himself believe it. In the end, I gave him a friendly pat on the back and wished him well.

It took some time, but I was genuinely able to forgive Samir because he was such entertaining company. To fast forward, in the winter of 2010, I invited him on a trip to Berlin with a few other friends. I always love to tour cities on foot, but on this occasion I wasn't able to walk around as it was freezing cold and the streets were covered with snow and ice. So, half-heartedly, we decided to take a look around some of the museums, mainly to stay dry and warm.

Unfortunately, we chose to visit the Egyptian Museum of Berlin, which I thought Samir, an Egyptian, would appreciate. As we strolled through the various galleries, I noticed my friend was becoming irritated. "What's wrong with you?" I asked him.

"Where are the police? I need the police," he said angrily.

"Why? What's the matter?"

"Haven't you seen the exhibits?"

"Yes, of course. What's the problem?"

"They've all been stolen from my country. They're all Egyptian antiquities. I want to report this to the police and press charges. This is theft. This is an outrage."

I couldn't help but laugh at Samir's silly rant. If he were intent on prosecuting this German museum, he would have to take on museums around the world, including the British Museum, stuffed with Pharaohonic artefacts and mummies, and New York's Metropolitan Museum of Art, that in 2010 agreed to return nineteen artefacts found in Tutankhamun's tomb.

I told him that he was getting worked up over nothing and explained that had those antiquities remained in Egypt, they would probably be un-appreciated, allowed to gather dust in some back room or sold to private collectors on the black market. At least in Germany they were secure in a place where people from all over the world could enjoy them. I must have been persuasive, because he ended up agreeing with me that they were better left in German custody.

* * *

The eighties had been good to Dubai and to me personally. My engineering company had been commissioned to build some of Dubai's most iconic buildings; I had opened my own marble factory to fulfil growing construction demands; our cars were flying out of the showrooms; and at last the Metropolitan Hotel was taking off in a big way thanks to the beach resort. I no longer had to worry about paying off loans. Most importantly, my wife and children were healthy and happy and so was I.

I was grateful, too, that I'd been given so many opportunities to meet interesting people, including an eccentric character, who in 1957 was dubbed the 'Richest Living American' by *Forbes* magazine – John Paul Getty.

In the 1970s, Sheikh Suroor bin Mohammed Al Nahyan, then Director of the Presidential Court in Abu Dhabi, had been invited to Mr Getty's English home and asked me to join him. We drove through the English countryside until we reached Getty's large sixteenth-century Tudor mansion 'Sutton Place' in Surrey, where he spent his last years in virtual retreat from the world. The gardens were stunning with lots of streams crossed by small ornamental bridges.

Getty, who was then an elderly man in his eighties, received us in one of the mansion's magnificent drawing rooms where a maid brought us a pot of tea. "Would you like me to serve you, sir?" I asked.

"Call me Paul, not sir," he answered, before picking up the teapot and pouring the tea into delicate bone china cups. At the time, I considered it quite an experience to have one of the richest men in the world pouring my tea. I didn't realise that this was a habit of the aristocracy.

The kid from Shindagha had grown up and successfully moulded his place in the world. The days when I watched the big ships pass me by were long gone; I was now captain of my own. Dubai was on an unstoppable upwards trajectory. Everything was just perfect, or so I thought. Little did I know that 1990, a year that began with so much promise, was about to become a nightmare shattering everyone's feelings of comfort and security. It was the year we lost our innocence; the year Arab was pitted against Arab.

Nothing would ever be quite the same again.

CHAPTER 14
The Mother of All Battles

"War may sometimes be a necessary evil. But no matter how necessary, it is always an evil, never a good. We will not learn how to live together in peace by killing each other's children."
— Jimmy Carter

2 August 1990 began like any other. The sky was cloudless and the mercury was rising like it does during most summer mornings in the Gulf. As I drove to my office in Deira, my mind was mostly consumed with the affairs of business. That was until I heard an astonishing announcement over the radio to the effect that Saddam Hussein had sent an army of occupation into Kuwait.

I didn't believe it at first. Iraq was invading Kuwait? Impossible! Maybe this was some sort of bad joke, like the 1938 'War of the Worlds' radio hoax that caused American listeners to flee their homes to escape alien invaders.

Everyone in the office was in shock; they could talk of nothing else. This wasn't some far, distant incident. It was happening now, right bang in the middle of our neighbourhood. The first thing I did was to telephone my friend, the US Consul-General John Limbert. If anyone knew what was happening, he surely would.

John is a veteran American diplomat who is no stranger to crises, after being personally held captive in the US embassy in Tehran, along with fifty-one of his fellow US citizens, in 1979. His understanding of the region is better than most Westerners and he's able to get along extraordinarily well with locals. I trusted his assessment of the situation more than anyone else's.

We arranged to see each other at the Metropolitan Beach Resort, where guests were eating, drinking, chatting and sun bathing, seeming oblivious to the potentially life-changing news.

As it happened, John was as dumbfounded and confused as I was. Saddam had kept his invasion plans so close to his chest that even most members of his inner circle weren't told about them in advance. Certainly, the Kuwaiti military wasn't on alert, even though Saddam had long been accusing the Kuwaitis of illegally tapping into Iraqi oilfields. Nevertheless, being able to talk to someone as wise and experienced as John was calming, and soon our conversation turned to more pleasant topics.

Aside from being furious at Saddam for attempting to annex Kuwait, which he had long claimed as part of southern Iraq, and feeling desperately sorry for the Kuwaiti people, I was worried that Saddam might turn his attention to the UAE. Relations between Baghdad and Abu Dhabi had been strained for some time over Iraq's criticism of the UAE's oil price-stabilising policy.

Saddam felt that such strategies employed by both Kuwait and the UAE placed a ceiling on Iraqi oil revenues, which he was keen to maximise for the purposes of post-Iran-Iraq War reconstruction. Historically, Iraq and the UAE had enjoyed cordial ties, and from the UAE's perspective Iraq was seen as a powerful bulwark between Gulf states and Iran. Iraqi troops were also massing on the country's southern border, threatening Saudi Arabia.

However, during the weeks leading up to the invasion when Saddam began sabre rattling against Kuwait, UAE airplanes had participated in a refuelling exercise with US jets, a joint exercise that was meant as a warning to the Iraqi regime. Even so, I don't believe that the UAE government took Saddam's threatening posture seriously.

Of course, when hostilities began, I knew little about the background story. I just knew from belligerent threats coming out of Baghdad that the UAE could be next on Saddam's list, and that according to reports Iraq was armed with chemical and biological weapons along with medium-range delivery missile systems, possibly able to deliver their deadly cargo on my country's shores.

Almost as soon as I got home, I took out my shotguns, handguns and machine guns that before that day were nothing more than collector's items. It had never occurred to me that the time would come when I would actually consider firing any of them, but on that day they represented safety and security. I then sat down to clean them one by one, before loading them with ammunition.

I might not be a trained soldier, but I wanted to be ready to defend my family and my country in case of developments. I am sure that many other UAE nationals were doing the same. It was a strange feeling to be propelled overnight from a peace-loving, family man to someone gearing up to become a warrior.

Kuwait's ground forces had fought the invaders bravely for two days, but they were no match for Saddam's armies. The Emir of Kuwait, Sheikh Jaber Al Ahmad Al Jaber Al Sabah, and several government officials fled to Saudi Arabia. Many ordinary Kuwaitis with the opportunity to leave did so.

On 4 August, Saddam set up the new Provisional Free Government of Kuwait, led by a dual Kuwaiti-Iraqi national, Ala'a Hussein Ali Al Khafaji Al Jaber. The puppet administration appealed to Kuwaitis to accept that "Kuwait should return to great Iraq, the motherland" and for "the hero, Saddam Hussein, to be our leader and protector of our march". Saddam's cousin, Ali Hassan Al Majid (later dubbed 'Chemical Ali'), a man with a reputation for terrible cruelty, was initially appointed governor of the newly-styled nineteenth province of Iraq.

When it sunk in that Saddam's ambitions may extend beyond the borders of Kuwait, I was fearful. Everyone in the UAE was, even if they didn't admit it. Every day, when I woke up for morning prayers, I would stare out of the window at the purple-black pre-dawn skies and would sometimes imagine that a moving light was a missile heading our way. I remember being so on edge that even the sound of a truck exhaust backfiring would be heart-stopping.

For several days, news reports in local newspapers and on local TV channels were scant on Kuwait, which was probably a government strategy to prevent panic; or it could have been that the authorities needed time to formulate a position. Not knowing what was going on was worse than being appraised of the facts. Much later on, Dubai television began relaying 24/7 news from CNN, which was the first time a foreign network had been allowed to broadcast within the country.

A strange and unsettling atmosphere of calm hung over Dubai. Outwardly, everything seemed normal, apart from new signs on bridges that read 'No fishing'. Behind the scenes, there was a run on the banks, as foreign investors and a few nationals began transferring funds abroad. It goes without saying that tourism began to dry up, but that was the least of my concerns; I was far more fearful of waking up one morning to find an apocalyptic landscape.

Western TV reporters started arriving in droves, mostly staying at the Hilton Hotel adjoining the World Trade Centre (WTC). They must have been instructed not to mention where they were, because their reports televised in front of a palm tree outside the WTC always ended with 'so-and-so reporting from somewhere in the Gulf'.

It was reassuring to know that almost the entire international community had condemned the invasion and within days of it, the United Nations Security Council passed UNSC Resolution 660, demanding the immediate withdrawal of Iraqi troops from Kuwait. That was swiftly followed by UNSC Resolution 661 that slapped Iraq with economic sanctions and UNSC Resolution 665 authorising UN member states deploying maritime forces in the area to inspect and verify ships' cargoes and destinations.

The Arab League called for an emergency meeting and in support of the Security Council's decision, issued a resolution to support the deployment of international coalition forces. It wasn't unanimous; Twelve Arab League member countries voted in favour, eight voted against.

I was very disturbed and disappointed to learn that Jordan's King Hussein and leader of the PLO Yasser Arafat both chose to back the Iraqi regime. In the case of Jordan, that news may not have been accurate. The US President at the time, George H.W. Bush, accused King Hussein of knowing of Saddam's invasion plans in advance and of providing the Iraqi leader with tacit support throughout.

King Hussein's account differs immeasurably. He later maintained that the first he heard of the invasion was during a phone call with King Fahd of Saudi Arabia. He said the news took him by surprise as Saddam had promised him that Iraq's disagreement with Kuwait was under negotiation and there was no military solution on the table. There is also evidence that the King worked hard to mediate a peaceful resolution, which was highlighted in a white paper that he published along with official documents to support his position.

There is no doubt, however, that Arafat made one of the biggest mistakes of his life by backing the wrong horse. Arab States took his pro-Saddam stance as an unforgiveable betrayal. Kuwait condemned him as a traitor, in light of the fact that the PLO had benefited greatly from Kuwait's generosity for decades – although it should be said that Iraq had been just as generous to the PLO and other Palestinian groups.

Arafat vehemently objected to any military intervention to free Kuwait by what he considered to be imperialist Western powers, and probably believed that a powerful, expanded Iraq would have more leverage against Israel. Arafat's error was to take sides. I am sure that he didn't approve of Iraq's aggression against a brotherly Arab country. He used to live in Kuwait City and used to tell everyone: "the meat on my shoulders is from Kuwait".

In the end, Arafat and the people he served were the losers. A greatly weakened Iraq was in no position to aid the Palestinians and Gulf states remained distrustful of Fatah for years to come. Some Middle East commentators are of the opinion that Arafat's new-found vulnerability was the opening to the 'peace of the brave' brokered by President Bill Clinton. In 1994, Arafat, Rabin and Shimon Peres were joint recipients of the Nobel Peace Prize in recognition of their efforts, which sadly came to nothing.

For me, there was no contest when it came to my respective loyalties towards Iraq and Kuwait. The Kuwaitis had supported poorer Arab countries for generations, and prior to the discovery of oil the Kuwaiti government had greatly assisted Dubai by sending teachers and doctors, building hospitals and offering loans for infrastructure. At the same time, the thought of Iraq, the cradle of civilisation, being invaded by Western armies was hard to take. A peaceful solution involving a total Iraqi withdrawal and payment of compensation to Kuwait was the only one acceptable to my mind.

The stories coming out of Kuwait were upsetting. Iraqis were breaking down the doors of homes to arrest men over sixteen years of age. There were reports of Iraqi soldiers cutting off ears, breaking limbs and gouging out eyes. Owners of houses marked with anti-Iraqi graffiti were executed. Civilians on the streets after curfew were gunned down. Resistance was met with torture and extrajudicial executions. Water and electricity plants were damaged, banks were looted and shut, foreign embassies were closed.

Many Kuwaitis and foreign nationals were incarcerated or taken to Iraq as hostages. Some 600 Kuwaitis are missing to this day. Up to 400,000 managed to escape the country for the US, Europe, Saudi Arabia and other GCC states.

Thousands arrived in Dubai, many with just the clothes they were wearing. Affluent families were caught out without access to their funds, which prompted the UAE government to offer each household a regular monthly stipend and free accommodation. Kuwaitis were treated as honoured guests by just about everyone in the UAE. We thought of them as family and wanted to do everything in our power to make them welcome and comfortable.

Unfortunately, a few took the UAE's generosity the wrong way: as charity – which it wasn't at all, as helping to alleviate our brothers' distress was not only our duty, but also a debt which Dubai, in particular, had long owed to Kuwait and its people. Wealthy Emirati property owners made unoccupied brand-new apartment blocks available to Kuwaiti families and hotels were open to them, including my own.

There were so many of them that I converted the hotel's Al Andalus Ballroom into a dining room. Everything in the hotel – rooms, food, laundry and medication – was provided to Kuwaiti guests on a complimentary basis, so I was a little surprised when I learned that a few were demanding better food and complaining about the service. But I didn't really mind because I knew what they were going through, homeless, penniless and uncertain about their futures and the future of their country. I didn't realise it at the time, but it should be mentioned that Sheikh Maktoum later compensated apartment and hotel owners for any losses they had incurred relating to the Kuwaiti guests.

I remember walking through the hotel with a prominent Kuwaiti, Dr Ahmad Al Rabie, who later became Kuwait's Minister of Education, when we came across a Kuwaiti man having a loud conversation with himself as he stood outside the barber's shop.

"What's happened to that poor person?" I asked Dr Ahmad. "Is he sick?"

"What do you expect after all he's been through? Anyone whose country was invaded by its neighbour overnight is liable to go crazy. Who can blame him?"

Amid all that worry and turmoil came one of the darkest days of my life; it was the day that Sheikh Rashid left us forever. He was in his bed when he slipped away at 10 p.m. on 7 October 1990. I had been anticipating this terrible event for years, but that didn't lessen the pain inflicted by the loss of a person I loved and admired. It was akin to losing my father all over again.

Although Sheikh Rashid had been too ill to carry out his duties for some time, just to know that he was there had been a great psychological comfort. Something inside me told me that such feelings were selfish. His work was done. He was tired and now it was his time to rest and enjoy the rewards of Paradise.

The next morning, I was enveloped by a black cloud of sadness that was almost palpable. I joined Sheikh Rashid's funeral process with a leaden heart. The mourners, led by Sheikh Zayed bin Sultan Al Nahyan and Sheikh Rashid's sons, included leaders from all over the region and the world, who wanted to show their last respects to a man who was truly exceptional in every way.

I still remember that my eyes were damp watching Sheikh Mohammed and Sheikh Hamdan, their faces etched with sorrow, lowering their father's body wrapped in a white cloth into the grave. I quietly said a prayer and bade him a last farewell. Sheikh Rashid was succeeded by his eldest son, Sheikh Maktoum bin Rashid Al Maktoum, who was subsequently appointed UAE Prime Minister and elected Vice-President by the Supreme Council of the UAE. Politically, the transition was seamless.

As war clouds loomed ever menacingly, expatriate managerial staff began sending their wives and children home, while a growing number of foreign workers flew back to their homelands. I told all my managers that whoever didn't feel comfortable staying should feel free to go. "You're under no obligation to stay in these circumstances," I said. Almost all chose to remain. One of my engineers, Mahmoud Khalid, engaged in extending the Beach Resort with new rooms, was panic-stricken. He asked me "What should we do?"

"I need you to pull out all the stops to finish the extension without any delay."

"But what about the war... the Iraqis are on their way. They will take over the UAE, they'll come to Dubai."

"No they won't," I said. "But whatever happens, we'll still be here. Where else will we go? We'll have to stay in our country." He tried to argue with me until I silenced him and told him to concentrate on his work. The wing was finished in just four months.

Mounir Tadros, the Metropolitan Hotel's General Manager, was one of those understandably cautious folk that chose to quit their jobs and leave. I was sorry to see him go, as despite his regular hot-tempered outbursts and slightly offbeat behaviour, overall his managerial skills were better than most.

Mounir was a person who hated to lose. He would claim to be a great windsurfer, but he could never manage to ride the waves for long. Whenever he landed in the water, he would make a fuss and come up with all kinds of excuses for his poor show.

On occasion, I played against him in tennis doubles matches. He had a strong serve, but most of the time his balls landed outside the court, although he would rarely accept what everyone with eyes could see. He would always insist they were in when we would get into long, loud arguments. When the yelling matches were over, he would shout at himself, saying, "How can I be a general manager? I'm an idiot, a donkey."

Quite a few 'donkeys' have wandered through the Metropolitan, a designation I use with some affection. One of our assistant general managers,

Hassan Wanli, was married to a woman who had a daughter from a previous husband. Two of his colleagues, Elie Tohmeh and Mounir Assi, were also married with stepchildren. One day, while dropping off his stepdaughter at the Emirates International School, Hassan came across the other two, realised that they were in the same boat and invited them for coffee at the Metropolitan.

Once they were all seated at the table, Hassan made an announcement. "Like you guys, I'm raising another man's child. I'm paying for her education, clothing and everything else. So now I plan to open an association, the Donkey Association. I've had printed all the stationery, posters and visit cards in your names. But there's one thing I insist upon. I must be the Chairman because I'm the biggest donkey of all."

News of the Donkey Club swept around the hotel and was soon a standing joke. One day, we were all sitting together on the patio of my bungalow, when Hassan decided to approach two ladies stretched out on the sands, to invite them to join us for tea. When they gave him the brush off, he returned to the bungalow to pick up a shovel. We had no idea what it was for, until we saw him digging up the sand around their beach umbrella, which he "accidentally" chucked in the direction of the women's feet. That may be a very unorthodox way to make someone's acquaintance, but it worked. Once the ice was broken, they came and had tea with us.

A few days later, I ran into one of those ladies by chance and was surprised to hear her ask, "Mr Habtoor, can you recommend my membership with the Donkey Association?"

"Sure," I said. "But why do you want to join when all the members are men?"

"Oh, that's perfect! I have a child without a father and urgently need a donkey to marry me."

There were many similar moments of levity during the build-up to military action. They were a good escape valve from all the pressure and worry everyone was under.

Some people, like Mounir, may have been in a rush to head for the airport, but many others, mostly American diplomatic officials, congressmen and US military honchos were either flying or sailing in on warships. The sight of monster black US airplanes on the tarmac of Dubai International Airport was an omen of the hostilities to come. I used to see those big beasts from my office window, but had no idea what purpose they served.

As keen as I was to see Saddam's forces ousted from Kuwait, and as reassuring as it was to know that the US fleet was close to our shores, I wasn't entirely happy about America's involvement in what I believed to be a regional problem better solved by Arab states. I met Ambassador Richard W. Murphy several times and we played at least one game of tennis. He was pleasant enough socially, but, frankly, his attitude to the area was such that he would have fit in nicely with Brits in India during the Raj.

One day, when we were sitting together talking politics, I was outraged when Mr Murphy said, "From now on, 'we' are responsible for regional security".

"What do you mean 'we'?" I asked, knowing full well what he meant.

"I'm talking about the United States of America," Mr Murphy said.

"Ah, I see. And who authorised you to take charge?"

"Nobody did. We inherited this role from the British."

"Oh, you did. Strange that we the people who live here are the last to know. Has the Gulf Cooperation Council been informed about this 'handover'?"

"No, I don't think so," he said. "This is a matter between the British and us."

I tried hard not to show how irritated and insulted I felt. What are we? I thought. Are we a flock of sheep handed over to a rancher? And all this time, we had been fooled into thinking that we had gained our independence from colonial powers.

At one point, I talked to US Consul-General John Limbert about my concerns, during one of our regular dinners together at the Metropolitan Hotel. I asked him about his country's primary role in the region and what US military power was doing here.

America's main interest in the region was to secure the flow of oil through the Straits of Hormuz and the Suez Canal, he told me.

"Don't you care about your friends?" I said. This question, given what I now know, must have come across as naive. The US government and its agencies work on one principle only – what's best for American interests. Friendship doesn't come into this equation.

"I can't really comment on that," he answered. "All I know is that our main priority is securing the flow of oil." At least, my friend was honest. Any other US diplomat in his place would have probably tried to bluff me.

I began to wonder whether the West had its eyes on Iraq for its oil all along and whether Saddam had been set up by the US and Britain to invade Kuwait, when those countries would have a rock solid pretext to control Iraq's oilfields. My mind went back to 1988, when UK's Foreign Minister Geoffrey Howe visited Dubai's British community. John Fulcher, the boss of Widnell & Trollope quantity surveyors, asked me if I would have liked to meet him and invited me to join the gathering.

I found myself seated next to Mr Howe. He was flanked by three Arabs and a Briton. He asked me why I didn't expand my business to Iran, adding that Iran was a rich and stable country bursting with business opportunities. I soon knocked that idea on the head. "I've no interest in opening any business in Iran because I fundamentally disagree with Iranian ideology," I told him.

He then asked whether I had Iraq in my sights. But before I could answer, he began to paint Iraq as a very dangerous state that posed a threat to the UAE. I found that statement odd, because at the time Saddam was a close ally of Western governments.

"Why is Iraq a danger?" I asked.

"Because Iraq has many scientists; when a country has too many scientists, it becomes a threat," said Howe.

"Scientists are dangerous?"

"Yes they are. It's the scientists who invent new deadly weapons."

I was appalled at his thinking. "It's a pity that a nation that values scientific achievement is seen as a potential danger," I said. "Personally, I respect a government that puts great store on education far above one that treats its population like dumb creatures." Perhaps it's no accident that numerous Iraqi scientists were assassinated during decades to come.

Despite my suspicions that America's motives were less than pure, I met quite a few very decent Americans at the Metropolitan Hotel and at the Beach Resort, which became a favourite with US diplomats, soldiers, marines and airmen. Although the US military men were instructed to wear civvies while out and about in the UAE, their short haircuts made them instantly recognisable.

Several became close friends and, before I knew it, I was accepted as one of the guys. Whenever a new ship or plane came in, high-ranking marines and pilots (the lower ranks were billeted in desert encampments) would invariably come to see me after hearing about me from their colleagues. When I had the time, I would invite the newcomers for dinner. I spent some fun times with those good-natured men, who would have preferred to be at home with their wives and children, rather than preparing for a possible war.

To show my appreciation for their mission, I provided offices with parking spaces, as well as water and electricity at my expense, for a facility on the ground floor of the Metropolitan Hotel adjacent to the Metroplex Cinema to be used as a branch of the United Services Organisation (USO). This was where they could get together over a drink at the bar, a game of snooker or gather around the television.

I also organised softball games and Happy Hours. The organisation received servicemen at the airport, showed them around Dubai and threw parties for them – including several in the Metropolitan Hotel and the Beach Resort. The USO assisted those in financial difficulty, offered psychological counselling and moral guidance. I was delighted when the USO made me an honorary member of its World Board of Governors, as I believed the organisation was doing an excellent job in boosting the morale of young men putting their lives on the line for the people of Kuwait. And I was especially proud to be the Board's only non-American member.

When my friends from the US Air Force learned that two of my sons were about to marry, they wanted to attend the wedding ceremonies and give the couples a celebratory salute by flying over the wedding venue. "Thank you. That's such a kind thought," I told them. "But please don't do it. You'll scare the wedding guests away."

Some of the big American ships and aircraft carriers that docked at Jebel Ali Port hosted regular parties for UAE nationals and expatriates to improve relations between the US Navy/Marines and the local population. At Christmas and New Year, families were encouraged to invite members of the American military to celebrate with them, which many were only too keen to do. The US Air Force also made efforts to woo the local media. Several reporters were invited to join air-born reconnaissance missions.

One of the guys I used to hang out with fairly frequently was an F-16 pilot called Colonel Michael ("Mike") Navarro, the Commander of the 388th Tactical Fighter Wing. He was a good person and over time we developed a close brotherly relationship.

One day, Karl, who was the base commander, told me that Col Navarro was intimately involved with an English girl, which I didn't think was any of my business since Mike had never mentioned her to me. But then the officer explained that such fraternisation with the civilian population was forbidden for pilots on a mission. He suggested I have a word with Mike and ask him to cease contact with the girl for his own sake. He hesitated to talk to Col Navarro himself, as the Colonel outranked him.

I spoke to Mike about it and he told me in no uncertain terms that as far as he was concerned, he was doing nothing wrong. I later came to know that Mike was being investigated by military intelligence, which put his promotion prospects at risk.

Hardly a day went by when I didn't see Mike for a coffee or a meal, but all of a sudden he disappeared. I paged him numerous times without any response and couldn't help but be concerned as to what might have happened to him. The mystery was solved when Karl made a surprise visit to my Deira office. "Where's Mike?" I asked him. "I've been trying to get hold of him for days."

Karl gestured to me to walk with him towards the window. "Look, all the black refuelling planes are missing," he said. That was when I came to know what they were for. "This means they are in the air refuelling F-16s on sorties over Iraq."

"You're not attacking Baghdad are you?"

"Not yet," he said, but I could see from his face that an attack was imminent. I was extremely upset when I heard that. Until then, I had been under the impression that the US-assembled coalition of thirty-four countries, that included Egypt, Saudi Arabia, Syria, the UAE, Qatar, Bahrain and Oman, was simply tasked with driving Saddam's army from Kuwait. I hadn't realised that major Iraqi cities and the Iraqi capital itself might come in for a battering.

Mike Navarro reappeared a few days later. I was relieved to see him in one piece. "I've been worrying about you," I told him. "Thanks Khalaf. You're a real brother," he said. He mentioned that the clock had begun ticking and therefore, I shouldn't expect to see him as much from now on. Within less than forty-eight hours, he was gone again.

Soon afterwards, a meeting of the Emirates Committee for Arab Solidarity was called, to which Dr Ahmad Al Rabie was invited. Naturally, the invasion of Kuwait and impending military action by US-led coalition forces dominated our discussions.

Taryam Omran Taryam was convinced that the Americans were preparing to bomb Baghdad and destroy its ancient Arab heritage. Knowing what I knew from Karl together with Taryam's credible fears prompted me to try to do something, anything to prevent Iraq's destruction.

"Gentlemen, I have an idea," I said. "We must immediately fly to Baghdad and demand to speak with President Saddam Hussein in private. We must talk to him in a friendly, brotherly way and in a down-to-earth street dialect. We must persuade him to surrender and pull out of Kuwait before his country is attacked and devastated, which none of us wants." I was desperate to do something positive before it was too late and sincerely believed that we might be able to change his thinking.

Both Dr Ahmad and Taryam stared at me as though I'd lost my mind, but I wasn't to be so easily deterred from my plan. "We can't just stand back and do nothing," I said. "He'll listen to the three of us. I'm happy to pay for the aircraft and all the costs for the journey." I had complete faith in my friends' powers of persuasion.

Indeed, shortly before, I had bumped into a prominent Kuwaiti, Yusuf Al Ghanim, who, when he learned that I knew Dr Ahmad, said, "I must warn you, Khalaf. If that man talked to a stone, it would get up and walk."

That advice might have been meant as a caution to me, but it was also a great compliment to Ahmad Al Rabie's negotiating talents. Mr Al Ghanim was absolutely right. Dr Ahmad possessed an exceptionally sharp, incisive brain and argued very persuasively. If anyone was capable of changing Saddam's mind, it was him. I kept on hammering home my point.

"You're joking of course," said one of my friends.

"No, not at all, I'm deadly serious."

"No way," said the other. "Saddam Hussein is a very scary guy. He even intimidates other Arab leaders. He's not going to listen to us. I saw him at a conference striding confidently along with two Arab presidents and a king running behind him like rabbits."

"It's worth a try," I insisted. But they were in no mood to listen. They were sure that the minute we landed at Baghdad's Saddam Airport we would be hauled off and executed at worst, or taken hostage to be used as human shields at best. "If you're that determined, you can go on your own," they told me. "There's no way that we're going to risk our lives by going into the lion's den and especially when Saddam won't take any notice of us anyway." So that was the end of that.

Everyone I knew was fearful in the days preceding the deadline for military action, mandated by one of the UNSC resolutions. Dubai Airport was packed with mainly Indian, Pakistani and Filipino workers trying to find a flight out, which wasn't easy as far fewer airlines were flying to Dubai by then. Emirates continued with its schedule throughout, but of course seats on Emirates were difficult to come by. There was little sign of panic, however, although I'm sure that a great many were feeling trapped inside a potential war zone and were panicking inwardly.

Several European embassies provided their citizens in the UAE with protective clothing against chemical warfare that included special boots and atropine injections. I recall some of the Brits complaining that their embassy hadn't bothered to afford British citizens with that kind of protection.

We all felt utterly helpless. All we could do was to monitor reports from CNN, which did an excellent job of bringing the war into our homes; this was the first conflict shown blow-by-blow on TV. CNN's Peter Arnett was the only Western television correspondent allowed to report freely from Baghdad and didn't hesitate to report on civilian casualties, belying the coalition's insistence that bombs dropped on the Iraqi capital were all surgical strikes.

Arnett was also the only reporter to gain an uncensored interview with Saddam and, because of that, he came to the attention of the CIA, which tried unsuccessfully to drive him out of the Al Rashid Hotel where he was based under the pretext that the Iraqis were operating a communications network in the basement. His response was to inspect the hotel's basement and when nothing was found, he refused to leave.

The coalition was further angered when Arnett insisted that "a biological warfare facility" destroyed by the US Air Force was a factory producing baby milk. Senior US officials said Arnett had been fooled, but the French company that had built the factory later announced that it was not equipped to breed pathogens and that its technicians who had been visiting the plant over the years to undertake routine repairs had confirmed that the only thing it produced was milk powder for babies.

"If we'd had the immediacy in Vietnam that we had in the Gulf War, it would have changed history," Arnett was to say later. "The Vietnam War could not have lasted as long as it did."

Christiane Amanpour and Wolf Blitzer also became household names, as did General 'Stormin' Norman' Schwarzkopf, then Commander-in-Chief of US Central Command; Colin Powell, Chairman of the Joint Chiefs of Staff; and Binyamin Netanyahu, who served as Israel's PR representative throughout the Gulf War.

Politics was never far from everyone's mind then. If I wasn't watching a political debate play out on TV or discussing the conflict with my friends in the US military, I was talking regional politics with one of the many visiting congressmen, whom I would often invite to enjoy the hotel's Beach Resort. I don't want to mention names, but whatever lofty position they held didn't deter me from telling them, "You guys are biased. Your administration is biased. All you do is support Israel unconditionally. You do nothing to help the Palestinians. All your presidents promise to bring about a Palestinian state and never do anything."

They usually answered that I was right, but there wasn't anything they could do to change things. One lawmaker told me, "When your presidents and kings visit the White House, they talk a different language. They don't want to involve themselves in the Palestinian problem. They say we'll leave this for the United States to solve." I couldn't help thinking that what he was saying was true.

The aerial war, code-named 'Desert Storm', billed by President Bush as purely defensive, began on 17 January 1991. Nothing could have stopped it because the US refused dialogue with Iraq, as long as there was a single Iraqi soldier remaining on Kuwaiti soil. Some 88,500 bombs were dropped on military and civilian infrastructure, including Iraqi command and control and anti-aircraft facilities, missile launchers, air force bases and warships.

Saddam's main line of defence was his arsenal of over 1,100 Scud missiles – purchased from Libya, North Korea and the former Soviet Union – with a range of approximately 1,000 km. Iraq's first launch of Scuds was on Thursday, 17 January. They were directed at Tel Aviv and Haifa, in hopes of dragging Israel into the war, and thus weakening the joint Western-Arab coalition. A total of thirty-nine Scuds were fired at Israeli targets, but caused few casualties due to the interception of Israeli Patriot surface-to-air missiles.

The Israeli government was champing at the bit to retaliate, but succumbed to heavy pressure from President Bush not to do so. Instead, the Israeli public was told to remain either in bunkers or in their homes where they were advised to seal all doors and windows with tape and keep door frames doused with water to dilute chemicals.

Iraqi Scuds were also fired at military and civilian targets in Saudi Arabia, Bahrain and Qatar. In Dubai, there was a rumour that one had landed in the sea off Jumeirah Beach, which turned out to be untrue. I asked a US commander whether the UAE was vulnerable to a Scud attack. He told me not to worry, as even if Saddam sent missiles our way, they would be knocked out of the skies before they could land. I suspected that his appraisal was overly optimistic, but nevertheless it put my mind at rest.

On 29 January, Iraq's forces invaded the town of Khafji in Saudi Arabia. Just days later, they were beaten back by Saudi and Qatari divisions. The conflict was now tipped in the allies' favour. 13 February was a day I will always remember with deep sadness. At 4 a.m., two 2,000-pound US laser-guided bombs were dropped on what the Pentagon claimed was an Iraqi command and control bunker in Baghdad.

In reality, this was the Al Amariya bomb shelter, a clearly-marked facility where more than 400 civilians, mostly women and children under fifteen years old, had taken refuge. The result was nothing less than sheer horror. Those on the upper level were incinerated, their bodies carbonised along with the walls; those sheltering on the lower floor were fatally scalded by boiling water from the facility's damaged hot water tank. Today, Al Amariya remains much as it was, following the attack as a shrine to the innocents who lost their lives.

On 22 February, President Bush issued Saddam with a twenty-four-hour ultimatum to withdraw his troops from Kuwait, else face a ground war. He ignored it. Two days later, coalition forces invaded Iraq and Kuwait simultaneously. In Kuwait, they encountered little resistance; not so within Iraq, where they were met with a fierce foe. But Iraq's military was no match for British and American forces, which took 500 prisoners in three hours.

By then, Saddam knew that the game was over. On 26 February, he ordered Iraq's withdrawal from Kuwait when the country's oilfields were torched, precipitating the dumping of millions of gallons of crude oil into waters of the Arabian Gulf. The smell of burning oil reached as far as Dubai, as did the black smoke which polluted our atmosphere for days, if not weeks.

What happened next was shameful. Retreating Iraqi soldiers were indiscriminately slaughtered by US airplanes and ground forces without mercy, on what came to be known as the 'Highway of Death'. One US pilot was quoted as saying, "It was like shooting fish in a barrel."

Those soldiers weren't withdrawing temporarily to fight again another day. They were on their way home. Thousands of incinerated or dismembered bodies and charred vehicles were discovered disfiguring Highway 80 from Kuwait to Basra. President Bush did his best to cover up this atrocity, but when real-time video was beamed around the world America's Arab coalition partners were horrified.

The Gulf War was finally over on 28 February 1991. For us in the UAE, this was the best news ever. I remember that just about everyone, nationals and expats alike, jumped in their cars and drove around Dubai waving UAE flags and honking horns. A great weight had been lifted from our shoulders. Kuwait had been liberated and now we could look forward to life returning to normal.

The UAE government wasted no time in tasking the army to transport desperately needed food, mineral water and medical supplies to Kuwait City. Kuwaitis had suffered great losses in terms of casualties and it would take time for them to fully recover from the psychological blow of witnessing the rape and devastation of their home. But now that the darkness had faded, the future was theirs. It was time to rebuild.

There is no doubt that George Bush senior was owed a debt of gratitude for intervening, but he was heavily criticised by human rights groups for the bombing of the Al Amariya shelter and the mowing down of retreating Iraqis on the Highway of Death. He was also condemned by some for failing to send ground troops into Baghdad to topple Saddam when he had the chance, a charge he responded to thus in his memoir, *A World Transformed*:

> Trying to eliminate Saddam [...] would have incurred incalculable human and political costs. Apprehending him was probably impossible [...] We would have been forced to occupy Baghdad, and in effect rule Iraq. There was no viable exit strategy we could see, violating another of our principles. Furthermore, we had been self-consciously trying to set a pattern for handling aggression in the post-Cold War world. Going in and occupying Iraq, thus unilaterally exceeding the United Nations mandate, would have destroyed the precedent of international response to aggression that we hoped to establish. Had we gone the invasion route, the United States could conceivably still be an occupying power in a bitterly hostile land.

Wise words indeed! It's a pity his son, President George W. Bush, who went into Iraq in 2003 to finish Saddam, failed to get the message.

It wasn't long after the war's end that Mike showed up. I was still angry over the bombing of Baghdad and upset over the images I'd seen of the carnage at Al Amariya and on the Highway of Death. I was also very relieved to see him in one piece. I was pretty sure that he'd survived because I'd been checking on US Air Force casualties almost daily.

The first thing he said to me was "Job's done". I was torn. On the one hand, I felt like welcoming him back with a hug. On the other, I feared that his bombs had killed Iraqi civilians. My fury took control of me. I swore at him before shouting, "You damaged Iraq. You destroyed the history of that great country. How could you do that?"

My harsh words wiped the smile from his face. "It's not my fault, Khalaf," he said to me. "I'm a military man. I have to obey the orders of my superiors who take their orders from politicians. None of this was my choice."

I knew that what he was saying was the truth. He was nothing more than a tool of Washington's powerful men in suits. My anger quickly dissipated. I invited him to my home to have dinner with the family and he brought with him all my officer friends who wanted to say goodbye to me before they headed home.

After the meal, I took Mike aside to ask him whether he knew that he was under investigation for his association with the English girl. He said he knew. As I had warned him, he lost his chance of promotion. To my knowledge, he submitted his resignation and left the Air Force for good, which was their loss. He was a fine man and a fine pilot. Once he was back in the States, he wrote a few letters to me, but as time went on we eventually lost contact.

It was to emerge later that the US may have given Saddam a green light to invade Kuwait in advance, if one takes at face value this excerpt of an Iraqi record of a meeting between Saddam Hussein and his foreign minister, Tariq Aziz, with US Ambassador to Iraq April Glaspie, published in the *New York Times*:

Hussein: The price [of oil] at one stage had dropped to twelve dollars a barrel and a reduction in the modest Iraqi budget of six to seven billion dollars is a disaster.

Glaspie: I think I understand this. I have lived here for years. I admired your extraordinary efforts to rebuild your country. I know you need funds. We understand that and our opinion is that you should have the opportunity to rebuild your country. But we have no opinion on the Arab–Arab conflicts, like your border disagreement with Kuwait.

I was in the American Embassy in Kuwait during the late 1960s. The instruction we had during this period was that we should express no opinion on this issue and that the issue is not associated with America. James Baker has directed our official spokesman to emphasise this instruction. We hope you can solve this problem using any suitable methods via Klibi (Chedli Klibi) or via President Mubarak. All that we hope is that these issues are solved quickly. With regard to all of this, can I ask you to see how the issue appears to us?

My assessment after twenty-five years' service in this area is that your objective must have strong backing from your Arab brothers. I now speak of oil. But you,

Mr President, have fought through a horrific and painful war. Frankly, we can see only that you have deployed massive troops in the south. Normally that would not be any of our business, but when this happens in the context of what you said on your national day, then when we read the details in the two letters of the Foreign Minister, then we see the Iraqi point of view that the measures taken by the UAE and Kuwait are, in the final analysis, parallel to military aggression against Iraq, then it would be reasonable for me to be concerned. And for this reason, I received an instruction to ask you, in the spirit of friendship – not in the spirit of confrontation – regarding your intentions.

As luck would have it, the UAE recovered from the economic effects of the conflict quickly. All eyes had been on the Gulf region for months; once the fighting was finally over, they were eager to get to know the area first hand. Tourism and investment levels soon returned to pre-Gulf War levels.

Emiratis felt extremely blessed to have remained on the periphery of the action. We had missed the bullet quite literally. For us, the conflict's end signified greater prominence for Gulf states within the international arena and a new climate of media transparency. MBC's launch of its free Arabic satellite news channel in 1991 paved the way for Al Jazeera, Al Arabiya and hundreds more which have made such a crucial contribution to Arab political and economic awareness.

Kuwait swiftly recovered too, although it took rather longer for Kuwaiti citizens to heal from their psychological scars. The quisling Ala'a Hussein Ali fled to Norway with his family where they lived under a new surname. A Kuwaiti court sentenced him to death in 1993 for treason, which was commuted to life imprisonment when he gave himself up to appeal. Ali Hassan Al Majid, charged with war crimes, crimes against humanity and genocide, was hanged in Iraq in January 2010. For the people of Iraq, the Gulf War marked one of the worst eras in their country's history. More than 20,000 Iraqis had died in combat and the lives of over 3,500 Iraqi civilians were lost. They probably were not aware of it at the time, but for Iraqis the suffering was far from over. It was only just beginning.

It wasn't long before we were beset with another kind of invasion. Citizens of the former Soviet Union and Russians began arriving in Dubai in greater and greater numbers. In 1990, Dubai received just 20,000 visitors from Russia. This statistic jumped to 50,000 in 1991 and 100,000 in 1992.

We started seeing Russian ladies in headscarves sitting at roadsides selling Russian-made manual cameras, watches and strings of tiny freshwater pearls. At the same time, Russians and Eastern Europeans were making frenzied purchases of containers full of vehicles, spare parts, electronic goods, fridges, washing machines and bales of cloth that were shipped to their home countries and were a material boost to the economy. Over the following years, a fledgling Russian business community was formed in the UAE and a sophisticated, well-heeled type of Russian and Eastern European visitor was seen frequenting hotels, malls and beaches.

* * *

Now that the business climate was once again healthy, in 1992 I formed a company called Dubai National Insurance and Reinsurance together with Saeed Juma Al Naboodah, Ahmad Saif Belhasa and my brother Sultan.

Before we went ahead, I went to see Sheikh Maktoum, who was in London at the time, to gain his support for the new venture.

On Sheikh Maktoum's instructions, the Ministry of Economy and Commerce was asked to assist us in opening our new company. The Legal Advisor to the Ruler of Dubai, Hamdi Abdul Majid, wrote to the Minister, Saeed Ghobash, setting out the details and also requesting his cooperation.

Back in Dubai, I waited and waited to hear something from the Ministry, before going with Ahmad Saif Belhasa to meet Mr Ghobash and his undersecretary, Abdul Raouf Al Mubarak. Instead of trying to smooth the way ahead, the two men seemed determined to complicate matters. They said they needed time to get approvals and clear red tape, giving the impression that we had a very long wait ahead.

I was irritated by such bureaucratic nonsense. "Well, in this case, you are ignoring the instructions of Sheikh Maktoum. If you don't proceed immediately, my colleagues and I will withdraw our written application and report this matter to His Highness."

"You know the way. You're free to report anything you want to anyone you want," responded the Minister.

I thanked him for his time and left. I didn't waste a second in calling Abdul Majid to let him know what happened. He immediately telephoned Saeed Ghobash and told him in no uncertain terms to give our request priority for the benefit of the country.

The way was miraculously cleared and we announced the company's formation in the media. We chose the office of Saeed Al Naboodah to hold our board meetings. As the company's Chairman, I nominated one of my friends at the time, Abdullah Al Shehhi, as a board member.

Rashid, my son, introduced me to a young finance graduate from an American university called Abdulrahman Al Awar, who was looking for a good job. He impressed me with his sharp mind so we employed him as Deputy Manager. He excelled in the post so it wasn't very long afterwards that I decided to promote him to General Manager. I was delighted to have such a hardworking, intelligent person in charge of the day-to-day running and thought of him as more of a friend than an employee.

As the business rapidly expanded and with an internal audit in the offing, I thought Abdulrahman deserved a qualified assistant to lighten his workload. To my surprise, he didn't warm to that idea and, moreover, his general attitude to me seemed to have cooled. I began to wonder whether there was something going on that I didn't know about.

I subsequently came to know that Al Shehhi and Al Awar may have been conspiring against me in cahoots with a few of my fellow board members, but I couldn't prove it, so I didn't say anything. In one of our regular board meetings, my suspicions were confirmed. Ahmad Belhasa surprised me saying, "Khalaf, we understand you're buying lots of shares from the market."

"So, what's the problem? Is it legal or isn't it?"

"In my opinion it is not legal," he said. "You shouldn't buy up company shares. In fact, you should sell what you have and keep only the shares you had when the company was first founded. Secondly, you should avoid interfering so much in the company's management. It's the General Manager's responsibility to execute board resolutions. He's under no obligation to refer to you."

"But someone has to follow up," I argued.

"There is no need for you to get involved. The General Manager has our full trust."

"I will leave that for the board to decide, but personally I disagree. How can we leave the General Manager to his own devices without any supervision? This is the people's money, the public's money. It's our duty to look after it." I didn't care that Al Awar was present or how he might take my comments. "So gentlemen, what do you think?"

Saeed Al Naboodah didn't say anything. My so-called friends, Abdullah Al Shehhi and Abdulrahman Al Awar, who wouldn't have been in the company at all if it wasn't for me, were quick to pipe up. They informed me that the board members weren't happy and because they were in the majority, I had no choice but to abide by their collective will.

"You've got that wrong," I said. "They're not in the majority. I am. It's not about how many people there are at the top, but how many shares they hold – or don't hold. And as I own more shares than anyone else here, I'm closing this meeting right now." The next thing I did was fire the GM.

Three of the board members, Al Shehhi, Ahmad Saif Belhasa and Saeed Al Naboodah, promptly resigned. According to Ministry of Economy and Commerce rules and regulations/company law governing public companies, the Ministry was obliged to take over the company until the next shareholders' meeting.

Not long afterwards, a representative from the Ministry came to my house for lunch. He told me that former board members had written something unflattering about me to the Minister. He asked me what was going on and I told him.

I called a shareholders' meeting within three days and with the consent of the shareholders I officially took over the company and then appointed a new board. The old board members were furious. They banded together to publish a defamatory statement in the newspaper, describing me as being dictatorial.

I was very disappointed with their behaviour. People often have differences of opinion or misunderstandings with one another, but they don't usually allow them to reach such personal lows, certainly not in a close society like the UAE, where prominent members of the business community are generally respectful to one another.

Ultimately, it was their loss. Thank God, nowadays, Dubai National Insurance and Reinsurance is under good management, board members get along well, and until now the company is surpassing all expectations.

CHAPTER 15
Lebanon of My Heart

"You were the lungs through which many Arabs breathed the air of freedom."

– Khalaf Ahmad Al Habtoor

Putting into words my feelings about Lebanon is a challenge. How does one define the complex set of emotions that human beings call fatal attraction? I've been to every continent. I've seen the wonders of the world. And I've been dazzled by magnificent cities. I've met with some of humankind's greatest minds. But this slim strip of land, 150 miles long and fifty miles wide, squeezed between Syria and occupied Palestine, with the Mediterranean lapping its western coastline, is for me the most amazing and exciting place on the planet populated with the most generous and hospitable people anywhere.

Steeped in history and scarred by sectarian conflict, civil war, invasion and occupation, she is an imperfect land. Her beauty doesn't only rest in her snow-capped mountains, emerald valleys and rugged coastline. It goes far beyond orchards laden with apricots, plums, peaches, figs, lemons and oranges, or its trellises of grapevines, mountainside stone houses, timeless villages and luxurious modern villas, apartments, malls and hotels.

It's greater than the poetry, songs and dance for which the Lebanese are famous, or the Roman ruins at Baalbek or Byblos where treasures of the Phoenicians remain 5,000 years on.

It's much more than the aroma of roasting lamb blended with the smoke from narghile, or the faint scent of cedar wood, thyme, mint and Greek sage, and the queenly Damask rose that unfolds its splendour each April. It's in the air; it permeates the soil, but most of all it rests in the unbreakable spirit of the Lebanese.

The Lebanese are a cultured, sophisticated, entrepreneurial people with an irrepressible appetite for life, whose optimism has always eclipsed the cloudiest of days. And for sure they've had more than their fair share of troubles, which is why their very DNA has been enriched with unusual resilience, stoicism and creativity.

There is no one Lebanon; it's a diverse land that is home to many different peoples. It's a place of contrasts offering something for everyone. It's where competing ideas, theologies and political agendas battle it out and is, sadly, a surrogate battlefield for big powers with competing ideologies and geostrategic interests.

The Lebanese poet Khalil Gibran, author of *The Prophet*, expressed his thoughts about his Lebanon in the poetic prose 'You Have Your Lebanon and I Have My Lebanon', writing:

> You have your Lebanon and its dilemma. I have my Lebanon and its beauty. Your Lebanon is an arena for men from the West and men from the East.
>
> My Lebanon is a flock of birds fluttering in the early morning as shepherds lead their sheep into the meadow and rising in the evening as farmers return from their fields and vineyards. You have your Lebanon and its people. I have my Lebanon and its people.

Now I will speak of my Lebanon.

My initial impressions of the country were via the cinema, at a time when Egyptian filmmakers, whose artistry was constrained by Cairo's nationalism of sectors of Egypt's film industry, began producing films in the more liberal atmosphere of Beirut.

Such Egyptian-Lebanese joint ventures were mostly light comedies or romances, but they provided a regional showcase for the country's God-given assets, as well as for Lebanon's talented actors and singers such as Sabah, Abdel Salam Al Nabulsy, Layla Karam, Fairuz, Nasri Shamseddine, Wadih El Safi and the legendary half Syrian-half Lebanese Egyptian national Farid Al Atrash. I had many Lebanese friends in Dubai, who loved to talk about their country non-stop. I thought I knew everything there was to know, but nothing prepared me for the real thing.

My first glimpse of Lebanon was in the late 1960s, during the country's belle époque – several years before civil war broke out. I travelled with Riad Sadik and Adnan Derbas, an engineer working in Abu Dhabi, to meet our friend Tarek Abu Samra who was based in Beirut.

My three companions, all graduates from the American University of Beirut, were great buddies. We stayed at the luxurious five-star Phoenicia (later destroyed but then completely rebuilt), where we remained until we met Ayoub Wazni, the owner of the Commodore Centre near Hamra Street, who offered us furnished apartments at a very generous rent.

Ayoub was one of those people with whom I instantly gelled and so I was pleased to take him up on his offer, especially since Hamra was then the city's intellectual and entertainment heart, lined with fashionable street cafés, pubs, bars, bookshops and boutiques. I was completely bowled over by Beirut and couldn't wait to go back.

The first time I took my family to Lebanon was in the early 1970s. From the moment we deposited our luggage in our apartment at the Commodore Centre, I could hardly wait to show them the sights. Beirut then was a magnet for the jet set, a place where the world's 'beautiful people' loved to summer as an alternative to the French Riviera. It was like stepping into the biggest non-stop party ever. Beirut was the archetypical city that never sleeps.

The rich would gravitate towards the iconic St Georges Hotel and Yacht Club, an exclusive French colonial hotel overlooking the downtown waterfront, or the nearby modern Phoenicia Hotel towering over the business and commercial district.

Wealthy foreigners and Lebanese tourists would grace the beaches by day in designer swimwear or take a suspended cable car from Jounieh to Harissa – a destination for pilgrims where a fifteen-ton bronze statue of the Virgin Mary holds out her arms – for spectacular views of the bay and pine-clad mountains. In the late afternoons, they would descend on the shops before changing into their smart evening attire, to head to one of many international restaurants dotting the Corniche downtown or the hillside of Mount Lebanon.

Nightlife at the time was dominated by a lavish subterranean restaurant, club Les Caves du Roy, housed in the Excelsior Hotel, that closed its doors in 1975, or the famed 35,000-square-metre Casino du Liban, sprawling across a hill overlooking the bay of Maameltein, Jounieh, partly camouflaged by a forest of conifers.

Packed with a fine-dining restaurant, a nightclub and a grand theatre, the Casino's Salle des Ambassadeurs was world-renowned for its opulence and its eighty-six electromechanical stages, facilitating entire sets and decor to be altered within seconds. The US magazine *Variety* described it as the number one entertainment provider of the world's best shows. 'Hello' was an over-the-top marvel of sound and light, involving 110 dancers, elephants, monkeys, horses and a tiger.

Such fantastical spectator journeys brought some of the planet's most eminent personalities to Levantine shores, such as Jordan's King Hussein, Shah of Iran Mohammed Reza Pahlavi, and the royals of Monaco.

It is said that there was almost a passenger mutiny on celebrity cruise ship *The Constellation*, when 300 passengers, including the American screen stars, Gloria Swanson, Hugh O'Brien and Joan Fontaine forced the ship's captain to change the ship's itinerary from Istanbul to Beirut so that they could watch a show called *S'il vous plaît* at the Casino. When the boat left Lebanon ten days later, it was virtually without passengers, as most had opted to stay behind.

Away from the glitz and the glamour of palm-flanked wide boulevards, majestic villas and the upscale neighbourhood of Raouché, was the downtown souk of Bab Idriss, a melting pot of Lebanese society and a microcosm of the Arab world, where modestly-dressed Gulf ladies and mini-skirted mademoiselles in high heels rubbed shoulders in search of vegetables, fruits and reasonably-priced fashions.

At the crossroads of the Mediterranean, where Europe meets the Arab world and the Near East, Beirut was – and still is – a den of international spies and Mossad agents. One of the most notorious was Shulamit Cohen, Israel's answer to Mata Hari, who ran an extended spy ring out of the Rambo Pub in Hamra Street from where she used young girls to lure secrets from top Lebanese officials.

Cohen and her gang were caught in 1961; a year later, she was sentenced to death, before being released during a prisoner exchange with Tel Aviv in 1967. In 2009, her story played out before Lebanese movie-goers in a movie titled *Shula Cohen the Pearl*. The black-and-white British film *Where the Spies Are* starring David Niven, filmed in Beirut and Byblos, illustrates the mysterious ambience prevalent in the country during the 1960s.

I must admit I came across quite a few dodgy characters myself during that first visit, which naturally made it all the more memorable. Every minute was more exciting than the next. You never knew who you might run into or what they might say or do. Everything was unpredictable, adding spice to my stay there.

The sheer energy of the place was staggering amid a thriving economy, energised by President Suleiman Franjieh, a right-wing pro-Syrian Maronite Christian. Franjieh laid the ground for a free economy by basically telling people to do what they liked and enjoy themselves, provided they avoid disturbing the country's security. He deserves an accolade for presiding over Lebanon's most glamorous glory days, dulled by the start of the civil war that began on his watch.

While at the Commodore, Ayoub Wazni introduced me to three members of President Franjieh's family: Sayed Franjieh, Antoine Al Jazzar Franjieh and Sarkis Shalhoub. They had also rented apartments there. Sayed and Antoine were in cramped studios, their living spaces made even smaller by stashes of guns and other weapons, just as many others in the building were. Sarkis, who had more disposable income than the others, had rented a much larger flat.

The three pals were young and good looking and, as eligible bachelors, two were always being eagerly pursued by young ladies. Sarkis was taken; he was dating a famous Egyptian actress who was clearly in love with him. They were not only fascinating companions, they also appointed themselves as my personal protection squad. I knew that as long as they were around, no harm would come to me or my family.

That said, I faced a few scary moments in their company. The first happened when I joined Sayed for coffee in the lounge of the Commodore Hotel, opposite the Commodore Centre. Our pleasant chat was rudely interrupted by a drunken Belgian man venting his hatred for Palestinians in English. I tried to ignore his offensive rant, but it impinged upon our conversation and continued for such a long time that I felt compelled to say something.

I approached the drunk to ask him to keep quiet for everyone's sake as well as his own. "You're in Beirut now," I said. "There are many Lebanese here who are pro-Palestinian. It would be better for you if you do not antagonise them."

Sayed Franjieh was oblivious to the man's insults, as he spoke only Arabic and that with a pronounced North Lebanese Zgharta accent, which half the time I couldn't fully comprehend.

"What was that foreigner saying?" he asked me, as soon as I returned to the table.

I knew how hot-headed he was and didn't want to stir up trouble, so I answered, "Nothing, nothing important."

"Nothing... then why did you go up to him? I don't believe you. I have a strong impression that he was cursing the Palestinians and the Lebanese. Is that true?"

"No, no. Just forget about it. He's quiet now." Sayed was like a dog with a bone, he just wouldn't let go, so I told him the truth. Clearly, my friend was in no mood to heed the words of Mahatma Gandhi who said, "The pursuit of truth does not permit violence on one's opponent".

"Khalaf, don't worry about anything. Just leave now and wait for me outside. Go! I'll join you in a few minutes."

"Okay, but why?"

"I just need a minute to put a bullet in his head and then we can go somewhere else for coffee."

It occurred to me that he must be joking. But one glance at his narrowed eyes and tight mouth, not to mention the huge gun in a holster hidden by his jacket, changed my mind. This was the real deal. The man I was with, my friend, was about to commit murder.

"I'm not moving an inch unless we go together," I told him. "The man's had too much to drink. He's an idiot, but he doesn't deserve to die for his hateful opinions. Leave him alone... please!"

To this day, I thank God for giving me the power to persuade the would-be assassin not to carry out the deed, else I'm certain what was left of the Belgian would have had to have been flown home in a casket. And in any case I would have been conscience-stricken for the rest of my life for translating the Belgian's idiotic diatribe.

Antoine Al Jazzar Franjieh was just as trigger happy. One day when we were together, he confided that he was severely cash-strapped.

"Look Khalaf, I'm in urgent need of money," he said. "A few thousand dollars will do. So I want you to do me a big favour."

"Of course, if I can help."

"Ask your government if it has enemies in Lebanon. If so, I'm prepared to finish them off for a fee. Anyone at all... I'm not bothered who."

I was appalled. I was speechless. How can any law-abiding person answer something like that? I don't remember what I mumbled in response, but I do recall thinking that my 'friend' probably wouldn't think twice about bumping me off if the price was right. That was the first and only time I had ever heard such a mercenary offer given in a matter-of-fact way, when what was at stake was a human life. Even now it's hard to believe there are people so ruthless in the world. But somehow I knew that he was deadly serious.

I should stress that the attitudes of those three were the exception rather than the rule. People unconnected with the feuding political elite were invariably warm, big-hearted and family-oriented, more interested in enjoying life to the full than spreading murder and mayhem.

The Beirutis I mixed with were always superbly dressed, coiffed and liberally perfumed. The scent of Paco Rabanne and Jean Patou's Joy lingered in the air. Everyone was so well turned out, that it was almost impossible to distinguish between secretaries and wealthy socialites.

Quite often, non-Lebanese Arabs would disparage this trend as superficiality or vanity; they would infer that the Lebanese were show-offs who spent most of their income on fancy cars, gold lighters and Paris fashions, never mind that their homes might be simply furnished. Between you and me, I think that was nothing more than a manifestation of envy in the way that foreign media attacks Dubai and its people today for striving to be the best.

The mood of gaiety and 'anything goes' in the Lebanese capital was a breath of fresh air, but if the visitor wasn't careful it could knock him off balance. I must admit that happened to me and what resulted is hardly my proudest moment.

The pencil-thin, chain-smoking young man who explored Beirut with Mahmoud Younes from Palestine and another acquaintance from Tripoli's Kabbara family had rarely felt so upbeat. Looking back, I can hardly recognise him as me.

As we ambled along without a care in the world, a gentleman drinking coffee outside his home caught our eye. He smiled, waved to us and invited us to join him. That was the way it was in those days; the ambience was so informal that it was unbelievably easy to make new contacts.

The man asked us what we would like to drink and we all asked for tea. Some minutes later, the tea was duly served by an exceptionally pretty and charming young girl who was introduced as our host's daughter. I could hardly prevent myself from staring at her.

"Where are you guys staying?" her father asked.

"I'm at the Commodore Centre," I said.

"Oh, I know it well. It's a nice place. It's owned by a friend of mine, Ayoub Wazni."

"Really... you know Ayoub! That's good!"

On the way back to my hotel-apartment, I was gripped with some kind of madness. I couldn't get the girl out of my mind. The first thing I did was to track down Ayoub and tell him about my encounter with one of his friends.

Ayoub listened to my story, when before I could stop myself I blurted out, "I need your help, Ayoub. I want you to get in touch with your friend."

"Why?"

"I need you to tell him that I'm interested in marrying his daughter and, depending on his response, would like to invite all the family to dinner so we can talk about it."

At that moment, it didn't cross my mind that I had just thrown common sense out the window. Instead, I tried to justify my decision to myself on the grounds that my religion and society allows it, and by then I could easily afford to look after another wife.

"No problem, my friend. I'll set everything up for you," he promised.

True to his word, Ayoub arranged everything. I went with him to a very nice restaurant to meet the young lady's parents and her extended family, who all seemed delighted with my proposal. There we all were chatting away and enjoying our meal as though we'd all known one another for ever, when the girl got up from her chair and excused herself to visit the restroom.

"Khalaf, escort your bride to the restroom," said Ayoub loudly in his strong southern Lebanese accent. I should mention that it was once customary in our part of the world to escort ladies wherever they went, both as a courtesy and to protect them from unwelcome attention.

Bride... what bride? That word doused me like a cold shower. The madness was instantly over. What was I thinking? I didn't want another wife. I was more than happy with the one I had. I imagined that all hell would break loose, were I to return to Dubai with two wives; it would destroy my peaceful home life and turn my kids against me.

Oh, the guilt, as I thought of Hamda and our young sons, Rashid and Mohammed, who were with me on that trip. I remembered how they smiled and waved to me from the balcony of our holiday apartment as I left them behind that evening. They trusted me implicitly; they relied upon me absolutely. They'd done nothing wrong, yet here I was, selfishly thinking of myself without a care for their feelings. I felt guilty about having inadvertently led on a sweet young woman and her fine family too.

I wanted to disappear, to run out of the door. There was no way I was going to marry that girl, or any other for that matter. I've rarely felt so ashamed of myself. I was embarrassed and guilt-ridden.

Ayoub picked up on my markedly altered mood, but he was having a good time and was in no hurry for the evening to end. Every few minutes, he would raise his glass and say, "A toast to the bride and groom," just to have the pleasure of watching me squirm. That must have been one of the longest and most awful nights of my life.

As soon as we dropped off the young lady and her parents outside their home, I sat back in the car and breathed a huge sigh of relief.

"What's wrong with you?" Ayoub asked me. "Are you ill?"

"My friend, I can't go through with this. I need to get out from this mess."

"But why... Why have you changed your mind?"

"Never mind why. You must help me. This arrangement must be cancelled as soon as possible. I need your help to sort out this horrible mistake."

"And how do you propose I do that? What should I say to those people without offending them?"

That was indeed a problem. In our culture, once a proposal of marriage is made, there needs to be a very good reason to retract it. I pondered for a while before saying, "I know how... It has to be done quickly before I'm in deeper. Please visit the girl's father tomorrow morning and tell him that I'm not a suitable groom for his lovely daughter. Make up any story you like. I don't care how bad it makes me look. Just find a way to get me out of this without upsetting those nice people or offending their dignity."

Ayoub gave a hearty laugh and told me that he would do exactly as I had suggested. He went to see the family the next day and blackened my name. When I next saw him, he enjoyed recounting all the awful things he had said about me. He had painted me as Rasputin, Casanova and Genghis Khan rolled into one. But I couldn't have been happier that my dilemma had been so efficiently dispensed with, without anyone getting hurt.

A year later, in 1975 Christian and Palestinian militias turned Lebanon into a blood-soaked war zone. Lebanese civilians were shot at by snipers or kidnapped for ransom. Beirut was divided into Christian and Muslim sectors. Terrified families abandoned their homes to reach safety in their sectarian heartlands.

In May 1976, President Suleiman Franjieh asked Syria to intervene, when Damascus received a mandate from the Arab League to retain up to 40,000 Syrian peacekeeping troops in country, tasked with preventing bloodshed. They did manage to subdue the sectarian conflict to a large extent, but were unable to prevent an Israeli invasion in 1978 ostensibly to drive the PLO out of South Lebanon.

Before Israeli forces withdrew later that year, they handed areas of the south to Major Saad Haddad's South Lebanon Army, that served as Israel's paid proxy to rid the area of Palestinian armed groups.

As the civil war raged on in ebbs and flows, on 17 July 1981 Israel added to the chaos by bombing buildings housing PLO offices and command centres, while the Israeli Prime Minister, Menachem Begin, and Defence Minister Ariel Sharon were formulating invasion plans.

By 15 June 1982, Israeli brigades were on the capital's doorstep. Condemned by the international community, Israel was persuaded by the US to sign a peace agreement with Lebanese President, Amine Gemayel. However, the Israelis merely withdrew to what they termed the 'Security Zone' in South Lebanon.

The 1989 Taif Accord paved the way for peace between the various Lebanese factions, but it wasn't until 1991 that the civil war came to a close, when the Lebanese Parliament gave amnesty to those who had committed political crimes.

Now that the Lebanese were left to pick up the pieces of their shattered lives, they had to confront a new unpleasant reality. The Syrian military was there to stay. Damascus, their invited friend and saviour, had entrenched itself as a pseudo-occupier and was giving most of the orders behind the scenes.

Needless to say, I was heartbroken watching the wanton destruction of such a beautiful land. So many good people had been caught up in the violence and died for nothing. All I could do was pray that the craziness was finally over.

Older and quite a bit wiser, during the winter of 1991–92 I decided to take the plunge and travel to Beirut to see for myself whether or not 'my Lebanon still existed. I was unable to imagine what it might look like after being shelled by Israelis, controlled by Syrians and carved up into militarised sectarian ghettoes by the Lebanese themselves.

On this occasion, I stayed at the newly-renovated Coral Beach Hotel where the UAE's embassy offices were situated. The hotel was owned by my friend Izzat Kaddoura from Sidon, a glamorous man-about-town with a reputation for being somewhat of a playboy, who did everything he could to make me feel at home. Purely by coincidence, I discovered that my cousin Mohammed Al Falasi, the UAE's acting Ambassador to Lebanon, was a fellow hotel guest.

Nothing in the city was the same as it once was. Official buildings, homes, shops and apartment blocks around Martyrs' Square in downtown Beirut were little more than rubble. Much of Ashrafieh's architectural heritage had been wiped out. Buildings around Hamra were pockmarked with bullet holes. The Phoenicia and the St Georges hotels had been destroyed along with the nearby Holiday Inn Hotel and many others. I was made to feel welcome in Christian and Muslim areas, but I hated going through those scary Syrian checkpoints.

I did succeed in getting in touch with a few of my old friends from Beirut. Some had left the country long ago, others had simply disappeared. I was very pleased to find that Ayoub Wazni was still on the scene, as by then he was frequently shuttling between his home in Beirut and his house in the Belgian city of Antwerp.

It was great seeing Ayoub again and I very much appreciated his offer to introduce me to the Speaker of the National Assembly, Nabih Berri, a public figure I used to admire. I invited Mohammed Al Falasi to join me on the journey, along with Ayoub and Habib Khalifa, then my legal advisor.

It was quite a long but pleasant drive to Nabih Berri's home in southern Lebanon. He received us with traditional Arab courtesy and hospitality, before escorting us into his gigantic majlis where over 100 men were seated talking and drinking coffee. I feared he would have to split his time between so many and we wouldn't have the chance to talk, but he proved me wrong.

He told me something of great significance at the time. "Please tell your government and all Arab governments to rally around Lebanon at this crucial juncture," he said. "I want to warn Arab leaders that Iran is pushing hard to control everything here. Believe me, the Iranians want to take over and are doing everything in their power to gain influence. The situation is extremely delicate. If Arab countries come forward now, without delay, to assist Lebanon's recovery, Iran won't be able to get a foot in the door," he told me.

Mr Berri was very honest. He spoke the truth in a straightforward way. I passed on his warning, but it wasn't heeded. The Arabs were too late responding. By the time they did, the Iranians bearing money and weapons inside a Trojan horse marked 'friendship' were luring proxies throughout Lebanon. I never had the chance of meeting him again, but his wise words have always stuck with me.

Around the same time, Mohammed Al Falasi made an appointment for me to meet with the then Lebanese Minister of Agriculture, Mohsen Dalloul, and accompanied me to the Minister's home where we were both courteously received. Mr Dalloul generously invited us to stay for dinner, during which I met one of our host's colleagues in the ministry, Ali Moussawi – a man who was later to become a great friend. Ali was casually dressed in blue jeans and a denim shirt, and was playing cards with his son when we were introduced.

The atmosphere was fine until Mr Dalloul asked his wife to bring us a plate of watermelon. When the fruit arrived, it was paler than the usual reddish-pink. When our host noticed that the melon wasn't up to standard, he yelled at his wife for serving it. We were shocked to hear him shout and embarrass her in front of guests. "Mohsen, please don't shout," I said, trying to diffuse the tense situation. "Nobody can know whether a watermelon is good before it is sliced, and in any case it has a nice taste."

Nevertheless, I was glad that fate guided me to that home on that day, as Ali and I clicked and became close friends. A few years later, I invited him to leave the ministry to work for me, which he was happy to do. He was a real asset, even though he wasn't experienced in business. His career until then had revolved around representing various departments of the Lebanese government, but he was a fast learner. He disclosed to me that during his government service, his influence increased when he used my name. I admired him for admitting that.

Ali was great company and a lively travelling companion. I convinced him to become an early riser and was pleased that he adapted to my lifestyle more quickly than most. Whenever my family visited Lebanon without me, Ali made sure they were comfortable. Even though he left my employment to form his own company, we often meet up when I'm in Beirut.

During that same 1992 visit, I travelled all over the country from north to south, west to east, when I had the opportunity to meet lots of other good Lebanese. Most were optimistic and excited to rebuild, but their natural light-heartedness had been dulled by internal scars. You could hear the tension in the voices and see it manifested on their faces.

When I learned just how much they had suffered over the past sixteen years, my heart went out to them. I met people who had lost mothers and fathers, sons and daughters, brothers and sisters; some had hardly left the safety of their homes for years; others had lost theirs and everything they owned, including family heirlooms and precious photograph albums.

I was humbled to discover that they were still able to smile and crack jokes. I wanted so much to stand with them, to be part of the new Lebanon that everyone hoped would rise up like a Phoenix from the ashes. Although the atmosphere in Beirut felt reasonably normal, the Israelis were still occupying parts of southern Lebanon, a stronghold of the Lebanese Shiites.

It wasn't until the year 2000 that Israel took the decision to withdraw from Lebanon, apart from a small area called Shebaa Farms, after ensuring its borders were protected by the United Nations Interim Force in Lebanon

(UNIFIL). But it continued bombing power stations and other infrastructure until the nth-minute, paralysing the country as much as possible.

Shebaa Farms remains a point of dispute, as Tel Aviv insists that Shebaa belongs to Syria. Beirut maintains that it's Lebanese. Damascus won't officially come down on one side or the other, which is unfortunate as Hezbollah successfully uses Israel's continuing occupation of that sliver of Lebanese territory as a pretext to retain its weapons.

The Israeli pull out heralded an exhilarating time for the Lebanese, who believed their problems were over. For days, the hills around Beirut resounded with gaiety, fireworks and music. People who had been holding on to their cash bought new homes, shops and businesses.

Each evening, downtown was packed with revellers drinking and eating around long trestle tables in the streets. Children grasping balloons and ice cream cones were able to be carefree. Trendy cafés like Casper & Gambini's were packed with the young latte-drinking crowd. Bargain hunters picked through the wares of an impromptu flea market. Downtown was once again Beirut's heart. Elsewhere, there were concerts, grand soirées and cultural festivals. That summer, the city was alive with tourists, many from Saudi Arabia and the Gulf.

Amid such optimism, I was undecided what kind of contribution I should make to the country's future now that it was stable – or so I thought. While I was investigating various avenues, I bought a piece of land in Sin el-Fil, a primarily Christian suburb of Beirut on the eastern side of the capital, separated from the rest of the city by a dried-up river bed, which Lebanese still refer to as Beirut River.

Several people recommended that area due to its fine class of people. Thankfully, even though I am a Muslim and a foreigner, people there made me feel as though I belonged. Occasionally, someone would remark with a raised eyebrow that my land was situated between two churches. That didn't bother me in the least; I don't discriminate on the basis of religion. Like any mosque, a church is a place where God-loving people go to worship.

It was a prime site, easily accessible to the north and south and close to the Beirut–Damascus highway, with the advantage of being some distance from the centre of Beirut congested with roadblocks and military forces. From a business perspective, I believed Sin el-Fil was less of a risk than some of the other suburbs. But, initially, I considered the plot to be a good investment, at least until I made up my mind how to use it.

I thought it would be a good idea to discuss my business plans with the Prime Minister, Rashid Solh, to whom I was introduced by the late Mr Wafic Ajouz, Middle East Airlines' President of Public Relations, a very active gentleman and a great friend of my country. We went together to the Prime Minister's residence, an upmarket, superbly decorated apartment that reflected his intellectual standing, personal history and culture. Our meeting was fairly brief, but I was left with the impression that he was a very nice man.

A not-so-nice man was the late Kamel Assaad, then Lebanon's Parliamentary Speaker. Habib Khalifa suggested that we see him and I agreed. I asked Mohammed Al Falasi to come with us and, once everything was set up, off we went.

Mr Assaad lived in an old building. A couple of casually dressed bodyguards were lounging outside the entrance gate when we arrived. They made us wait until they received the okay to let us in. The man himself looked like he'd just woken up; he was still half asleep when Habib introduced us to him.

Once the usual formalities were exchanged, I said, "It's an honour to meet with you Sir."

"Where are you from?" he asked me.

"I'm from Dubai in the United Arab Emirates."

"I see. What's the name of your President?" To say I was shocked when I heard that was an understatement; it took great self-control not to show him how amazed and angry I was. It had never crossed my mind that there was anybody in the entire Arab world who had never heard of Sheikh Zayed, a leader greatly loved for his generosity and good works.

"Sir, did I hear you correctly? You don't know who the President of the United Arab Emirates is?"

"Yes, that's right. I don't! Who is he?"

"My President, Sheikh Zayed bin Sultan Al Nahyan, Sir, is the most generous, well-respected and beloved Arab leader in the world. His philanthropy is legendary. He is a man who gives to the needy irrespective of their religion, race or colour," I answered proudly. "He is the wisest man I've ever met."

Before he could say anything else, I stood up and excused myself before we all stormed out. Habib couldn't stop apologising to me; he thought I was upset with him for initiating the meeting. Of course, I wasn't at all. I explained to him that, as far as I was concerned, he wasn't responsible for Kamel Assaad's ignorance and disrespect that had so ignited my fury.

It was the late Rafik Al Hariri who encouraged me to use my land in Sin el-Fil for a hotel project. He was a very successful businessman and also a well-known philanthropist before he became Lebanon's Prime Minister.

My first visit to him was through arrangements made by the UAE Embassy. I was honoured to make the acquaintance of such a charismatic, well-loved internationally-known figure. Out of all Lebanese leaders before him and after him, he was the most trustworthy.

We talked on several subsequent occasions over a meal and later on I met with him in his prime ministerial office. Overall, we developed a great relationship. He always boosted my enthusiasm to create jobs for the Lebanese and help to energise Beirut's economy.

At the same time, he would caution me. "You're not in Britain or a GCC country now," he once told me. "Here, you have to be very careful. Make sure you hire the best lawyers and don't you dare sign anything unless you've read through it line by line." His advice was later echoed by President Emile Lahoud, who also told me to consult a respectable law firm, cautioning that "Lebanon is not the UAE".

I knew what they meant. The Lebanese are honest in friendships; they'll give you the shirt off their back. But in business you have to keep checking to make sure you're still wearing it.

Unfortunately, not all Lebanese lawyers can be trusted either, as I found out at my cost. I had been used to dealing with Western and UAE lawyers and had never had cause for serious complaint, so it took me some time to wise up to the antics of Hussein Dalle (not his real name), our Lebanese legal advisor in the UAE.

I had never seriously considered employing an in-house legal advisor; I only did so on the urging of others. It was a big mistake. The minute Hussein was taken on, we were inundated with cases that invariably ended up in arbitration. It occurred to me that this turn of events was strange, but nevertheless, I would tell myself, if you can't trust your own lawyer who's being paid to take care of your interests, then who can you trust?

Each time, Hussein would assure me that our documentation was perfect and our case would be successful. Whenever I would ask him how long we would have to wait for the decision, he would say "just a few months"; but those months always dragged on into years. Every so often, he would ask me for cash in connection with a specific case, which I would usually hand over without querying what it was for.

Then, to my great dismay, I discovered that he was taking bribes to lose cases and sharing my money with arbitrators, who, little did I know, had been paid to decide against me. Not only did I incur losses, I ended up having to pay the fraudulent claims of successful litigants. I've never taken on another in-house lawyer since. I prefer to use the services of prestigious international law firms with proven credentials and impeccable reputations.

To be fair, Lebanon doesn't have the monopoly on crooked lawyers; they're all over the world, but it is true to say that the Middle East, where rogue lawyers can operate freely without checks and balances, has more than its fair share.

In Britain, for instance, any solicitor who isn't scrupulously honest is stricken off the Law Society's register, while any barrister implicated in graft would be disbarred. Moreover, it's no accident that most countries in the world – and especially developing countries – insert a clause in their contracts accepting litigation by British courts.

Disputes in Arab countries often end up being mediated within the UK's independent judiciary system. I've discussed this anomaly with businessmen and intellectuals throughout the Arab world and until now nobody has been able to explain why Arabs prefer US, UK and German courts over their own – or, more to the point, how this can be rectified. When it comes to legal matters, the West is a hundred light years ahead of us.

The Egyptian actress Ilham Chahine told me of her own bad experience with cheats, when she stopped for a drink in the Candles Lounge of the Metropolitan Palace Hotel in Beirut. I was sitting with my brother Sultan and one of our friends, Abdullah Al Hathboor, as she arrived to vent her frustration.

"You won't believe what happened to me," she said. I went for an interview here in Lebanon and the interviewer persuaded me to buy some jewellery, for which I paid 20,000 dollars. When I flew home and showed it to a trusted Egyptian jeweller, he told me than it was barely worth 1,000 dollars. I've been conned."

Some time afterwards, she came to Dubai, where she was similarly swindled. Sultan and Abdullah happened to be with me when she told me that story, which felt a bit like déjà vu.

Abdullah, who didn't like the idea that any visitor to Dubai had been taken for ride, asked, "Who stole from you in Lebanon?"

She answered, "Lebanese".

"And who stole from you in Dubai?"

"Also Lebanese," she said.

"*Alhamdulillah* (Thanks be to God) that it was the Lebanese who stole from you," said Abdullah. "You're an Egyptian and the con men were Lebanese. Thank God we Emiratis are innocent."

I knew I had to stay alert at all times, but I was determined to invest in the Lebanese hospitality industry. The first thing I did was to hire a Lebanese consultant. I told him to award the job of building my hotel to a Lebanese contractor, despite the fact that I own the largest construction company in the region. I did this to provide opportunities to Lebanese companies, so their staff could go home each month with a pay packet.

I next asked my management team to draw up a quota of prospective employees from a variety of religious and political backgrounds without differentiating between them. I was determined that all applicants would be fairly treated and would receive an equal chance of employment, based on their qualifications and skills. Until now, my Lebanese managers have a strict rule they must follow. Politics or religion must play no role in any of my businesses or be allowed to create disputes between employees.

When Rafik Hariri succeeded Rashid Solh as Prime Minister in October 1992, he helped me greatly by speeding up building permits and approvals. He even charged one of his advisors to assist my team in wading through bureaucratic hurdles. Lebanon was lucky to have a leader who led by example.

It was thanks to the public company he conceived and founded, Solidere, that Beirut's downtown district was restored to its former glory. I know that some of his critics maintain Mr Hariri was only taking care of his own pocket; I don't believe that. No doubt his personal interests were tied up with his efforts to beautify the capital, but his own interests and those of his people coincided; they were inextricably linked.

One day, after I saw him being harshly interrogated in Parliament, I went to see him. "How can you bear such disrespectful treatment?" I asked him. "You are Rafik Hariri, well recognised and well respected by the world. Why do you put up with insults from such inconsequential troublemakers?"

"Someone has to do it for the sake of the people," he said. "I just try to do my best."

I was very proud of my five-star, twenty-one-storey Metropolitan Palace Hotel, which has more than lived up to its tagline, "an oasis of opulence", and has been the recipient of numerous prestigious travel industry awards.

It took a massive investment to bring it up to high world-class standards, with a range of international restaurants, state-of-the-art conference facilities, a 1,000-capacity grand ballroom, a fully-equipped business centre, health club and swimming pool. To my eyes, it was the best hotel in Lebanon. Getting the word out was our main challenge, as Sin el-Fil was a residential area slightly off the usual tourist track.

When the hotel was still under construction, influential Lebanese were always promising to support our effort by giving us business and sending their guests to us. Few, if any, lived up to those promises. I felt let down and phoned Prime Minister Hariri to complain about those people's failure to stand by their commitment to host all their business visitors and visiting acquaintances in my new hotel. He said he would look into the matter, but nothing came of that call.

Although I was concerned, I decided not to bother him. He had enough on his plate working to lift his country out of financial straits. He resigned from office on 20 October 2004 and was succeeded, briefly, by pro-Syrian Prime Minister Omar Karami.

On 14 February 2005, St Valentine's Day, Rafik Hariri's life was cut short. He was assassinated by a bomb that killed eight others and injured over 100, leaving a smouldering, blackened crater behind it.

I had just finished playing tennis in Dubai and was cooling down in my chalet on the beach watching television, when news of the explosion broke. As smoke blackened the skies over Beirut, no one knew for sure if Rafik Hariri had been in the convoy, or if he had survived death or escaped injury.

When officials confirmed his demise, I gasped. As I watched his body being carried away, a friend who was with me at the time noticed the blood draining from my face. "Why are you so upset?" he asked. "So what if another politician has been assassinated in Lebanon? His death is no different from all the others."

"You're wrong. I know him well. He's a good man. He's irreplaceable," I said. "His death will change the country. Lebanon will be affected for years to come. He's an extraordinary man, an extraordinary businessman and an extraordinary Prime Minister. I will go to Beirut immediately. I can't just sit here. I must be there to show my respects to his family and the Lebanese people," I said.

My friend tried to dissuade me from going, on the grounds that the country was now more unstable than ever following the killing, and open to all kinds of reprisal attacks. "It's not safe for you to go," he said.

"I don't care. Now's not the time to worry about my own safety. I have no choice. I can't just sit here and do nothing," I said. "He was my friend. His family will be devastated. I should be with them. It's the duty of everyone who loves Lebanon to make their feelings known about this terrible tragedy and to show support when the country's at its weakest."

By the time I joined my wife, sons, daughters and grandchildren at home, I was overcome with grief. I wept openly in front of them like a lost child, not only because Rafik Hariri had been cut down in his prime. I cried for the country and its people.

My thoughts were racing. Who would look after the Lebanese now? Who would take care of their children, their education, their emotional well-being and their future? Who would protect them from outside aggression or insiders paid by foreign powers to destabilise their own land? Who could continue my friend's fight against corruption or keep the greedy among the elite from creaming off Lebanon's wealth?

Rafik Hariri had committed himself heart and soul to bring prosperity and stability to his country. That's why he had so many enemies. Unfortunately, most of those enemies were Lebanese of differing backgrounds and faiths, with foreign-manufactured agendas.

If people around me at the time thought my fears were unfounded, they've been proved wrong. Even as I write these words, Lebanon is being dragged down by clashes between political and religious parties, as well as armed militias attempting to brand the country with their ideological stamp.

Before taking the plane, I telephoned Rafik Hariri's sister, Mrs Bahia Al Hariri, and her late brother's friend Fouad Al Siniora, then the Chairman and Managing Director of Hariri's banking group, Le Groupe Méditerranéen, as I wanted to express my condolences and to let them know that I was on my way.

Almost as soon as the flight touched down, I drove straight to the Hariri family house where I was received by Rafik Hariri's closest friend, Assaad Diab, a businessman. The poor man was in deep distress, his eyes swollen and red.

I tried hard to be of comfort, but there was nothing anyone could say or do to lessen his grief. He was also consumed by anger, casting suspicion on all kinds of people from all over the political spectrum as having instigated the assassination.

"Now is not the time to pinpoint blame," I told him. "For now, we must control our emotions. We must ask God to bless him and allow his soul to rest in peace. Until the investigators have done their work, it's up to all of us to do all we can to calm people's nerves. Our first priority is how to prevent the country lapsing into another civil war."

When emotions were less fragile, I had a calm discussion with Fouad Al Siniora and Mrs Bahia Al Hariri on how we could lighten the country's mood from one of despair to optimism. They decided that they needed to put on a brave public face to encourage everyone else to do the same. They suggested that a walkabout should be organised involving sympathetic Lebanese politicians in honour of Mr Hariri, to show that although he may be gone, his principles live on. I considered that to be an excellent tribute to his name.

I went back to Dubai, but returned a month later with the Chairman and Founder of the Rotana hotel chain, Nasser Al Nowais, and other UAE entrepreneurs, to participate in an organised walk led by Hariri's sister, family and politicians.

The starting point was the site where his life was robbed by terrorists. The spot where his blood had soaked the earth was ironically where he had been poised to embark on a government contract to construct shopping malls, hotels and the biggest conference centre in the country.

It was a very hot summer's day. I was wearing the national Emirati dress, that was soon drenched in sweat. Notwithstanding my discomfort, being able to pay tribute to my friend in that small way made me feel good inside. Like me, my colleagues from UAE's business community were happy to show their solidarity with Lebanon and their continued faith in the Lebanese people. We all wanted to assure them that we would stand by their side in good times and bad.

Prior to setting off, I had gone to Mrs Bahia's Beirut home to warn her against some politicians whom she believed in and trusted, and who were falsely claiming to have been her brother's closest colleagues and friends. I didn't trust their motives and time proved me right, but nothing could convince her that they weren't honest friends of her late brother. I also reiterated my caution about rushing to lay blame for Rafik Hariri's killing until investigators had reached their studied conclusion.

The political ramifications of Rafik Hariri's assassination were vast. At first, all fingers were pointing at the Syrian leadership. However, in spite of a long-drawn-out United Nations-backed inquiry into the killing, until now there has been no firm resolution. It seems the Special Tribunal for Lebanon no longer claims Syrian involvement; its investigators have concluded that members of Hezbollah were behind it, which the group forcefully denies. In July 2011, the Tribunal released the names of four Hezbollah members wanted in connection with the assassination, along with indictments and arrest warrants.

The only positive thing to emerge from that criminal tragedy was in the aftermath. Enraged at what was then believed to be Syrian complicity in Hariri's assassination, millions of 14 March patriotic pro-government demonstrators took to the streets all over the country to demand Syria's exit. A UN Security Council Resolution reinforced their demands, with which Syrian President Bashar Al Assad chose to comply rather than condemning his country to international pariah status. By 26 April 2005, Syria's twenty-nine-year-long peacekeeping presence in Lebanon was over. On 19 July that year, Fouad Siniora, whom by then I considered a friend, was asked to form a government.

When I asked Prime Minister Siniora to be kind enough to help me obtain a 'restricted fixed deposit' bureaucratically frozen by one of his government departments in relation to a branch of Dubai National Insurance and Reinsurance, he promised to facilitate its repayment, but neglected to follow through.

The Lebanese branch of my insurance company, opened during the mid-1990s, had turned out to be an unprofitable venture. We did our best to keep it going and recoup some of our losses, but finally we took the decision to close the company and cancel the licence, thereby freeing our deposit and bank guarantees. Well, that was the idea even if it didn't quite work out that way.

Once the necessary documentation required to wrap up the company was completed, I asked my representative, Ali Moussawi, to show the legal papers to Prime Minister Siniora and remind him of his promise to accelerate the cancellation of permits and the return of our restricted fixed deposit, which was no small sum. As he knew me well, I was sure he would do his best to help. I was, therefore, surprised to learn from Ali that the Prime Minister clearly wasn't open to our request.

"Well, if he's not willing to assist that's up to him," I said. Siniora could have facilitated the immediate release of our money; he was the key. Instead, we were made to wait five years before it was returned.

In all honesty, without a scythe by way of connections to cut through the government's complicated – and often petty – rules and regulations, a foreigner trying to do business in Lebanon is a bit like the mythological

Greek fellow Sisyphus, compelled for all eternity to roll a boulder up a hill, only to see it roll down again.

Before I constructed the Habtoor Grand Hotel, Convention Centre and Spa adjacent to the Metropolitan Palace in Sin el-Fil, I was meticulous about obtaining relevant approvals, because that's how we do things in the UAE where not even one brick can be laid without authorisation.

Then after the hotel was finally inaugurated in 2005, during a parliamentary session, certain MPs complained that at thirty-two storeys, it was so tall that it might interfere with the flight path of passenger jets. That was utter nonsense. It's nowhere near as high the Burj Al Arab hotel or the much higher Burj Khalifa in Dubai – and in any case, since I bought the land, I've hardly seen a large insect flying around, let alone airplanes.

Soon afterwards, the media turned up the heat with opposing opinions being offered in newspapers, magazines and on television networks. I was quite anxious when all this was going on. I didn't relish having to lop off a couple of floors. Luckily enough, the free publicity worked in my favour. Thanks to the media, the new hotel's fame grew along with its popularity.

For some reason, I never allowed those kinds of obstacles to deter me from investing in Lebanon. One of my biggest investments in the country was Habtoorland, a vast themed amusement park inaugurated in the autumn of 2004.

Situated on a 107,000-square-metre plot on a mountain slope in Al Jamhour near Baabda – a ten minute drive from the capital – it was designed to reflect the Mediterranean Phoenician civilisation from Tyre to Sidon, Byblos, Carthage and Phoenician settlements in Spain, Sardinia and Sicily.

It was an ambitious venture, even for me, with spinning roller coasters, a rapid river experience and other nail-biting rides engineered by German experts. Attractions were geared towards all ages, including a monorail, musical fountains, laser shows, fine dining and fast-food outlets, and a large 1,800-seat amphitheatre for concerts.

Habtoorland's turnover was estimated to be substantial in the months following the grand opening. Things were going better than I'd hoped. Everyone loved the place because it was a novel concept and provided somewhere fantastical for all the family to spend their leisure hours in a joyful atmosphere.

* * *

From 1992 until the present, I have been back and forth to Lebanon more times than I can count, mainly for business but also on pleasure. Quite often, I take friends along with me. However, it's rare that I find a travelling companion who can adjust to my set-in-stone early-to-rise, early-to-bed daily routine. The amusing thing is to what lengths some of them will go to try and fool me into thinking they are going along with my schedule.

One such is Ziad Hasbani, an educated, well-mannered and respectful person from a good Lebanese family, a man I've known since my 1992 visit to Beirut, when together with Ali Moussawi, we opened a production company – yes another one. I have no idea what possessed me after the previous production company in Dubai had failed so spectacularly and I had promised myself never to go into partnership again.

Ali and Ziad believed there was a fortune to be made producing TV series or soaps. They lacked experience, but were so enthusiastic, that I was persuaded to hire them and invest a sum of money that they used to produce two series for television. Nobody was queuing up to ask us to produce any more and I ended up losing the capital invested in that company.

The lesson is never to go into a business unless it's something you know inside out. '*Give your bread to the baker even if he eats half of it,*' goes an Arabic proverb.

We shrugged off that loss and Ziad and I have continued our friendship until today. Whenever I visited Lebanon during the early 1990s, we would keep each other company most of the time. We often stayed at the Palm Beach Hotel in Ain el-Mreisseh. Each morning we would meet for breakfast. Whereas I was bright and breezy, his lids were heavy and he couldn't stop yawning. As each day passed, dark rings began to appear under his eyes. I was a little worried about him until I found out what was going on.

Each evening when I thought he had gone to bed, he had instead slipped out of the hotel to go partying. He would usually ensure he returned just in time to meet me for breakfast. He was young and wanted to enjoy himself.

He's a delightful person, but he has one awful habit. Whenever we went out for a walk, he was always stepping on my toes; on quite a few occasions, my toes were painful and swollen. After he married his lovely wife, May, I thought I should warn her to keep her feet as far away from his as possible. She smiled when I told her; she thought I was joking or exaggerating. Now she's the one complaining. She tells me that Ziad is always stepping on her toes too. They're such a great couple!

My travelling companions, Danny Hamadeh and Salim Wanli, were just as devious about hiding from me what they were up to. In 2002, we were all staying at my Metropolitan Palace hotel. After lunch, I would leave them to take my siesta and would usually advise to get some rest themselves. "Oh no," they would say. "We don't sleep in the afternoons. We're going to work out in the gym".

For the first few days of our stay, I believed them. I had no reason not to. But gradually I began having doubts. I decided to see for myself. I couldn't find them in the gym, so I checked their suite – and lo and behold, there they were sleeping like dead cows in their rooms. I don't know if they had been trying to impress me with their athleticism or what!

Those were fun times, when it was easy to visualise Lebanon regaining its reputation as the 'Paris of the Middle East' sooner rather than later. Sadly, though, Lebanon's misery days were far from being over after all.

Less than two years after the opening of Habtoorland, on 12 July 2006, Hezbollah militants killed three Israeli soldiers and abducted two to be used as bargaining chips in a prisoner exchange. Israel didn't respond as expected. The result was thirty-four days of all-out war between Israel and Hezbollah, involving everyone in Lebanon.

While Hezbollah fighters in the south were exiting their tunnels and bunkers to destroy Israel's Merkava tanks and firing Katyusha rockets at Israeli towns, the Israeli Air Force (IAF) was bombing civilian infrastructure such as TV stations, bridges, highways, electricity and sewage plants. Fuel stations and commercial enterprises were destroyed by Israeli bombs and shells, along with schools, hospitals, ambulances – and tens of thousands of homes.

The devastation was so great that Hezbollah leader, Hassan Nasrallah, loudly requested Prime Minister Siniora and the Arab League to ask the US and the UN Security Council to stop Israeli attacks. But time and again the US President, George W. Bush, and the British Prime Minister, Tony Blair, blocked ceasefire negotiations to give Israel time to complete its deadly mission.

Israel used munitions such as white phosphorous and cluster bombs that are internationally banned for use in populated areas. Over 1,200 Lebanese civilians were killed in that conflict. A report by Human Rights Watch dated 6 September 2007 stated most of the civilian deaths were as a result of "indiscriminate Israeli airstrikes", alleging that Israeli warplanes targeted vehicles carrying civilians trying to flee combat zones.

Israel failed in its aim of eradicating Hezbollah and Israelis did some soul searching as to the effectiveness of the Israeli Defence Forces, going as far as to institute the Winograd Commission to investigate the military's failures.

Israel's former Defence Minister Moshe Arens admitted that Israel had suffered a defeat at the hands of "a very small group of people" that could have "some very fateful consequences for the future". Nasrallah announced he wouldn't have approved the kidnapping of Israeli soldiers if he had known that action would spark a major Israeli assault.

Both Hezbollah and Israel declared victory, when in reality, the biggest loser was Lebanon in terms of human life and monetary losses. Direct and indirect losses, including infrastructure (power stations, bridges, tunnels, roads etc.), together with lost business opportunities and potential foreign investment were estimated to have been between 10 and 20 billion dollars. In spite of Hezbollah's celebratory post-conflict posturing, sorry to say, by every measure imaginable the Lebanese were the greatest victims of that war.

Since 2006, it seems Hezbollah has entered into some kind of accommodation with Israel. It's no longer a resistance organisation; it has morphed into a de facto guardian of Israel's northern border. This might seem outlandish to some ears, but there is evidence. Since that devastating war, on each occasion guns or missiles are fired from southern Lebanon into Israel, Tel Aviv is the first to let Hezbollah off the hook by accusing other groups. I believe history will prove that Hezbollah is an agent for Iran which covertly cooperates with Israeli intelligence; a premise that I've outlined elsewhere in this book.

Once again, the Lebanese people were left to pick up the pieces of their shattered hopes. The protagonists were publicly boasting of their respective successes, when all that had been achieved was massive destruction. When the bombs were dropping, Fouad Siniora had appeared on television weeping. He pleaded with George W. Bush and US Secretary of State Condoleezza Rice to call for a ceasefire in the United Nations Security Council, which they refused to do until the eleventh hour to allow Israel time to finish the job.

Aside from the human cost to Lebanon, the country's infrastructure and economy were wrecked. The war damage cost billions of dollars to repair. Countries in the Middle East and beyond were shipping in humanitarian aid. A donor conference was held in Stockholm, attended by representatives of sympathetic countries, the UN, the World Bank and the IMF. Lebanon also lost untold billions from lost revenue, from tourism, agriculture and industry.

From a personal perspective, the war was painful to watch. I was angry with all sides for their wilful destruction of lives and property. Businesswise, the war and its aftermath were like a hurricane indiscriminately devastating everything in its path.

I kept Habtoorland and the hotels going as long for as I was able, but international tourism dried up and the Lebanese were in no mood for fun weekends or vacations. I had no alternative but to lock the gates of Habtoorland for an indefinite period of time. I also closed my hotel the Habtoor Grand for a while, leaving the Metropolitan Palace operating with under 50 per cent occupancy rates.

I worried a lot about my employees. I continued paying their wages; some were relocated to Dubai to work in my hotels there until Lebanon could get back on its feet. I absolutely hated the thought of putting loyal staff out of work, especially those with families to feed.

As if the war wasn't crippling enough, from 1 December 2006 Beirut was sliced apart by political demonstrations and sit-ins, stirred up by the pro-government 14 March coalition and the pro-Syrian pro-Iranian 8 March alliance led by Hezbollah, Amal and Michel Aoun's Free Patriotic Movement. Gun battles regularly broke out between the feuding sides, Martyr's Square became an occupied 8 March tent city; access to the airport was blocked for a time and business life was also virtually brought to a standstill.

So incensed was I at the senseless cycle of violence in a country I believed in that I called a press conference to urge unity among sectarian groups. I told reporters that I wished my investments were mobile as in that case I would definitely transfer them elsewhere until Lebanese politicians quit squabbling amongst each other instead of working towards better days.

Furthermore, I informed the media that I was mulling over suing the Lebanese state for developing an unfriendly investment climate together with other investors under the rules the United Nations Commission on International Trade Law (UNICITRAL) or the International Centre for Settlement of Investment Disputes (ICSID).

I was so disheartened that I complained bitterly about the lack of law and order and Lebanon's antiquated confessional political system that has contributed to political, social and economic stability.

Since the emergence of the modern Lebanese state in 1943, cabinet positions, parliamentary seats and jobs for government bureaucrats have been allocated according to candidates' faith rather than on the basis of experience or qualifications.

Until today, the President must be a Maronite Christian, the Prime Minister a Sunni Muslim and the Parliamentary Speaker has to be a Shiite Muslim. All efforts to replace this divisive sectarian system with one that is more pluralistic and democratic have so far failed.

"I think the only fault I committed was that I believed in Lebanon," I announced at the time. I penned my frustration and anguish in an article headed 'Have Mercy on Lebanon', as follows:

> Let any entity in Lebanon take the trouble of investigating the losses inflicted on the Lebanese economy during the near past. Do they know that Lebanon's losses stand at billions and that this loss is expected to increase even further due to the paralysis of the country? Do they know how many investors were planning to invest or expand their investments in Lebanon and cancelled their plans? Who is the loser? Definitely there is a big loser, and there is no winner. The loser is the Lebanese citizen, the Lebanese economy and the Treasury. And who is responsible? Isn't it the Lebanese political class?
>
> It is no secret that nobody will help Lebanon if it does not help itself... I do not regret writing this message and I do not consider it an intervention in your affairs because I am not neutral towards what happens in your country. I am with you. When you bleed, I bleed too. The end of the tunnel is within reach and clear but it needs a brave decision that's unselfish. I am sure that Lebanon abounds with that quality of leaders and people... but when?

But when push came to shove, I refused to give up on Lebanon. Habtoorland and the Habtoor Grand were both reopened; former employees that were still available returned to their jobs. Things were quiet for a while, but peace is a precious commodity in Lebanon, as it is so rare.

In May 2007, a conflict broke out between an Islamic militant organisation called Fatah al-Islam and the Lebanese Armed Force in Nahr al-Bared, a Palestinian refugee camp run by UNRWA in Tripoli. Some 446 soldiers and militants died, many refugees fled to other camps. That month, there were several terrorist bomb blasts in the capital. I had two emotions about all this. The first was a sinking feeling of 'here we go again'; the second was one of concern for the terrible plight of those living in the camp.

On 10 June 2007, the intolerable situation of the Palestinians in Nahr al-Bared prompted me to write to Prime Minister Siniora and the Palestinian President, Mahmoud Abbas, primarily to call for the creation of an Arab Construction Fund that would supply Palestinian refugees in Lebanon with decent housing.

Second, I asked Lebanon to allow Palestinians to hold decent jobs on Lebanese soil.

Third, I requested Lebanon to facilitate the "travel and passage of Palestinian refugees" and for them "to be treated with dignity and respect".

And lastly, I reminded the Lebanese Prime Minister that the Lebanese Army must protect all residents, including Palestinians, and must apply strict control of unauthorised weapons possession.

At the time of writing, nothing has changed for generations of Palestinian refugees living in squalor without any prospects or hope. Their anger is understandable. They've been patient for too long. All they want is to live like everyone else. The way they've been treated is shameful and through no fault of their own; it's a stain on Lebanon's human rights record. Providing refugees with acceptable living conditions, the freedom to travel and job opportunities so they can feed their families will not only benefit Palestinians, but will also bring increased stability to Lebanon, not to mention economic benefits as employed individuals pay taxes and are consumers of goods and services.

* * *

On 9 November 2009, Rafik Hariri's son, leader of the Future Movement and the 14 March coalition, Saad Hariri, succeeded Fouad Siniora as Prime Minister. I decided to go and see him regarding a problem I had with a parcel of land I owned in Al Jamhour, on which I wanted to build a house for me and my family.

The trouble was I couldn't get a building permit, because when I applied I was informed that a planned highway to Damascus, the 'Arabian Highway' or the 'Autostrade Al Arabi', was to run bang smack through my plot.

That sounded nonsensical to me; indeed, there was no possibility whatsoever of that happening. Somebody in the ministry hadn't done their homework. There are two reasons why the idea was impractical: the first is that the main power station is adjacent to the land and the other concerns several residential buildings that have been built on it.

I explained my reservations to Prime Minister Hariri and asked if he would be kind enough to send someone to check the land and report on his findings, i.e. that it isn't suitable for a major highway. He was receptive and nominated one of his staff, Fadi Fawaz, to look into the matter.

Unfortunately, Mr Fawaz didn't bother to do any proper research and merely came back with "The highway is going ahead as originally planned and construction will begin as soon as funding becomes available". Saad Hariri has an excellent business mind and he's gained experience since I first knew him, but you cannot be a strong, successful leader without a good team. He should have evaluated the people in his team to ensure they were knowledgeable advisors rather than clerks.

Unwilling to give up that easily, I arranged a meeting with the Minister of Public Works, Ghazi Al Aridi, in the hope that I could convince him to see the light. When I entered his office with my Executive Director, now Al Habtoor Group's Managing Director Maan Halabi, and Ahmad Hamadeh, then our Beirut lawyer, Mr Al Aridi didn't bother looking up at us.

He was standing engrossed in reading a letter. He knew that we were waiting for him to acknowledge our presence, but he carried on reading.

His lack of common courtesy was hardly an encouraging start to our interaction to say the least. He was still studying the paper in his hand, when I called out in a loud voice "*Assalamu Alaykum*". He deigned to answer me with a casual "*Ahlan*".

Once we were seated, he asked us to wait until he'd finished reading. I felt like leaving immediately, but when I remembered why we were there I decided not to be impulsive.

As soon as he was free, I told him about my reservations concerning the proposed highway through my land, but before I could finish explaining he changed the subject by launching into a political critique of his own government. I thought his behaviour more than odd, especially since this was the first time we had ever met. I told myself, Khalaf, leave now.

We'd only been in his office for seven minutes or so, but even in that short time, I was convinced that he either couldn't digest our case or couldn't be bothered to understand what we were saying. What a waste of time, I thought, as we thanked him for his time. In fact, it wasn't a waste of time at all. It was a blessing in disguise, because prior to that day, I'd admired Mr Al Aridi from afar in the mistaken belief that he was a clever man who was loyal to the nation he served.

Meeting him was the straw that broke the camel's back. On that day, I decided never again to personally seek out any Lebanese politician, preferring to leave such contacts to my staff in the event there were outstanding issues needing to be resolved.

In the end, I cancelled the entire 20 million-dollar project, for which I had planned to contract Lebanese construction, interior design and landscaping companies. That was a great pity as the project would have created many new badly-needed job openings. Some people advised me to talk it over with the Prime Minister, but given my past experience with him and his people, I preferred to cut my losses.

Perhaps it's old-fashioned to demand respectful treatment. If that's the case, then I'm happy to be called old-fashioned. Today's generation of politicians may be well-educated in the world's most renowned foreign universities, but some could do with lessons in old school manners.

Following my unfortunate encounter with the Minister of Public Works, I couldn't help but contrast his behaviour with that of former Lebanese President Emile Lahoud. I had first visited him in 1998 to congratulate him on taking office and to inform him about my projects and how many Lebanese I planned to employ.

Our meeting had been scheduled to take place at Baabda Palace, the official residence of the President of Lebanon. I took Ali Moussawi and my sons, Rashid and Ahmad, along with me. As soon as we went in, we were received by President Lahoud's Director of Protocol, Maroun Haimari, who was instantly likeable, welcoming and courteous. He walked with me to a waiting room where I was greeted by the Chief of the Presidential Guard brigade, General Mustafa Hamdan; he greeted me like an old friend, and strangely enough I felt that I'd known him for a long time.

General Hamdan went out of his way to offer his assistance even before I had asked. "Please, anything you need from the palace or if anyone is causing you problems or delaying documents, let me know. I will inform the President and we'll take it from there."

President Lahoud certainly knows the importance of surrounding himself with good people, I thought. And when at last I came face-to-face with him, I understood why. He was an absolutely wonderful person himself. Meeting him was an amazing experience. He embraced me like a brother and chatted with me as he would to a close family friend. There was no barrier between us at all. President Emile Lahoud's hospitality was pure Arab.

When we had finished talking, he escorted me as far as the palace steps. "My dear friend Khalaf, if there's anything at all you need, you can call me on my personal mobile. If you don't get an immediate answer, telephone any of my assistants whom I'll instruct to assist you in any way they can."

Thereafter, we remained in touch. Later, when I faced several problems concerning the construction of Habtoorland, President Lahoud and General Hamdan were the only ones who helped me solve them satisfactorily. One in particular centred on a shooting range right next to Habtoorland that nobody had thought to tell me about, until I began building. It was all a great fuss about nothing. I won't go into the details, but suffice it to say that President Lahoud's kind intervention did the trick.

As the years have passed, I miss the leadership of Prime Minister Rafik Hariri more and more, because, frankly, his successors haven't matched up. In early 2012, the UAE's Ambassador to Lebanon Yousef Osaimi informed me that Prime Minister Najib Mikati who took office on 13 June 2011 had invited me to lunch. I was pleased to accept the invitation and went along with the Ambassador Osaimi and my son Ahmad. The venue was impressive, a palace surrounded by striking architectural gems from bygone eras. Mr Mikati received us warmly and told us that we would be eating "a homemade meal".

In Lebanon, as in many parts of the world, homemade meals are often delicious and involve so much time to prepare that they are rarely served in restaurants. This particular homemade meal consisting of the famous Lebanese *Moujaddara* (rice cooked with lentils and onions), salads, stuffed courgettes and yoghurt was simple yet tasty, the kind of informal fare that a Lebanese might offer a close friend who had popped in to say hi rather than to a formal invitee. He certainly didn't pull out all the stops for us in the way that even the poorest of Lebanese families would have, even if it cost them their last penny. I smiled to myself recalling an earlier disappointment. One of our Lebanese friends, who knew that my brother Sultan loves to eat fried *Asafeer* (small birds), a culinary Lebanese delicacy, promised to send him some. Sultan was delighted and looked forward to enjoying one of his favourite meals that isn't always available. What a surprise he had to find that our friend's messenger turned up bearing a small bag, which Sultan initially assumed contained a letter informing us that the birds would be delivered shortly. When he opened it up, to his amazement he found twelve tiny birds, hardly sufficient for two persons at one sitting.

After lunch, the Prime Minister and I sat down to talk. He is a nice enough person, but I couldn't help but draw comparisons between my host's personality and that of the late PM Hariri, his son, Saad Hariri and the Parliamentary Speaker, Nabih Berri, all natural-born leaders. A telecommunications billionaire appearing on the Forbes List as the richest living person in Lebanon, Mr Mikati is clearly a successful 'trader' in business. But in my view he lacks the aura associated with the head of a nation. He doesn't have sufficient leadership presence or personal magnetism to be a source of inspiration required to bring people together and guide them towards the right track.

Despite the mismanagement of successive governments, Lebanese people are hospitable, friendly and helpful. However, most things are out of their hands. In this country of Sunnis, Shiites, Druzes, Alawites, Isma'ilites, Armenians, Catholics, Orthodox, Maronites, Chaldeans, Assyrians, Copts and Protestants, so-called 'democracy' isn't workable, as most vote on religious or sectarian lines.

Adding to the confusion are numerous political parties that alter their core principles and allegiances at the drop of a hat – or, rather, each time they throw their hats in the parliamentary or presidential ring. They're shape-shifters. Just when you think you're familiar with their manifestos and who they represent, before you know it they've changed sides.

One minute the Druze leader, Walid Jumblatt, detests Hezbollah; the next he's praising the organisation. Likewise, nobody could have predicted that the formerly anti-Syrian Maronite head of the Free Patriotic Movement party, Michel Aoun, would ever forge an alliance with pro-Syrian, pro-Iranian Hezbollah. Those are just two examples of shape-shifters; there are many, many more.

The Lebanese would be better served by implementing a GCC-type system, whereby a president is elected as decision-maker and it is up to him to appoint a Prime Minister and a loyal military commander. This way of doing things ensures that everyone in government is on the same page and pulling together rather than pulling the state apart.

The problem with our dear Lebanese is that they believe their thinking is more advanced than people of other Arab nationalities; but they should look around and ask themselves how their 'superior intellectual capacity' is working for them. They all think in a similar vein. From the President, ministers and bankers, to bakers, taxi drivers and garbage collectors, they all have a similar mentality. With few exceptions, they mistake ignorance for knowledge. Their understanding of the world from the man in the street up to the man sitting in the presidential chair is broadly the same, which, unfortunately, tends to be either flimsy or close to zero.

The Lebanese are all 'experts' in politics and they're all 'smarter' than Arabs, and no one is more elegant or smooth. I know many who are still living the dream of the 1960s and early 1970s, when most of their counterparts in the Middle East and Gulf were barely subsisting. Things have changed since then. Other countries have hurtled forward in terms of standard of living and lifestyle, while Lebanon has been stepping backwards. It's as if the Lebanese have been frozen in a 1960s time capsule while the world has moved forward. Until they're able to understand where they truly stand in the world and figure out ways of catching up politically and economically, they are destined to fossilise.

In order for the Lebanese to move their country forward in a positive way, they must first get to grips with the issue of spurious titles thrown like confetti on people, who half the time don't deserve them. So many unworthy people are addressed as "Your Excellency", "Your Highness" and other lofty titles.

The Shiites, for instance, award special titles to certain families due to their alleged relationship to the grandsons of the Prophet's cousin and son-in-law Ali ibn Abi Talib – Al Hasan and Al Husayn. It's worth mentioning that while Sunnis respect Ali as the fourth and last Rightly Guided Caliph, Shiites consider him as the First Imam. The heads of such self-anointed families – an example being Hezbollah leader Sayyed Hassan Nasrallah – are usually addressed with the title 'Sayyed', meaning 'Master'.

This is particularly irksome for those of us who know only too well that many with such elevated status aren't Arab, and hold allegiance to the Iranian mullahs, while half of them don't even speak Arabic. If anyone is a direct descendent of Ali ibn Abi Talib, he would be either from the Arabian Peninsula, Yemen or the Hashemite Kingdom of Jordan, individuals whose antecedents are well-documented. The strangest thing is that we only find these 'Sayyed' in Lebanon, among our Shiite brothers!

Unfortunately, the memories of those unwilling or unable to change are stuck in the good old days; they refuse to take a long, hard look at reality. If they did, they would be able to free Lebanon from often-repeated mistakes that impact upon the country so negatively. Frankly, it's probably simpler to learn how to read a Chinese encyclopedia than it is to unravel the Lebanese political system and the mindsets of the various actors. So I'll leave it there.

It's been a struggle, but I'm very proud of my two hotels in Beirut, whose names were respectively changed in 2011 to the Hilton Beirut Habtoor Grand and the Hilton Beirut Metropolitan Palace, following an agreement I signed with Hilton Worldwide to develop and operate the properties under the Hilton brand.

I will always cherish the knighthood bestowed on me by the President of Lebanon, my honorary doctorate degree in Humane Letters from the American University of Science and Technology and the fact that I was elected as 'Man of the Year 2003 for Foreign Investors'. They are prestigious accolades that I'm sincerely proud of, but nothing would make me prouder or happier than to see a patriot in charge of Lebanon, who loves the country and who wants to see it forever peaceful, prosperous and beautiful, as much as I do.

CHAPTER 16
Travelling Tales

"TRAVEL IS FATAL TO PREJUDICE, BIGOTRY AND NARROW-MINDEDNESS."
– JIMMY CARTER

I've been very lucky in life to have made lots of good friends from all over the world. Many of them have accompanied me on my frequent journeys abroad. I rarely travel alone, as shared experiences are always more enjoyable and it's nice to be able to look back on them with someone who was there. As much as I love seeing new places, it's the people around me who make a journey special.

The best way to know a person is to take a journey with them. It's at those times I discover whether or not I can get along with someone. If I don't feel altogether comfortable in their company, I never upset them by showing my feelings, but make a mental note never to invite them again. A few of my travelling companions have been disappointed that I'm not up for late night partying or clubbing even though I always tell them upfront that kind of life isn't mine.

Everyone has memorable travel stories. I hope to amuse you with some of mine.

Don Camp, a professional photographer from California who has flown many thousands of miles with me, is one of the best travelling companions I've ever had. Tall with somewhat of a paunch, he always sees the funny side of life, has boundless energy and is one of those rare individuals who is cheerful from morning till night. Whatever minor problems we encounter on our journeys, he never fails to make me laugh. I've rarely seen him without his camera; he shoots anything and everything wherever we go. I'm sure it's almost as dear to him as his children.

In the summer of 2007, I travelled with Don and a bunch of other friends to France via the Belgian capital, Brussels. We took a fast train to the Gare du Nord, one of the six main train stations in Paris. Like all transport hubs all over the world, there were all kinds of people milling around.

As we were walking out of the station, we came across several homeless people; some were sleeping curled up on the floor, one or two were clutching bottles of liquor.

It wasn't a pretty sight, but the scene – a pitiful real life cameo of poverty and addiction – caught Don's sharp photographic eye. While we waited, he removed his camera from its bag and began clicking away, illuminating their startled faces with his flashlight.

Those unfortunates didn't appreciate having their misery captured or being woken up by bright flashes as we soon discovered. A few of the indigents were enraged and leapt up shaking their fists. The last thing we wanted was to be involved in an ugly brawl. In those situations, there is a saying in Arabic that translates to 'run away as fast as a gazelle'. We were in such a hurry to get out of there that a cheetah would have had difficulty catching us – all except Don, who was ready to brave being punched in the nose if it meant he could take a few more pictures.

Besides being an exceptional photographer, Don is also an artist, a pianist and a singer. I may not have a professional ear, but I've always enjoyed his renditions and, to my mind, he's very musically talented. Don is crazy about music, unlike my Lebanese friend Ali Moussawi, who frequently accompanies me on my trips. There's only one thing that irritates Ali more than squandering money, and that is being forced to listen to music – especially classical, opera or jazz. He says that kind of music is torture for him.

In 2008, we went back to Paris for a few days to explore the city on foot and relish the kind of fine dining experiences that are uniquely French. It's a pleasure to dress up in the evenings and savour exquisitely prepared dishes in one of the world's top restaurants.

I love Paris. It's such an inviting and exciting city of contrasts. Every quarter has its own special flavour and, because I don't want to miss anything, I seldom take a taxi, preferring to walk anywhere and everywhere. You can't smell the aroma of freshly-baked croissants or soak up the romantic ambience behind the windows of a vehicle.

Each morning I stroll along the Champs-Elysées for hours, taking in the shop windows and the sounds of a dozen languages being spoken. I particularly enjoy wandering around the perfumery section of one of the Sephora stores just to breathe in the infusion of heavenly scents. People in the Gulf are mad about perfumes, which are part of our culture. We are proud that our perfume shops are the best in the world in terms of quality and variety, but I'm sure if Gulf Arabs ever visited a Parisian perfumery, they would change their minds.

Sometimes, I sit down outside a café just to watch the world go by or find somewhere to have lunch before walking back to my hotel. One of my favourite Paris restaurants that I make sure to visit each time I'm in Paris is Le Dali. It's in the hotel Le Meurice on the Rue de Rivoli; the chef is a real maestro, so it's little wonder that it's earned three coveted Michelin Stars. I wouldn't exactly call myself a gourmet or even a foodie, but I appreciate the rich yet subtle flavours of French cuisine at its best.

On this occasion, we strolled from our hotel to the recently renovated Le Meurice – an imposing and elegant hotel of a similar style to the opulent Plaza Athénée and the Paris Ritz. Its spacious opulence attracted the Nazis during Germany's occupation of France in World War II, when it was sequestered by the Nazi Military Command for a time.

As it was still too early for dinner, we sat for a while in the lounge listening to an African-American jazz singer and pianist; his voice sounded much like Louis Armstrong's. What was literally music to our ears was painful to Ali's who made his agony known. Don was busy savouring his James Bond signature drink – a Martini with two olives, shaken not stirred – and snapping away between sips. But even he noticed that Ali was squirming in his seat like a death row inmate strapped to the electric chair.

"It's too noisy here. Let's ask them to tone it down," Ali eventually said. We didn't take any notice of him, so he said it again. Don thought Ali was being a real killjoy when the rest of us were enjoying our time. He waited until the jazz man sang a slow sentimental song to teach Ali a playful lesson.

He took on a soulful expression and with misty eyes he told us that this particular song held a very special significance for him before feigning a few sobs. "Oh my God, this is too emotional!" he said. "I can't take it anymore." At that point, I had no idea what he was up to. I'd never seen him like that before. I began to mentally count how many Martinis he'd downed. He could usually handle his drink. Sometimes alcohol made him sleepy when he would have a short power nap and wake up as energised as ever. That was the first time he'd gone to pieces in my company. What's wrong with him, I wondered?

Then, without any warning, Don leant over to grab Ali's tie and used it to blow his nose – or rather, pretended to do so. We were stunned. We thought he'd done it for real. And, more to the point, so did Ali. We were all concerned when he stared at Don with killer eyes, his face turning tomato red with fury, as he checked his tie for evidence of the crime. Just as I was expecting blood to be spilled on Le Meurice's plush, thick-pile carpet, Ali cottoned on to the prank and, once he had composed himself, took it in good humour.

Another of my regular travel buddies was a British friend called Jerry Morgan. The strange thing was that on each occasion we flew to New York or Miami, I would complete immigration formalities in under a minute, while he would be kept waiting for half an hour or more. I asked him why someone holding a UAE passport would receive preference over a British national. "Well, that's probably because the trans-Atlantic relationship is so strong that Uncle Sam's authorities want to extend their hospitality to us Brits," he joked. Of course, that was before 11 September 2001 attacks. Since then, Arab passports send red lights flashing in US airports.

Jerry is a great guy, but he's allergic to leaving big tips. Once, we ordered cakes and pastries in the coffee shop of a famous New York hotel and when the bill came, he left a 15 per cent tip, which would have been appreciated in a similar standard UK hotel. Imagine our astonishment when, minutes later, we were accosted by an irate waiter on the street asking, "Did I do something wrong? Did I insult anyone? Please let me know what mistake I made?"

"You did nothing wrong. The service was excellent," said Jerry.

"Then why did you only leave a 15 per cent tip?" the waiter asked accusingly. "You should have left 21 per cent. That is the minimum."

We were taken aback by his audacity, but nevertheless we paid the extra. If a waiter were to hassle customers for inadvertently undertipping in one of my hotels, there would be repercussions. For that style of restaurant, reputation is everything and it only takes one member of its staff to destroy the hard work of everyone else.

* * *

In late 2010, whilst in Vienna with some friends, I booked a table for seven in a new Italian restaurant, the San Carlo, opposite the Bristol Hotel where I was staying, on the recommendation of one my travelling companions, Abdullah Mazrooie. The restaurant seemed nice, but our table was in a stuffy room without windows or natural light. We sat for a few minutes until I decided that I didn't want to have my lunch in a prison cell. I told Abdullah to politely ask the manager to move us to a table near a window.

I have no idea how such a simple request could have sent the manager into such a rage. He started yelling like a madman. Abdullah and another of my friends, a young Lebanese-American called Hussein Chami, tried to calm him down, but he wouldn't let them get a word in. Eventually, he ordered us out. Abdullah tried to get him to change his mind, until I said "Leave him. It's alright. Let's go."

Everyone saw the funny side. We don't often get kicked out of restaurants. Hussein was the most indignant. On those evenings we had dinner at our hotel, he would go out onto the street for a cigarette. He would stand outside the entrance to the San Carlo and puff away as hard as he could. His futile efforts to ensure the smoke wafted in through the restaurant's door made us laugh.

* * *

Whenever I travel with a group of friends, I usually take along a capable person who knows how to take care of hotel bookings, immigration, luggage and car hire. Hussein was my 'Mr Fix It' at one time. He has a great sense of humour and is experienced at handling such boring details that no traveller can escape – or so he claimed. So I would bring him along whenever I travelled with a large party of friends and would tell everyone that Hussein had everything under control.

Once when we flew from Paris to Luton Airport in the UK, Hussein mistakenly offloaded the luggage of Noura Badawi, the Director of Media and Communications at the Al Habtoor Group, who was transiting in Abu Dhabi en route to her home in Dubai. Upon arrival at my English country house, we found Noura's suitcases mixed up with our own. Noura called me from Abu Dhabi Airport sounding quite upset. "Please don't be angry with Hussein," I told her. "Your luggage is safe with us; it was offloaded in Luton by mistake." Poor Hussein could never boast about his efficiency again, but I forgave him and warned him to be more careful in future.

As it turned out, Hussein's American passport came in useful when our private plane landed in Bari, Italy. We headed for immigration, but there wasn't a single immigration officer on duty and all the gates were open. One of my party suggested we just walk through without clearance to our cars that were waiting for us outside the airport. "We can't do that," I said. "That wouldn't be right and in any case we'll have problems with immigration when it's time to leave." Thirty minutes later, no officer had turned up.

There was nothing for it but to go in search of them. We eventually found them huddled together in a small office chatting away.

The problem was they didn't speak a word of English. Hussein handed our passports to one of the officers, but instead of making a move to process them, he just set them down on a desk and continued conversing with his colleagues as though we didn't exist. We left the office leaving Hussein to sort things out. He turned up sometime afterwards, waving his American passport. "Where are ours?" I asked. "They've still got them," he said, shrugging his shoulders.

By then I was annoyed. We had unnecessarily been hanging around the airport for over an hour, so that immigration officers could enjoy a cosy chat. Adding insult to injury was the fact that the sole American among us had got his passport stamped, while we were still waiting for ours.

"Hussein, go back to those people now. If they have so much respect for an American passport, flash it at them, show them that you are angry and demand the immediate return of our passports. They won't understand what you're saying, but never mind. Just scare them." He did just that and sure enough, within a few minutes he came back with everyone's travel documents.

I've rarely had problems clearing immigration or customs, but there have been a few uncomfortable moments. The first was when I flew with six others by private plane to Le Bourget Airport just outside Paris. When we landed, immigration officers boarded the aircraft and stamped our passports. A car was waiting for us outside the customs terminal, but just as we drove off we heard loud police sirens before we were flagged down and blocked by two police cars. Two tall black Frenchmen and a short policewoman approached our vehicle. My heart sank.

At least, their manner was polite. One asked, "Do you speak French, messieurs?" I told them we didn't, so they switched to broken English. "Did you remember to declare how much currency you're carrying?" When I explained that we hadn't and didn't know about the rule, they told us that we had violated the law.

One of my companions offered to go back into the terminal to complete the necessary form, but they said we could do that next time. Instead, they asked to see all the money we had with us so they could count it. When they saw how much currency we had with us, they were clearly suspicious, until I explained that we were a party of seven and needed ready cash for our hotel and travel expenses.

"Why don't you speak French?" asked the tallest policeman accusingly.

"There are a lot of English people in my country and we're more used to speaking English," I explained.

"You should get yourself a French girlfriend to teach you."

"Do you have someone in mind?" I bantered before they finally allowed us to go on our way.

Few of my countrymen speak French, as most people in the UAE consider Britain as their second home, due to the long relationship between the two countries. British visitors to our country are welcomed and respected and, likewise, we are well-received by the UK authorities. I did, however, have one bad experience. Once, when I was going through customs at London Heathrow after a trip to Brazil, a young customs officer asked us where we had flown from.

"Good morning, Sir," I said. "We've just arrived from Brazil."

"Where is your passport?" he barked.

I was travelling on a special passport at the time and handed it to him for inspection. He hardly glanced at it before throwing both our passports onto a luggage conveyor belt. "He's deliberately insulting us," whispered my friend. "Let's just remain calm and quiet," I told him, because ultimately those guys have absolute power. We could have shouted or become aggressive, but it would not have done us any good. Boiling internally, we stood helplessly watching him rummage through all our suitcases, allowing all the contents to spill out. When we asked if he would kindly help us to get everything back in, his rude response was "Do it yourself!". That kind of disrespect from personnel working at Britain's airports is unusual, but I suppose there is always the exception that proves the rule.

* * *

In accordance with my usual summer routine, in 2006, I flew to Paris with Hussein, Ali Moussawi and other friends. One evening, we had dinner in one of the city's most renowned restaurants, Le Jules Verne, on the second floor of the Eiffel Tower. It only seats 120 and so it's not always easy to get a reservation, as visitors to Paris clamour to enjoy fabulous cuisine as well as spectacular views. Le Jules Verne is exceptionally stylish – and also exceptionally expensive. We arrived at 7 p.m., my usual time to dine wherever I am in the world, and had a lovely meal as usual.

When it was time to leave, Ali asked for the bill. I always asked Ali to carry the money on our trips for expenses, as he's very careful with cash and hates wasting his own or anybody else's for that matter. Hussein, on the other hand, is afflicted with typical Lebanese millionaire-style spending habits, never mind that he rarely has a penny in his pocket. As Ali began scrutinising the bill, I saw him change colour. I guessed it was high and laughed at his reaction. I asked him how much it was. I don't recall the exact amount, but I do remember that it was around three times higher than a similar one-Michelin-star Paris restaurant.

Ali grudgingly took out a wad of euros and placed them one by one on the plate, looking as pained as if a dentist was pulling out all his teeth. As far as he was concerned, we were being royally ripped off. Of course, Hussein didn't see it that way. He compounded Ali's agony by asking, "How much pourboire did you leave? Remember the kind of place we're in."

Ali was infuriated. "It's none of your business," he told him. "If you're so worried about the tip, why don't you dig into your own wallet for a change?" Ali and Hussein were constantly arguing like cat and rat over what was an appropriate tip. I usually stayed out of it, but for some reason this time I asked Ali the amount. "I left around fifty euros," he admitted unhappily. "That's more than enough for those French."

"What? You only left fifty euros?" interjected Hussein. "That's not nearly enough. You're supposed to leave at least 20 per cent."

To be honest, Hussein was right in that 20 per cent is the norm in France, but, if he had to fork out that sum himself, it would be one of his life's blackest moments. In the end, I supplemented the pourboire with a generous sum, which delighted Hussein but sent Ali into a sulk. He didn't say anything because he has too much respect for me to second-guess my decision, but I could tell that he was seriously annoyed.

I understood both sides of the coin. There was a time when I had to count the pennies myself and nobody likes to feel exploited. But as a hotelier, I could easily imagine the massive overheads incurred by a restaurant in such a prime location. We could have had a perfectly adequate three-course twenty-euro 'menu' in one of the hundreds of Paris bistros, but if you want the best it comes at a price. Most importantly, I'm always aware how much reliance waiters put on tips to supplement their income.

Ali's sulk didn't last long. It was cut short by a hair-raising experience. The avenue Gustave Eiffel was far away from our hotel in the Place de l'Opéra, so rather than walk we flagged down a couple of taxis. Taking a taxi in Paris is often an adventure on its own. The driving can be so erratic that the cabbies would feel at home on the streets of Cairo or Mumbai. Some of the drivers – both male and female – are real characters. There are the surly ones and those at the other extreme who want to talk your head off even when you don't understand a word they're saying. Occasionally, you'll get into one, only to find the driver's pet dog occupying the front passenger seat. But this was the night I would meet the driver from hell.

I got into the back seat of one of the cabs and was joined by Ali and Noura Badawi; the rest of my party followed in the other one. Our taxi driver was a talker. He said he was Algerian and, the moment he knew we were Arabs, he gave us a hearty welcome as though we were blood brothers. Almost before Ali finished saying *"L'Opéra s'il vous plaît,"* the driver put his foot on the gas and the ride of terror began.

In the mistaken belief that we would enjoy listening to blaring North African music so late at night, he produced a CD, inserted it into the cassette deck and turned up the volume to the maximum ear-splitting level. We could have done without that, but when he began dancing in his seat we were horrified. As he swayed his body, waved his arms and clicked his fingers, the taxi zigzagged from one side of the road to the other. We had stepped into a nightclub on wheels. Thankfully, at that time of night, the traffic was fairly light.

As we sat in white-knuckled stony silence, Ali and I exchanged looks that meant 'God help us!' Ali then started chatting with the loony Algerian to divert his attention from the rhythmic sound, in the hope he would slow down a little... but no such luck.

"How do you like the music?" he asked. We managed to raise a smile and nod our approval. By his tone of voice, we could tell that he was anxious for us to get into the swing of things and join the party.

Fearful of upsetting this manic character, the three of us decided to show him that we were going with the flow – cheering, clicking our fingers and jiggling about, like suddenly animated waxwork figures from Madame Tussauds. That drive seemed like it went on forever. Once we got to the hotel, we couldn't get out of the taxi fast enough and swore that we would never again dine anywhere that wasn't within walking distance of where we were staying. Never again would we leave ourselves to the mercy of taxi drivers in Paris, we pledged.

* * *

Most of my travelling companions rebel against my written-in-stone daily routine, as I've mentioned before. They especially dislike having to sleep early to rise at dawn, and are unused to eating dinner in the early evening. In my part of the world, night owls outnumber early birds. However, one of my friends, Fouad Tarabey, is a man after my own heart – a real exception, who understands the importance of getting up early.

Fouad and his family are among several Lebanese with whom I've maintained a long friendship. They are genuine, honest people and a pleasure to know. My family loves them too, so we sometimes invite them to spend a few weeks with us at our home in England. At other times, I invite them to join my travelling party.

I have circled the world with Fouad numerous times. He's a very respectable man from a well-known and highly respected family from the village of Tannourine that nestles in a scenically beautiful north Lebanese mountain region. I never cease to be impressed by his smart attire and his high standards in personal hygiene. He always meets me for breakfast well shaven and well dressed, ready to start his day. I suspected he was a self-disciplined person like me. His timekeeping is impeccable. Whenever we arranged to meet, he would usually arrive at least fifteen minutes early. But after we had made a few trips together, I came to know that Fouad's disciplined ways that I considered admirable were an annoyance to some of my less disciplined buddies.

A long journey I took together with my brother Sultan, Abdullah Mazrooie, Karim Alayli, Ibrahim 'Bob' Tahlak, Fouad Tarabey, Bill Kalchoff and Jawa in the winter of 2010–11 was one of the most memorable of my life. It was first stop Egypt, where I inaugurated the Khalaf Ahmad Al Habtoor Football Stadium and Track in the American University of Cairo. From there we flew to Kazan, the capital of the oil-and-gas-rich Republic of Tatarstan, to study investment opportunities at the invitation of the government.

I knew next to nothing about Tatarstan when my plane took off and had no preconceived ideas about the place other than it stands on the banks of a river that flows into the Volga and that it is considered to be Russia's Oriental capital as well as its cultural and sporting heartland. As it turned out, I was completely bowled over by the place.

I was amazed at the stunning one-thousand-and-one-nights baroque and contemporary architecture of that pristine city, so rich in history and culture. Minarets, cupolas and spires dominate the skyline and the city's historical Kremlin was nominated as a UNESCO World Cultural Heritage Site. The highlight of my stay was a visit to one of Kazan's forty-five mosques, where the names of all the prophets were inscribed on the walls and where children were being taught stories from the Qur'an with the aid of pictures, objects and costumes. I liked that unusual interactive method of religious teaching, which clearly kept the youngsters interested.

Eating out at some of the plush, older established restaurants, some resembling the private quarters of the Tsar's palace, felt like stepping back into the early part of the last century. I've never in my life seen such extensive à la carte choices; it would take most people an age just to read through their menus.

I was even more amazed at the hospitality we received, from the President Rustam Minnikhanov, down to his ministers and passersby on the street, who smiled and waved at us. The President, a commodity expert and economist, is intelligent and dynamic. During our forty-minute discussion, it was clear that he really cares about his multiethnic, multireligious citizenry and is pulling out all the stops to turn his homeland into a success story.

He and his ministers were sincere, down-to-earth men without pretensions. They couldn't do enough for us. It was refreshing to meet people who haven't adopted social masks. Their warmth and inherent courtesy reminded me of the way we Arabs were before we caught the fast train. I was so relaxed in their company I could almost have been sitting on my porch among my own family members.

Bill Kalchoff made us laugh when he spoke to the President's aide for international affairs, Timur Akulov, about a new trading relationship between Tatarstan/Russia and his country, the United States. "We'll trade our women, just the old and fat ones, for young and slender Russian ladies." The Minister enjoyed the joke. "Thank you for the compliment," he said laughing. "But that trade won't work as we prefer to keep our own women."

Our last port of call before flying home was Chicago, Illinois, where I had been invited to attend a Lingerie Football League match and event. It was phenomenal! It was the first time that I had ever witnessed girls playing such a rough game. When I saw them before they began kicking the ball, they looked sweet and angelic. But once in action they were tougher than most professional wrestlers.

All in all, a good time was had by all on that marathon trip and every one of my friends appreciated having such original and fascinating experiences.

However, I had no idea of the scenario that had played out behind the scenes. Hussein and Abdullah waited until we were home in Dubai before telling me. I invited them both to my office for coffee and a chat shortly after our return. Hussein was the first to arrive.

"Abu Rashid (Father of Rashid), I want to thank you very much for laying on the journey of a lifetime," he said. "But I must tell you something. I have newfound admiration for Fouad Tarabey." There was something in his voice that told me Hussein was just being polite in the lead-up to a complaint.

"I admire him too. Fouad is great, but what are you trying to say?"

"Before I proceed, would you mind ordering coffee? This is a tale that should be told over a cup of coffee," he said, before greeting Abdullah who had just walked in. I ordered espresso macchiato for the three of us. Hussein and Abdullah exchanged a conspiratorial grin before Hussein launched into the story.

"As soon as you excused yourself at 10 p.m. each evening, we would plan to wind down from the day watching TV in the lounge or just chatting over a drink. But once you'd gone to bed, Fouad would turn into a headmaster. 'Yalla, yalla (Arabic for 'let's go' or Vamonos in Spanish), it's time to go to your rooms. It's time to sleep. Come on, lights out.' And like kids in boarding school, we would all head to our hotel rooms with our tails between our legs," Hussein explained.

The thought of grown men trooping off at Fouad's command made me laugh out loud; yet, at the same time, my respect for Fouad had grown by leaps and bounds. "Is that true?" I asked Abdullah.

"Yes, it's absolutely true," Abdullah said. "But wait, Abu Rashid... Wait to hear this!"

Actually, I was anxious to hear the rest, because it sounded like something I've been tempted to do myself in the past when such a lot of my friends sleep so late that they have to drag themselves out of bed in the mornings and spend the rest of the day yawning and yearning for a siesta. Being in the company of people who are half-asleep isn't much fun for someone like me who is wide-eyed and active all day. And so he went on...

"Every night, before we went to bed, we would meet in Hussein's suite to talk about our day. Unfortunately, every time Fouad found us there, he would shout: 'Abdullah, go to your room!' And he would say to Karim Alayli 'You, kid! Go to your bed... Yalla, yalla.'"

If Hussein and Abdullah thought I would be outraged at Fouad's bossiness, they were wrong. I could hardly drink my espresso for laughing.

"That's not all," Hussein interjected. "Once he had kicked everyone out, he would say to me, 'Go to sleep, Hussein. Don't forget that we have to get up early tomorrow morning.' And the funniest thing was I would do as I was told and close my eyes."

"Wait to hear what he did in the morning," added Abdullah.

"What was that?"

"I'll tell him," Hussein said. "Every morning at 4 a.m. sharp, he would burst into the suite, yelling 'Hussein, wake up! It's time to get up. Now! You need time to shower and brush your teeth before breakfast.' I would beg him to let me close my eyes for another few minutes, but he always refused. One morning, he woke me up at 3 a.m., and when I complained that it was still early, he said 'I know that but we're travelling today.' 'Please let me rest for another hour,' I pleaded. 'What should I do in the meantime?' he asked. 'How about going back to sleep yourself,' I said. To my amazement, he said 'okay' and left me alone. Victorious at last, I felt quite pleased with myself. Unfortunately, my victory was short-lived. At 4 a.m. on the dot, he returned to complete his mission. Can you believe it? He actually stood over me when I was cleaning my teeth. I tell you, Abu Rashid, I've never served in the military, but I'm sure that soldiers get more sleep than I did during that trip. Fouad behaved worse than a sergeant major in the army."

I tried to show as much sympathy as I could. In truth, though, their tale of woe was wasted on me other than for its humour value. Fouad had been elevated in my eyes. At last, I'd found someone with a more disciplined character than all the friends and travelling companions I've known over the years – someone who, in that respect, was very much like me.

* * *

I only wished that I had invited Fouad to join me on my first trip to Morocco with Abdullah, Ali, Sari Al Mansouri, Ibrahim 'Bob' Tahlak, Jamal Al Odeidi, my son Mohammed – and a very respectable, instantly likeable Emirati friend from Dubai, the late Fawzi Al Falasi. They could have done with some organising.

The guys booked a hotel beach villa and went ahead of me; they received me at Rabat-Salé Airport a few days later. The next morning, I got up at my usual 6 a.m. and then woke up everyone else, because I had arranged cars for 7.30 a.m. to take us to Marrakech. In retrospect, I realise that was crazy planning, as Marrakech is over a four-hour drive from the Moroccan capital.

I couldn't understand why every single one of my friends came down to breakfast wearing dark glasses looking like actors auditioning for *Men in Black*. I later discovered they had been out enjoying themselves until five in the morning. Naturally, they slept all the way to Marrakech, all except Fawzi, who wasn't used to the modern, high-speed cars I'd rented. Every so often, he would shout at the driver, "Are you trying to kill us?", or "Why do you accelerate when you see a car or truck and slow down when we're on an empty road... What is wrong with you?"

I sat back and relaxed, gazing out of the window. Morocco in spring was resplendent with greenery, rose bushes and wild flowers. We drove past green valleys, alive with flocks of sheep and goats – and, as I caught a glimpse of the snow-capped Atlas Mountains, I remember thinking that the landscape was reminiscent of parts of Europe. The more southerly we drove, the more the land was arid.

At last, we arrived at this unique ochre-coloured former imperial city at the foot of the High Atlas.

There's nowhere else quite like the labyrinthine old part of town, with its narrow alleyways and traditional *riads* – walled two or three-storey houses built around a courtyard, which in recent decades have been turned into guest houses or snapped up by wealthy Europeans. Many international celebrities have fallen in love with this mysterious desert city, including Sir Richard Branson, who built a fabulous mountain retreat nearby in Berber style.

Winston Churchill often stayed in the majestic Mamounia Hotel; he described his balcony there as the loveliest spot in the whole world and captured the view in watercolours. John Paul Getty Junior and Yves Saint Laurent owned magnificent homes in the medina, and today it's the place to spot famous movie stars, fashion designers, writers, artists and musicians.

We didn't come across the rich and famous on the day we were there. Like all first time visitors to Marrakech, we headed to the Djemaa el-Fna square to see the acrobats, dancers, magicians and street peddlers selling everything from herbal remedies to oriental perfumes, leather pouffes, slippers, kaftans and glazed pottery. It was all very entertaining, until I noticed an 'enforcement steel bar' around 1.5 metres long, rising out of the ground some distance away. "What's that steel bar doing there?" I asked someone. "That's no metal bar. It's a snake," he said with a grin. I wasn't laughing and to make things worse, I began to notice those slithering creatures all over the square.

That was it! I couldn't wait to get out of there. I didn't know then that the square is the favoured haunt of snake charmers. I was later told that the snakes are harmless, they never hurt anyone; but as someone who is no fan of slippery serpents – whether reptilian or human – I wasn't convinced.

Fawzi was terrific company on that journey. We got to know each other well. It seems his fear of erratic driving was justified. Sadly, around five years ago Fawzi, who was nervous and uptight travelling by road, lost his life in a car accident in which his wife also died. I have very good memories of Fawzi and I still smile when I remember a phone conversation we once had.

I called him to ask where he was. He said he had just put down the phone after talking with his friend Majid (also known as 'Abu Awad', the father of Awad). "A funny thing has just happened," he told me. "In an earlier call, Abu Awad said he couldn't talk now because he was about to land a plane at Charles de Gaulle airport in Paris. 'Please call me later once I've landed,' he said. I was stunned because, firstly, I had no idea that Majid was a pilot and, secondly, I'd seen him in Dubai two hours ago. How could he reach Paris in less than two hours?" said Fawzi. "When I called him back, he said he was busy guiding the aircraft along the runway. The third time I called, he was breathing heavily. 'Thank God we landed safely,' he said. I asked him how he flew from Dubai to Paris in a couple of hours. 'That's easy,' he said. 'I've been playing Flight Simulator on the computer.'" Fawzi yelled at him and called him crazy; we later found out Majid was known for his eccentricities – and that's putting it politely.

* * *

Some years ago, the President of Kazakhstan, Nursultan Nazarbayev, invited me to his country to talk about potential investments. It was winter, so I knew it would be very cold there, but that didn't bother me at all because I love cold climates. The colder it is the better, I thought. I flew by private jet to Astana, the Kazakh capital, with the Kazakh Ambassador to Saudi Arabia Baghdad Amrayev (at that time there was no Embassy of Kazakhstan in the UAE), together with top members of my management team. As the plane began its descent, I glanced out of a window and could hardly believe my eyes. The ground below was carpeted with snow and ice that looked just like an endless 360 degree sheet of glass.

We were met at the airport by a Minister and several government officials. "Welcome to Kazakhstan, Mr Al Habtoor," said the Minister. "Thank you. Is it always this cold?" I asked him, trying to stop my teeth from chattering.

"You're lucky that you came today; the temperature is only –20 °C. It was –40 °C yesterday." I love cold weather, but until that day I didn't know what cold meant. I could hardly draw breath. I regretted wearing leather shoes and thin cotton socks; I should have packed a pair of fur-lined boots.

Then, much to my surprise, the Minister asked us "Do you have a visa?"

"No, sorry, none of us have visas. Because we were invited by the government, we thought visas were unnecessary," I answered.

"But everyone who comes to Kazakhstan has to have a visa," he said, with an almost imperceptible frown.

"Well, the ball's in your court. Are you going to invite us into your country or not? We'll gladly re-board our plane and take off now if that rule is unbreakable." He quickly changed his tune and told me there was no problem at all. Just leave your passports with us and we'll drop them at your hotel later on, he said. He suggested that we might like to have a few hours rest. Before we were driven to the hotel I was warned that the entire city from where we stood to the coast was under layers of ice. All the rivers were frozen. People were apparently making small holes in the ice to catch fish.

When we finally reached the hotel, I showered and changed into a smart suit, thinking I was about to meet with the President and Vice-President. Instead, our hosts offered to show us around Astana, which they explained had recently become the Kazakh capital instead of Almaty – Kazakhstan's largest city and major commercial centre. While waiting for everyone in my group, I asked a pretty hotel receptionist with oriental features, "Are you Chinese or Japanese?"

"Excuse me?"

"Where are you from... Japan or China?"

"Neither," she said, looking very offended. "I am Kazakh."

I was just trying to make small talk to pass the time, but I said the wrong thing and she wrongly thought I was trying to insult her. This visit hasn't started off very well, I remember thinking.

The promised tour of the city turned out to be a walking tour. Our government-appointed guides bought us very glamorous and expensive Russian-style fur hats straight out of *Doctor Zhivago*. I don't normally wear hats, but anything to prevent icicles forming on my ears was gratefully received. The more we walked, the more the cold penetrated my bones. My nose and feet were so numb I couldn't be sure they were still there.

I pride myself on my ability to withstand cold weather, but this time it got to me. I was unable to walk any further. I could no longer move my limbs, I could hardly feel them. When the government officials noticed my distress, two of them held me under the shoulders and hoisted me a few inches off the ground. In this way, with my feet dangling in the air, I was transported all the way back to the hotel. I've rarely felt so embarrassed in my life, especially as so many people were staring at the undignified spectacle; they probably thought I'd had one too many glasses of Russian vodka.

Later that day, I met with the Vice-President and was scheduled to have a meeting with the President the following afternoon. As much as I had looked forward to that, the only thought in my head was how quickly I could get back to the warmth of Dubai.

Despite the fact that I was anxious to go home, I appreciated that the Vice-President had laid on a very generous lunch that included *ouzi* (a slowly roasted whole lamb) and venison. He and his colleagues thirstily downed warm vodka and were soon relaxed enough to open up about themselves. The Vice-President revealed that he had been a wrestler in his youth which was easy to believe. It hadn't escaped me that he had a larger and more muscular body than most politicians. I was, however, startled when he told me that the President was also an ex-wrestler. I've nothing against that profession, but that sealed my decision. This wasn't the place for me. Let me get out of here in one piece, I thought with a silent chuckle before making an excuse to cut short the lunch.

"Look, we'll have to come up with an excuse to leave immediately," I told my team. "I don't want to be impolite, but I can't stay here another day." Everywhere was cold and damp; we were shivering even inside the hotel. It's not like Europe, where even when the temperature drops to minus thirty you can survive, because most hotels, offices and homes are centrally heated.

I told my hosts that I was sorry I couldn't stay to meet the President, but due to an emergency in Dubai I had to get back. They said President Nazarbayev would be upset if I left without seeing him. "Please relay my apologies to him and assure him that I'll return as soon as I can," I said.

The next morning, very early, I gave everyone's luggage to our American pilot and told him to take it to the aircraft. We followed soon after. It was fifteen minutes into the flight before I finally defrosted. To be fair, the people we met in Kazakhstan were pleasant and generous, but I just wasn't physically able to withstand that kind of extreme cold. I'm sure it's a lovely city; if we'd gone in summer, I would have appreciated it a lot more.

* * *

If you've ever read Jules Verne's novel *Around the World in Eighty Days* or seen the film, you'll have heard of Passepartout, the hero's valet who provided his boss with comic relief, but was always getting himself into scrapes. One of my 'Mr Fix Its', Sami, was a Lebanese version of that funny character.

I first met him in the 1980s. Sami's name kept cropping up in conversations with my sons Rashid and Mohammed and others who raved about the manager of one of our restaurant outlets. They all enthused about how clever this manager from South Lebanon was, how smart, how elegantly dressed. So one day I decided I had to see this genius for myself.

I asked Walid Abu Al Hassan, a Lebanese gentleman, to come with me to the restaurant. It was late afternoon. The terrace was so packed with customers that a special table had to be squeezed in for us. Walid ordered tea and *zaatar* with olive oil for both of us and then Sami, who had no inkling then that I was the restaurant's owner, came up to ask whether everything was alright.

In truth, he looked more like a president of France or a British prime minister than a restaurant manager. His face was glistening like he had just stepped out of a spa, his nails were well manicured and he wore an impeccably-cut suit and a crisp shirt set off by expensive cufflinks. As soon as we told him what we'd ordered, he said, after he realised who I was, "No, no. I don't recommend that. I can bring you better food from my home." That wasn't something any restaurant owner would like to hear from one of his employees. But I didn't say anything. We drank our tea and left.

I found his manner intriguing because his outer appearance didn't suit the part. That same evening, I told my driver to invite him to join me and some friends for dinner. He came across as someone who was bold, overly confident and an extrovert; all in all, he was quite the entertainer. However, I disagreed with my sons who were wowed by his intelligence. I wasn't taken in. He told me that he used to be a policeman in Qatar. It wasn't until much later on that I found out he had been working *for* a policeman in Qatar.

On another day, I drove to the restaurant at around 11 a.m. and was surprised to find Sami asleep on a sofa with everyone tiptoeing around him or doing the cleaning in silence. As soon as I came through the door, one of the waiters, who wasn't aware I was the owner, signalled to me to whisper so as not to wake him up.

I went close to him and called out his name in a loud voice. He jumped up looking irritated at first and then embarrassed. "Sorry, I wanted to have a short nap before the lunchtime crowd arrived. I'm very tired. I went to bed very late last night." I'm not sure why I didn't sack him there and then. Something held me back; probably his PR value, because, if nothing else, he seemed to make a good impression with customers.

Later on, he asked me to find a job for his son, who I hired as a Sales Manager in my trading company, one of the companies I had established and which failed. That was a mistake. The young man kept disappearing every morning to have breakfast in my restaurant with his father, who coddled him like a baby. I reached the conclusion that Sami might act more responsibly in a more challenging position – and somewhere where I could keep an eye on him. And so I transferred him to the Head Office under the supervision of the Director of Operations of Hotels Gopi Bhawnani, who asked Sami to do a feasibility study on the potential location of a new branch we planned to open.

Gopi, a very astute professional, was suspicious of Sami from the start, and more so when he started reporting to work in the morning only to leave shortly afterwards, and to show his face again just before the close of our working day. I assigned an office staff to check if he was actually checking out suitable restaurant premises and locations or up to something else.

I told him to go to Sami's apartment building, hide and wait to see if Sami drove up in his green Honda. Sure enough, it wasn't long before he called me to say, "Sami's just parked his car, opened his jacket, removed his tie and gone up in the elevator." I told him to wait there until 1 p.m. to see if he came out again. He didn't. I called those managers of my hotels who had some free time to meet me in the lounge of the Metropolitan Hotel to witness how Sami was going to wriggle his way out of this one, more for a laugh than anything else. But I also thought it was time to put Sami on the spot, in the hope he would finally learn his lesson.

I phoned Sami and told him to join us. When he arrived, I asked whether he had found a nice location. "Yes, I have," he answered, before launching into a descriptive tissue of lies about the merits of this place and that.

"Tell me exactly what you did and where you were from the minute you left the office this morning until now," I told him. He didn't blink. He just continued with his imaginary account like the accomplished liar he was. His fibs were mostly harmless and there were times when I actually enjoyed them; this wasn't one of those times.

"I'll tell you what you did today," I said, and proceeded to do so in great detail. He must have thought I'd been reading the coffee cups, although I had to draw on my knowledge of his character and my imagination to describe what happened once he had entered his own front door.

"Your wife put on the air conditioner and turned down the lights. You removed your jacket, threw your tie on the sofa and slept." That was exactly what he'd done. He reacted with amazement at first, which morphed into shame. "Oh, I'm really sorry," he said. "I was desperate for a nap."

When I saw his eyes begin to moisten, I forgave him. By then, I understood that he was a compulsive liar; someone who had trouble distinguishing reality from fantasy. I'm sure there were times when he believed his own lies. Again, I held back from firing him, because I could see that he had untapped potential – and besides it was fun to have him around. Then again, maybe I'm just too soft-hearted.

As time wore on, it became evident that Sami wasn't suited to an eight-to-five structured office environment, so I hired him as a paid travelling companion. Unfortunately, that wasn't exactly his calling either. He was more like Mr Bean than Passepartout.

I took him with me to New York once, together with Jerry Morgan. Once there, we were invited to dinner in a restaurant close to the hotel where we were staying, by British supermodel Naomi Campbell. The restaurant had a no-smoking policy, so when Naomi's secretary wanted a cigarette after we'd finished eating, she went outside and Sami went with her. Little did I know then that Sami was giving the secretary the third degree, bombarding her with personal questions about her boss, such as: How much money does she make every year? How much does she have in the bank? What stocks and shares does she own? And who knows what else.

At the end of the very pleasant evening, I thanked our hostess and walked back to the hotel. The following day, Naomi phoned sounding extremely upset. When I asked her why her voice sounded strange, she said, "Your assistant has been asking my secretary how much money I have and..." She was furious.

Naomi is a very sweet person but she's gained notoriety for occasionally losing her temper and hurtling missiles at the object of her displeasure. If Sami had been within bopping distance, I wouldn't have blamed her. I would have been just as angry had the roles been reversed and her secretary had interrogated Sami about my financial affairs. I explained to her that, first of all, Sami is not my assistant, but rather a paid travelling companion who mostly makes me laugh but sometimes does stupid things that make me want to scream. "Don't take any notice of him," I told her. "He's just an idiot." We'd had a great evening and Sami went and spoiled it all.

From New York, we flew to Houston, Texas so that I could catch up with some of my old friends. One evening, Sami told me he didn't feel very well, so he stayed in his room to rest, while I went out with my friends to dinner. I came back around 10 p.m. and went to his room to make sure he was alright, but he wasn't there. I was concerned that something might have happened to him, so I searched for him around the hotel. He wasn't in the reception or any of the restaurants. As a last resort, I went to the bar and asked whether anyone had seen Mr Sami.

"No, he hasn't been here," said the head waiter. "Do you mean Mr Al Habtoor?" he asked.

"No, I'm looking for Mr Sami who's with Mr Al Habtoor's party."

"Why don't you ask Mr Al Habtoor whether he's seen him; he's sitting over there at the bar."

The waiter led the way to the bar where Sami was perched on a high stool holding court surrounded by up to thirty new friends, both male and female. He was so engrossed that he didn't spot me. One of his newfound admirers turned to me with a smile and asked, "Would you like me to introduce you to Mr Al Habtoor?" "That would be very nice," I answered, secretly enjoying the joke.

Sami's eyes almost popped out of his head when I walked up to shake his hand. I expect he thought I would embarrass him by giving the game away, but I allowed him to continue playing the role for a short while longer. Of course, I was landed with the bill when I understood why he was so popular all of a sudden. He had invited all those people to drink and eat on his account – or rather my account. He had spent over 3,000 dollars at that bar in under two hours.

Nothing gave Sami more pleasure than giving away money that wasn't his. Once, while we were staying at the Pierre Hotel in New York, I gave him 200 dollars to keep in his pocket, just in case we went out and stopped somewhere for coffee. He broke 100 dollars into smaller denominations and then began spreading it around like confetti to strangers who looked down on their luck, giving away five dollars here and ten dollars there – not because he sincerely empathised with their plight, but simply because he liked to show off and pretend he was a wealthy benefactor.

I didn't mind until the news of Sami's generosity spread like wildfire and all of a sudden, while walking along Fifth Avenue, we were surrounded by tens of beggars. They wouldn't leave us alone. When we tried to get away from them, they chased after us. As we sprinted along the pavement, I called Sami an idiot and quite a few unprintable expletives, until I saved myself by running inside the entrance of a big store.

When it was time to leave Houston, I told Sami to ask the hotel concierge to book us a flight back to New York together with my friend, the UAE composer Ibrahim Juma'a and Fawzi Al Matni, a Lebanese lawyer. I left all the arrangements to Sami and all went smoothly, until we were seated on the aircraft awaiting take-off, when a flight attendant announced the flight was going to New Ark (Newark), not New York. I thought I must have misheard or didn't understand her accent, but to my horror I soon learned that I'd heard right.

We were on our way to Newark. I had no idea where it was; I feared it might be a city on the west coast and was very relieved to be told that it was in New Jersey, not too far away from New York. That was more luck than judgment on Sami's part. Left to him, we could have found ourselves in Alaska. I promised myself that I would never again entrust Sami with organising anything, and from that day on I never did.

Sami sometimes complained of feeling unwell, and his behaviour was so odd at times that, during one of our many visits to Houston, I took him to St Joseph Hospital for a full check-up and left him in the capable hands of Indian-born Chief Neurologist Dr Athar H. Sayed – known by his American patients as Dr Arthur – who was also a friend of mine. Later that afternoon, Sami came back to the hotel with the doctor.

"Well, doctor, how do you find Sami?" I asked him.

"Sami is great," he asserted enthusiastically.

"Did you check everything out? Did you find anything at all?"

"I checked his head and didn't find anything."

"That's excellent. You didn't find anything at all?"

"No, there was nothing to find. Beneath his skull, there's nothing but empty space."

We laughed, even Sami, but I concluded that Dr Athar was very astute. It didn't take him long to sum up what kind of empty-headed person Sami was. Dr Athar loved a joke. In my experience, some of the best doctors in the world are of Indian origin – in fact, I might not be here today if it wasn't for Dr Chin, who operated on my perforated ulcer in Dubai. But not everyone is aware of the quality of Indian doctors, as evident from the story recounted by Indian heart specialist Dr Madaiah Revana and by Dr Imtihan Jawdat, a cardiologist from Iraq.

It seems a member of the Saudi royal family travelled to Houston for a consultation with one of the world's top Indian-born heart specialists. Apparently, the Indian doctor himself greeted the royal gentleman and his entourage, and politely asked them what they would like to drink. "We don't want any drinks, we've come for a check-up," answered the royal patient.

"Yes, of course, but what would you like to drink first? Can I offer you coffee, tea or something cold?"

The Saudi became annoyed thinking the help was making an attempt to socialise and was behaving in an over-familiar manner, unbefitting his lowly station in life. "I told you before. I don't want anything to drink. Go fetch the doctor now!"

Some of the best doctors in the world gravitate to Houston, which has become somewhat of an international medical hub. Several American doctors and others hailing from India and the Arab world are good friends of mine, including Iraqi cardiologist Dr Imtihan Jawdat, who treated me for dizziness in the 1970s, when he practised in Abu Dhabi before moving to the States to complete higher studies.

We lost touch until he sought me, claiming that he had borrowed a sum of money from me some time back and was now in a position to pay back the loan in the form of a transfer. To be honest, I didn't remember lending him money, but I appreciated that he'd gone to the trouble of tracking me down and admired his honesty and integrity. I discovered that he is a very generous and caring man who takes care of a large extended family; in that respect, he's a traditional Arab. At the same time, he's embraced the American dream. He's always impeccably dressed and enjoys collecting cars, especially sports cars.

After that we became good friends and began to meet up in either Dubai or Houston fairly frequently. It was Dr Imtihan who introduced me to Dr Athar, Dr Samir Touma – a Palestinian who was specialising in internal medicine – and also to well-known heart surgeon Dr William 'Bill' Kalchoff, who has an unusual way of walking and a laugh so quiet that you can only tell he's amused by his body language.

In 1995, my doctor friends held a reception for prominent men and women from the business community, at which I was the guest of honour. The atmosphere was great. We laughed so much. I appreciated meeting so many high-calibre interesting people and remember that visit to Houston as one of the happiest.

I'm still in close touch with Dr Kalchoff, who is quite the ladies' man. I found that out during a visit to Los Angeles in the late 1990s to attend the graduation of my youngest son, Ahmad. I invited Bill to join the celebration at a restaurant in Orange County and, while we were there, we saw a long stretch limousine driving up to the entrance. Out of the vehicle stepped six men and one exceptionally stunning young woman looking like a celebrity about to walk the red carpet. I was curious to know who she was.

"Who's that woman, Bill?" I asked.

"I don't know. Would you like to meet her?"

"I don't mind, but didn't you notice she has six men with her?"

"Don't worry about them. Leave it to me."

As soon as they were seated, he walked to the restroom and paused at their table on the way, to introduce himself to the young lady. "Hi, I'm Dr Bill Kalchoff," he said. "I would love to introduce you to my friend Khalaf from Dubai – a beautiful place that I'm certain you've never visited." I was astonished when within a matter of minutes, he brought her to our table to say hello.

On another of my many visits to Houston, Dr Bill and Dr Imtihan took me to a men's club; it was the first and only time in my life that I've been to such a place. As we sat watching the gyrations of scantily-dressed dancing girls, he was shocked to find that one of them was his current girlfriend. He had no inkling that she was an exotic dancer. She had told him that she was a cash-strapped student and he had been helping her financially to complete her 'studies'. I don't know what he must have felt inside, but I admired his cool. Most Arab men in those circumstances would have turned the evening into a major drama. Westerners are able to control their emotions more than us hot-blooded Arabs.

I've rarely met anyone with Dr Bill's confidence. That's one of his many strong points; he has the kind of personality that attracts people to him wherever he goes. His latest love is Brazil. He's always inviting his friends there. He's a great age now, but he's still a very capable doctor; his hands have remained steady judging by some sharp and perfectly composed photographs he took himself and forwarded to me on his iPhone.

* * *

Towards the end of the 1990s, I was invited to lunch at Jean Paul Getty II's 2500-acre Buckinghamshire estate where a charity cricket match was being held on a pitch modelled on the London's famous Oval ground. Getty Junior had taken British citizenship and heartily embraced English traditions, including cricket. He had been honoured by the Queen with a knighthood and was now known as Sir Paul Getty.

I took Jerry Morgan, my very own Mr Bean, Sami, a doctor from Sudan and two other friends along with me. We were graciously received by Sir Paul and his elegantly-dressed, beautiful third wife, Lady Getty, formerly Victoria Holdsworth, the daughter of a Suffolk farmer. The first thing that struck me about Paul Jr was his ugly psychedelic tie, which I later learned was his trademark attire left over from his flower power days.

He seemed like a very nice man, but when lunch was served I began to wonder whether he had inherited some of his father's famous parsimonious traits; it consisted of tasteless frozen chicken, semi-stale bread and cheap Austrian wine – or so the connoisseurs at our table whispered to me.

However, that was an unfair assumption on my part, as unlike his father Sir Paul was an enormously generous person who donated large sums to the British museums and art galleries as well as to the British Film Institute, Lord's Cricket Ground, a fund for striking miners, the Conservative Party and to various English cathedrals.

Lunch was in a marquee giving out onto the cricket pitch. We were guided to the main table where Prince Philip, American model Jerry Hall and the Chairman of the construction company, John Laing, were seated. Unfortunately, the occasion was spoilt by my companions.

When the meal was finished, the Sudanese doctor moved around taking snaps of the VIPs and celebrities like a paparazzo. Of course, such crass behaviour is frowned upon in those kinds of circles, where people fiercely guard their privacy. He soon got the message. When he tried to focus his lens on Prince Philip, security men grabbed him and threw him out.

The embarrassment caused by my friends didn't end there.

Sami spent most of his time standing in a field viewing the grounds with his hand shading his eyes from the sun, making no effort to socialise. When the meal was finished, Prince Philip walked over to him to ask whether he was enjoying the match. "Match... what match?" he answered. Prince Philip's face registered surprise – or it might have been irritation as it's well known that the Queen's husband doesn't suffer fools gladly.

"Are you a fan of cricket?" he asked.

"Cricket... Oh no, I don't like cricket," Sami replied. "I'm just enjoying the sight of those gorgeous cows."

* * *

Once, I left Sami with some of my travelling companions to reclaim our luggage at Terminal 2 in Dubai Airport. He called me while I was in the car on my way home to say, "Abu Rashid, help me. I've been arrested."

"What! How's that possible? I've just left you."

"The police stopped me as I was walking out of the airport and they arrested me."

"Why? What have you done?"

"I don't know," he said. "They won't tell me."

I told him not to worry and that I would try to find out what was going on. But before I could, he called again. This time he was crying. "I'm in handcuffs," he said. I phoned my nephew Faisal, who worked with me at the time, and asked him to go to the airport to see what could be done. Then Sami called a third time sounding really terrified.

"Help me! I'm in a police van. I don't know where they're taking me."

It took some time, but we eventually tracked down the police station where he was being held and after much discussion with the officers, we managed to get him out on bail. That was lucky for him as all this happened on a Thursday, the start of our weekend. If we hadn't acted swiftly, he would have remained behind bars until Saturday.

Thankfully, he was no murderer or rapist. He'd taken out a bank loan and purposely defaulted on the repayments, in the certainty that if he were arrested for non-payment I would bail him out of jail and settle the outstanding amount on his behalf. He hadn't realised that his default would automatically place his name on an airport watch list. I had no choice but to buy the problem. I settled the outstanding loan on his behalf so that he could avoid a court sentence.

Sami was indeed a very troublesome and expensive 'entertainer'. Something similar occurred later, involving another of my Lebanese friends, but I won't go into that. Suffice it to say that I made the decision that before I make friends with anyone, I must order police and credit reports first.

Although I've always known that Sami is inherently selfish and loves no one but himself, as he proudly admits, I've kept in touch with him. I've never expected much from him and believed nothing he could do or say would shock me. I was wrong. Recently, I made a call from Dubai to his home in Lebanon just to check whether he was alright. Since he left my employment and returned to his own country, I usually invite him to dinner during my frequent visits to Beirut and help him out financially. When he heard my voice, he greeted me in Arabic with his usual "Abu Rashid, my brother, you are the master of all men (*Sayed Al Rijal*)," adding that he missed me a lot.

"In that case, come to Dubai," I said. "It's only a three-hour flight away. I'll send you the ticket."

"Abu Rashid, I can't do that."

"Why can't you?"

"Well, I have to confess something to you. I hate Dubai and I hate every Gulf country."

I could hardly believe what I was hearing. This must be a joke, I initially thought.

"But Sami, that can't be true. You always said that the meat on your shoulders is from the Gulf," I said.

"It is true. I hate the GCC and I hate all the Sunnis in the world."

Sami is a Shiite from southern Lebanon who has been close to me for a great deal of my life. I was speechless, so I hung up on him. I sat shaking my head as it sank in that my friend Sami had officially lost his mind. Better that than to conclude I had allowed a disguised viper to slither into my circle and remain for years.

* * *

Besides unruly friends, I've got one or two unruly relatives. One of them, Majed, used to be a military cargo pilot and he still goes around as though there's a war on, getting into fights over nothing occasionally with his superiors. Sometime during the 1980s I went with my family to London for a medical check-up. We stayed in the Britannia Hotel where we met Dr Moussa, a skinny, Palestinian-born gentleman with a limp who unusually spoke proper standard Arabic, *Al Fousha* (pronounced 'Al Fous-ha'), without any recognisable dialect.

I told him that I had an appointment for a medical examination at Saint Thomas Hospital and Medical School and he offered to come along. I rather liked his company so I invited him to Dubai, sent him an airline ticket and put him up in my Dubai Metropolitan Hotel. One day, over a meal, he told me that he had bumped into one of my relatives around the swimming pool. When I heard that, I immediately became tense.

"What was his name," I asked?

"He said his name was Majed."

"Whatever happened, I hope it was nothing serious," I said with a sinking heart.

"Nothing happened, but I found him to be one of the stupidest people I have ever met in my life," the doctor said in perfect, pure Arabic. "If you cut him open, he will bleed stupid and sweat stupid."

"You're not going to see him again are you?" I said, adding, "Doctor, when are you flying home?" before he had a chance to respond.

"I'm going back tomorrow."

"Try to avoid him, but if you do come across him, please don't tell him your opinion of him," I pleaded. I felt a twinge of relief that Dr Moussa – who, as my guest, was my responsibility would soon be gone from the country and couldn't bask in that feeling until he was actually out of harm's way. Majed loved lounging around the hotel pool and often annoyed our guests, but his reputation as a troublemaker was so well known that everyone, including me, was afraid to tell him off.

Hours after the doctor flew off, I rang Majed to get his version and shortly afterwards he came to see me.

"Did you meet Dr Moussa?" I asked him.

"Yes, I did. But he speaks funny. He was very nice, but he never smiled.

"Do you know what he said about you?"

"No, but he seemed nice."

"He said he has travelled all over the world but has never met anyone like you."

"Thanks."

"You won't thank me when you know what he said. He said, "I found him to be one of the stupidest people I have ever met in my life. If you cut him open, he will bleed stupid and sweat stupid." I didn't, of course, mention that those were my thoughts entirely. Just as well. His reaction made me back away; it was scary.

"What's his room number?"

"Why?"

"I will kill him and then I will call the police to let them know what I have done."

Although I'm his uncle and he's generally been okay with me, I was rather frightened.

"Do you have his phone number?" I asked.

"No."

"Oh... Thank God!"

I've never heard from Dr Moussa since. I hope Majed never got his hands on him.

* * *

There are two men who have travelled with me in terms of hours more than any other – my drivers.

In 1974, when the civil war in Lebanon was raging, I brought a man from south Lebanon called Hussein Murad to Dubai to be my personal driver. He was very friendly and seemed nice enough, so before long I began to think of him more as a friend than an employee. I put him up in a house within the walls of my family compound, and he stayed there with his wife and kids. I educated his sons and daughters in the same schools as my own children and sent the brightest to the best universities, such as the American University of Beirut – and I must say they made me proud with their serious aptitude for their studies. Unfortunately, their father didn't match up.

In the first place, all he wanted to do was sleep. Sleeping was his life's passion. Whenever I left him in the car even for five or ten minutes, I would come back to find that he'd nodded off. No matter what time of day, as soon as I left him for a meeting or a social occasion, he would lie back and close his eyes until I returned and woke him up. This is too much, I thought, worried that he might nod off at the wheel.

He had a problem with his nose and sometimes, when we were driving along, he would actually snore. That would always make me jump fearing he might have dozed off. Just about everyone in my family would refuse to get in the car with him, mainly because he made them depressed with his negative world view and bleak attitudes to everything.

For some reason, I put up with him, until the 1979 Islamic revolution in Iran that brought the Ayatollah Khomeini to power. He woke up then and became obsessed with politics. It turned out that he was a big fan of Khomeini and never ceased to praise the revolution, which really annoyed me because not only did I not share his enthusiasm for Iran's new leadership, I thoroughly disliked everything about it. I'm not interested in dictating to people what they should think or not think, but I certainly don't want to be in the position of being their captive audience – and especially when my opinion is poles apart from theirs.

I almost preferred Hussein the heavy-lidded to Hussein the opinionated bore. "Enough Hussein, just drive," I would say to him to stop him droning on and on in his praise for the ayatollahs. But because we had always treated him like one of the family, he didn't listen to me. Once, I got so upset with him trying to stuff his politics down my throat that I told him to stop the car in the middle of a road leading from the Clock Tower roundabout in Dubai, and then I kicked him out of the car. I told him to take a taxi and then drove myself home.

Shortly afterwards, I replaced Hussein with Lourduswamy Amalanathan, who still drives me today. It was one of the best decisions I've ever made. He never gabbles away about nothing, he only speaks when he has something real to say. His given name was too much of a mouthful, especially for my parents whom he used to drive around, so we gave him the nickname 'Jawa'.

Jawa, who is originally from India's Garden City, Bangalore, has worked for my family for more than thirty years. His mother used to take care of my mother and he used to help my father groom and feed the camels until he learned to drive, when my parents took him on as a driver. When we used to stay at our house in Hatta, he used to buy the meat in the market and start the barbecue. I began to notice that whenever Jawa was around to attend to the details, everything tended to go smoothly.

As a young man, Jawa was a fast learner and was willing to try his hand at everything. He was also very bright and speaks fluent Arabic and English, besides his mother tongue. When he came with me to England, his role was substantially broadened to include food shopping, cooking, cleaning, laundry, booking appointments with the dentist and organising tickets and travel. But even this paragon of efficiency has his imperfections like the rest of us.

Around ten years ago, when I'd had enough of Sami and others in the same irresponsible mould, I decided Jawa should come with me when I'm travelling abroad as he's more organised, reliable and active than just about anyone I know. At that time, I was very impressed with his social and PR skills and knew he would never embarrass me or let me down in any way.

When, in the spring of 2010, I travelled with a group of friends to Illinois College in Jacksonville to receive my honorary doctorate and meet up with my good friend Paul Findley, Jawa's enthusiasm to please everyone was unbounded. En route to Illinois State, we stopped off in New York, where we stayed in the Ritz-Carlton Central Park Hotel for three days to recover from jet lag and adjust to a different time zone.

We hadn't been at the hotel more than a few hours, when I noticed that Jawa had the hotel staff in the palm of his hand. We dined in one of the Ritz-Carlton's fine restaurants on the first evening of our stay and it soon became clear that the waiters were hanging on his every word, anxious to do his bidding. I wasn't that surprised as I'm aware that Jawa is naturally sociable and very likeable.

That first morning, I met my companions for breakfast in the hotel's coffee shop. Most American hotels don't lay on a buffet breakfast in the way that most five-star hotels in Europe and the Middle East tend to do. Selecting my breakfast à la carte is fine by me when I'm on vacation and don't have urgent appointments to keep.

I ordered my usual simple and healthy start to the day, papaya followed by fried eggs; one of my friends chose a plate of fresh mixed berries and a cup of plain yoghurt. Everyone else in my party ordered fairly modest breakfasts by American standards – or Middle Eastern, for that matter. No one minded having to order from the menu and waiting to be served, with the exception of Jawa.

He didn't complain at the time, but, being used to the amazing buffet breakfasts available at our hotels in the UAE, he didn't approve of our relatively spartan morning's fare. As far as he was concerned, the small portions of everything served were little better than samples.

The following morning, I was more than impressed to find that Jawa had already chosen the best table and ordered our breakfast ahead, on the basis of everyone's preferences the day before. We found the table covered with huge platters of papaya, strawberries and all kinds of berries, as well as an enormous bowl of yoghurt. That suited me, because I rarely eat anything for breakfast other than fruit and eggs, but the friend who had ordered berries and yoghurt the day before didn't look too pleased. He had planned to order something completely different, but decided to eat what was available rather than waste food.

Once we'd finished eating the fruit and yoghurt, leaving enough to satisfy the inmates of a small-sized health farm, I tried to order fried eggs. But for all my calling out and waving, I was unable to attract the waiters' attention, as they were all too busy hovering over Jawa as though he was a maharaja and we his inconsequential entourage of hangers-on.

The same story played out at dinner; whenever we attempted to order something, we were ignored and ended up having to channel our requests through my friend from Bangalore. We were impressed at Jawa's ability to attract sycophants – and if truth be told, also slightly intrigued by the way he had grabbed centre stage with his 'commanding presence'.

I was quite mystified by the effect Jawa seemed to have on the hotel personnel, until I saw the bill for our breakfasts, which was the highest I'd ever seen in my life. Jawa had assumed breakfast was included in the room rate, which is why he had felt free to order what he liked in large quantities. Moreover, as he held the cash for our expenses, he was seen as the biggest spender of our group. As the object of so much flattering attention, he didn't need much encouragement to order whatever the maître d' or the waiters suggested in an effort to fulfil their targets or gain sales commission. Jawa had been well intentioned, but had gone overboard. I pointed out to him the error of his ways and he promised to temper his enthusiasm in the future.

I thought Jawa had reformed, but he just can't help getting carried away on occasion. In December 2010, between Christmas and New Year, I travelled with friends to the magnificent Hungarian capital, Budapest. We arrived at our hotel in the afternoon and just had time to shower and dress for dinner in the hotel's restaurant. Once again, every time someone chose from the menu, the head waiter would turn to Jawa for approval before writing down their order. I remembered New York and laughed. In this case, he hadn't enough time to befriend the hotel's staff and anyway I was sure he'd learned his lesson, which left me to assume that fair-skinned Hungarians admire people with darker complexions than their own, especially since some of them could hardly take their eyes off him.

The same thing happened at Dubai International Airport's VIP terminal and at airports abroad, where porters and waiters gathered around Jawa, waiting for his signal to move a certain piece of luggage or serve coffee to one of my group. It so happens that in Dubai most airport porters are

Asian; many are from Jawa's homeland. I persuaded myself that they probably feel a natural affinity with Jawa because of their shared culture and language, which explains why even when he doesn't actively seek the limelight, it shines upon him anyway.

Back in Dubai, the mystery was solved. I soon learned that Jawa had been playing the part of Lord Bountiful throughout the journey, liberally tipping airport and hotel staff with fistfuls of notes, so they would go the extra mile in taking care of us. The problem was that, in their eyes, he was the man with the cash and the one they went out of their way to please. I'm not against generous tipping in principle, but, as we Arabs say, if someone wants to be generous, they shouldn't do it by dipping into someone else's pocket; in this case, mine. But this is such a small gripe – it just goes to show how perfect Jawa is in every other way.

He's a master at everything he turns his hand to. He is honest and trustworthy, as is his wife, Francina (we know her as Helen), who is also employed by our family and is highly respected for her work ethic, which has been inherited by their two daughters – one of whom, Jennifer, I've sent to London to complete her education.

If there's anyone I would trust with my life, that would be Jawa. I will always support him and his family, not out of charity, but because I owe him a debt of gratitude for his unstinting devotion and loyalty to me and my parents, and, later, to my wife and children ever since I can remember. More than a driver, a valet or a travelling companion, Jawa is the walking definition of a tried and true friend – and those, according to my experience, are as rare as the Koh-i-Noor diamond.

* * *

Travelling the world is much more than an opportunity to sightsee. It's also a character-building experience. Human beings are naturally tribal, gravitating together according to their colour, ethnicity or religion because we are born with a fear of the 'unknown other'. We are brought up and indoctrinated by our societies to believe that we are the best, that our way is the only way, the right way, and rarely take the trouble to see the other side of things. But once we step out of our familiar comfort zones, we soon realise that, regardless of our origins, we are all members of the same human race with similar hopes, fears and desires. Getting to know people of other races, religions and cultures, gaining the ability to see beyond the colour of their skins or their religious beliefs and allowing ourselves to step into their shoes for a brief moment in time is an important path to a harmonious, peaceful planet.

Having friends from all over the world has opened my eyes to the fact that we could all get along if it were not for the interference of agenda-led politicians. Some of my dearest friends are Christians and Jews. For instance, I feel blessed to have been recently introduced to three fine men, variously of Catholic and Jewish extraction: Sztanó Tamás, the proprietor of a Hungarian restaurant chain; Nimrod Rinot, the Honorary Consul of Montenegro in Israel; and Péter Kovás, the Honorary Consul of the Republic of Uganda in Budapest.

I first got to know Sztanó Tamás socially, through the husband of my friend Balázs Tariczi, a former professional tennis player. I was immediately struck by Tamás' strength of character. Unfortunately, he is wheelchair-bound, but his personality is so forceful that anyone meeting him for the first time swiftly forgets his disability. Sztanó – or Tamás, as I like to call him because his first name is too difficult to pronounce – went out of his way from day one to ensure I felt welcomed and appreciated in Hungary. Tamás later introduced me to Nimrod in October 2011 when I was contemplating buying one of his hotels and, through them, I met Péter Kovás.

Since then, I've been overwhelmed by their generosity and kindness to me each time I visit Hungary, which, thanks to my three new friends, is a country I love more and more. Whenever I'm in the country with friends, Tamás and Péter show us around and take us out to dinner each evening. When I travelled to Europe in December 2011, I made a point to see my new friends in Budapest and was astonished and delighted to find Tamás on the tarmac when I exited the plane – together with a troupe of gypsy musicians he had hired to give me a rousing welcome.

My warm relationship with those three fine human beings of different faiths to my own is just one example of how travel can facilitate the opening of the heart and eradicate negative preconceptions about those who don't look like us, talk like us or pray like us. God didn't create our Earth with borders or checkpoints. Mankind made those artificial divisions, which can be rearranged or even torn down, but, perhaps, the most difficult barriers of all to dismantle are those in our minds. It's only when we can overcome our subconscious barriers to realise that we are all the children of God destined to share this one planet, will we be able to avert wars and conflicts that are tearing our world apart.

CHAPTER 17
Views on Our World

As someone who keeps abreast of political and economic fluctuations, I would like to share my opinions on some of the twenty-first century's most earth-shattering events.

As the new century approached, there was hope in the air that human-kind was evolving away from conflict, racism and the abuse of human rights. South Africa's monstrous apartheid regime had collapsed in 1994 and China had opened up to allow its citizens greater freedoms, subsequent to the international backlash over the Tiananmen Square massacre, and was fast becoming an economic powerhouse rivalling the United States.

Brussels had begun negotiating with ten eastern and central European countries seeking EU membership and, on 1 January 1999, the European single currency, the euro, was introduced initially for transactions, with notes and coins in use by twelve countries in January 2002.

NATO had, rightly in my opinion, bypassed the United Nations Security Council to intervene in the former Yugoslavia to quell ethnic conflicts in Bosnia and, in particular, the ethnic cleansing of Albanian Muslims in Kosovo. I was very appreciative of the Clinton administration's role in this humanitarian war. I was proud that the government and citizens of the UAE had donated medicines and food to alleviate the suffering and set up field hospitals, temporary schools and shelters. During his visit, Sheikh Mohammed bin Rashid ensured the commitment of the UAE Armed Forces to the KFOR operations.

Overall, US President Bill Clinton did a good job. He was one of the most sincere American presidents who used his considerable personal charm to display the superpower's softer demeanour abroad. Upon leaving office, his approval rating was higher than any other president since World War II.

Clinton worked to improve relations with China and was the first American president to visit Vietnam since the Vietnam War. He also made great strides towards a Middle East peace process, bringing Palestinian leader Yasser Arafat and Israeli Prime Minister Ehud Barak to Camp David for face-to-face negotiations, rudely cut short when Clinton and Barak were succeeded by hard-line right-wingers, George W. Bush and Ariel Sharon.

Anti-Iraq sanctions
There was one thing for which I found it hard to forgive Bill Clinton. And no, I'm not talking about the Monica Lewinsky scandal and the subsequent attempt to impeach him for trying to cover up his private life (perjury under oath) – to my mind, the brouhaha over that indiscretion was politically motivated. There's a long list of US presidents and world leaders who have committed worse crimes than telling a lie.

Clinton's biggest mistake was his administration's continuation of United Nations sanctions against Iraq that destroyed lives and children's futures. An entire population was punished for ten years with shortages of medicines, medical equipment, educational tools and even food. Sanctions were responsible for an increase in poverty, illiteracy rates, infant and child mortality, malnutrition and diseases caused by a bar on the import of chlorine, resulting in a lack of clean water.

The United Nations UN Humanitarian Coordinator in Baghdad, Denis Halliday, was so disgusted with the effects sanctions were having on ordinary people, that he quit saying, "I don't want to administer a programme that satisfied the definition of genocide".

UNICEF estimated that sanctions had led to the deaths of up to 576,000 Iraqi children and like many others I was appalled when in a televised interview US Secretary of State Madeleine Albright, who was questioned, said, "We think the price is worth it" (to prevent Saddam from developing weapons of mass destruction). The irony is that Saddam's nuclear weapons programme and stockpiles of chemical weapons were effectively destroyed in 1991.

Although I had several good friends in the US Army, Navy and Air Force from the 1991 Gulf War days, my conscience didn't allow me to remain on the Board of Governors of the United Service Organisations (USO) and on 11 November 1997 I wrote the following letter to Mr Duane W. Acklie, Chairman of the USO, in protest:

Dear Mr Acklie,

Over the past years, it has been my pleasure and my honour to be associated with the USO and to be on your Board of Governors. I have enjoyed meeting the American servicemen and women and those working for the USO who are all excellent people.

However, as you are of course aware, at present the situation in Iraq and in the Arab world as a whole is very delicate. There are very strong feelings towards what is happening in Iraq, not only from all the Arab countries and the Muslims, but from many other countries in the world. There is a feeling that the sanctions on Iraq are harming its people and not the authorities and they are seen as an aggression towards the Iraqi people.

This has put me in a very awkward position and I think that it will now be inappropriate for me to be connected to the USO. As an Arab and a Muslim my loyalties must, of course, be with my people.

I therefore regret to inform you that I feel compelled to resign from the Board of Governors.

Your input is important to try to ease the tension between Iraq and the US military, the consequences of which are potentially damaging for both sides. What is the guilt of the Iraqi people or of the US servicemen and women to be engaged in a battle that will benefit nobody except the enemy of peace?

Your positive contributions with the decision-makers can help to put an end to the continuing pressure which is on the Iraqi people.

Yours sincerely,

Khalaf Al Habtoor

Cc: Gen Carl E. Mundy Jr – President

I was certain that I had done the right thing, when in December 1998 the US and the UK ratcheted up the pressure on Saddam with a four-day bombing campaign, 'Operation Desert Fox', that was loudly condemned by Saudi Arabia, Bahrain, the UAE, China, Russia and France. Some 100 Iraqi sites were destroyed by cruise missiles and bombs, ostensibly to downgrade Saddam's weapon-making capability.

Towards the end of Clinton's presidency, the international community seemed to have reached a consensus on either relaxing or dropping the sanctions. However, the mood changed when George W. Bush became the forty-third President of the United States on 20 January 2001, defeating former Vice-President Al Gore, controversially with the help of the Electoral College, although his adversary had a larger percentage of the popular vote.

President Bush surrounded himself with neoconservatives – Vice-President Dick Cheney, Defence Secretary Donald Rumsfeld, Deputy Defence Secretary Paul Wolfowitz, Assistant Secretary of Defence Richard Perle, and Chief of Staff to the Vice-President Lewis 'Scooter' Libby – who were members of a Washington-based think-tank called the PNAC (Project for the New American Century).

In September 2000, the PNAC laid its cards on the table in a report titled *Rebuilding America's Defences: Strategies, Forces and Resources for a New Century*. Essentially, this paper promoted American global hegemony and full-spectrum dominance. Its core message was the US should "fight and decisively win multiple, simultaneous major theatre wars" and it was clear that Iraq featured prominently on its list of targets.

The report was clear on the PNAC's ambitions towards Iraq. It mentioned that "While the unresolved conflict in Iraq provides the immediate justification [for US military presence], the need for a substantial America force presence in the Gulf transcends the issue of the regime of Saddam Hussein."

In Section V of the report, under the heading 'Creating Tomorrow's Dominant Force', was this: "The process of transformation, even if it brings revolutionary change, is likely to be a long one, absent some catastrophic and catalysing event – like a new Pearl Harbour."

The day the world changed

That "catastrophic and catalysing event" happened almost exactly one year after the report was published. On 11 September 2001, symbols of US wealth and power were attacked by nineteen Arab men, who used passenger jets as weapons.

I won't elaborate on those strikes on the World Trade Centre's twin towers in Manhattan or the Pentagon because they are well known; suffice it to say that like almost every other human being on the planet, I was deeply pained to see people leaping out of windows before the 110 floors of those high buildings turned to dust, and to see panicked New Yorkers fleeing from an Armageddon-type landscape. Almost 3,000 innocent people lost their lives on that terrible day.

It was no surprise when President Bush visited 'Ground Zero' in Manhattan shortly afterwards, with a bull horn vowing to root out the evildoers. I was, however, astonished to learn that a member of the Saudi bin Laden family, Osama bin Laden, was the apparent mastermind who was also connected with the 1998 bombings of US embassies in Kenya and Tanzania and the USS Cole in October 2000, while it was harboured in the Yemeni port of Aden. Prior to 9/11, I had never heard of a terrorist organisation called Al Qaeda ('the Base').

All I knew about Osama bin Laden was that he was the black sheep of a prominent and well-respected family based in Jeddah, whose business interests were independent of his brothers when their inheritance was divided after the death of their father, Mohammed bin Awad bin Laden, a developer who built his fortune from zero.

In fact, I had met Mohammed bin Laden briefly in my youth when he came to Dubai. I went with Mohammed Saeed Al Mulla to see him in his hotel, in connection with a road his company was constructing to link Sharjah with Ra's al-Khaimah, as Mr Al Mulla's company was one of the subcontractors engaged in that project.

My memory is vague on that meeting, but I do recall that the elder bin Laden was a simple but clever man of slight build, who was thought highly of by the Saudi Royal Family. Soon afterwards, in 1967, he died in a plane crash caused by pilot error.

It was only after the 11 September tragedy that I came to know that one of his fifty or more children, Osama, had been a freedom fighter during the Russian occupation of Afghanistan, when the so-called 'Afghan Arabs' had worked closely with the CIA to rid that country from the Soviet military presence. It appears that his hatred of the West was born from his disapproval of US troops on Saudi soil, which he saw as a "profanity" that led to the Kingdom revoking his citizenship.

Afghanistan

There's no doubt that President Bush needed to react to the attack and while I understood the reasons behind the 2001 invasion of Afghanistan, I thought 'getting bin Laden' who was being hosted by the Afghan Taliban could have been effected without so much bloodshed using special ops and human intelligence.

However, George Bush added another casus belli to that war, which was to bring down the ruling Taliban that had run the country on archaic lines since 1996 and held it in an iron fist, forbidding television, computers, movies, paintings, kite flying, chess, girls' dolls, dancing and nail polish.

Girls were barred from education, females were forbidden from working or leaving home without a male relative and were forced to totally shroud themselves and sit in their own homes behind blackened windows. Men were obliged to keep their hair short and grow beards. Yet it should be said that under the Taliban Afghans enjoyed personal security and because there was a clamp down on poppy-cultivation, the streets of Western capitals weren't flooded with Afghan heroin.

Laura Bush and Cherie Blair were enlisted to launch a televised campaign to champion the rights of Afghan women and promised their coming emancipation – which never happened, because the opposition Northern Alliance warlords outside the capital Kabul had a similar repressive mentality as the Taliban. And although Afghans gained the right to vote, elections have been manipulated and the Hamid Karzai-led leadership generally deemed corrupt.

As for Afghan women, a June 2011 study conducted by TrustLaw based on a poll of 213 gender experts, cited Afghanistan as the world's most dangerous country for women, with females being bartered, one in eleven dying in childbirth and 87 per cent illiterate. Mrs Bush and Mrs Blair may have been well intentioned, but even they would have to admit bringing women's rights to Afghanistan has hardly been a success story.

Bush's willingness to dispense with international laws and treaties, as well as the Geneva Conventions, to incarcerate and torture Afghan, Pakistani, Arab and other detainees in wire cages open to the elements at a US base, Guantanamo Bay on the island of Cuba, was blasted by international lawyers and human rights groups. Guantanamo has housed up to 775 detainees; only three were ever convicted of anything by a military tribunal. As of April 2012, there were 169 remaining, even though many of them are considered to be entirely innocent of any crime.

While I didn't fully approve of the invasion and occupation of Afghanistan, I was horrified by the Bush administration's disingenuous attempts to link Iraq to Al Qaeda and other terrorist groups. If you recall, in September 2002, Defence Secretary Donald Rumsfeld – who had expressed his disappointment at the lack of targets to bomb in Afghanistan – said such a link was "accurate and not debatable".

Shock and Awe
Yet, later, the US commission investigating the 9/11 attacks found "no credible evidence" of any such relationship, which indicates that the administration had used false propaganda to sell the 2003 invasion of Iraq, dubbed 'Operation Iraqi Freedom', to the American public. General Wesley

Clark, the former Commanding General of US Military Command, said just days after 9/11 he heard of a Pentagon plan to invade seven countries in the Middle East and North Africa within five years, including Iraq.

Then Secretary of State Colin Powell, who at the time was respected and admired to the extent that he could have been a successful presidential contender, was basically Bush's patsy. Charged with making a hard sell for war in a speech before the UN Security Council, much of the 'proof' he produced, that included mobile chemical labs that were actually weather balloon facilities and pilotless drones that looked hardly bigger than a child's toy, was laughable.

In 2005, Powell admitted that he had been "a reluctant warrior", describing his speech as a "blot" on his record. "I'm the one who presented it to the world and it will always be a part of my record. It was painful. It is painful now," he told ABC News.

There is evidence that Britain's Prime Minister Tony Blair, widely dubbed as Bush's 'poodle' for his eagerness to dance to the President's tune even when this meant going against the wishes of the British public, had also deliberately distorted and exaggerated intelligence to make a case for war, as millions of Britons took to the street in protest.

In 2011, Major General Michael Laurie, who was the Ministry of Defence's Director General, Intelligence Collection, from 2002 to 2003, told Britain's Iraq Enquiry that he and his colleagues had come under pressure from Downing Street to beef up intelligence on Iraqi WMD to reinforce the case for war in Tony Blair's infamous "sexed-up" dossier. He said making a case for war was "exactly its purpose".

An earlier Number Ten dossier, now known as the 'Dodgy Dossier' purporting to be serious intelligence, included tracts from a student's twelve-year-old thesis lifted with typographical errors and all from the Internet. The embarrassment was such that Tony Blair's spin doctor, Alastair Campbell, wrote a letter to Intelligence Chief Sir Richard Dearlove to apologise for discrediting the service.

Whether Mr Bush and Mr Blair genuinely believed that Iraq was a clear and present danger to their country's interests, we'll never know; despite the fact their choices led to the death of up to one million Iraqis and thousands of coalition service people, the international community has no appetite to investigate those men and their motives, let alone put them on trial.

Nobody has been held accountable for the rape of the Cradle of Civilisation that almost destroyed Iraq's Arab heritage, attracted foreign extremists and set its people – Sunnis, Shiites and Kurds – against one another, whereas they were formerly good neighbours who socialised together and often intermarried. US troops stood by watching as government ministries were burned down and museums were looted. Entire families in cars were shot and killed at checkpoints for hesitating to identify themselves or for driving too close to military vehicles.

Footage of a small Iraqi boy called Ali who lost his parents, almost all his close relatives plus his arms during a missile attack on Baghdad, melted hearts around the world. Videos of toddlers' corpses piled into a wooden cart and resembling broken dolls were horrifying evidence of man's inhumanity to man – young children who had been playing with their friends or sitting on their mothers' laps before their lives were robbed.

No-bid construction and security contracts were handed out to US companies with crony connections to Dick Cheney and others in the Bush administration. Billions of dollars went astray, as Iraqis were left without clean water and electricity for years.

Mercenaries from private security companies paid up to 1,000 dollars per day were hired by the US/UK authorities; with immunity from prosecution, they adopted a shoot-first-and-ask-questions-later policy, creating terror among the civilian population.

Iraqis who were in the wrong place at the wrong time were bundled into US-run prisons, such as the notorious Abu Ghraib, where they were tortured, humiliated, physically and sexually abused, dragged around on dog leashes, burnt with cigarettes and, in some cases, even murdered. Explicit photographs of the abuse revealed in 2004 on the US television news show *60 Minutes II* caused worldwide revulsion and disbelief.

Donald Rumsfeld assured the Senate Armed Services Committee that those who committed wrongdoing would be brought to justice, characterising the abuse as "un-American" and "inconsistent with the values of our nation".

However, no high-ranking US service person or interrogator was convicted for the abuse and murders; only eleven low-ranking soldiers were sentenced on related charges, although there is documentary evidence that they acted according to guidelines from the highest authority in the Department of Defence.

As you know, no WMD was found in Iraq and the invasion was pronounced illegal and in breach of the UN Charter by UN Secretary-General Kofi Annan, but until now neither Bush nor Blair have said they regretted their decision, citing how crucial it was to topple "a brutal dictator" and bring "freedom and democracy" to the Iraqi people.

Failed wars

In truth, the Bush years could hardly be considered as America's finest hour. At the time of writing, the US and NATO are still battling the Taliban, that still controls much of Afghanistan; the government has little credibility with its own people, and away from Kabul there has been little reconstruction; furthermore, opium and heroin production has greatly increased, the revenues used to buy weapons for the Taliban.

It's a similar woeful tale in Iraq, primarily because, as both the US and the UK have admitted, when operation Shock and Awe was first launched, there was no plan for the day after, with two of their greatest mistakes being the dismantling of the Iraqi military and the exclusion of former Ba'ath Party members from government office and jobs. For all the West's sophistication, it appears their finest brains were unable to figure out that men, angry that the occupiers had robbed them of being able to feed their families, would likely take up arms and fight.

Seven years after the invasion, in 2010, Iraqis on the streets of Baghdad were chanting "no water, no electricity in the country of oil and the two rivers"; an incredible state of affairs when following the devastating 1991 Gulf War, Iraqis had those services up and running within a year.

Even today, Iraqi children are being born with deformities due to the coalition's use of depleted uranium tank shells and almost every week one reads of deaths resulting from insurgents' bombs and other explosive devices.

American-style democracy hasn't worked in Iraq either. Without debating the issue of whether or not democracy can flourish under occupation, the problem is that power has switched to Shiites, who take their marching orders from Tehran, which has naturally caused resentment among Sunnis. Sectarian violence has resulted in millions of Iraqis being displaced internally or condemned to border camps or impoverished lives in neighbouring Syria and Jordan.

One of the greatest ironies is that the US has inadvertently or otherwise gifted Iraq to the country that has purportedly been its sworn enemy since the 1979 Khomeini revolution. Ridding the country of Saddam removed Iran's most feared foe in one fell swoop, leaving the way open for the Iranian leadership to spread its ideological tentacles around the Gulf and throughout the Middle East. Saddam was far from perfect, but, whatever his faults, he was a true Iraqi patriot and a proud Arab, which cannot be said for many of those who took his place.

Iraq's current Prime Minister, Nouri Al Maliki, also the Secretary-General of the Dawa Party, lived in Tehran from 1982 until 1990 and has made official visits to Iran since taking office. The current Iraqi President, Jalal Talabani, Founder of the Patriotic Union of Kurdistan (PUK), sided with Iran during the Iran–Iraq war in the 1980s.

One of the country's two vice-presidents, Adil Abdul Mahdi, who held office from 2005 until May 2011, once disseminated the Ayatollah Khomeini's philosophy in France and was once a member of the Supreme Council for the Islamic Revolution in Iraq – a Shiite political party and militia formed in Iran.

From the perspective of an Arab and a Gulf national, Iraq's sway towards Tehran is bad news. Without an Iraqi buffer to thwart its ambitions, the Iranian government has formed a close bond with Syria, backs Hezbollah and Hamas with cash and weapons, is attempting to cement close relations with Egypt and is pouring fuel on the embers of Shiite–Sunni sectarianism in Bahrain.

Arab heads of state – and GCC leaders in particular – should consider rescuing Iraq from the current ruling elite that have crawled into Tehran's pocket. Otherwise, the day will soon come when Iran and Iraq will unify to form a single, powerful federation with domination over our airspace and coastlines, as well as control of overland traffic heading our way.

If our rulers continue to bury their heads in the sand on this issue, all of us who live in GCC countries will suffer the consequences. An Iraq–Iran federation would allow those two countries to hold the world's economy hostage using their massive combined oil reserves. With that kind of clout, they can buy the backing of the international community. Gulf states would then be left with zero influence, when we'll lose our hard-won independence and be followers, just as we were in the old days.

Troubled by the ongoing carnage in both Iraq and Afghanistan, in 2010, I wrote to President Obama and Prime Minister Gordon Brown, outlining my concerns as to the costs of the ongoing occupations, both human and financial, and enclosing advisories, 'Iraq: Pathway to Peace and Security' and 'Afghanistan: Strategies for a New Dawn', on both Iraq and Afghanistan, compiled by myself with the assistance of the Al Habtoor Research and Information Centre (The advisories can be read on page 553 and page 546 respectively of this book).

Unfortunately, I didn't receive the courtesy of a response from President Obama. I was so surprised that I asked a friend of mine in an official position to track down the letter to ensure it reached the White House. I did at least receive an acknowledgment from Mr Brown.

In June 2010, I forwarded an updated 'Afghanistan: Strategies for a New Dawn' to Prime Minister David Cameron under cover of a letter urging the British government to work towards a political solution by negotiating with the Taliban. I received both an acknowledgment from Number Ten and a detailed written response from the Ministry of Defence (published on page 551 of this book).

A year later, in June 2011, came the news that the US had engaged in preliminary talks with the Taliban, prior to a scheduled drawdown of troops. This had been advocated by the new Afghan leadership shortly after the 2001 invasion, but Donald Rumsfeld refused to entertain the idea. What a pity the Bush administration didn't listen to sense then. We'll never know how many lives could have been saved if it had.

There's no getting away from it, the direct and indirect fallout from 9/11 was worse than the tragedy itself, harming millions of people. Not only were there untold numbers of fatalities, many more were injured, maimed, widowed and orphaned. People in Afghanistan and Iraq lost their homes and livelihoods. America suffered great losses too. Over 4,801 US service personnel have been killed in Iraq and over 7,000 US and other coalition troops have died in Afghanistan as of early 2012. The cost of those wars has tipped more than 1.3 trillion dollars.

Unlike the West's intervention in the former Yugoslavia, which was a humanitarian rescue, Afghanistan and Iraq have been pointless wars. None of the occupiers' aims have been achieved in either case, while Afghans and Iraqis who have suffered death, destruction, homelessness and humiliation will ultimately be left to pick up the pieces.

Islamophobia

Another unfortunate by-product of 9/11 was how some citizens of Western countries altered their perceptions of Muslims. Suddenly, the world's 2 billion Muslims, who are overwhelmingly decent and law-abiding men and women, were being tainted with the same brush as the nineteen hijackers. US newspapers were constantly running opinion pieces urging Muslims to publicly condemn terrorism or extremism, as though all followers of Islam were somehow to blame, which was rather like all Christians being asked to apologise for the Vietnam War, the Nazi genocide or the Spanish Inquisition.

In the months following 9/11, thousands of American Muslims were rounded up and detained without access to family members or lawyers. Islamic charities were closed down and American Muslims were often harangued in the streets or lost their jobs. Others were treated with suspicion at airports or offloaded from passenger planes.

Mosques were attacked and there was a marked rise in hate crimes against anyone who looked Middle Eastern – and also against non-Muslims perceived to be Arab, such as turban-wearing Sikhs, as Hollywood has created a stereotypical link between turbans and Muslims. Later on, stories of innocent Muslims being abducted for rendition to countries that routinely practise torture began to emerge.

I am certain that decent people all over the world, including many Americans, were relieved when George W. Bush's second term of office came to a close and were hopeful that Bush's brand of neo-imperialism was dead when Barack Obama, an eloquent liberal who had spent part of his childhood in a predominantly Muslim country, Indonesia, was inaugurated as President on 20 January 2009. The thinking went that America's new leader would, at least, have some understanding of Islam and would not harbour negative feelings towards Muslims.

It was gratifying to hear his speech delivered in Cairo University on 4 June 2009, reaching out to the Muslim world and, in particular, to receive his acknowledgment that tension between the US and Muslims around the world has been "fed by colonialism that denied rights and opportunities to many Muslims and a Cold War in which Muslim majority countries were too often treated as proxies without regard to their own aspirations".

In the same speech, he also admitted that the attacks of 11 September 2001 and the continued efforts of extremist groups to use violence against civilians "has led some in my country to view Islam as inevitably hostile, not only to America and Western countries, but also to human rights. This has bred more fear and mistrust. This cycle of suspicion and discord must end," he said.

Superficially, the anti-Islamic mood has subsided in the US as the years have passed and memories faded, but it still exists. This was highlighted by demonstrations held all over the country in September 2010 against the opening of an Islamic Cultural Centre and Mosque in Manhattan, not far from Ground Zero; and as I mentioned in an earlier chapter, by the announcement of Florida-based preacher Terry Jones, calling for an 'International Burn a Qur'an Day', cancelled at the direct request of the White House. More recently, in September 2012, Jones actively promoted a disgusting anti-Islamic video produced by a convicted Californian fraudster; amateurish trash that set the Muslim world aflame, triggering the revenge killing of the US Ambassador to Libya among others. To my mind, people like Jones are nothing but attention-seeking, sick bigots who should be ignored. Islam is strong; it protects the believers and doesn't require defending from insults from the mouths of the insignificant, ready to do just about anything, no matter how despicable, for fifteen minutes of fame.

Obama's message of hope

Unfortunately, Obama's promise to personally pursue a two-state solution for Israelis and Palestinians "with all the patience the task requires" has not been taken seriously enough and, at the time of writing, has come to naught. While I believe that pledge was sincerely made early on in Obama's presidency, I don't think he fully understood the influence of the pro-Israel lobby on lawmakers, or the intransigent mindset of the Israeli Prime Minister, Binyamin Netanyahu, who had done nothing in pursuit of peace besides paying lip service to the concept, under US pressure.

I would love to meet with President Obama face to face to talk about the stalemate in Middle East peace, because I have the feeling that he's not receiving an accurate picture from his national security team. As long as Israel expands Jewish settlements and ousts Palestinians from East Jerusalem, a two-state solution will no longer be viable.

While the Israelis need to make compromises and yield land for peace, the Palestinian Authority, which has lost credibility since the death of Yasser Arafat, should admit that it has been ineffective. It should instead agree to become a caretaker authority tasked with the day-to-day running of the territories and relinquish any involvement in the peace process.

No one can say President Mahmoud Abbas and his team haven't tried hard, but the fact is that they've failed to get anywhere and, judging from the 'Palestine Papers' leaked by Al Jazeera, they have become so desperate and demoralised that they're willing to accept anything Israel throws their way.

I would strongly suggest that the PA should hand the role of negotiator to a committee made up of carefully vetted prominent Palestinian individuals, chosen on the basis of their respectability, patriotism, successful track record and reputations, rather than on the size of their bank accounts or their crony connections. Such a committee could also include a senior representative of the GCC to add greater international clout. It's also time for responsible Arab States to quit fence sitting and focus on this issue in a meaningful way.

A referendum could be held on the West Bank, Gaza and in the Diaspora, to lend further legitimacy to the committee under the supervision of UNRWA, with which all Palestinian refugees are registered.

Once the committee is approved by the majority, a framework for negotiations should be agreed broadly on the following lines:

a. A Palestinian state based on 1967 borders with East Jerusalem as its capital.
b. The right of return for Palestinian refugees that is enshrined within UNSC resolutions.
c. The dismantling of Israel's apartheid wall.
d. The evacuation of Jewish settlements, which should not be demolished but handed to the PA to house the growing population.
e. The drawing up of a 'Marshall Plan' with those countries responsible for the Palestinian catastrophe being the main financial contributors.

Global economic meltdown

One of the biggest earthquakes that occurred under George W. Bush's watch caused tremors just about everywhere on the planet – and three years after, its aftershocks can still be felt. The 2008 global financial crisis heralded by the collapse of Freddie Mac and Fannie Mae – two US mortgage giants – and the bankruptcy of the mighty Lehman Brothers was due to the industry's practice of handing out mortgages to recipients whose credit worthiness hadn't been properly vetted during the property boom of the 1990s.

It came as a bigger surprise to ordinary investors just how vulnerable the international banking system was. The saying 'When Washington sneezes, the rest of the world catches cold' was never so true. US banks had bundled risky loans with other assets into sellable securities and paid ratings agencies to lend their seal of approval to those, often complex, securities. As borrowers began to default, there was an increase in repossessions.

When the bubble began to burst, it became clear that in the absence of regulation, banks and hedge fund managers had been taking unacceptable risks that bordered on throwing dice at a roulette table. An ensuing credit crunch cut interbank and consumer lending hurtling currency, commodity and financial markets into instability. What resulted was what some economists have described as the worst financial crisis since the Great Depression of the 1930s. Ordinary Americans blamed greedy bankers and Wall Street sharks for initiating the crisis.

The International Monetary Fund (IMF) forecasted that American and European banks would lose up to 2.6 trillion dollars from toxic loans and bad assets. Iceland, whose banks had assets eight times greater than GDP, was particularly hard hit, bringing the country to the verge of bankruptcy. Ireland, formerly dubbed the Celtic Tiger for its strong economy, had to recapitalise three Irish banks and has yet to recover from the crisis.

The first bank to fall in Britain was Northern Rock that was ultimately nationalised; others wobbled like ninepins. The share prices of hitherto reputable banks went into free fall. Consumer–investor confidence was at such a low that the British government was forced to guarantee savings and bail out The Royal Bank of Scotland and Lloyds TSB, adding up to 1.5 trillion pounds to the burgeoning national debt, with the result Britons were asked to tighten their belts for years to come.

My dabble with fire

As the contagion swept around the planet, few companies and individuals went unscathed, and I was no exception. During the period between the liquidity crunch and the disastrous 2009 financial crisis, like most others, I didn't fully comprehend the gargantuan nature of the calamity, soon to become a worldwide economic tsunami. As an eternal optimist, I saw opportunity in adversity. Almost immediately, my team and I set ourselves a task, which was to identify an investment to suit the following criteria: low P/E (price/earnings ratio); high dividend yield; well diversified, thus inherently hedging its risk; sound management, with an impeccable track record; high liquidity; low volatility; operating in a safe legal and tax jurisdiction; and available at a distressed price.

Ours was not an easy task by any means. But even with the limits of such self-imposed strict criteria, we managed to identify a few potential targets before honing on one in particular, which involved breaking my own rule never to invest in stocks. After intensive research, attracted by a 15 per cent ROI (return on investment), I decided jointly with my Group's directors to buy a large number of shares in Barclays Bank from my personal funds, that would provide us with an almost 2 per cent share in the bank.

Once we had made our choice, the next step was to arrange financing, which was essential to greatly enhance our yields; plus we knew that the leverage would provide us with an imperative foreign currency risk hedge.

What remained was to select the right brokerage platform partner who would assist us in achieving our ultimate objective with the least amount of market disturbance, which we did with relative ease.

Very soon, we were on the market; and although we were the new kid on the block, we struck a minor but significant strategic stake in Barclays, one of the financial industry's top names; an achievement that was, perhaps, one of the defining moments of my career. At the close of the first year, we were delighted to receive substantially more than the forecasted dividend, that was just as healthy in the first two quarters of 2008.

We were elated that our strategy had worked so well. However, as the global crisis showed its vicious face, our joy was short-lived. We were taken completely by surprise when the stock began to lose value and the fluctuations started to widen. The shareholders' yearly dividends dived to 2.5 pence from 34 pence. Initially, we stood strong and held our breath, hoping the situation would swiftly turn around for the better.

Markets were choppy and were no more governed by tried and true fundamentals or the efficient market hypothesis. We could no longer count on the old rules; the game had changed. Suddenly, we were at the mercy of one and all. Sometimes, I felt that even a trivial remark from a street barber could negatively affect the market that seemed to have taken on a life of its own.

As someone with nerves of steel when it comes to a business that I know inside out, I had to admit that this roller coaster ride was something I was not prepared for. All my life, I have been in control of my decision-making and investments. Now, I felt incredibly vulnerable as it slowly sunk in that my investment was entirely out of my control.

I spent many long hours with my directors and advisors during those rocky times, studying the market indices, when our mood would swing in tandem with fluctuating stock prices. Green was, of course, our favourite colour that always made us smile briefly; but with the dreaded colour red ever-lurking on the horizon, we enjoyed hardly a moment's relaxation. I used to spend every day on tenterhooks, wondering which way the stock price was heading, and when I was informed of the direction I would speculate as to why it was going up or down, although I knew full well that no logic could be applied to its movements either way.

Without doubt, that was one of the most stressful periods of my life; I shudder to think about it now. For me, it was a war of nerves that affected my health and well-being and adversely impacted others around me. Throughout, my family was wonderful. Everyone stood firmly alongside and accepted my whimsical moments with patience and understanding.

During those volatile times, we held on to the stock and made money by taking advantage of the swings, but we also lost some fantastic opportunities due to liquidity issues. I can never forget the day we took the decision to save ourselves from daily anxiety. Besides, pondering the issue had eaten up too much time at Board meetings and I feared our preoccupation with one investment could be detrimental to my other businesses. We divested.

While it's true that I did lose a little money, I emerged from the crisis rich in experience. The damage could have been much worse, but for whatever good deeds I have done in my life, in the end I came out well and certainly better than most. This had been one of the not so 'up' moments of my career in business, but we all learned an important lesson. Fire is a strange thing. It can cook, it can envelop us in its warmth... but we must never forget that it can also burn!

Financial crisis hits Dubai
The UAE was impacted by the downturn, though Abu Dhabi, cushioned by oil revenues, escaped relatively lightly from its effects. Dubai, which has the most globally-integrated economy in the Gulf, was soon caught up in an unexpected tornado, as tourism and the demand for new property dwindled. In what was considered the region's financial, tourism and construction epicentre, building projects were put on hold or cancelled completely, causing many to lose their jobs.

Foreign investors and creditors became nervous when Dubai World, the emirate's investment vehicle, laid off up to 10,500 employees worldwide and announced that it planned to restructure 26 billion dollars of its total 59 billion-dollar debt, which the government of Dubai declined to guarantee.

Then, in February 2009, Abu Dhabi, through the Central Bank, intervened to halt speculation with the purchase of Dubai bonds worth 10 billion dollars and subsequently provided Dubai with a 10 billion-dollar facility via two Abu Dhabi-based banks, NBAD and Al Hilal. Abu Dhabi's support went a long way to calming things down.

Adding to Dubai's woes were pessimistic reports from ratings agencies that had played a big part in the sub-prime mortgage crisis and gleeful foreign columnists spewing doom and gloom for Dubai's future prospects on the pages of newspapers. If I were a conspiracy theorist, which I am not, it would have been easy to make the case that elements were conspiring to bring Dubai down.

Western pundits criticised Dubai's government for its glitz, glamour, ambitious programmes and what they described as excessive opulence; it seemed to me that these were the sort of people who would dance on someone's grave or the kind who simmer for years with envy, just waiting for the day they can put the boot in.

Every negative word they wrote went some way to erode investor confidence in Dubai, whose debt was negligible in comparison to most other countries and whose financial infrastructure was still intact.

The sheer nastiness of A.A. Gill, whose article 'Dubai on Empty' was published in *Vanity Fair*, almost leaps off the page. "Dubai has been built very fast. The plan was money. The architect was money. The designer and the builder was money. And if you ever wondered what money would look like if it were left to its own devices, it's Dubai," he writes, after accusing Dubai of "gigantism – a national inferiority complex that has to make everything bigger and biggest". The rest of it is too offensive to republish.

If mankind had adopted that attitude, there would be sand where the Egyptian pyramids now stand, a parking lot instead of the Empire State Building. Such stunning edifices such as Granada's Alhambra Palace, London's Westminster Abbey, Moscow's Kremlin and Istanbul's Blue Mosque wouldn't exist – and the acceptance of mediocrity would not have propelled man to send rockets into space or walk on the moon.

Simon Jenkins writing in *The Guardian* luridly predicted Dubai's "luxury apartments will become tenements to an ever-shifting army of refugees from the torments of the Islamic world... Its fantasy islands will be squatted or will rot and sink back into the sea. Where fresh water will come from, who knows? But before the desert sands close over it, Dubai's lesson should be learned... the short route to folly is the belief that what goes up need never come down." The vitriol behind this ridiculous commentary is palpable.

What happened to Dubai was not of its own making. No one knew that US banks had been selling bad mortgages under cover of fake ratings to financial houses around the world, while paying their executives' multi-million-dollar bonuses, or that Wall Street was riddled with fraudulent practices. No one could predict that tent cities would be set up outside US cities to house the growing homeless, whose homes had been repossessed, or that 40 million would have to rely on food stamps.

I penned several columns in English and Arabic warning readers of those out to hobble Dubai's recovery with weasel words. But all that's now water under the bridge.

As time marched on, those of us who believed in Dubai and knew that the downturn was a temporary blip were proved right. In 2011, Dubai's economy expanded by 3.4 per cent and is anticipated to post 5 per cent growth in 2012. Contrast that with the IMF's April 2012 forecast for the US economy expected to grow by just 2.1 per cent in 2012, while the British Chamber of Commerce slashed its 2012 growth forecast to just 0.1 per cent. Portugal, Spain and Italy are still struggling to get back on their feet, while Greece has been obliged to institute harsh austerity measures resulting in civil unrest and an increase in suicides. Some economic pundits believe the eurozone is in danger of breaking up.

In hindsight, it's easy to say that Dubai could have done some things differently, such as creating a cushion for a rainy day, but lessons have now been learned the hard way. This does not mean to say that Dubai should not continue pursuing excellence or deviate in any way from the government's grand plan.

Probably the greatest the UAE and other GCC countries have learned from Bush's military interventions and the global downturn is that we must become self-sufficient as possible. Even together, GCC states form a small nation and, unless we stick together, we will be fragile to outside influences.

I believe the GCC should metamorphose into a federation rather than a cooperative body, provided governments and their peoples agree. We should collectively form a modern, well-equipped Gulf military to protect our borders, and a rapid-reaction force that could join with others to help Arab League member countries with internal and external threats upon request. Such forces would also act as a deterrent to our foes, including Iran, that uses proxies to interfere in Arab affairs and makes unfounded territorial claims on the Arabian Gulf and the states which surround it.

Our rulers should continue to develop trust and transparency with one another and encourage their citizens to look upon others in the federation as one family, in the tradition of our fathers and grandfathers, when rulers consulted with people and gave them a say in the country's development.

That would allow us to carry one flag high, to show our strength, to ensure our enemies understand our collective power. We may be some of the richest countries in the world with vast reserves of our planet's essential resources, but until now we've not exercised any muscle. I don't mean we should use oil, a gift from God, as a weapon; we are stronger than oil.

As it is, we rely on Western protection from our enemies and are restricted from printing our own money without the West's supervision. We've walked on egg shells long enough worrying about what other nations think. No foreign state should be allowed to threaten our stability and security.

In order to gauge opinions, UAE nationals should feel free to express themselves openly in our Arabic language newspapers; writers should voice their uncensored opinions, but unfortunately the editors of Arabic papers shy away from anything controversial and practice unnecessary self-censorship, unlike their English language counterparts.

There is no official discrepancy between the editorial freedoms enjoyed by the English language press and the Arabic press from an official standpoint. But I've noticed that the editors of Arabic papers are reluctant to take advantage of the freedoms open to them, preferring to remain in the bland zone rather than rattle cages that need to be shaken up.

There is one exception, my friend Ahmad Al Jarallah, the Editor-in-Chief of the Kuwaiti papers *Al Seyassah* and *Arab Times*. I admired his courageous writing long before I met him a few years ago. He is brave enough to put thoughts to paper that others think, but are too scared to write. He doesn't beat about the bush; he goes straight to the point. He's not only a great editor and writer, he's also a great person to know, friendly, sociable and possessed of the ability to make people laugh. Two other Arab writers that I appreciate very much for their fearless, straightforward columns are Tariq Al Humaid and Abdul Rahman Al Rashid.

Personally, I would like to see the UAE become more proactive in regional and international geopolitics, like our much smaller neighbour, Qatar, that has been punching above its weight in recent years and has gained the respect of the international community. Even if not everybody agrees with all Qatar's foreign policy decisions and interventions, at least Doha is prepared to go out on a limb to make a difference.

Here in the Emirates, we should agree on how our country is presented abroad and choose our ambassadors according to their personal calibre and education. All ambassadors should be well screened to ensure they are worthy of representing our nation.

Since the UAE's birth in 1971, the country has been run on the lines of a corporation, a policy that has been very successful in creating wealth; but in order to avoid some emirates having to sell government bonds or take out high interest loans, we should consolidate our income and resources and make sure our economy is well managed. GCC countries are rich with oil and gas and if economies are properly run, there would be no need for states to issue bonds or take loans to support government projects.

Frankly, I don't understand where the oil revenue goes. It should be very simple; if states suffer a deficit in one area, they can balance that with cash flow in another and draw up payment schedules to satisfy their business partners. This system would erase financial commitment from fiscal balance sheets and will make them solid and respected.

Conversely, not everyone trusts in bonds, which are basically pieces of paper that could end up in the bin. For instance, if the US comes close to defaulting on its Treasury bonds, what guarantees do the holders have? This is why it's important that Gulf states keep within their budgets. I just hope the people in charge of such matters read my words and understand that this advice comes from someone who loves his country and its Gulf neighbours.

Here, I will echo the message I've been telling the media for a long time. Now is the right time for all GCC states to spend on infrastructure, which will generate jobs and wealth, when all citizens will benefit. They should not delay because the cost of labour and materials has gone down since 2008 and now is the time to take advantage before prices rise again. The veins of GCC economies require new blood, which such projects will pump. Visible growth will also encourage foreign investors to come, learn how we do things and gain confidence in our business environment.

Moreover, it's also beyond time that we took our rightful place in the world, which we cannot do by remaining politically neutral. There is no such thing as neutrality in today's day and age. It's time that we made a vital decision to preserve our stability, security and autonomy. United with other GCC countries, we can form an influential bloc. Together, Gulf states must choose between being either a wolf or a goat – and since most goats are destined for the pot, it's really a no-brainer.

Concerning scenario

The greatest potential threat to Gulf states comes from Iran. However, there is the possibility that even greater danger may be brewing or may emerge at some point in the near or distant future. There was a time when the US, Israel and Iran were covert allies and I can't help wondering whether the enmity between America/Israel and Iran today is part cinema and, if so, what are the implications. You're probably asking yourself: what possible motivation could the trio have for creating a deceptive facade?

Keeping up the pretence – if that is what is, indeed, occurring – allows Israel to play victim, faced with an existential threat from Tehran, thus enabling it to flout international laws without repercussions. Iran uses anti-Israel slogans to elevate its standing in the Muslim world – and the US has a pretext to maintain its military footprint in the Gulf. Whatever the truth, there is a symbiotic relationship between the three powers, based on keeping Arab states under the boot.

You may be surprised to learn that the Islamic Republic of Iran, for all its fiery rhetoric against Israel, helped Tel Aviv to bomb Iraq's nuclear reactor with use of its airspace as well as photographs and plans of the Tuwaitha facility. During the Iran-Iraq War, Tehran purchased Israeli weapons.

Likewise, the Reagan administration secretly sold US arms to Iran, discovered when the Iran-Contra Scandal broke. Moreover, more recently, the Iranians offered to train the Afghan army under US supervision and helped persuade the Shiites in Iraq not to take up arms against the occupying forces.

I've noticed too that anti-Iranian sanctions to deter Iran from enriching uranium have not dealt a serious blow to the Iranian economy like those that crippled Iraq, and whereas a nuclear-armed Iraq could in no way be tolerated by the US, there is no such international fervour to discipline Tehran.

No doubt, there are Arabs who have swallowed Iran's propaganda hook, line and sinker that Iranians are their brothers. Not so, says Dr Abdullah Al Nafisi, a specialist on Shiite affairs. He maintains that Iranians are primarily Persian nationalists who use their faith to reach Arabs through Shiite Arab minorities.

Al Nafisi points out that Iranian officials, from the Supreme Leader to members of the Revolutionary Guard, once hung on the teachings of Abdollah Nouri, an Iranian cleric who expounds his view that all Gulf states belong to Persia, while advocating retribution on Arabs for destroying the mighty Persian Empire. That opinion may hold water when the Iranian government impedes its citizens from speaking Arabic, giving their children Arabic names, constructing Sunni mosques – and still occupies islands that belong to the UAE.

It's particularly telling that when Jewish Iranians are treated well, enjoying representation in the Iranian parliament and freedom to build synagogues, so well that they resist the lure of Israel cash incentives to immigrate to Israel, Iranians of Arab origin are looked upon as second-class citizens.

Tehran has discriminated against the Arabs of Al Ahwaz – formerly Arabistan, now Khuzestan – since the Shah's annexation of Al Ahwaz, and has rejected the Ahwazi demand for autonomy. In an area rich with oil and gas, stretching between the Zagros Mountains to the north and the east, Iraq to the west and Kuwait to the south, the Ahwazi people suffer from a shortage of drinking water, electricity, plumbing, telephone connections and even sewage.

Some 50 per cent have been abandoned to poverty; 80 per cent of Ahwazi children are malnourished, as the Director of the Ahwaz Education and Human Rights Foundation reported to the UN some years ago. The Ahwazi Arabs are also underrepresented in Parliament and accuse the government of racially-based political and economic prejudice. If Persians genuinely considered Arabs as their brothers, this would not be the case.

You may further be surprised that until today, Iran does business with Israelis. In mid-2011, the Israeli website, *Ynetnews*, revealed that "Israel-Iran trade ties are thriving" with "dozens of Israeli companies secretly engaging in relations with the Islamic Republic through third parties".

The article quotes the Chairman of the Israeli-Arab Friendship Association, Yehoshua Meiri, as saying, "Despite what is seen on the ground, the secret relations with Iran total tens of millions of dollars a year... Even when harsh statements are made on both sides, business thrives. Relations with the Iranian colleagues are excellent and political statements are ignored."

Around the same time as that article was published, Tehran's Trade Ministry had to answer to Iranian exporters/importers who claimed Israeli apples and oranges were being sold in the country's markets. Indeed, it's an open secret that Israel buys marble, cashews and pistachios from Iran, while Iran imports organic fertilizer, hormones to boost milk production, irrigation pipes and seeds from Israel.

In light of Binyamin Netanyahu's loud calls for tougher economic sanctions against Iran, you would be forgiven for dismissing the possibility that any trading exists between the two countries. But as Yossi Melman explains in *Haaretz*, "Netanyahu, who endlessly preaches the need for firm action against Iran to prevent it from acquiring nuclear arms, is not lifting a finger to stop Israeli companies and individuals indirectly trading with Iran."

One of Israel's largest corporations, Ofer Brothers Group, faced allegations that it had routinely traded with Iran in June 2011, when it became public knowledge that it had sold a tanker to the Islamic Republic of Iran Shipping Lines and its ships had been docking at Iranian ports for a decade, thus contravening US sanctions. In their own defence, the Ofer family insisted that their dealings with Iran had been on the Israeli government's behalf, but later either decided – or were squeezed – to change their tune.

The Ofers were not the first to be embroiled in scandal over Iran dealings. In 1997, a former IDF paratrooper, Nahum Manbar, was imprisoned for sixteen years after being tried behind closed doors for selling components used to make mustard and nerve gas to Iran. Manbar claimed that his transactions with Iran were approved by Israel's intelligence community and was angered that the Ofers would probably be allowed off the hook. "The establishment took revenge on me while they, the Ofer Brothers, have connections in government and nobody is touching them," he complained.

In a nutshell, the Israel/US–Iran relationship is murky and may not be what it seems to be at first glance. Should you care to delve further into this, may I suggest that you read a book written by Trita Parsi, titled *Treacherous Alliance: The Secret Dealings of Iran, Israel and the United States* (Yale University Press, 2007) which is very illuminating. My own feeling is that whatever the truth may be, Arabs should prepare for the worst case scenario.

Let's suppose that Iran does succeed in enriching its own uranium and begins producing nuclear bombs. In that case, isn't there a strong possibility that the West could adopt the view 'if you can't beat 'em, join 'em'?

What if, in the future, Washington, Tel Aviv and Tehran formed an alliance such as that existing when the Shah was in power? How would that impact the independence of Gulf states? This may never happen, but our Arab governments should wake up and smell the pistachios before there's even the slightest risk that Iraq's tragic fate could becomes ours.

Total War with Islam

A troubling exposé, revealed by the BBC and credible British newspapers in May 2012 and which came as a shock, was given scant coverage in the US. I could hardly believe what I was hearing and reading. Even more disturbing was the absence of any riposte from governments of predominantly Muslim countries that host American military bases. As someone who is committed to mend fences between the West and the Muslim world incinerated by Bush's wars, and to facilitate non-Muslims' greater understanding of Islam, I was shaken to learn that US military commanders and officers had been attending a year-long course at the Joint Forces College in Virginia, given by Lt Col Matthew Dooley, advocating 'Total War with Islam'.

Dooley taught on the premise that there is no such thing as "moderate Islam". "This barbaric ideology will no longer be tolerated," he told his classes. "Islam must change or we will facilitate its self-destruction" with nuclear attacks on Mecca and Medina without regard for civilian casualties.

Believe it or not, the course was advertised on the Pentagon's own website. It has since been cancelled and condemned by the Pentagon's top brass. However, it emerged that a similar course was being taught at a second military college, complete with anti-Islamic slides approved by former CIA Director, James Woolsey, and two three-star generals. The Pentagon portrays Dooley as a rogue instructor whose teaching had nothing to do with US government policy, yet, instead of being drummed out of the military in disgrace, he has retained his post.

Since, the FBI has been driven to vet its own course materials when it was discovered that counter-terrorism agents were being taught that "American Muslims are likely to be terrorist sympathisers" whose charitable donations equate to a "funding mechanism for combat". FBI materials refer to the Prophet Mohammed (PBUH) as a "cult leader".

Likewise, as revealed by *The New York Times*, the New York Police Department (NYPD) has been infiltrating mosques and Muslim community centres. The department's officers were shown a documentary called *The Third Jihad*, contending that the Muslim leadership in the US harbours ambitions to "infiltrate and dominate" in which the NYPD's chief participated. The film was also endorsed by NYC former mayor, Rudolph Giuliani.

In the Arab world, we've become used to dismissing crimes perpetrated by US soldiers in Iraq, Afghanistan and Pakistan as 'mistakes' that run counter to official US policy. However, I have a hard time accepting that those courses were unauthorised when they appeared on the Pentagon website, were taught in military schools, were signed off by generals as well as a CIA director and are somewhat mirrored within the FBI and the NYPD. The thought that the US government knew nothing about this philosophy of hate doesn't ring true.

Given the turmoil in Arab countries, ostensibly in pursuit of American-style democracy that was partly instigated by US non-governmental organisations (NGOs), the potential for slicing apart Iraq and Libya in the same way that Sudan has been split, and the possibly orchestrated divisions between Sunnis and Shiites (to the detriment of Sunnis), it's possible that the US has a clandestine policy of inciting Arabs to destroy each other as a continuation of imperialist Britain's 'Divide and Rule'. After all, that was effective in tearing Syria, Jordan and Palestine asunder.

Without any convincing explanation or apology from the White House, my suspicions have been raised that the US may be a wolf in sheep's clothing vis-à-vis Muslims and Arabs. I don't have proof, but I can't help wondering whether the Al Assad regime in Syria, Hezbollah in Lebanon and the Iraqi Badr Brigades – all Iranian satellites – have been commissioned by the US to kill Sunnis, thus reducing the numbers of Muslims, eroded by the invasions of Afghanistan and Iraq that caused up to one million deaths. If they haven't been endorsed by the US behind the door, then why has America gifted Iraq to Iran, failed to prevent the massacre and torture of Syrian civilians, including women and children? And why is it that the mighty US hasn't leant on Hezbollah's military wing – an army outside state control – to relinquish its weapons?

This is one time I hope I'm wrong. I don't want to even imagine that America is secretly plotting the destruction of Islam and its believers or manipulating Shiites and Sunnis to kill one another. The very idea is hurtful to me when, in a small way, I have striven to bring all of the Prophet Ibrahim's children together in peace; notably with my gift to Dubai, the Al Farooq Mosque that welcomes visitors of all faiths, the Khalaf Al Habtoor Leadership Center in Illinois College, and the Al Habtoor Football and Track Stadium enjoyed by students at the American University in Cairo.

Some of my dearest American friends are convinced that Washington has no such anti-Islamic policies in place and say the bigoted strains, permeating the military, intelligence and law enforcement are renegade. I would like nothing more than to give their assurances the benefit of the doubt, but I refuse to sleep when there is potentially so much at stake.

With the future of our children and grandchildren on the line, I can only reiterate my call for the GCC to become a federation and build an independent, powerful military capability as a deterrent against all threats no matter where they're from.

As President Abraham Lincoln, a man who has my full admiration, once said, "You can fool all of the people some of the time, and some of the people all of the time, but you can't fool all of the people all of the time." The peoples of the Middle East and the Gulf have been fooled long enough. It's beyond time we wizened up and made preparations for any eventuality.

CHAPTER 18

Hopes and Fears

"HOPE AND FEAR ARE INSEPARABLE. THERE IS NO HOPE WITHOUT FEAR,
NOR ANY FEAR WITHOUT HOPE."

— FRANÇOIS DE LA ROCHEFOUCAULD

The family I am most worried about nowadays is my greater Arab family,
the Arab nation, which I'm not even sure still exists other than words on
paper. The 'Arab Spring' or the 'Arab Awakening' has brought about sudden
change throughout the length and breadth of the Arab world, culminating
in political, civil and social uncertainty. No longer can we rely on the past to
predict the future. Everything we thought we knew has been hurled into a
tailspin. This may or may not be a good thing.

It began in Tunisia when a twenty-six-year-old street seller immersed
his body in inflammable liquid and set fire to himself on 17 December
2010 in his hometown of Sidi Bouzid, in response to his produce-laden
wheelbarrow having been confiscated by a municipal official. His act of
suicide was the catalyst for major public protests against corruption, rising
prices and a lack of job opportunities that led to the ousting of President
Zine El Abidine Ben Ali, who reluctantly sought exile in Saudi Arabia
together with his wife and three children.

It wasn't long before the wave of public discontent spread to Egypt.
25 January 2011 began a youth uprising centred about Cairo's landmark,
Tahrir (Freedom) Square, resulting in the capital's downtown becoming
a war zone, when pro-regime thugs attacked protesters. Demonstrations
spread to Alexandria, Suez, Port Said, Tanta and other cities. People of all
political persuasions and from every strata of society eventually joined in.

Muslim and Christian pro-democracy activists erected tents in the main
squares and chanted for President Hosni Mubarak to step down, which
he was forced to do on 11 February, when his powers were given to the
Supreme Council of the Armed Forces (SCAF) that swore to uphold
revolutionary principles. For a time, the country was lawless. The police

and security forces left the streets and the army wasn't trained to adopt policing duties. Prisons were besieged and thousands of criminals and politicians walked free.

All over the country, ordinary people fearing for their lives and property joined vigilante groups tasked with keeping their homes and families free from harm, until law and order could be restored. The economy took a hit as tourists stayed away, investors took fright and striking workers downed tools. The government closed banks to prevent a run and propped up the Egyptian pound, and the Bourse shut its doors to stop stocks going into free fall. This policy of containment was largely effective.

The Tunisian and Egyptian 'revolutions' have been hailed worldwide as success stories due to their overwhelmingly peaceful nature, although it's true that hundreds were martyred. With offers of aid and debt relief flooding in from the West and Gulf states, democracy in the purist sense has so far remained elusive.

Both Tunisia and Egypt are enduring roller coaster periods en route to democracy; those who joined hands in the squares are no longer united. Democracy isn't just ticking off a ballot. It relies on an educated population that understands the issues at stake and can flourish within an atmosphere of free speech, the right to gather and the presence of an uncensored media. Creating the right climate for democracy cannot happen overnight.

In Egypt, there is a rift between modernists and Islamic parties such as the Muslim Brotherhood, that despite showing a moderate face early on, have long harboured the goal of forming an Islamic state based on Shari'ah law. Others resent the SCAF which went out of its way to placate protesters during the months following the revolution. On 12 August 2012, President Mursi declared the retirement of the Commander-in-Chief of the Armed Forces, Field Marshall Mohammed Hussein Tantawi, following demands for his resignation for what some deemed his betrayal of the revolution.

Tantawi couldn't win; he was damned if he did and damned if he didn't. Many of his former supporters (and President Mohammed Mursi's former presidential rival, Ahmad Shafiq) accused him of manipulating the vote in response to threats from his Muslim Brotherhood backers to reignite the street in the event their man lost his bid. Those same critics believe the US has a sinister agenda; they are convinced that the Obama administration's push for a swift and total democratic transition with power resting with the new president is a prelude to Washington's tagging of Egypt as a terrorist state. They have concocted an Iraq/Afghanistan scenario that would result in Egypt being divided into two states – one for the Copts – along with the oil-and-gas rich Sinai Peninsula being gifted to Israel. Tantawi has officially turned over SCAF's powers to an elected president, but many are relieved that the military is still the hand that rocks the cradle behind the scenes.

My fears for Egypt are many; they include the potential for civil war between progressives and religious extremists, as well as a violent face-off between the civilian population and the army. Egypt stands at a crossroads. It can either go forward stronger and more prosperous than ever to retake its role as leader of the Arab world – which right now isn't looking feasible – or it will face an economic and security nightmare for many years to come.

Egyptians held the future in their own hands during 2012 when they voted in parliamentary and presidential elections. The result was an Islamist-dominated upper and lower house and a President drawn from the Muslim Brotherhood's Freedom and Justice Party, a man with an engineering background without diplomatic, administrative or geopolitical know-how.

Egypt's new President, Mohammed Mursi, took office in June 2012 when he softened his former hard line rhetoric, resigned from the Muslim Brotherhood and promised to be a leader for all Egyptians, including moderates and Coptic Christians. Moreover, he announced that he would respect all existing international treaties, including Camp David, Egypt's peace treaty with Israel. In spite of my reservations, I admit to being impressed with the substance of the new leader's inaugural address delivered at Cairo University. He's a man who knows what he wants and how to achieve his aims, which may bode well for the future. He and his wife are simple folk. His wife rejects living in a palace and refuses to be called First Lady, preferring First Servant or *Umm Ahmed*. However, the jury's still out on whether he is able to convince the moneyed elites, the business community and investors of his seeming impartiality. His is a balancing act between satisfying the demands of his base – mainly the poor and uneducated – with everyone else's. He must tread carefully to avoid confrontation with the military and work to maintain diplomatic relations with countries that matter. And as long as there are Egyptians going hungry, he must prioritise the economy over and above any personal ideological convictions he might hold that could deter investors and tourists. He must also bear in mind that he is bound by constitutional principles that separate religion from the state.

President Mursi took office as a leader without a job description, a leader of a country where a constitution has yet to be drafted. It is thought that a backroom deal has been struck between the new president and SCAF that limits his presidential role. For instance, although SCAF officially handed over its powers, in theory Mursi isn't free to make sweeping legislative changes or take the country to war without a green light from SCAF's head honchos, which is somewhat of a relief to me personally. I can but hope that President Mursi will live up to his pledges and that he won't disappoint those Egyptians who gave him their trust. In the interim, all I can do is to wish the Egyptian people all the best.

At the time of writing, Hosni Mubarak is back in the fearsome Tora prison's clinic after being near to death in a military hospital subsequent to being sentenced to life in prison, in connection with the deaths of revolutionary martyrs. Newspapers reported that his health markedly deteriorated when he heard that his nemesis, Mohammed Mursi, had taken over his old presidential office, which he considered the ultimate insult to his dignity. The only vice-president he ever appointed, former army officer and intelligence Chief Omar Suleiman, died while undergoing medical tests in the US on 19 July 2012. Dubbed 'the Black Box' by the media, he took his secrets with him.

It saddens me that Egyptians have been focused on taking revenge on members of the ousted regime, many of whom are undergoing trials, when they should be concentrating on the future, patiently working towards bringing their vision of democracy, freedom and increased economic opportunity into fruition. Their number one priority should be the economy, because if the country goes bankrupt, no leader will have the wherewithal to make good on his pledges.

I understand that they will never forget the decades of oppression under emergency law. I understand that almost half of all Egyptians have been living below the two-dollar-a-day poverty line, while many don't have access to decent homes or clean water. I understand that change is urgently needed.

But I don't understand their desire to severely punish and humiliate their former leadership, especially their president of thirty years, who served with honour as a pilot during the 1973 October War and who, despite his failures, provided his country with decades of peace and security. President Mubarak made serious mistakes for which he should be held accountable, but I don't believe he should be humiliated.

Instead, Egypt's future would be better served with a South African style Truth and Reconciliation process, whereby officials admit their wrongdoing and ask forgiveness. Just as bad is their determination to pursue business people who used the prevailing culture of corruption to the benefit of themselves and their enterprises. Egypt was – and to a large extent still is – operating on graft from top to bottom. Singling out entrepreneurs discourages investment and will ultimately put employees out of work. From here on, corruption should be dealt with severely, but dredging up the past benefits no one.

I hope and pray that Tunisia and Egypt live up to the ideals and aspirations embraced by the revolutionaries, but I'm not optimistic. The Tunisian constituent assembly made a bad decision when they opted for President Moncef Marzouki, who formerly worked closely with banned Islamist organisations. A Tunisian court has sentenced former President Ben Ali to life imprisonment in absentia and has also passed sentence on his interior minister and thirty-eight other former government officials.

If a fledgling democracy begins life with a wrong decision, what will follow is likely to be more of the same or worse. The same applies to Egypt where almost 52 per cent of voters chose an Islamist-dominated parliament and a leader rooted in the Muslim Brotherhood. When I knew that, I initially mourned Egypt's future. The Brotherhood has ties to Hamas which is one of its many offshoots and is open to being wooed by Tehran. Nevertheless, if Mohammed Mursi can put the well-being of his compatriots before his allegiance to the Brotherhood and operate from a basis of real politic, there is hope. As a person, he inspires confidence, but we'll see.

Both Egypt and Tunisia are vulnerable to their enemies, which could easily take advantage of the chaotic days ahead to sow division and violence for their own ends. In particular, a weakened, divided Egypt will be a gift to both Israel and Iran and may result in the Arab nation's death knell.

Amid such political and social instability within Egypt, it seems to me that the Arab League headquarters should be relocated to a GCC country – possibly Saudi Arabia or the UAE – that enjoys stability and security. I also don't think that the League's secretary-generals should automatically be Egyptian, as, sorry to say, none of them have done a very good job; they have all proved to be tasteless, colourless and resultless.

Ideally, the secretary-general should be from the GCC states; someone who is just and strong, someone who can share our vision and speak on our behalf. Alternatively, the post should revolve, giving an opportunity to candidates from all member nations.

It's 2012. The Arab world is unrecognisable to the extent an Arab world barely exists. In February 2011, unrest spread to Libya where a civil war raged between the regime of Colonel Muammar Gaddafi and anti-government rebels headquartered in Benghazi. The Arab League and the UN Security Council sided with the Libyan opposition. UNSC Resolution 1973 was passed under Chapter VII, authorising a no-fly zone over Libya, the freezing of Libyan assets abroad, an embargo on arms imports and permission for UN member states to use military means to protect Libyan civilians.

Subsequently, NATO launched a bombing campaign targeting military sites, command and control centres as well as Gaddafi's compound. There were several international diplomatic efforts to persuade Colonel Gaddafi to go into exile, all to no avail. Gaddafi swore to remain until the last drop of Libyan blood was spilled, including his own. The International Criminal Court (ICC) issued an arrest warrant in his name, yet months into the NATO campaign, there was no sign of the Libyan dictator relinquishing power.

He was eventually driven out of the capital to his hometown, Sirte, where on 20 September 2011, he was dragged out of a large drain pipe, abused, taunted and shot in the head by rebel fighters. His body was placed on public display in a vegetable market alongside those of his Defence Minister and one of his own sons, where people lined up to take photographs of their battered former leader on their mobile phones. Gaddafi was eventually buried in an unmarked grave under the desert sands.

You only have to look at his country's lack of infrastructure, schools and hospitals to see that he failed his people. Libya is rich with oil and gas, yet the country resembles some of the poorest in the developing world. But I would have preferred if the opposition had kept him alive to answer for his crimes before a court of law. It was interesting to note that, unlike most other 'Arab Spring' countries, a secularist party, the National Forces Alliance, won the majority of parliamentary seats by a substantial margin.

Yemen similarly fell apart with fierce clashes between pro and anti-regime tribes. There were massive anti-government demonstrations and counter-demonstrations, with some calling for President Ali Abdullah Saleh's resignation and others venting their support for him. In early June 2011, there was a rocket attack on the presidential palace, as a result of which the President and five leading members of his government suffered injuries; they were immediately flown to Saudi Arabia for medical treatment. But President Saleh wasn't to be frightened off. As soon as his health improved, he returned home to face yet more public protest. His quest to hang on to power ended on 27 February 2012, when he put the country in the care of his deputy, Abd Rabbuh Mansur Al Hadi, and stepped down.

Likewise, the ruling Allawite family's hold on Syria may be coming to an end. A year and a half into a violent uprising, opposition fighters reached Damascus where they bombed the regime's inner sanctum, the National Security Building, killing the Defence Minister, Assad's brother-in-law, the Deputy Defence Minister and other senior figures. There have also been high-level political and military defections. It's not over yet, but the writing is on the wall for the Syrian dictator.

The regime of President Bashar Al Assad has shamed the Arab nation more than any other by committing genocide on the very people it swore to defend. The Allawites (a Shiite sect) are a minority, yet they have re-mained in control of the country since January 1971, when President Hafez Al Assad came to power. Protests there began on 26 January 2011 and by March had escalated into a mass uprising. Demonstrations were prompted by socio-economic factors, human rights and an absence of freedom of expression.

As in Egypt and elsewhere, activists demanded the cessation of emergen-cy laws and a pluralistic political system. Rather than seriously consider the population's just demands, the Syrian government, led by President Bashar Al Assad, blamed armed gangs, Islamist extremists and foreign governments for the uprising and used its military to ruthlessly crack down on demonstra-tors with tanks, fire from helicopter gunships and snipers. There have been mass arrests, widespread torture and detentions. Some towns were deprived of water and electricity to deter dissent. Thousands fled to neighbouring countries such as Turkey and Lebanon.

It seems to me that Bashar, a Western-educated eye doctor, is more inhu-man than his father Hafez Al Assad, infamous for his brutal repression of civilians in 1982, when his army, commanded by his brother Rifaat, quelled a Sunni revolt killing up to 40,000 in the town of Hama. Like father like son, Bashar remained silent as his security forces killed children, whose life-less bodies were discovered bruised, broken and in some cases minus limbs or genitalia.

Despite harsh UN, US and EU sanctions, the leadership appears deter-mined to keep Syria under the thumb of the ruling Allawite minority that would certainly lose power and privilege following democratic elections. Should Syria descend into civil war, Israel could become emboldened, leav-ing the Lebanese and the Palestinians more vulnerable than ever.

It's of note that while the West didn't hesitate to intervene in oil-rich Libya, its leaders have done little to alleviate the suffering of Syrians. The same goes for the leaders of Arab states, if truth be told, although kudos should go to Saudi Arabia and Qatar for pushing for serious action on the diplomatic front and supplying weapons to the opposition. A group of seventy countries, including the US, Britain, France, Germany, Canada, Australia, Egypt, Qatar and the United Arab Emirates, came together under the umbrella Friends of the Syrian People in an attempt to find a solution. Three conferences were held, but produced nothing but empty talk.

Ironically, Iraq numbers among the so-called friends of the Syrian people. Iraq's Shiite-dominated government led by Prime Minister Nouri Al Maliki has steadfastly supported the Assad regime at the direction of its master Tehran. Al Maliki would naturally prefer Damascus's pro-Shiite government to remain, in order to bolster the Shiite triangle stretching from Iraq to Lebanon. He has proved his disregard for Sunni lives in his own country. Iraq has urged the 87,000 Iraqi refugees in Syria to return home due to increased incidents of murder and assault, yet the country's foreign minister ridiculously blames Al Qaeda for the violence. Doesn't he have eyes? Hasn't he seen the helicopter and tank shelling that destroyed entire sections of Homs and Hama shown on videos put out by activists? Hasn't he heard the chilling first-hand accounts by witnesses who are in no doubt who the aggressors are?

I was appalled at the group's inaction amid documented reports of massacres by Syrian forces. In the town of Houla, militias loyal to the regime calling themselves 'Shabiha' went on a rampage going house to house to murder entire families. Even babies and young children weren't immune. At least thirty-two children under ten years old were either shot or hacked to death. The village of Tremseh that lies within the province of Hama was the site of a similar killing spree. More than 220 villagers were killed as a result of being bombarded by helicopter gunships, tanks and artillery – or were executed by Shabiha militiamen.

Western powers made their disgust known, but did nothing apart from drafting UN Security Council resolutions with the foreknowledge that any Chapter Seven resolution predicating military intervention would be vetoed by Moscow. I realised that the lack of a UNSC resolution authorising the invasion of Iraq was no barrier in 2003, when the US formed the 'Coalition of the Willing' to wage a war of choice based on a cooked-up premise. Is this another example of oil being considered more valuable than blood?

Throughout, Al Assad has remained arrogantly indifferent to the disgust of the outside world as he relies on Syria's allies, Russia and China, to thwart humanitarian military intervention. Russia and China have steadfastly opposed military interference in Syria as well as attempts to topple Al Assad, as both powers view Syria as part of the geopolitical spheres of influence and have major trade and economic relations with the regime.

Russia has been flexing its muscles, hinting that any military intervention on the part of the West could trigger a third world war. President Vladimir Putin has ignored appeals from the UN and countries such as the UK and Turkey to step back. On the contrary, Moscow supplied the Syrian regime with attack helicopters and air defence systems. "Russia's concern is to deny victory to the West" was a headline in the *Financial Times*. That seems to be the case. I'm exasperated by Russia's intransigence, seemingly oblivious to the Syrian people's suffering, but I'm not surprised. Let's not forget that President Putin was the First Chief of the Soviet Union's KGB Directorate. The KGB was universally feared because of its brutal crushing of internal dissent as well as anti-Soviet uprisings in Hungary, Czechoslovakia and Poland. Indeed, how can anyone expect Russia to respect human life when Russia's bombardment of the Chechen capital Grozny robbed 27,000 civilians of their lives, including 5,000 children? Just as is happening in Syria today, Russian soldiers committed torture, summary executions and prevented humanitarian assistance from reaching civilians in need.

It pains me greatly to say this, but I'm left to reluctantly conclude that the Syrian regime's viciousness towards the people it's supposed to care for together with the failure of the Arab world to come to their aid, has stripped Arab countries of a moral platform when criticising Israel. It's undeniable that the Assad gang has gone beyond red lines even Israel would think twice to cross in its treatment of the Palestinians. In my view, people that kill, mutilate and displace their own brothers and sisters are humanity's dregs, undeserving of being ranked human beings. The one thing that separates humans from animals is the soul – and it's evident that those barbarians in the finest bespoke suits have made a pact with the Devil in a futile attempt to keep their wealth and position.

There were sporadic protests in Jordan, Algeria and Morocco that subsequently died down on their own. Bahrain, however, was plunged into turmoil when the minority Shiite population, stirred up by Tehran camped out in Manama's Pearl Square, calling for an end to the monarchy. Violence erupted bringing the tiny state to a standstill, resulting in Saudi Arabia and other Gulf states sending troops to restore security on the basis that Bahrain is a crucial buffer between Saudi Arabia and Iran. It's important to differentiate between genuine uprisings against dictators and tyrants and those demonstrations instigated by foreign powers, such as Iran, designed to create chaos and further their influence.

To sum up, I have mixed feelings about the Arab Spring. Overall, I believe change could be good for Arab republics, where people have been subjugated by dictators more interested in milking their country's resources for their own ends rather than heed the concerns of the people. But once their revolutions are over citizens should put old hatred and grievances aside. Now is the time for smart thinking, planning and discipline, so those countries unnecessarily plagued by poverty can transform, which experts from First-World nations should assist them in so doing.

In 2011, we witnessed economically and socially-driven civil uprisings in Europe, the US, Britain and Israel, many of which have led to violent confrontation between protesters and police, as well as the destruction of property. In my view, citizens of Gulf states have little to complain about and I would have no sympathy for anyone who tried to cause trouble in this part of the world.

We benefit from tried and true systems of governance going back hundreds of years. Gulf countries, including the UAE, are the envy of the world; they have been peaceful and secure for generations. In particular, the people of the UAE enjoy comfortable lifestyles in a free and open, investor-friendly climate. There is every opportunity for UAE citizens to get ahead in a place with unparalleled infrastructure and leisure facilities.

Our leaders, whose roots are deep in the soil, are respectable and responsible. They are patriots who sincerely love their countries. As they say, if it isn't broke, why fix it? That isn't to say there isn't room for improvement. We should never say that's it; we should always strive to do more.

I would, however, like to see Gulf rulers become closer to their people so as to include them in the decision-making, in the way that the UAE's founding fathers, the late Sheikh Zayed and Sheikh Rashid, always did. Such close collaboration and transparency is crucial during these turbulent times, when there are omnipresent threats from Iran, other neighbouring countries and terrorist groups. Speaking with one voice will help protect us from outside dangers and assure not only our future, but also that of the Arab nation. We must be one hand with our leaderships to ensure the security of our children and grandchildren. United we'll stand, divided we'll fall.

Gulf states must also work to preserve their people's identity and traditions. There is no doubt that expatriate experts and workforces have greatly contributed to building our countries, which is why they have been welcomed and appropriately remunerated. We owe a lot to foreign expertise, but we must be very careful when it comes to awarding citizenship even to those who purport to love their host country.

There are two kinds of love for a country. The first is inherent and permanent as it derives from an individual's roots in the land of his or her birth. The second depends on how much personal benefit a person derives from being in a certain place and is liable to fluctuate according to circumstances.

For example, I don't love the UAE any more or any less now than I did in the days it had little material to offer and when the only foreigners present were those who had been lured by high salaries. My fear is that some of our new nationals harbour dual loyalties and it is my hope that the government understands how important it is to screen applicants for citizenship as to their motives and backgrounds well before nationality is awarded.

I wish I could end on a positive note vis-à-vis the Palestinians. But tragically, although thousands of exceptional minds have written articles, essays, papers and books on the two-state solution, that if placed end to end would probably circle the earth a number of times, we are no further forward now than we were in 1967. If anything, the Palestinians are in a far worse plight.

On the one hand, Hamas – an extremist Palestinian organisation, an offshoot of the Muslim Brotherhood, supported by Iran – has hijacked Gaza and does not believe in holding peace negotiations with Israel which it refuses to recognise on any terms. And on the other, Arafat's successor, President Mahmoud Abbas, seems to have thrown in the towel after hitching his people's fortunes to Washington, getting nothing at all in return.

In a last ditch resort, against fierce opposition from the US and Israel, he took his case to the United Nations hoping that the international community would recognise the Palestinians unilateral declaration of a state and allow it full membership of the UN General Assembly. The only UN Security Council member state to block that attempt using its power of veto was the US, which many thought was the ultimate in hypocrisy when, in the early days of his presidency, President Obama had championed a Palestinian state based broadly on 1967 borders with land swaps and had loudly condemned Israel's ongoing expansion of Jewish settlements on the West Bank as well as its incessant demolition of Palestinian homes in East Jerusalem.

It's a tendency in the West to blame the Palestinians for the impasse, even though we learned via papers leaked to Qatari news channel, Al Jazeera that Abbas and his negotiating team led by Chief Negotiator Saeb Erekat had made unprecedented concessions to Israel in December 2009, which were turned down by the Israeli Foreign Minister, Tzipi Livni.

I was stunned when I heard that such secret concessions made by the Palestinian leadership included the 'biggest Jerusalem in history', joint Israeli-Palestinian supervision of the Haram al-Sharif – and an agreement that any future Palestinian state would be demilitarised. Palestinian negotiators were allegedly willing to accept Israel's annexation of all Jewish settlements on the West Bank barring one and discussed the transfer of Israeli Arabs to the new state.

The credibility of the Palestinian leadership has been shot. Israel has been exposed as the side that can't say yes. Western newspapers are writing obituaries on the death of the peace process. Barring a miracle, 'where oh where do we go from here?' Gaza is still under a total Israeli blockade and is vulnerable to regular Israeli air strikes. Thousands of Palestinian detainees are locked inside Israeli prisons without being charged or tried under the Jewish state's monstrous policy it calls administrative detention; more than a thousand have been on a prolonged hunger strike in protest. In June 2012, President Mahmoud Abbas accused Israel of deliberately destroying any chance of a two-state solution with its settlement policy and pronounced the peace process as "clinically dead".

Where is my old friend Arafat when he's needed? Probably spinning in his mausoleum in Ramallah. A 2012 Al Jazeera-instigated investigation indicates that he may have been slowly poisoned with Polonium-210, a radioactive isotope that can only be manufactured by governments, after a Swiss laboratory tested his clothing and found traces of the poisonous substance. If he was assassinated, then whoever was behind it thought they had consigned both Arafat and the peace process to the same grave. If so, they were wrong. As long as there is a single olive tree struggling to survive in Palestine, the Palestinian people will never give up on their own struggle, no matter how long it takes.

I'm only one man, but I won't give up either. On 5 July 2012, I wrote the following letter to President Jimmy Carter:

To President Jimmy Carter
Dubai, 5 July 2012

Dear Mr President,

I apologise for not being able to see you in Europe during your visits. I hope you and your family are in good shape and health.

I enclose a proposal and its essence and main points I believe warrant further debate. I would very much like to ask your opinion on how we can progress the points I make in some form of dialogue.

My idea is to bring together like-minded colleagues from Palestine, Israel, Egypt and the GCC in a conference to be held at a mutually acceptable location, and hammer out these points to form a solution to be presented in a cohesive document.

I would value your comments on this idea and your suggestions for participants. I look forward to progressing this very important issue.

Best regards,
Khalaf Ahmad Al Habtoor

An excerpt of my proposal, published in its entirety on page 561 of this book's appendices, is as follows:

Palestinian/Israeli Resolution

Plan B

I would suggest a meeting to discuss the following stipulations, keeping in mind that these points will not take away from the fact that Palestinians will always consider Palestine as their motherland.

The meeting agenda will discuss:

1. The 'refugee' status must be lifted and Palestinians must be allowed to be true residents in the country in which they presently reside.
2. They must have access to first-class education and training so that they can gain skills that can benefit both their families and their newly adopted homelands.
3. Creating a Housing Fund, supported internationally, for the construction of homes for Palestinians in the appropriate designated homeland.

4. A reasonable/feasible approach should also be taken with respect to Israel, again for the sake of Palestinians. So rather than battling over this sacred soil beloved by all Abrahamic prophets, Israelis and Arabs must find a way to peacefully coexist.

5. A committee should be appointed made up of respected Palestinians, Israelis and selected representatives from Arab states to negotiate directly with the Israeli government.

6. Talks should be without preconditions on both sides with one exception: Israeli settlement expansion should come to a halt; the reasons for this are obvious.

With hope of success I suggest this, but if all fails or an independent Palestinian state is no longer practical in the light of realities on the ground, Palestinians should be offered the choice to pursue either a 'one-state solution' or an autonomous region within an Israeli/Palestinian federation.

We must work together to try and give our Palestinian brothers a decent life, an existence which we take for granted. Likewise, a good outcome from this will affect Israelis positively and will allow them to live peacefully with the Palestinians instead of living behind isolating high walls.

I am currently involved in discussions with the Carter Center as to the best way of bringing my proposal into fruition. I trust President Carter. I know for sure that he is passionate about finding solutions to this more than six decade-long impasse.

If a business plan is clearly unworkable, it is shredded to make way for a new one. Talks between Israel and Palestinian negotiators – whether direct or via US intermediaries – have produced nothing. So it's nothing short of madness to continue down that same twisting path to nowhere. The old paradigm hasn't worked because:

a. Israel prioritises retaining land and security concerns over peace concessions and has become comfortable with the status quo.

b. The international community either cannot or will not come together to hold Tel Aviv accountable for its numerous breaches of international law.

c. The US can't be a just broker when president after president has sworn before AIPAC to safeguard Israel's interests and is wary of falling foul of America's estimated 40 million Christian Zionists who hold that the return of Jews to Israel is a prerequisite to the Second Coming of Jesus.

d. The Palestinian National Authority has little clout and few bargaining chips.

e. Palestinians have no effective leader and are split between Fatah and Hamas. This means Israel has no single partner for peace who enjoys the support of all the Palestinian people.

Palestinians must accept that alone they lack enough power to their elbow to negotiate successfully with the Israeli/American virtual monolith. They've tried long and hard. They need to appoint decision-makers among their ranks, flexible individuals, to work with representatives from Gulf States to form a negotiating committee that might also include leading lights from politically stable Arab countries as well as Israelis who genuinely believe in a two-state solution and who sincerely crave peace.

Israelis should realise that the 'Arab Spring' has produced a more hostile and unpredictable neighbourhood. The clouds of war are gathering in the distance. I would ask the Israeli people to use their imaginations; and to envision full diplomatic and economic relations with all twenty-two Arab League countries, open borders, cultural exchanges and business opportunities. Israel would no longer need to spend 7 per cent of its GDP annually on defence. Israeli mothers would no more be forced to hand their sons and daughters as conscripts to the military.

I would ask the Israeli people to put aside their preconceptions about Arabs, go beyond the anti-Arab propaganda long enough to talk with us, truly see us for what we are. People who suffer, hope, fear, pray; people who love their parents and children; people with ambition who dream of a better world. People just like them.

CHAPTER 19
Today and Tomorrow

"LEARN FROM YESTERDAY, LIVE FOR TODAY, HOPE FOR TOMORROW. THE IMPORTANT THING IS NOT TO STOP QUESTIONING."

– ALBERT EINSTEIN

One of the highlights of my annual calendar is the renewal of my acquaintanceship with Her Majesty Queen Elizabeth II at the annual Royal Windsor Cup polo challenge, held at the Guards Polo Club in Windsor Great Park, where we jointly present the winning trophies.

I've met several kings, princes and presidents over the decades, and had the privilege of spending time with the Queen's daughter, Princess Anne, and her ex-husband, Captain Mark Phillips, during the 1980s, when I hosted them at the Metropolitan Hotel, where they participated in an equestrian event. The Princess later invited me to a celebration at London's City Hall, which I attended with my wife. Among all the selected invitees, we were the only Arabs. But she went out of her way to make us feel comfortable by including in her speech: "We have friends that have come a long way to attend this event".

I've also enjoyed several meals with the Queen's cousin, Prince Michael of Kent; the last one was at Kensington Palace where, in June 2009, a lovely lunch was served in a tent erected in the palace grounds. "Khalaf, you will not feel that you are a stranger," he told me and indeed I was reminded of our days in the desert (except that there were clean toilets on hand). It was an opportunity to get to know businessmen from all over the world and to discuss the state of the economy and various global trends with the Prince.

However, I must admit that the first time I was introduced to the great lady herself, Queen Elizabeth, I was nervous. Not because she is of royal blood. To me, she is not only a living legend, but also the personification of female dignity and honour. Since 2 June 1953, she has dutifully and selflessly served her nation and the Commonwealth without once taking a wrong step.

I think of her as the Queen of the World and can't help but feel sorry that some of her subjects fail to appreciate the important role the British monarchy plays in differentiating the UK from its European neighbours, and I'm saddened that a succession of British governments have put pressure on the Royal House to trim its expenses. Expecting the head of the Royal Family to live on a shoestring budget will eventually shatter the House of Windsor's mystique.

You only have to remember what a boost the 2011 wedding of her grandson Prince William to Kate Middleton and the Queen's Diamond Jubilee, celebrated in 2012, were to Britons' spirits at a time of economic hardship, to understand that the British royals earn every penny they receive from taxpayers.

I wasn't at all sure how Queen Elizabeth should be addressed and was thankful when the fine points of protocol were explained to me by one of her aides, who said she should initially be addressed as 'Your Majesty' and subsequently as 'Ma'am'. I'm sure that most people feel as I did before meeting the Queen, but she has the knack of putting people at ease almost immediately with the warmth of her smile, her gracious charm and natural wit. To whomever she speaks, she looks them straight in the eye and for a fleeting moment makes them feel that they are the most important person on the planet.

I'm always amazed at her incisive knowledge of polo and her enthusiasm for the game. When she saw my grandsons challenging my sons during the Royal Windsor Cup, she asked me about my family and noted that, since we have two teams of Al Habtoors, we don't need to hire players from outside.

I thanked her for her encouragement and sent her a letter upon my return to Dubai, saying how honoured I would be should she consent to visit my family and I at home during her next visit to the UAE. She answered immediately to acknowledge my invitation. I don't know if she will be able to fit such a visit into her busy schedule, but, if it ever happens, it will be the greatest honour of my life.

I sense that family is everything to the Queen as it is to me. I have twenty-five grandchildren at the latest count, aged between one and twenty-one, and I get to see many of them daily when I'm in Dubai. The eldest, Tariq and Habtoor, both twenty-one years old, are mad about polo and are excellent players.

Rashid's son Tariq, whose mother is English, served for a year in the British Army and is now doing a degree in mechanical engineering at

Kingston University. Tariq is one of my favourite grandsons. I am very proud of him because he has shown himself to be a very responsible young man. I always try to see him whenever I'm in the UK. He doesn't stay in my English home as it's too long a drive to his university, but I always make sure that he comes to the house and spends a few days with me when I'm there. I miss him greatly and am thrilled when we get quality time with him in Dubai, which is often. I love the children of Rashid and his wife dearly, but don't see them as regularly as I do the others, primarily because they live away from the family compound.

Habtoor, the son of my son Mohammed and his wife Aysha, affectionately known as 'Knight', is equally special in my eyes; he's my pride and joy. He is very much his own man. He has his own ideas about everything. He's handsome, strong and very confident. He's also a health and fitness nut like me. He reminds me of myself when I was his age in so many ways. He relishes all kinds of sports and is the most accomplished polo player in the family. He wants everyone in the family to be as fit as possible and is currently on his Uncle Ahmad's case.

Ahmad's doctor has advised him to work out regularly in the gym to build up his strength and Habtoor has taken it upon himself to monitor his uncle's progress. Even when he's out of the country, he'll call Ahmad's personal trainer to make sure his uncle doesn't slack – and woe betide Ahmad should he miss a session when Habtoor harasses him until he promises to make up for lost time.

Habtoor likes to do things his own way. When he played in the 2011 Al Habtoor Royal Windsor Cup, he wore his hair long like some of the 'glamorous' Argentine players. I told him that I disapproved of his new style. As far as I'm concerned, long hair detracts from a man's masculinity and, unless it's kept scrupulously clean, isn't very hygienic.

I tried my best to convince him to have a haircut. He promised he would, when he returned to Dubai. "I'm sure that there are excellent coiffeurs here in the UK," I told him. "Maybe," he replied. "But my personal hair stylist is in Dubai and I'm afraid those guys will ruin my look." If I had dared to grow my own hair long when I was young, my father or elder brother would have given me a clip around the ears and a short back and sides.

Knight's latest craze is boxing, which he took up instead of weight lifting so as to stay lean and fast on his feet. Not long ago, he joined me on the terrace of my beach bungalow and told me, "*Abouya* (my father), I've become very good at boxing. What would you think if I became a boxing champion?" I must admit that I was taken aback. "Who are you? Mohammed Ali? Polo is a great sport. You should concentrate on excelling at that," I said.

Habtoor enthusiastically argued his case, saying boxing was a manly profession, adding "If I am strong, I can protect the family." "Protect the family by using your brains, not your fists," I told him laughing. I'm sure he'll change his mind if he finds himself walking around with a cauliflower nose or a blackened eye one of these days.

After he completed his first year at university, I told him that I wanted him to marry and that I would be happy to choose his wife. I wasn't serious; I just wanted to test the waters and get his reaction.

"Do you have a nice girl in mind, Habtoor?" I asked him.

"No *Abouya*, I'm single and ready to mingle." That's his favourite line nowadays; he uses it all the time. Only Habtoor could come up with such an answer. I still laugh every time I think of it.

On an earlier occasion, while I was hosting dinner in my private majlis for a group of friends, Habtoor popped in to greet my guests. I told everyone there about his upcoming move to Los Angeles for his studies when, instead of introducing himself as my grandson, he described himself as my friend.

"Is that right?" I asked him.

"Of course, we will travel together and go out. I am going to be your wingman," he announced with a grin.

My second youngest grandchild, Mohammed's three-year-old son Khalaf, has me wrapped around his little finger and there's nothing I can do about it. He's cute, chubby and loves to eat. We call him 'Tike', because each time his siblings try to take food from his hand, he would hit them and make them cry. That reminded me of the lovable bulldog in *Tom and Jerry*, who would bite anyone that dared to go near his bowl.

Since almost the day Tike was born, I would cuddle him on my lap and Eeda, his nanny, would bring him for breakfast to receive his morning kiss. It was a real pleasure for me, because he was a baby who smiled and gurgled more than he cried. Nowadays, Tike is brought to my office each morning, where he amuses himself pulling pens out of my pocket and playing with objects on my desk; sometimes he attends my morning briefing to the directors, sitting all the while on my lap.

As soon as he gets bored, he walks around calling for his nanny in a deep voice as if he's commanding her to follow him because "I'm leaving". I've never been one to play with young children for more than an hour at a time, but Tike I just can't resist. He doesn't allow me to walk away from our games; he always gestures for me to stay and, nine times out of ten, I give in.

Tike has started to call everyone he knows named Khalaf – and there are many Khalafs in our family – 'Katan'. I don't know how he came up with this nickname, nobody does. As soon as I came to know this, I instructed everyone not to call me 'Khalaf' or '*Abouya* Khalaf' in his presence, so I don't end up with this weird nickname like my unfortunate namesakes. My plan worked. I was pleased. But it was short-lived.

Lately, I have set up a play area for Tike and his cousin Khalaf bin Ahmad within our office gym, a place where they can entertain themselves while waiting until I'm free each morning and where they won't disturb my employees. It wasn't long before young Tike barged into my office with his nanny and cousin in tow. He was laughing and clearly happy about something. I dotingly smiled back until my worst fear manifested. "*Abouya* Katan, *Abouya* Katan, *Abouya* Katan," he said over and over. Somebody must have blown the whistle.

Mohammed's daughters, Noura, Shamma and Hamda are all very different from one another. Noura is quiet and calm and never raises her voice. She is very close to both of us, but especially to my wife. Shamma is very pretty with beautiful facial features and has a similar personality to her father.

Whenever my granddaughters want something, Shamma is their appointed spokesperson. If the girls plan to go somewhere, she is the one who decides where they will go and what they will do. The youngest of Mohammed's girls, Hamda, is petite and used to be pale and sylphlike. I used to call her 'Pascale', because she reminded me of a star in a movie with the same name.

I have another grandson called Khalaf – my daughter Noura's son Khalaf Al Qamzi, whom I spoke about in an earlier chapter. He's the most highly spirited one of the family. He's almost six now, but when he was younger he would drive my wife mad breaking things in the house and hitting anyone who got in his way. Now that he's older and has taken to football, he's even worse. He goes around kicking everyone. I tell his mother that she should start looking for a good lawyer to deal with 'Al Qamzi's' troubles with the law when he grows up.

Noura has four daughters, Oosha, Hamda, Maryam and Meera, who is Khalaf's twin; and two sons – twelve-year-old Mohammed and, of course, the lovable imp, Khalaf.

My daughter Amna, whom we know as 'Dina', has a wonderful daughter called Hamda aka 'Hamham'. As I mentioned earlier, we call her 'the Princess'. She's dignified, serene and clever – and loves working on her computer. I know Hamda very well because she and her mother live with us in the same house and, due to her exemplary character, I consider her to be especially precious.

Ahmad, my youngest son, is married to my cousin Fatima Al Otaiba. They have three daughters, Noura, Maryam and Hamda; and one son, Khalaf, a four-year-old quiet and deliciously sweet child. Whenever I see him smile showing a mouthful of new teeth, I can't resist the urge to hold him close and kiss him. As young as he is, Khalaf's passion is cars. Once we were together being driven through London, and he was visibly excited at seeing so many cars, animatedly pointing with his tiny forefinger at the smartest, saying over and over, "Look *Abouya*! *Sayyara* (car) up, *sayyara* down. So many *sayyara*!". The little guy must have inherited his love of vehicles from his father, who heads Al Habtoor Motors.

Whenever Tike and Khalaf come to my office in the morning, it's evident they're like chalk and cheese. Tike makes a lot of disturbing noise, while shy Khalaf smiles, cuddles me and attracts everyone with his considerable charm. I refer to the two Khalafs as 'the brain and the muscle'. Of course, 'the brain' is Khalaf bin Ahmad and Khalaf bin Mohammed is 'the muscle'.

I always remind Ahmad of the words of the Prophet Mohammed (PBUH), who said: "He who provides good upbringing to three daughters shall go to Paradise." Whenever I ask Ahmad about his daughters, I say "Where are the *debab al assal* (a Gulf term for 'pots of honey')?" Ahmad's wife is an excellent mother, who has brought up her daughters to be exceptionally ladylike and well behaved. Noura, the eldest, is only ten years old but she is organised and polite to everyone. When she was younger, I used to call her '*al walida*' (the mother), as she was named after my mother. She is very creative; she writes plays and calls her sisters and cousins to act under her direction. I was invited to one of Noura's productions and came away impressed with her talents.

Her sister Maryam was given the nickname '*al khalah*' (the aunt) because my mother's sister had the same name. Maryam reminds me of Hillary Clinton; she's very much the boss and, on occasion, I catch her soberly sitting like a fifty-year-old woman. She made me very proud in 2012 when I took her and my grandson Mohammed Al Qamzi to the Al Habtoor Royal Windsor cup to meet the Queen. When Her Majesty arrived, I introduced her to my grandchildren who had both been standing tall awaiting the honour. I was pleased that Maryam curtsied properly, but was astonished to hear her say "Congratulations on your Diamond Jubilee, Your Majesty" with amazing grown-up confidence. It was a real surprise because no one had coached her in advance. The Queen gave her an exceptionally warm smile and, judging by the glint in her eyes, was clearly impressed by Maryam's level of maturity at such a young age.

My friend Kyra Nagy, the well-known Hungarian tennis player, loves to visit Ahmad's daughters, especially Maryam, her favourite. Once, during the Holy month of Ramadan, when Maryam was just five, she told Kyra not to wear shorts when playing tennis with me. "It's Ramadan so you must cover up with long sleeves and trousers," she said with an air of seriousness.

Kyra laughed before replying, "You're right, but it's so hot nowadays that I need to wear shorts when I play. What can I do?" Maryam in her wisdom shot back with these words: "Easy, when you are hot you can pull your shirt away from your body by the waist so that the wind can enter and cool you down." Hamda's nickname is associated with her beautiful dark complexion. I'm always teasing her to see her lovely smile; she's an ebony princess, a family jewel, who's stolen my heart with her good-natured sense of humour.

My youngest daughter Meera is married to my cousin Abdullah Khalaf Al Otaiba (the brother of Ahmad's wife Fatima), and, as mentioned earlier, lives in Abu Dhabi. She is the only one of my children who isn't nearby. Their six-year-old son Khalaf and four-year-old daughter Metha are both adorable. Metha, aka *'umm al gatagit'* (a term of endearment literally translated to 'mother of the curly-haired') is so attached to her mother and father that she doesn't like to be around anyone else. I give her plenty of hugs whenever I see her, but she usually makes me laugh by telling me, "I don't like you." I'm not at all offended, because she feels the same way about everyone else. Metha's mother and grandmother recently took her on a holiday to Beirut and, when an old friend of theirs who has always treated Metha like her own granddaughter knocked on the door, she shouted "You! I don't like you." Metha doesn't care for anyone, a stage she will no doubt grow out of shortly.

Meera's youngest son, Mohammed, who is a little over seven months, is full of energy. He is a bundle of joy and once you see him, you have to fall in love with him, because the smile never leaves his face.

It's probably occurred to you that two of my children, Ahmad and Meera, are married to Al Otaibas. Ahmad's wife, Fatima, and Meera's husband,

Abdullah, are the children of Khalaf Ahmad Al Otaiba, one of my maternal uncles. I was happy to share my future bloodline with his own because I have always felt very close to him and very much enjoy our discussions on the UAE's economy and various political issues. Just being with him is an education in itself. He is intelligent, sharp-minded and quick to find solutions to problems. Like me, he has raised sons and daughters that have turned out to be well-educated adults enjoying respect within the community. I've rarely come across a father who has devoted so much time and thought to the education of his children or known sons and daughters who look up to their father in such an admiring and respectful fashion. Ours would be a better world if all parents concentrated on imbuing their young ones with knowledge and wisdom in the way that he's done. Without doubt, any father would be honoured to have children like Khalaf Ahmad Al Otaiba's and anyone would be privileged to be blessed with such a great man for a father.

I have a single hope for all my grandchildren: that they will be unafraid to pursue their dreams and wherever their paths take them, they will enjoy happy, healthy and fulfilled lives. I feel blessed that I'm still young and energetic enough to keep up with them.

Those rare times when all my children and my grandchildren come together are some of the happiest. It's on those occasions that I realise what the word 'immortality' truly means. None of us can live forever; we can extend our time on earth with a healthy lifestyle. Those who commit their bodies to a frozen state in cryogenic centres in hopes of being revived in the future simply don't get it. Immortality rests in one's genetic make-up that is passed on through the generations as well as the legacies and good works we leave behind us. At the same time, I don't understand those people – often gifted people with everything to live for – who seek to end their lives prematurely when each moment is a God-given gift to be appreciated and savoured.

However, if some genius were to invent a pill guaranteeing eternal life, I would consider taking it only if I were certain that I could continue to alleviate pain and suffering around the world, which is what I've always tried to do within the limits of my capacity. I would welcome the opportunity to combat hunger, ensure all children had access to medical treatment and education, and give the less fortunate opportunities to excel. For instance, if I were given control over the zakat collected from Muslims, I would take that pill and pledge that no child would go to bed with gnawing hunger pains or be deprived of an education. Otherwise, I would happily throw that pill away and look forward to meeting my Maker.

I think my greatest achievement in life has been being able to help others all over the world. Whether it's giving help in a small way to a distressed individual, or a donation towards improved health and education, or aid to the victims of natural disasters, this is what gives me more pleasure than anything else in life.

I am also very proud of my sons' achievements and the men they've become. I'm proud of my daughters for their intelligence, pure hearts and the caring way they bring up their children. I am also proud of my businesses, which I built from zero to become one of the largest and strongest Group of Companies in the Middle East. I feel lucky to work with wise and experienced board members to whom I sometimes turn to for all manner of advice, and very much appreciate my capable and loyal English personal assistant, Elizabeth 'Liz' Tidd, who, since she joined me in 1990 at the age of twenty, has always called me 'Mr K.', because in the early days she was unable to pronounce my name. I consider Liz, who now has a family of her own, a member of mine; my wife and children all adore her.

In one sense my companies are an extension of my family. A company is like a baby. When it is first born it requires 24/7 care and attention. When it's ailing it needs to be nurtured. When it's successful it requires constant supervision. It's a living, breathing entity, into which its founder has poured energy and creativity. As long as its parent is mentally agile, physically fit and well, it should never be abandoned.

It goes without saying that sometimes a person has no choice but to retire due to advanced age or incapacity. Before that day comes, he should delegate responsibilities to his successors, so that he can keep a close eye on their executive and management skills. If the time arrives when my job no longer gives me personal or professional satisfaction, I'll consider retiring.

An article by William Wolff, published in *The Times* under the heading 'Retirement kills love, it kills dignity and it kills people' delves into this topic: "The tales of men who were fit and healthy on their pensionable 65th birthdays and dead before their 66th are too many to be airily dismissed as anecdotal," he writes. "With retirement their lives had suddenly lost their meaning. And with that loss of purpose, direction and structure, the will to go on living seeped out of them." George Bernard Shaw once said, "A perpetual holiday is a good working definition of hell." I second that.

I can never forget that my group of companies employs thousands, which is an enormous responsibility. To ensure the longevity of my companies, I plan to launch IPOs (first sale of stock to the public) as soon as I consider the market to be stable enough. This might happen in 2013 depending on 2011 and 2012 financial results. Public companies don't die. They continue with their new owners, the shareholders. Problems with family-owned companies can arise with the demise of the proprietor, which often leads to family in-fighting. So many thriving businesses are destroyed in that way and all too often a company's name is buried with its founder. I want my companies – my babies, if you like – to flourish generation after generation. But all that is for tomorrow.

Right now, I have many business plans for the future; some are already in the construction phase, others are still on the drawing board.

One of the most challenging and worthwhile projects that is still under construction is the biggest hotel complex in Dubai that will be sited on 1 million square feet alongside Sheikh Zayed Road where the Metropolitan Hotel, now demolished, once stood.

The project encompasses three large five-star hotels offering 1,675 rooms and suites, an entertainment theatre and 500,000 square feet of landscaped gardens. The hotels – Dubai's first St Regis Hotel, a stylish W Hotel and a Westin – will be operated by Starwood Hotels and Resorts Worldwide Inc. Each hotel will offer distinct food and beverage outlets and signature spas.

Scheduled to open towards the end of 2013 is my 324-room resort hotel on the man-made island Palm Jumeirah to be operated by Hilton Worldwide's luxury brand Waldorf Astoria Hotels & Resorts – the brand's first resort in Dubai. As long ago as 1932, arguably the planet's best-known hotelier, Conrad Hilton, wrote 'The Greatest of Them All' on a photograph of the New York Waldorf Astoria because it epitomised his dream. I can relate to how he felt because in many ways the new hotel will bring to life a vision I've long been nurturing.

I first bought the land when its reclamation from the sea began in 2001, but I didn't want a rushed job. The setting is so beautiful that I knew my new hotel had to be something special, something aesthetically unforgettable. It is designed for guests seeking the highest standards in terms of facilities and quality, which is why I was keen to tie up with the internationally acclaimed Waldorf Astoria, a brand associated with impeccable service and old world elegance. Surrounded by the Arabian Sea, the hotel will offer panoramic views of the city, its own private beach, a serenity spa, a health club incorporating a state-of-the-art gym, swimming pools, tennis and squash courts – plus six themed restaurants.

Whenever I travel abroad, whether on pleasure or business, I constantly assess a destination's investment potential and business-friendly climate. In June 2012, my group acquired the 218-room historic Le Méridien Budapest, set close to the River Danube in Hungary's capital city. I fell in love with the property, already an important city landmark, at first sight and was pleased when feasibility studies supported my instinct to buy it. Also in 2012 I entered into an agreement with Hilton Worldwide to operate my two hotels in Beirut that have now been renamed The Hilton Beirut Habtoor Grand and the Hilton Beirut Metropolitan Palace respectively.

On the construction front, I would like to see the Habtoor Leighton Group going global. I would love for that company, managed by Leighton Holding Australia, in which Leighton is a major shareholder, reaching all four corners of the globe. I know that Habtoor Leighton is poised to expand its operations and has a great future ahead of it.

It warms my heart that the Al Farooq Omar Ibn Al Khattab Mosque and Centre, from which I hope people from all over the UAE and the world will benefit, opened its doors just before the 2011 Holy Month of Ramadan. It is acknowledged to be the UAE's most beautiful mosque in terms of exterior and interior design and is the country's second biggest, the Sheikh Zayed Mosque in Abu Dhabi being the largest.

With classrooms, a lecture hall and a library, it aims to spread the true word of Islam, not the distorted version espoused by fanatics and extremists. It is the third in the UAE that welcomes visits from non-Muslims keen to learn about the world's fastest-growing religion. Its motto is 'moderation', which means that the mosque and associated facilities exist to illuminate worshippers' hearts and souls, not to indoctrinate them with fake interpretations or coercive methods, for there is no coercion in Islam.

I was pleased to see that an excess of 3,500 attended its inauguration on 29 July 2011 and over 5,000 prayed inside and outside the mosque during Laylat al-Qadr (the holiest night of Ramadan, when the first verses of the Qur'an were revealed to the Prophet). Each Friday, worshippers pack its interior for Friday prayers and I am gratified to have made this small contribution to my Emirati brothers and sisters, as well as the residents of the UAE and vistors, both Muslim and non-Muslim, which will live long after I am gone. I'm delighted to say that the mosque receives calls from the organisers of tour groups to book visits in advance of the foreign visitors' arrivals. Calls and e-mails have come from all over the world, from as far away as Germany and Japan.

The media interest has been phenomenal and overwhelmingly positive. Newspapers enthuse about the large sixty-man-strong team of Moroccan craftsmen and calligraphists, flown specially from Fez to Dubai to paint carved panels and affix mosaics of glazed tiles. Writers wax lyrical about its thirty-metre-high central dome resting on twenty-one half and full smaller domes, and its four majestic sixty-metre-high minarets.

One of the most heartfelt write-ups was written by a blogger calling herself Mich Café. Under the heading 'Dubai gets its Blue Mosque', the writer says, "The closer you get, the more splendid the mosque looks. The size is breathtaking and I had difficulty getting the four sixty-metre-high minarets in one photo frame. The domes are of different sizes and the stained glass windows sparkle in the morning sun."

The blogger visited the mosque in the middle of the morning "so as not to interfere with prayer times" and thanks a helpful security guard for shadowing her and lending her an abaya to wear while inside the mosque. "I walked around Dubai's blue Al Farooq Mosque for more than an hour, and kept discovering inscriptions, patterns, designs, mosaics and other little wonders," she writes. "As it starts to write its own history, I like to think that in the centuries to come, in the entries about the Al Farooq Mosque, I played a minuscule role in treading its new carpets." I know how she feels.

All in all, I have few regrets. Even the hard times have served me well. If you have never known a sour taste, how can you recognise what is sweet? Like everyone else, I've made mistakes, but consider each one to be a learning curve and I've done my utmost not to make the same mistake twice. Of course, I haven't fulfilled all my dreams, but God willing I still have plenty of time to get through most of my personal wish list.

Unfortunately, I never managed to attain my life's dream of meeting President Gamal Abdel Nasser, but I count myself fortunate to have known two of the greatest men of our time: Sheikh Zayed bin Sultan Al Nahyan and Sheikh Rashid bin Saeed Al Maktoum. I couldn't have asked for better role models to guide me through life.

Likewise, I appreciate having had the opportunity to spend time with President Jimmy Carter. Meeting people of such calibre is an education in itself. You can learn so much from such smart and intelligent men.

There are a few outstanding personalities that I hope to have the pleasure of talking with face to face one day. Topping the list is King Abdullah bin Abdulaziz of Saudi Arabia, who has made a lot of positive changes on behalf of his people, providing them with jobs, education and affordable housing. And also the former Malaysian Prime Minister, Mahathir Mohammed, who stabilised his country's economy and helped his nation prosper. During his time in office, Malaysia boasted zero unemployment and was a fearless, honest voice on the world's stage.

Prime Minister Recep Tayyip Erdoğan of Turkey is someone else I admire, especially because of his principled forthrightness and his determination to keep his people's interests at heart, whatever he does. Thanks to him, Turkey has regained its role as a regional leader and gained respect for being a moderate, progressive predominantly Islamic country that many consider should be a template for others in the area. He and his colleagues have overseen a booming economy, improved Turkey's relations with its neighbours and are fervent champions of a Palestinian state. The Arab world has much to learn from Turkey's example in my opinion.

You may be surprised to learn that the successful entrepreneur cum, former Italian Prime Minister Silvio Berlusconi is on my list because he is such a controversial figure; people either love him or hate him. I don't know much about his political achievements, but my admiration for him rests mainly on his ability to live life with a capital 'L', his sense of fun and love of beauty in all its forms. He's not afraid of doing his own thing and doesn't hide his love of women like most other politicians do. Some time ago, I sent the former Italian PM a letter inviting him to Dubai and enclosed a compilation of some of my articles in the form of a book. I was pleased to receive a reply acknowledging the book and thanking me for my invitation. I wish other world leaders were as courteous.

There is someone in my own field that I would like to meet. Wait for it... Donald Trump! In truth, I'm not a big fan of his personality or his world view, but I admire his positive attitude as well as his ability to bounce back time and time again from adversity.

Nelson Mandela is another great man I would like to meet, after learning all about his struggle against apartheid and his rare quality of being able to forgive those who imprisoned him for twenty-eight years and treated his fellows like lesser humans, undeserving of respect. To be able to forgive and move on for the greater good is something Mr Mandela shares with Mahatma Gandhi, who refused the spilling of blood to give India its independence from the Imperialist British Raj. I wish we could embrace a similar way of thinking in our Arab world. If only we were able to forget our hatred against others, forgive their faults and put all our efforts into a brighter tomorrow for everyone. I wonder will we ever learn, if not to love one another, at least to accept one another with clear, clean hearts.

I am proud of my generation who knew the meaning of hardship and struggle in a way that is incomprehensible to the youth of today. I recently lost one of my greatest friends and peers, the Emirati businessman, former diplomat and poet Mohammed Khalifa bin Hadher, known to me as 'Abu Khaled', who passed away suddenly while on holiday in Paris.

He was a walking encyclopedia on Arab history, culture and tradition. There was little he didn't know about the Arab world and he always had great respect for his Arab heritage. The UAE has lost one of its finest patriots and classical poets – and I am still mourning the absence of someone who was as close to me as a brother. I have urged Dubai's government to erect a monument to Mohammed bin Hadher, not only to remember him for his beautiful romantic poems that speak of the highest and purest forms of love, but also as a symbol of the principled men who helped change a small fishing and trading town into a byword for excellence worldwide.

We, my generation, did whatever we could and now we must get ready to pass the torch to those that come after us. It is my fervent hope that they in their own way will strive to keep it burning bright.

* * *

Everyone who reads this memoir will take something different from it. For some, it will be a small insight into the history of the Arab world and, in particular, the United Arab Emirates. Others may enjoy learning about our Gulf culture and traditions or be interested in my opinions on a range of topics from geopolitics to religion. Yet others will judge it to be a 'rags to riches' story, although even in the days when money was tight, blessed with dear parents, siblings, close friends and good health, I never for one minute thought of myself as poor. Perhaps a few will be inspired to pursue their ambitions even when they seem unattainable. I hope so!

I'll be happy if my stories about people I've known and the experiences and challenges that life has thrown my way have, at the very least, lifted your spirits a notch and has given you pause for thought.

My Life in Pictures

Aerial view of the districts of Deira and Bur Dubai, Dubai, 1952.

Aerial view of the Creek, Dubai, 1952.

My father, Ahmad bin Mohammed Al Habtoor (left) with my maternal uncles and my maternal grandfather, Ahmad bin Khalaf Al Otaiba (fourth from left).

The signing of the Abu Dhabi Petrol Concession Agreement in 1939. My maternal grandfather, Ahmad bin Khalaf Al Otaiba (left), my uncle Abdullah Ahmad Al Otaiba (far left in the back), Sheikh Shakhbut Al Nahyan, Ruler of Abu Dhabi (second from left, sitting), my maternal uncle, Rashid bin Ahmad Al Otaiba (right, sitting) and the British Petroleum (BP) representative (right, foreground).

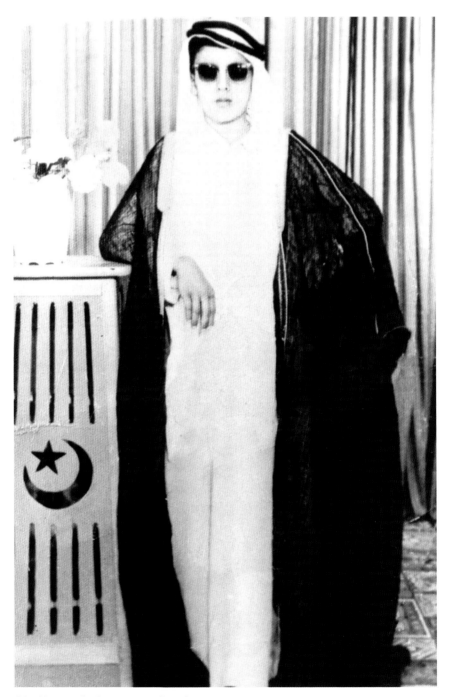

Myself, posing for the camera, in the early 1960s.

The majlis of Dubai's ruler Sheikh Saeed bin Maktoum, in the 1950s, filled with dignitaries. Present are my maternal grandfather Ahmad bin Khalaf Al Otaiba (on the facing wall, second from the left side) and my father Ahmad Al Habtoor (on the right side of the room).

Myself taking a ride on a donkey in Al Buraimi, Al Ain, in the late 1950s.

With my brother Sultan (left) during a trip in Denmark in the late 1960s.

With my brother Sultan (standing) in Parklands, my house in the UK, in the 1990s.

With my brother Sultan (centre) and my nephew Faisal Jassem (right) in Lebanon in the late 1960s.

With Said Saif bin Thaleth (centre) and Ismail Al Jarman (right) in Ra's al-Khaimah in 1963.

With Saif Mubarak Al Nakhi (left) on a visit to Egypt in the late 1960s.

With Obeid bin Butti Al Mulla (right) in front of the Telefric (cable car) in Jounieh, Lebanon, in the late 1960s.

With Saif Mubarak Al Nakhi (right) near the Pyramids in Egypt in the late 1960s.

In the late 1950s with some of my school colleagues and teachers in Al Shaabiya school. I am in the last back row on the left.

Sheikh Rashid bin Saeed Al Maktoum (left, foreground) at the opening of Al Ittihad Private School in 1975. I am sitting to his left and my daughter Noura is in the foreground.

In discussion with Sheikh Rashid bin Saeed Al Maktoum (left) and a dignitary (right) in the 1970s.

With Sheikh Rashid bin Saeed Al Maktoum (right) at the opening of Al Ittihad Private School in 1975.

Attending the ground breaking ceremony of the Dubai Petroleum Company in the early 1980s. On the right, in the foreground, is Sheikh Rashid bin Saeed Al Maktoum. Handling the shovel, to his right, is Yusef Shalabi, the engineer, and the President of Continental Oil Company, USA (far left of the picture).

Sheikh Rashid bin Saeed Al Maktoum (centre) with my maternal uncles Mohammed and Buty bin Ahmad Al Otaiba (far left), and my father Ahmad Mohammed Al Habtoor (far right) in the 1950s.

Sheikh Rashid bin Saeed Al Maktoum and Sheikh Zayed bin Sultan Al Nahyan to my far right and left at a celebratory event in the late 1970s.

Looking at plans with Sheikh Rashid bin Saeed Al Maktoum at the ceremony for laying the foundation stone of the Dubai Petroleum Complex in the early 1980s. On my right is engineer Yusef Shalabi; behind us is the President of Continental Oil Company, USA and far back is Riad Sadek.

> Sheikh Rashid quickly warmed to Abu Dhabi's new ruler, Sheikh Zayed, as an honourable man of like mind with a similar visionary outlook. Together they spearheaded the United Arab Emirates and closely cooperated to ensure the flourishing of the new federation comprising seven emirates, with Abu Dhabi as its capital.

Accompanying Sheikh Rashid bin Saeed Al Maktoum (centre right) at the ceremony for laying the foundation stone of the Dubai Petroleum Complex, in the early 1980s, along with the President of Continental Oil Company, USA (left).

With Sheikh Rashid bin Saeed Al Maktoum (right) and engineer Yusef Shalabi (left) reviewing plans at the ceremony for laying the foundation stone of the Dubai Petroleum Complex in the early 1980s.

In deep discussion with Sheikh Rashid bin Saeed Al Maktoum, the late ruler of Dubai, UAE Vice-President and Prime Minister.

Enjoying the view with Sheikh Rashid bin Saeed Al Maktoum (left)at the top of the World Trade Centre when it was under construction.

With Sheikh Rashid bin Saeed Al Maktoum (left) at the official opening of the Metropolitan Hotel on Sheikh Zayed Road in 1979.

> For someone who was brought up in a virtual village locked into earlier centuries, Sheikh Rashid was an exceptional visionary. Without his innovative approaches, my hometown wouldn't be the thriving, high-profile, modern wonder it is acknowledged to be today.

With Sheikh Rashid bin Saeed Al Maktoum (left) at the official opening of the Metropolitan Hotel on Sheikh Zayed Road in 1979.

My father Ahmad Mohammed Al Habtoor (centre) with Sheikh Rashid bin Saeed (left) in the 1950s.

Accompanying Sheikh Rashid bin Saeed Al Maktoum (right) at the ground breaking of the Dubai Petroleum Company in the early 1980s. The President of Continental Oil Company, USA, is behind me to my right.

With Sheikh Khalifa bin Zayed Al Nahyan, President of the UAE and Ruler of Abu Dhabi, in the late 1980s.

Sheikh Zayed's son, Sheikh Khalifa bin Zayed Al Nahyan, President of the UAE and Ruler of Abu Dhabi, is continuing his father's tradition. He has launched the Zayed Humanitarian Award in his father's memory, which recognises outstanding philanthropic works worldwide.

With Sheikh Hamdan bin Mohammed Al Nahyan, then Deputy Prime Minister (left) and Sheikh Abdul Aziz bin Mohammed Al Qassimi (centre), brother of the Ruler of Sharjah, in the late 1980s.

With Sheikh Hamad bin Mohammed Al Sharqi, Ruler of Fujairah (left), at the Al Habtoor Motors showroom opening in Fujairah in the 1990s.

With Sheikh Maktoum bin Rashid Al Maktoum at his majlis in the 1980s.

With Sheikh Mohammed bin Rashid Al Maktoum (left) at my sons Rashid and Mohammed's wedding in the early 1990s.

With General Sheikh Mohammed bin Zayed Al Nahyan, Crown Prince of Abu Dhabi and Deputy Supreme Commander of the UAE Armed Forces (left).

“Each year, I pay a courtesy visit to Sheikh Khalifa and his brother, Sheikh Mohammed bin Zayed, to show my respect and my appreciation of the way they are taking care of the country and faithfully holding on to their father's generous spirit.”

With Sheikh Hasher Al Maktoum (right) during the Horse Jumping show at the Metropolitan Hotel in the 1980s.

> On the prompting of my son Rashid, I had opened a horse racecourse within the hotel's grounds. Children and novices came for horse-riding lessons and adults wishing to ride into the desert or along the Jumeirah beach would hire a steed on an hourly basis. There was hardly a week when there wasn't something or the other going on.

With Sheikh Ahmad bin Saeed Al Maktoum, now President of the Department of Civil Aviation, CEO and Chairman of Emirates Group(left), and my brother Sultan Al Habtoor (right).

With Sheikh Hamdan bin Rashid Al Maktoum (left) in Newmarket in the UK.

With (in order, from my left) Sheikh Sultan bin Khalifa bin Zayed Al Nahyan, Sheikh Hamdan bin Rashid Al Maktoum, Sheikh Nayahan Mabarak Al Nahayan, Mohammed Khalifa Al Suwaidi and Mohammed bin Mijrin at the wedding of my sons Rashid and Mohammed in the early 1990s.

With Sheikh Mohammed bin Rashid Al Maktoum at my majlis in Dubai.

With Sheikh Sultan bin Khalifa Al Nahyan (second from the right) and Ahmad Al Badi, Minister of Health (left), at one of the Al Habtoor Group Anniversary parties.

With Sheikh Maktoum bin Rashid Al Maktoum, then Ruler of Dubai (second from left), Sheikh Hamdan bin Rashid Al Maktoum, then Finance Minister (second from right) and Sheikh Mohammed bin Rashid Al Maktoum, then Defence Minister (right).

With Sheikh Hamdan bin Rashid Al Maktoum, UAE Minister of Finance and Industry, and Deputy Ruler of Dubai (left). In the background, Sheikh Nahayan Mabarak Al Nahayan.

In discussion with Sheikh Hamdan bin Rashid al Maktoum (right) and Majid Al Futtaim (left).

At a social event with Sheikh Mohammed bin Rashid Al Maktoum.

I appreciate the way that Sheikh Mohammed bin Rashid continues in the spirit of his father, Sheikh Rashid, by encouraging people to work by giving them projects rather than cash handouts, while at the same time taking care of those who cannot care for themselves.

Enjoying a light moment with Sheikh Nahayan Mabarak Al Nahayan (right) in his palace in Abu Dhabi in October 2009.

"Sheikh Mubarak's son, Sheikh Nahayan Mabarak Al Nahayan, has inherited his father's good character. He is one of the most generous and welcoming hosts I know. He's always inviting people to his house for meals and he goes out of his way to make them feel at home, smiling and talking to everyone. He's also one of the most caring and energetic people I've ever met. He faithfully visits the sick to ensure they're being well taken care of and he often helps those afflicted with illness to get treatment abroad."

With Sheikh Nahayan Mabarak Al Nahayan (right) in his palace in Abu Dhabi in October 2009.

With Sheikh Hamdan bin Zayed Al Nahyan, Ruler's Representative in the Western Region of Abu Dhabi, in his palace in Liwa in Abu Dhabi in October 2009.

During a visit to Sheikh Hamdan bin Zayed Al Nahyan in his palace in Liwa in Abu Dhabi in October 2009, along with my brother Sultan (far right).

With Sheikh Hamdan bin Zayed Al Nahyan (right) in his majlis at his palace in Liwa in Abu Dhabi in October 2009 (with my brother Sultan and others).

With Sheikh Khalifa bin Zayed Al Nahyan, President of the UAE and Ruler of Abu Dhabi, in the Presidential Palace in 2010.

With (from right) my brother Sultan Al Habtoor, Sheikh Nahayan Mabarak Al Nahayan and Mohammed Al Habtoor in the Al Habtoor Head Office in 2010.

With Sheikh Sultan bin Mohammed Al Qassimi (right) at the American University of Sharjah (AUS) Career Fair in March 2011.

Accompanying Sheikh Mohammed bin Rashid Al Maktoum (centre) at the ATM, Dubai. My son Mohammed is second to the right.

With Sheikh Mohammed bin Rashid Al Maktoum (left) in my majlis during Ramadan in 2011. My brother Sultan Al Habtoor is on the right.

Posing for a photograph with my children: carrying my second daughter Amna, with my hand around Rashid. Next to him Noura and Mohammed; in Lebanon in the late 1970s.

Carrying my daughters Amna (right) and Noura, in Lebanon in the late 1970s.

Noura bint Khalaf (right) and Amna bint Khalaf.

My father Ahmad Mohammed Al Habtoor (centre) with my son Rashid (right) in the 1980s.

"My father never judged anyone based on
their monetary worth. He would always
tell me that I was as good as anyone else
regardless of their wealth or position. 'Don't
be intimidated by anyone!' Father would say.
'When you meet someone, whoever they
are, never cast your eyes downward. Look
them in the eye!"

From the left, my children Amna, Ahmad, Noura and in her lap Meera, in the early 1980s.

With my brother Mohammed (right), my father Ahmad Mohammed Al Habtoor (second from left) and Abou Saeed (nicknamed Shayboub, left) in my house in the UK in the 1980s.

My children Rashid (top right), Mohammed (left) and Noura in the late 1970s.

My estate in the UK.

With my son Ahmad in California while he was there studying in the 1990s.

“I am very proud of my sons' achievements
and the men they've become. I'm proud of my
daughters for their intelligence, pure hearts and
the caring way they bring up their children.”

With my son Ahmad (on the left) and his cousin Suhail Khalifa Al Habtoor at their graduation from California State University of Long Beach in 1999.

With my grandsons Tariq bin Rashid (left) and Habtoor bin Mohammed (right) at the Habtoor Grand Resort & Spa, Dubai, in April 2011.

With my grandson Habtoor in my house in Dubai in the winter 2010.

With my grandson Tariq in my house in London in the spring 2011.

Photographed with some of my grandchildren at Al Khawaneej Farm in 2010.

"Family is everything to me. I have twenty-five grandchildren at the latest count, aged between one and twenty-one, and I get to see many of them daily when I'm in Dubai. The eldest, Tariq and Habtoor, both twenty-one years old, are mad about polo and are excellent players."

With the Honourable Paul Findley, Former United States Representative at the 20th Congressional District of Illinois and member of the House of Middle East Committee (centre), taken during one of Mr Findley's lectures at the Metropolitan Hotel in the 1990s.

At the 181st Annual Commencement Ceremony at Illinois College, Jacksonville, Illinois, in May 2010, receiving my Honorary Doctorate of Humane Letters.

At the 181st Annual Commencement Ceremony at Illinois College, Jacksonville, Illinois, in May 2010, after receiving my Honorary Doctorate of Humane Letters.

At the Tree Dedication and Planting Ceremony at Illinois College, where Paul Findley (centre left) and I planted two white oak trees in front of the Whipple Hall, now hosting the Khalaf Al Habtoor Leadership Centre, in May 2010. Here with (from left) my son Rashid, President Stever and his wife.

> "The Khalaf Al Habtoor Leadership Center is a venue for lectures as well as home to a library containing Lincoln papers, memorabilia, furniture and personal items that Paul has donated to the college."

With my son Rashid (second from right) and Paul Findley's family in Jacksonville Illinois, in
May 2010.

In my house in Dubai with Paul Findley (centre right) and his family, with Dr Axel Steuer,
President of Illinois College (fourth from left, in the back) and his wife Loreli (centre, standing);
Novak Djokovic and his fiancée Jelena (right) and a group of friends.

During a meeting of the Dubai Chamber of Commerce. Seen in the picture are Sheikh Hasher Al Maktoum (right), Majid Al Futtaim (centre) and Abdulla Al Futtaim (left).

From left: Diab bin Hilal Al Nahyan, my maternal uncle Abdulla bin Ahmad Al Otaiba, Mohammed bin Ahmad bin Dismal, my father Ahmad bin Mohammed Al Habtoor, my maternal uncle Buty bin Ahmad Al Otaiba, Yusef Al Duwais, Hamed Al Ghaith.

With Habib bin Mohammed Ridha, Undersecretary of the Ministry of Information (left) and Mohammed Abdul Rahim Al Ali, Assistant Undersecretary of the Ministry of Defence (right).

Enjoying a meal at the Al Ain branch of Al Mulla, with Abdul Aziz bin Hadef (left), Khalil Awad (second from left) and Sultan Khalifa Al Habtoor (second from right), in the late 1960s.

With my cousin Otaiba Abdulla Al Otaiba.

With my friend composer Ibrahim Jumaa (right), standing in front of my house in the UK in the early 1980s.

With Ahmad Khalifa Al Suwaidi (left), Taryam Omran (second from left) and my uncle Khalaf bin Ahmad Al Otaiba (right).

With my old friends Saeed bin Majed Bilyohah (right) and Mohammed bin Hadher (left).

With Dr William Kalchoff (right) and Dr Athar (aka Arthur, left) in Houston, Texas.

With Dr Imtihan Jawdat at the graduation ceremony of my son Ahmad from California State University of Long Beach in 1999.

With Abdul Wahab Galadari.

With (from left) Hmouda bin Ali bin Hmouda, Minister of State for Internal Affairs, Khalfan Al Roumi, Minister of Information, Sheikh Humaid Al Mualla, Minister of Planning, and Sultan Al Owais, one of UAE's biggest traders and founder of the National Bank of Dubai, at my sons Mohammed and Rashid's wedding.

With British Actor Oliver Tobias (centre) at an event in the Monkey Island Hotel, UK, in the early 2000s.

Actor Bruce Willis with my son Mohammed Al Habtoor at the Metropolitan Palace Hotel, Dubai.

Model Cindy Crawford with Sultan Al Habtoor during her stay at the Metropolitan Palace Hotel, Dubai.

The Metropolitan Hotel's guests included royalty, politicians, celebrities and Hollywood movie stars, including Omar Sharif, Bruce Willis, Wesley Snipes, Patrick Swayze, Jean-Claude Van Damme, Sylvester Stallone, super models Cindy Crawford and Naomi Campbell – and not forgetting Princess Anne and her first husband, Mark Phillips.

NBA player Rony Seikaly with Mohammed Al Habtoor at the Metropolitan Palace Hotel, Dubai.

With Apollo 11 astronaut Buzz Aldrin at my residence in the UK in 2007 (on 20 July 1969 Buzz was the second human being to set foot on the Moon, following mission commander Neil Armstrong).

With actress and musician Anita Harris and England cricketers David Gower (left) and Allan Lamb (right) at a charity cricket match held at Sir John Paul Getty II's house in Buckinghamshire, UK.

With Sir John Paul Getty II at a charity cricket match held at his house in Buckinghamshire, UK.

With actor Jean-Claude Van Damme at the hotel Prince De Galles in Paris in the 1990s.

With Sir David Frost in 2011 at my residence in Parklands, UK.

Like most people I spoke to in the UK,
Sir David was highly critical of Silvio
Berlusconi's affairs concerning various
young women. 'What's the big deal?' I told
him. 'I've never met Mr Berlusconi, but I
admire his appetite for love and life.' After all,
he's a son of one of the world's most free-
living, romantic countries.

With actor Omar Sharif at the Metropolitan Beach Resort (now Habtoor Grand Resort & Spa) in the 1990s.

With actor Don Johnson in 2011 at the Habtoor Grand Resort & Spa, Dubai.

With Ahmad Al Jarallah, Editor in Chief of the renowned Al Sayassah Newspaper *in Kuwait, at my majlis in Dubai during Ramadan 2011.*

With Imran Khan, the famous Pakistani cricketer turned politician, at the Metropolitan Hotel in Dubai in the late 1990s.

Sheikh Rashid bin Saeed Al Maktoum inaugurating the Metropolitan Hotel in Dubai in February 1979.

With Sheikh Rashid bin Saeed Al Maktoum (centre) at the inauguration of the Metropolitan Hotel in February 1979.

> The Metropolitan Hotel was finally inaugurated in 1979 by Sheikh Rashid. When I asked him whether he was pleased with the finished result, he said 'It's lovely, but I can't help thinking it looks like a donkey tied up in a swamp.'

With Sheikh Rashid bin Saeed Al Maktoum (right) and Dhahi Khalfan at the official opening of the Metropolitan Hotel on Sheikh Zayed Road, in February 1979.

With senior executives from Mitsubishi Motors in Dubai in the early 1980s.

With senior executives from Mitsubishi Motors in Dubai in the early 1980s.

With Reijiro Kuromizu, executive Vice-President of Mitsubishi Motors Corporation (centre right) opening Al Habtoor Motors showroom in Dubai in October 1997.

With Sheikh Hamad bin Mohammed Al Sharqi, then Ruler of Fujairah (centre), at the opening of Al Habtoor Motors showroom in Fujairah in October 1994.

> With the Mitsubishi franchise, Al Habtoor Motors was born. In the years that followed, we added Bentley, Rolls Royce and Aston Martin to our stable. More recently, the Turkish coach and truck manufacturers Temsa, McLaren sports cars, and the crème de la crème of luxurious, high-speed cars, Bugatti were great additions to our showrooms.

With Sheikh Mohammed bin Rashid Al Maktoum at the inauguration of the Metropolitan Hotel on Sheikh Zayed Road in February 1979.

With Osamu Masuko, President of Mitsubishi, at the Dubai Motor Show in November 2007.

Our Japanese partners knew that we were
a young, energetic and enthusiastic team
and saw how successful we had been
in construction and in our other business
ventures. We were always transparent with one
another, which laid a solid foundation of trust.

The ground-breaking ceremony of the Metropolitan Palace Hotel (now Hilton Beirut Metropolitan Palace) in Beirut, Lebanon, in the late 1990s.

With super model Naomi Campbell presenting awards to graduates of Emirates International School with Mohammed and Sultan Al Habtoor (first and second from right).

Speaking at the fortieth anniversary of Al Habtoor Group gala dinner in April 2010.

With a Japanese group visiting me in my office at Al Habtoor Engineering in Deira in the late 1980s.

With my PA Liz and Riad Sadik at the Employee Excellence Award in January 2008.

With Captain Mark Philips (left), Sultan Al Habtoor (right) and Ambassador John Limbert (second from right) at an event held at the Metropolitan Hotel in Dubai.

With Sheikh Mohammed bin Rashid Al Maktoum visiting Metroplex Cinema in the late 1990s.

> I am proud of my businesses, which I built from zero to become one of the largest and strongest Group of Companies in the Middle East. I feel lucky to work with wise and experienced board members to whom I sometimes turn to for all manner of advice.

With Sheikh Mohammed bin Rashid Al Maktoum cutting the ribbon at the official opening of the Metropolitan Palace Hotel in Deira, Dubai, in the 1990s.

With the President of Kazakhstan, Nursultan Nazarbayev (centre) and Saif Ahmad Al Ghurair (left).

President George H.W. Bush, the 41st president of USA, being greeted by Mohammed Al Habtoor during a visit to the USO offices at the Metropolitan Hotel Dubai in the mid-1990s.

*With Benazir Bhutto, former Prime Minister of Pakistan, at the World Forum held in April 2007
at the Habtoor Grand Resort & Spa, Dubai. She is holding an Arabic edition
of* My Vision: Challenges in the Race for Excellence *by HH Sheikh Mohammed bin
Rashid Al Maktoum.*

> As a young boy, my biggest ambition was
> to one day own my own shop. Never in
> my wildest imagination did I ever envisage
> that I would one day be the Chairman of a
> respected international group of companies
> employing thousands; or that I would mingle
> with royalty, world leaders, politicians,
> tycoons, bankers and intellectuals.

With HRH Prince Michael of Kent during his visit to my office in Dubai.

With President Jimmy Carter at my farm in Khawaneej, Dubai, in 2009.

With HRH Princess Anne as my guest in Dubai and Sheikh Hasher Al Maktoum (second from left) attending the horse show at the Metropolitan Hotel in Dubai in the 1980s.

With HRH Prince Philip, Duke of Edinburgh, at a charity cricket match held at Getty II's house in Buckinghamshire in the UK.

With HE Rustam Minnikhanov. President of Tatarstan, during a visit to Tatarstan, November 2010.

I was positively surprised at how intelligent, energetic, easy-going and down-to-earth President Carter is, but what impressed me most were his human qualities. He is a person with genuine concern for humanity's problems and is a good human being.

With President Jimmy Carter and some of my grandchildren at my farm in Khawaneej, Dubai, in 2009.

With Gerhard Fritz Kurt Schröder, Chancellor of Germany from 1998 to 2005, in Berlin, in the early 2000s.

With Prince Khaled bin Talal bin Saoud (centre) and my son Mohammed Al Habtoor in my residence in Dubai in the 1990s.

With Dr Abdul Salam Al Majali, Prime Minister of Jordan, in my residence in Dubai.

With the late Palestinian leader Yasser Arafat.

Greeted by Prince Turki bin Abdullah bin Abdulaziz in Beirut Airport in October 2009.

With Sheikh Subah Al Ahmad Al Jaber Al Subah, President of Kuwait, at the Habtoor Grand Hotel in Lebanon 2010.

With the Emir of Qatar, Sheikh Hamad bin Khalifa Al Thani at an event in Dubai in the early 2000s.

With my brother Sultan Al Habtoor (left) visiting Sheikh Hamad bin Jassim bin Jaber Al Thani, the Prime Minister of Qatar, in Qatar in 2010.

With the Palestinian leader Yasser Arafat in the 1970s.

❝ When Arafat was given permission to address the United Nations General Assembly, his legitimacy opened the door for the PLO to forge relationships with world leaders. 'Today, I have come bearing an olive branch and a freedom fighter's gun. Do not let the olive branch fall from my hand,' he famously told UN delegates. ❞

At the first Al Habtoor Tennis Challenge in 1998 with Sheikh Hasher Al Maktoum (left), my brother Sultan (fourth from left) and the winner Kira Nagy (centre).

At the Al Habtoor Tennis Challenge 2003, with singles match winner, former #1 Jelena Jankovic, WTA Ranking 2003, 2008 (centre). Also seen in the picture are Sheikh Hasher Al Maktoum, President of the Tennis Federation of the UAE (second from left), and my brother Sultan Al Habtoor.

The Al Habtoor Tennis Challenge 2003 singles match winner, former #1 Jelena Jankovic, WTA Ranking 2003, 2008.

At the thirteenth Al Habtoor Tennis Challenge 2010, with singles match winner Sania Mirza, world #27, WTA ranking 2007, and runner up Bojana Jovanovski, world #50, WTA Ranking 2011.

At the Al Habtoor Tennis Challenge 2007, with singles match winner, Maria Kirilenko, world #14, WTA ranking 2012 (centre right), and Sheikh Hasher Al Maktoum, President of the Tennis Federation of the UAE.

The Al Habtoor Tennis Challenge 2007 singles match winner, Maria Kirilenko, world #14, WTA ranking 2007, 2012.

"Over the years, I've partnered some of the world's top-ranked tennis players in doubles matches. They include the Serbians' former World Number One players, Novak Djokovic and Ana Ivanovic. Russian players Svetlana Kuznetsova, Vera Zvonareva and Maria Kirilenko, and Victoria Azarenka from Belarus as well as the Australian Jelena Dokic are all well-known players that I've been lucky enough to team up with."

With Vera Zvonareva, world #2, WTA ranking 2010, playing tennis at the Habtoor Grand Resort & Spa in 2009.

With Novak Djokovic, world #1, ATP ranking 2011, playing tennis at the Habtoor Grand Resort & Spa in 2010.

With Ana Ivanovic, world #1, WTA ranking 2008, relaxing after playing tennis at the Habtoor Grand Resort & Spa in 2009.

With Svetlana Kuznetsova, world #2, WTA ranking 2007, playing tennis at the Habtoor Grand Resort & Spa in 2009.

With Victoria Azarenka, world #1, WTA ranking 2012, playing tennis at the Habtoor Grand Resort & Spa in 2010.

With Novak Djokovic (world #1, ATP ranking 2011) and his fiancée Jelena, at my residence in December 2010.

❝Tennis is well and truly in my blood. I always play hard to win, just as I do in life. Challenge is a real adrenalin rush for me and winning is an affirmation of the lynchpin of my life – a can-do philosophy that never accepts second best.❞

Dinner with John Varley, CEO of Barclays (left), along with executives of Barclays and of the Al Habtoor Group at the Habtoor Grand Resort & Spa in October 2009.

With Brady Douga, CEO of Credit Suisse Group in my office in Dubai.

In discussion with Dr Josef Akermann, Chairman of the management board and the group executive committee of Deutsche Bank, at the Habtoor Grand Resort & Spa in November 2008.

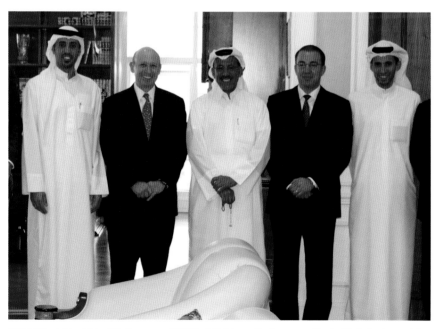

With Lloyd Blankfein, Chairman and CEO of Goldman Sachs at my office in Dubai, along with executives of the Al Habtoor Group and Goldman Sach, in January 2010.

With Stuart Gulliver, Group Chief Executive of HSBC (centre), along with executives of HSBC and of the Al Habtoor Group, at my office in Dubai in 2009.

With James Gorman, Chairman and CEO of Morgan Stanley (centre), along with executives of Morgan Stanley and of the Al Habtoor Group, at my office in Dubai in 2009.

With Jamie Dimon, Chairman of the board and CEO of JP Morgan Chase & Co., at my office in Dubai in 2009.

A company is like a baby. When it is first born it requires 24/7 care and attention. When it's ailing it needs to be nurtured. When it's successful it requires constant supervision. It's a living, breathing entity, into which its founder has poured energy and creativity.

With Stuart Gulliver, Group Chief Executive of HSBC, at my office in Dubai in 2009.

With Christopher Nassetta, President and CEO of Hilton Worldwide, announcing the partnership between the Al Habtoor Group and Hilton at a press conference in October 2011.

With Baron David de Rothschild, Chairman of NM Rothschild and Sons, at my office in Dubai in 2010.

With Carsten Kengeter, member of the group executive board and co-CEO of the UBS Investment Bank at my office in Dubai in 2009.

All too often a company's name is buried with its founder. I want my companies – my babies if you like – to flourish generation after generation.

With Serge Dassault, the Chairman and Chief Executive Officer of the Dassault Group, at the Dassault Group offices in Paris, February 2012.

With Shahbaz Sharif, Chief Minister of Punjab Province in Pakistan in my majlis in Dubai,
during Ramadan 2011.

With Michael Corbin, US Ambassador to the UAE (left) and US Consul General Justin Siberell
(right) at my majlis during Ramadan 2011.

With Richard Olson, US Ambassador to the UAE before leaving his post (right), Justin Siberell, US Consul General (left), and Mohammed Al Habtoor at my office in Dubai in April 2011.

Politics was never far from everyone's mind then. If I wasn't watching a political debate play out on TV or discussing the conflict with my friends in the US military, I was talking regional politics with one of the many visiting congressmen, whom I would often invite to enjoy the hotel's beach resort.

With Rafik Hariri, Prime Minister of Lebanon, during the Conference of Arab Investments in the Arab World held at the Metropolitan Palace Hotel Beirut in the early 2000s.

With Nabih Berri, Speaker of the House of the Lebanese Parliament, in Lebanon in the 1990s.

Holding a lunch for former Prime Minister Salim El Hoss at the Metropolitan Palace Hotel Beirut, in December 2001.

Paying a visit to Rafik Hariri, Prime Minister of Lebanon, at the Hariri residence, in 1992.

With Rafik Hariri, Prime Minister of Lebanon, visiting the Metropolitan Palace Hotel Beirut, in the early 2000s.

With Rafik Hariri, Prime Minister of Lebanon, at the Metropolitan Palace Hotel Beirut, in the early 2000s.

With President Emile Laboud at the Presidential Palace in Lebanon, in the early 2000s.

With HM Queen Elizabeth II, Queen of Great Britain and Northern Ireland, at the Al Habtoor Royal Windsor Cup in June 2012.

With HM Queen Elizabeth II, Queen of Great Britain and Northern Ireland, along with (from left) Rashid Al Habtoor, Mohammed Al Habtoor, Tariq Al Habtoor and Habtoor Al Habtoor during the Al Habtoor Royal Windsor Cup 2009 at Guards Polo Cup, UK.

With HM Queen Elizabeth II, Queen of Great Britain and Northern Ireland, during the Al Habtoor Royal Windsor Cup 2010 at Guards Polo Cup, UK.

With HM Queen Elizabeth II, Queen of Great Britain and Northern Ireland, congratulating Habtoor Al Habtoor during the Al Habtoor Royal Windsor Cup 2011 at Guards Polo Cup, UK.

With HM Queen Elizabeth II, Queen of Great Britain and Northern Ireland, during the Al Habtoor Royal Windsor Cup 2008 at Guards Polo Cup, UK

Receiving an award from the World High Tech Forum, UK, in October 2010. Here with Lord Ahmad, British MP.

> I will always cherish the knighthood bestowed on me by the President of Lebanon, my honorary doctorate degree in Humane Letters from the American University of Science and Technology and the fact that I was elected as 'Man of the Year 2003 for Foreign Investors'. They are prestigious accolades that I'm sincerely proud of, but nothing would make me prouder or happier than to see a patriot in charge of Lebanon.

President Dr Hyam Sakr bestowing upon me an Honorary Doctorate Degree in Humane Letters from the American University of Science & Technology (AUST) in Lebanon in July 2005.

After receiving an Honorary Doctorate Degree in Humane Letters from the American University of Science & Technology (AUST) in Lebanon in July 2005.

Presented with the Gulf Excellence Award by Sheikh Khalifa bin Salman Al Khalifa (left), in appreciation of pioneering spirit and achievements for the UAE at the 4ᵗʰ Gulf Excellence Forum in Bahrain in February 2005.

At the awarding ceremony of the prestigious International Peace Price from the United Cultural Convention of America in my office in March 2004.

At the awarding ceremony of the 'Grand Ambassador of Eminence' award from the American Biographical Institute of the USA in my office in May 2004. I was chosen as a representative of the institute for the UAE.

Receiving a hand-made sand board (picturing a falcon and made from sand collected from the seven emirates) from Dr Tayeb Kamali, Vice Chancellor, Higher College of Technology & Dubai Men's College, United Arab Emirates University, in December 2008.

Presented with a knighthood by the Lebanese Consul General to Dubai by the president of Lebanon in 1995.

Recognised by the Arab American Medical Association (Houston Chapter) for the significant contributions to the Association at the 1st annual 'Ben Khaldoun' awards, in Houston, Texas, USA, in the 1990s.

> All in all, I have few regrets. Of course, I haven't fulfilled all my dreams, but God willing, I still have plenty of time to get through most of my personal wish list.

Elected 'Man of the year 2003 for foreign investments' during the ceremony of 'Woman and Man of the Year 2003' in Beirut, Lebanon, in February 2004.

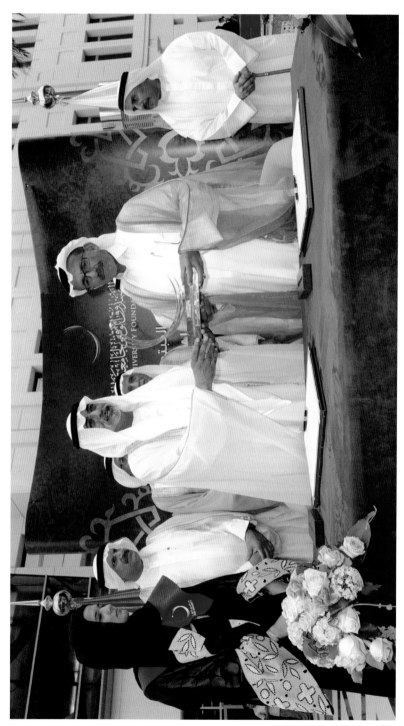

With Sheikh Nahayan Mabarak Al Nahayan, Minister of Higher Education and Scientific Research and President of Zayed University, at the signature of the endowment agreement of Dhs 10m. The agreement established the Khalaf Ahmad Al Habtoor Chair for Business Sciences at the University in May 2011.

At the inauguration of the 'Khalaf Ahmad Al Habtoor Football and Track Stadium' at the American University of Cairo (AUC) in 2010.

With Sheikh Nahayan Mabarak Al Nahayan at the opening of the Khalaf Al Habtoor Assistive
Technology Resource Centre located in Zayed University, in April 2012.

We, my generation, did whatever we could
and now we must get ready to pass the
torch to those that come after us. It is my
fervent hope that they in their own way will
strive to keep it burning bright.

APPENDICES[1]

Covering Letter to President Obama

Thursday, October 29, 2009

President Barack Obama
President of United States of America

Dear Mr. President,

On that historic day in June, when I saw you in Cairo University reaching out to Muslims and Arabs, I realized to what extent we both share the same values. We may be very different in terms of background, culture and experience but we both firmly believe in peace and the sanctity of human life. That common belief inspired me to write to you, today, so as to communicate my thoughts on how best to address the ongoing conflicts in Iraq and Afghanistan.

I take pleasure in presenting to you my enclosed papers 'Iraq: Pathway to Peace and Security' and 'Afghanistan: Strategies for a New Dawn'. Both are roadmaps to swiftly and successfully ending wars you inherited and for which your servicemen and woman are paying a terrible price each day.

I appeal to you, Mr. President, to carefully consider the solutions they proffer towards peace and security for these two nations in turmoil. Their implementation needs a visionary leader like you, who has the courage and the political will to take the right decisions for the good of all concerned.

Lastly, I take this opportunity of wishing you all the best in your noble endeavor of making the world a better place for your two lovely daughters and all the world's children.

Congratulations on your well-deserved Nobel Peace Prize!

Yours truly,
Khalaf A. Al-Habtoor

C.C. President Jimmy Carter
Enclosures: i) "Iraq: Pathway to Peace and Security" ii) "Afghanistan: Strategies for a New Dawn".

---

[1] The appendices have been reproduced in their original form to preserve authenticity. The publisher is not responsible for typos, errors in content and views expressed.

Covering Letter to President Carter

Thursday, October 29, 2009

President Jimmy Carter
Former President of United States of America

Dear President Carter

Thank you for your hand written Letter which I have received with pleasure.

Your visit to me at my farm was an honour and all my family were delighted to meet you and show you the animals and horses..

I hope to see you some time soon.

Mr President I am enclosing an idea, a copy of the letter addressed to President Obama and attachments.

I hope you will read it carefully and if you meet President Obama to discuss this important topic to save the lives of innocent servicemen and women of NATO and USA and people and civilians of Iraq and Afghanistan.

Thank you Sir I wish you all the best and my Best Regards to your family.

Khalaf Al Habtoor

Enclosures: i) "Iraq: Pathway to Peace and Security" ii) "Afghanistan: Strategies for a New Dawn".

Covering Letter to Prime Minister Gordon Brown

Thursday, October 29, 2009

The Rt. Hon. Gordon Brown MP, Prime Minister,
10, Downing Street,
London, SW1A 2AA
United Kingdom

Dear Mr. Brown,

Armistice Day is always a solemn occasion but it was particularly poignant this year when so many young Britons are losing their lives in Afghanistan and so many have died in Iraq. As I watched the laying of wreaths at the Cenotaph, your demeanor spoke of the heavy burden you carry as a premier pursuing a cause that exacts so much sacrifice. It is evident that you are an honorable man endeavoring to bring an unpopular conflict to a peaceful conclusion, who may sometimes feel that his task is thankless. Yet, the strength of your convictions is such that you are willing to forego the lure of electoral gains for what you believe is right; it's a quality you share with one of your predecessors Sir Winston Churchill – and, for that, I salute you.

You may not be able to please all the people all of the time but everyone I know agrees that your career as a politician has been based on a bedrock of principles and conviction. We may be very different in terms of background, life experiences and culture but I am certain that we both firmly believe in peace and the sanctity of human life. That common thread inspired me to write to you with my thoughts on how best to turn the page on Afghanistan and Iraq. Motivated by contributing a new perspective to ending conflicts that have taken such a heavy toll in terms of blood and treasure, I respectfully enclose the following 'roadmaps':

"Afghanistan: Strategies for a New Dawn" and;
"Iraq: Pathway to Peace and Security".

With respect to the latter, while I realize that the United Kingdom no longer has troops in Iraq, it is certainly within Britain's strategic interests to ensure that Iraq emerges whole, economically viable and secure, in collaboration with its U.S. ally.

As a national of the United Arab Emirates who considers England as my second home, I wish for nothing more than to end the pain for people on all sides of the conflicts. I would, therefore, appeal to you, Prime Minister, to consider the solutions proffered by these 'roadmaps' that require implementation by a strong and courageous leader like yourself with the courage to take hard decisions. Your feedback would be greatly appreciated.

Lastly, I take this opportunity of congratulating you on your struggle to make the world a safer place and would like to thank you for your visionary leadership in stemming the global economic downturn, which has been acknowledged worldwide.

Yours sincerely,
Khalaf Ahmad Al Habtoor

Enclosures: i) "Iraq: Pathway to Peace and Security" ii) "Afghanistan: Strategies for a New Dawn".

Covering Letter to the Rt Hon David Cameron MP, Prime Minister

PRIVATE & CONFIDENTIAL
The Rt Hon David Cameron MP
PRIME MINISTER
10 Downing Street, Whitehall
London, SW1A 2AA
Ph: 020.7276 1234
by fedX
Wednesday, June 30, 2010
Re: Solution for Afghanistan

Dear Prime Minister,

Firstly, I would like to congratulate you on your Prime Ministerial appointment, and for your decisive leadership of Britain's new Governing Coalition. I particularly admire your positive energy at this time of economic crisis, and the transparent way you are communicating how your Government intends to tackle existing problems. Although I am a national of the United Arab Emirates, I have long owned a house in the English countryside and consider Britain as my second home.

Congratulations too, on your Government's emergency budget that is tough enough to get the country's economy back on track without hurting low income families; and which offers incentives to small businesses. I am particularly pleased at the way you are dealing with the abuse of housing benefits and disability payments that deplete the UK's coffers, and admire your determination to encourage people who live permanently on social security to return to work.

Mr Cameron, it was with great sadness that I learned last week of the death of the 300th British serviceman serving in Afghanistan. As you said before Parliament, although every single serviceman or woman to lose their lives doing their patriotic duty is a terrible loss, the 300th represents a tragic milestone in this lengthy conflict. Since you spoke those words, regretfully, a further nine have fallen. Moreover, the longer a British military presence remains in Afghanistan, the more challenging it will be for the Government to explain those deaths to a concerned public that has difficulty understanding the reasons behind this presence.

At a time when ordinary Britons are being asked to tighten their belts for at least five years - if not more - it would seem right for the British Government to consider options for a speedy withdrawal of troops from Afghanistan ... that as I am sure you know has the deserved reputation of being the 'Graveyard of Empires'. Unfortunately, your Government has inherited this conflict, which many including myself consider a waste of Allied and Afghan lives, as well as fiscal resources, amid a growing consensus that the solution is political rather than military.

To this end, I have prepared a comprehensive advisory titled "Afghanistan: Strategies for a New Dawn" (attached); an earlier version of which I sent to your predecessor Gordon Brown. I would respectfully request you to peruse this report that offers fresh perspectives on the conflict, as well as ways of bringing it to a satisfactory conclusion for both Britons, Afghans and the world.

I realize how busy you must be, but I would be grateful if you could spare a few moments from your hectic schedule to communicate your thoughts on the enclosed advisory, and in this connection I look forward to hearing from you in due course.

In the meantime, keep up the excellent work! It's comforting to feel that, at last, this great country is in safe and capable hands.

Kind regards,
Yours sincerely,
Khalaf Ahmad Al Habtoor
Chairman

Enclosure: Advisory paper on Afghanistan

Afghanistan: Strategies for a New Dawn

Preamble
The following 'Strategies for a New Dawn' in Afghanistan were inspired by the seeming lack of progress in Afghanistan in terms of security, societal cohesion, women's rights and reconstruction. Afghanistan isn't dubbed 'the Graveyard of Empires' for nothing and the danger is the longer NATO forces remain, the more bogged down in an endless conflict they will become.

Moreover, as the death of NATO soldiers is announced without anything tangible to show for their sacrifice, public opinion in the various member nations is souring. Unless, the US, which leads NATO in this particular conflict, does a policy U-turn, its war will become a harder and harder sell at home.

An August, 2009 Washington Post-ABC news poll shows that a majority of Americans now see the war in Afghanistan as not worth fighting, while a Populus poll of 1509 British adults indicates that 68 percent of Britons want their troops withdrawn within a year.

While it is true that Afghanistan's capital Kabul has benefited from the 2001 invasion in terms of security, modernization and individual freedom, this cannot be said in relation to the rest of the country. A recent report by a respected London-based think tank The International Council on Security and Development displays a map suggesting that the Taliban now control as much as 80 percent of Afghanistan. And it is true to say that they are being funded by the poppy crop that ends up on the streets of Western countries in the form of heroine.

At the same time the credibility of central government has diminished with the recognition that the results of the 2009 election are seriously tainted. This is a blow for democracy. Indeed, Afghans perceive President Hamid Khazai as being Kabul's president and believe that the conservative religious group that once rules them has been replaced by a cabal of thugs, such as the brutal warlord General Abdul Rashid Dostum and Mohamed Qasim Fahim, accused of being involved in criminal gangs and weapons smuggling.

President George W. Bush's promises to Afghan women that they would no longer the subjugated under the heel of religious extremism has also come to naught. According to the Revolutionary Association of the Women of Afghanistan (RAWA) every 30 minutes an Afghan woman dies during childbirth, over 87 percent of Afghan woman are illiterate, 80 percent of young woman are forced into marriage, a third experience physical, psychological or sexual violence, while all Afghan woman can look forward to a life expectancy of only 44 years.

The sad but inescapable truth is that, to date, the US and NATO have not succeeded in their aims of capturing Osama bin Laden and Taliban chief Mullah Omar and neither have they succeeded in bettering the lives of Afghan women, eradicating the Taliban or bringing security to the country overall. This is not for the lack of trying, however. The question now is: should more US and NATO troops be poured into Afghanistan, as some White House advisers are advocating, or will their presence be inflammatory, offering the Taliban insurgents even more targets?

In light of the grip which the Taliban wields over most of the country and the inherent dislike of foreign occupation felt by most Afghans, another way of ensuring that Afghanistan will not revert to being a danger to the US and its allies should be considered.

'Strategies for a New Dawn' was devised following careful analysis of the country's history, conservative ethos, ethnic make-up, terrain and strategic importance.

History
Founded by the Pashtuns - today Afghanistan's largest ethnic group - the word Afghan first saw the light in 982 AD. The modern state was created

in 1747 by a Punjabi Ahmad Shah Durrani. Throughout centuries, it was conquered by Medians, Persians, Alexander the Great, Seleucids, Indo-Greeks, Turks and Mongols. In 1979, the Soviets invaded to prop-up the then socialist government only to withdraw under rebel pressure in 1989 leaving a series of civil wars in their wake. In 1996, a hard-line Pakistani-backed movement the Taliban took power to quell the in-fighting. Their rule was crushing but those who abided by their extremist diktats enjoyed security and they did curtail the growing of opium poppies.

Conservative ethos
The Pashtuns rose up against the Durrani rulers in 1978 when the country was named The Democratic Republic of Afghanistan. Once in power, the People's Democratic Party of Afghanistan moved to permit freedom of religion and attempted to bring women into politics. But the secularist nature of the new government was rejected by conservative villagers who preferred to live under Islamic law. It is worth recalling Western leaders' surprise when, subsequent to the 2001 invasion, Afghan women chose to retain their burkas.

Ethnic make-up
Afghanistan's population of close to 29 million is made up of Pashtun – 42%, Tajik – 27%, Hazara – 9%, Aimak – 4%, Turkmen – 3%, Baloch – 2%, and other 4%. Their cohesion is mostly based on tribal loyalties.

Terrain
Afghanistan's rugged, mountainous terrain and harsh extremes of climate have generally deterred foreign invaders unused to prolonged physical hardship.

Strategic importance
Landlocked and bordered by China, Iran, Pakistan, Tajikistan, Turkmenistan and Uzbekistan, Afghanistan is strategically located. It is a bridgehead to the oil, gas, copper and gold-rich Caspian republics, which was why it was coveted by the Soviets, and it serves as a buffer between nuclear-ambitious Iran and nuclear-armed Pakistan.

The above factors illustrate the difficulties of waging a prolonged war in Afghanistan where the terrain, topography and climate is as unforgiving as the fiercely proud people, whose tribal loyalties transcend recognized borders. This explains why the predominately Pashtun Taliban receive so much support in largely Pashtun North West Pakistan. (Note: Pashtuns comprise over 15.42 percent of Pakistan's population)

A stable Afghanistan would not only be beneficial to the Afghan people but would also cool tensions among pro-Taliban Pakistani sympathizers. Most importantly, a viable Afghanistan at peace with itself and its neighbors would open the door to the homecoming of US and NATO forces, while allowing earmarked funds to be spent on reconstruction instead of security.

Aims and objectives

1. To bring peace and security to Afghanistan while minimizing combat and civilian deaths.
2. To curtail the stay of NATO forces in Afghanistan.
3. To ultimately free up donor money for rebuilding purposes rather than security.
4. To contribute to the stability of Pakistan and the overall region.
5. To win Afghan hearts and minds so that the country will reject extremist foreign elements and their training camps in future.
6. Relieve the government of Pakistan from pressure to take-on Pakistani Taliban, which could ultimately result in a civil war or the emergence of an extremist government with its finger on the nuclear button.

Concrete steps forward

A. Set a timetable for the withdrawal of US-lead NATO forces, which would bring hope to the Afghan people as well as to the families of NATO soldiers, who fear their loves ones may be embroiled in a conflict without end.
B. Ask a reliable neutral country, such as Turkey or Qatar, to broker discrete US negotiations with what are considered "moderate Taliban" on a pre-withdrawal political settlement, whereby they would be included in the democratic future of their country in return for laying down their arms.
C. Continue combating and extracting members of Al Qaeda and affiliated terror groups using either special service forces, such as Britain's SAS and America's Green Berets, or highly trained contractors.

D. Work with those countries bordering Afghanistan to ensure all borders are either sealed or closely monitored to avoid the free movement of elements hostile to Western interests.

E. Prior to the exit of NATO forces, the US and its allies should call a free, fair and monitored presidential election that would be opened up to all contenders including Taliban members with whom an agreement has been reached.

F. Once security has been established, the US and other Western countries should help with democracy building, reconstruction, and the supply of essential services such as potable water and electricity to remote regions while making certain that any donor monies are not siphoned off to line the pockets of corrupt officials.

G. Gradually invite Afghanistan into the international community, help it develop the export of its natural resources, such as natural gas, petroleum, coal, copper, sulfur, lead, zinc, iron ore, salt and precious as well as semi-precious stones while offering cash incentives to farmers not to grow poppies.

H. Assist Afghanistan is developing a well-trained and equipped national army as well as a sophisticated police force.

Conclusion

Military might is useful in certain theatres but Afghanistan isn't one of them due to its tribal allegiances, hostile topography, and anti-Western sentiment made worse by the growing number of civilian casualties. Using force to quell the rise of the Taliban has proven unsuccessful because as commanders often report as soon as they clean out a village from Taliban insurgents and move on, the Taliban re-take their original positions. A mountainous, arid country spanning some 653,000 square kilometers could only be subdued by millions of troops rather than thousands.

When Dr. Marc Sageman of the Foreign Policy Research Institute based in Philadelphia was asked by a Congressional committee on the war whether he backed an Iraq-style troop surge in Afghanistan, he replied thus:

"Let me answer that with an old Middle Eastern proverb. "It's me and my brother against my cousin. But it's me and my cousin against a foreigner. So if we send 40,000 Americans…that will coalesce every local rivalry; they will put their local rivalry aside to actually shoot the foreigners and then they'll resume their own internecine fight…"

Instead the US and its allies should take a hearts and minds approach and agree to brokered negotiations with the Taliban, who are probably just as weary of fighting as US and NATO soldiers surely are.

Once the US and its NATO allies have completed ceasefire agreements with Taliban, warlords and tribal sheikhs (that would provide US special forces the right to stay in country to rout out Al Qaeda for a fixed period), they should call for and monitor a presidential election. Thus, Afghans would be free to choose their own leader instead of one that was initially imposed from outside and who now claims power on the back of a rigged ballot.

Britain's most senior commander in Afghanistan Brigadier Mark Carleton-Smith announced, last year, that the war in Afghanistan cannot be won militarily, and suggested that talks with the Taliban might lead to "precisely the sort of progress" required to end the insurgency.

His conclusion was supported by the U.N. Special Envoy to Afghanistan Kai Eide, who said, "We all know that we cannot win it militarily. It has to be won through political means. That means political engagement." The author of this advisory paper holds the same view.

Letter from Ministry of Defence, London

Operations Directorate
Afghanistan Team
Ministry of Defence
Main Building
Level 5, Zone A, Desk 01
Whitehall, London SW1A 2HB
United Kingdom

Our Ref: TO/2010

Mr Khalaf Ahmad Al Habtoor
PO Box 25444

Dubai
United Arab Emirates

Date: 19 August 2010

Dear Mr Khalaf Ahmad Al Habtoor,

Thank you for your letter dated 30 June 2010 to the Prime Minister and your proposal for a solution for Afghanistan in pursuit of a lasting peace in Afghanistan. Such commitment is both worthy and important indicators of a majority of individuals who only want the best for the people of Afghanistan and the wider region.

The UK national strategy involves protecting the civilian population from the insurgents, supporting more effective government at every level, and building up the Afghan National Security Forces as rapidly as feasible.

We want to see the Afghans take control of their own security. As the Prime Minister said in his statement to Parliament on 14 June 2010, 'Our Forces will not remain in Afghanistan a day longer than is necessary.' President Karzai has made clear he wants to see Afghan Forces assume full responsibility for security by 2014. G8 leaders have endorsed this objective and NATO Allies have agreed that we should seek gradually to transition lead security responsibility from ISAF to Afghan forces, province by province as conditions on the ground allow. So the objective is withdrawal from a combat role by 2015 – and the entire focus of our effort and that of our international and Afghan partners is creating the conditions that will allow that withdrawal.

We are focussing our efforts on building the capacity and capability of the Afghan National Security Forces (ANSF). As this happens, more parts of the country can transition to Afghan control. [Kabul already controlled by the Afghan National Army (ANA)].

With regards to governance, the Kabul Conference has built on the process of transition to Afghan lead and ownership established by the London Conference in January. The Kabul communiqué clearly demonstrates the decisive progress towards good governance that the Afghan Government has made in the six months since London.

The Government of Afghanistan has demonstrated some impressive progress since the London Conference, particularly through economic and electoral reform, the establishment of a High Peace Council to take forward work on reconciliation and reintegration, the introduction of measures to reduce corruption, and the signing of an Afghanistan-Pakistan trade agreement.

However, as you have surmised it is clear that we will not bring about a more secure Afghanistan by military means alone. President Karzai has said that he is willing to reach out to all of his countrymen, providing they cut ties with Al Qa'ida, end violence and live within Afghanistan's constitutional framework. We support him in this. Since the London Conference, the Afghan Government has made good progress on the development of a reconciliation and reintegration programme. The international community can play a role in support of that if requested, for example, through providing funding to help finance this initiative; however, it is important that this is an Afghan process. Therefore whilst your pledge of support is welcome any additional help would be inappropriate at this time.

Yours sincerely
Mark Revell
Assistant Head Operations Directorate

Iraq: Pathway to Peace and Security

Preamble

The following 'Pathway to peace and security' in Iraq was created due to the prevailing turmoil and violence in that country, which has robbed the lives of over 4,600 American military personnel, and untold numbers of Iraqi civilians. With the bulk of US troops set to withdraw from Iraq in 2011 – as per the Status of Forces Agreement signed by Former President George W. Bush – it is imperative that law, order and security be maintained following their departure. A strong leader and a united government are urgently needed to prevent Iraq from descending into anarchy, becoming an inter-factional battleground, and/or becoming a hostile state allied with an increasingly powerful, anti-Western Iran.

This blueprint was devised bearing in mind Iraq's cultural donation, political history, ethnic make-up, strategic importance and global asset-value in terms of oil-wealth.

Cultural donation: The land on which present-day Iraq stands was formerly Mesopotamia (Land between the rivers.) It is revered as "The Cradle of Civilization" because it was here that the world's oldest writing, artworks, glass and metallurgical objects were discovered. Over the centuries it was culturally enhanced by the Hellenistic, Parthian, Sassanid, Roman, Rashidun, Umayyad, Abbasid, Ottoman and British empires.

Political history: The independent state of Iraq was founded in 1932 under the rule of King Faisal bin Al-Hussein bin Ali Al-Hashemi. On July 14th, 1958, the Hashemite monarchy was overthrown when the country was ruled by a succession of Sunni presidents. On 17th of July 1968, the Arab socialist Baath Party took power and held ruling monopoly until the 2003 invasion.

Ethnic make-up: Arab 75% - 80%, Kurdish 15% - 20%, Assyrian, Turkoman or other 5%. (Note: Until 2003, people of different ethnicity lived together, worked together, prayed together and often intermarried in what was considered a secular Arab state)

Strategic importance: Iraq has borders with Saudi Arabia, Jordan, Syria, Turkey, Iran, Kuwait and the Shatt Al-Arab waterway at the head of the Arabian Gulf. Until 2003, it was considered by Western powers as a buffer to the military ambitions of neighboring Iran, while its unified existence allayed Turkish fears of an impending Kurdish state on its borders. Its stability and security, therefore, affects the entire Middle East region.

Global asset value: Reserves of 112.5 billion barrels of crude oil and, 3.17 trillion cubic meters of natural gas, proved to be commercially recoverable.

On all the above counts, Iraq's continuation as a unified, independent and peaceful nation is imperative and it should not be abandoned to the ongoing chaos and bloodshed. Maintaining Iraq as a Democratic entity is a laudable ideal but it may not be feasible at this juncture in the country's history when voters are subjected to threats and intimidation, while others cast their ballots according to the diktats of religious, party or tribal leaders. It's, therefore, felt that a temporary moratorium on democracy – say three to five years – should be instituted in favor of an appointed authoritarian leader whose main responsibility would be to combat the insurgency and to keep his people and his country safe.

Once painful wounds are healed and divisions mended, Democracy's true spirit can then be re-introduced to Iraq, whose people, known for their education, sophistication and culture, will be ready to embrace it.

Aims and objectives

1. To save lives of the brave US and NATO servicemen and women and innocent Iraqi people;
2. To bring peace, security, stability and, ultimately, Democracy in its truest sense, to Iraq.
3. To ensure that Iraq does not become a terrorist haven.
4. To re-create Iraq as a military buffer to potential Iranian ambitions in the Gulf.
5. To release the United States and its coalition allies from their post-invasion responsibilities – both militarily and financially - a US burden which has already exceeded US$ 700 billion.
6. To re-mould Iraq as a strong ally of the West and to enable it to protect US and GCC interests throughout the Middle East, the Subcontinent, and South-West Asia.

Concrete steps forward

A. The calling of a State of Emergency in light of the burgeoning violence and death toll. (*From the 16th October – 25th October, insurgents' bombs in Nineveh Province and Baghdad killed more than 170 and injured over 600*)
B. The dissolution of Parliament and the stripping from office of the incumbent Prime Minister and Presidents, Nouri Al Maliki and Jalal Talabani respectively. (Note: As head of the Dawa Party (*a former militant Shiite group that supported Iran's Islamic Revolution) and in light of his self-exile in Iran as well as his former ties to Hezbollah, Mr. Al Maliki should not be Iraq's custodian. Likewise, Mr. Talabani who is a non arab and a minority leader, cannot be said to have a unified Iraq at heart when he has spent his career in the Patriotic Union of Kurdistan (PUK) pursuing Kurdish independence*).
C. The appointment of an interim caretaker president and prime minister with a military background prepared to wield an iron fist in a velvet glove. They should share the goals of peace and security as well as that of a unified, secular Iraq seeking an equal partnership in the community of nations. (*These individuals should be anointed based on their overall popularity, patriotism, secularism, and ideals rather than their ethnicity or religious affiliations. Ideally, the President should be drawn from the Arab Sunni community, who do historically have experience over centuries of high position and governance and does not harbor any allegiance to Iran.*)

D. The awarding of interim ministerial posts to mainly Arab Sunnis as well as to Arab Shiites and Kurds, who have proved that their first loyalty is towards a united, secular Iraq rather than their respective parties, sheikhs, tribal leaders or neighboring powers.

E. The relaxation of current regulations that bar former Baath Party members from rising to high office. (*Note: During Saddam Hussein's rule, becoming a nominal Baathist was the only option open to talented ambitious individuals who sought to rise up through the military and civil ranks. However, in most cases, their membership does not indicate that they necessarily shared the party's principles or supported Saddam's ruthless tactics. For all its faults, the Baathists did bring to Iraqis personal security and a high standard of living that prior to the country's 1991 invasion of Kuwait was enviable.*)

F. The reconstitution of Iraq's national army/navy/air force to include commanders, officers and service personnel who served in the military prior to 2003. Anyone who ever served in Iraq's armed services should be invited to re-join and enabled to do so once they have been carefully vetted. (*Note: Disbandment of Iraq's military has been acknowledged by US officials to have been a wrong step. It has led to individual exclusion, anti-US feeling, joblessness, and provided an armed pool of insurgent volunteers*).

G. The firm sealing of the Iraqi/Iranian and the Iraqi/Syrian borders and the close monitoring of all other borders to exclude the illegal import of weapons and bar would-be terrorists from entering the country.

H. The setting up of a 'Truth and Reconciliation' process South-African-style that would facilitate forgiveness rather than revenge and provide renewed optimism for future societal cohesion.

I. The international monitoring of Iraq's fiscal funds to reduce corruption and to ensure that Iraq's funds are spent on reconstructing infrastructure, electricity/water supplies, and medical facilities.

Conclusion

There can be no freedom in an atmosphere of fear while democracy cannot flourish among the weeds of violence. Such lofty and worthwhile ideals should be postponed until Iraqis feel secure on their own soil. Iraq needs strong, impartial leadership to guide it safely through the current quagmire of insecurity and mistrust. An Iraq that functions under the rule of law and order is a prerequisite of democracy.

A unified, secure and secular Iraq brought about by temporary authoritarian rule would not only benefit the Iraqi people but also Gulf States suspicious of Iran's long term agenda. Furthermore, an open door to former Baath members to aspire to ministerial level and above would go a long way to dissolving grudges. Likewise, a Truth and Reconciliation commission would dampen hurts and the desire for revenge.

Moreover, once Iraq is in a position to defend itself with a highly-trained and well-equipped experienced military, it can once again stand as a buffer to Iran's ambitions, combat extremists and terrorists and work towards restoring regional stability. In this way, the US can rightly declare victory and walk away in the knowledge that although the invasion itself has been widely acknowledged as a blunder, the final result was, in the end, worthwhile.

Finally, while it is recognized that the above 'Concrete steps forward' represents a departure from US policy on Iraq to date, severe problems sometimes require courageous solutions that may appear drastic to some. The US currently has a small window of opportunity to make brave decisions that can change Iraq's fate – and its own place in history – forever.

Have Mercy on Lebanon

A neutral monitoring of political and parliamentary activities over the world prove that such activities would be bustling with life only due to differences in visions, opinions and analyses among the many trends that forms the nerve of the political scene in any nation.

Such differences must be founded if they do not exist, so as to reform performance. Furthermore, the change of governments is a very important matter to rectify the efforts, the civic, political and economical life in all countries.

All countries realize this fact, and submit to its natural rules that focus on political pluralism, contradicting ideological currents. Every civic, political or ideological community, throughout history abound with diversified currents that are sometimes contradicting.

However, differences in opinions in the civilized democratic world, never led to serious structural and economic cracks as is the case presently in Lebanon.

Let's take the UK for example - a country that is the mother of democracy, experienced several discords among its parties and political entities. But these differences were always solved via the institutions and the final judgment came from the Parliament, which is binding. There is nothing in the UK history that shows any reference of such discords to the public in the streets, although the public, with their inflammatory nature could be easily used.

Shouldn't we derive a lesson out of that?
Several years ago, Britain's capitol, London, suffered from the bombings and subversive acts of the IRA. Didn't those terrorist operations affect life in general in the UK? The answer is a definite "yes".

British press and media took a united stand despite their differences, and – without coordination – carried front page headlines that continuously promoted security and stability, stressed the importance of continued production and work. This helped national economy to continue to grow despite those bad days. The media did not resort to scaring residents, whether British or expatriates, nor did they try to frighten the tourists and investors.

I have no intention of hinting, or making you guess. I am talking directly about the Lebanese media that was for a long period the sight, the press and the TV of the Arabs.

I want to say to Lebanese media, which I respect and have good relations with: "Stop the incitement, focus on the cultural face of Lebanon far from the flames of politics".

Months ago, out of fear for Lebanon, I made an appeal stating that the continuation of this state of factionist would lead to something that is similar to a revolution of the hungry, as a result of the expansion of unemployment.

Wouldn't such state lead to an impasse? The gap between the leaders and the people is widening, and the wound is becoming deeper and would become in the near future, God forbids, incurable.

Many employees lost their jobs in the past 6 weeks, and more are expected to join them, which means that a lot of Lebanese families will join the world of poverty and instability.

Who is responsible for that?

Let any entity in Lebanon take the trouble of investigating the losses inflicted on the Lebanese economy during the near past.

Do they know that Lebanon's losses stand at billions, and that this loss is expected to increase even further due to the paralysis of the company?

Do they know how many investors were planning to invest or expand their investments in Lebanon, and cancelled their plans?

Who is the loser? Definitely there is a big loser, and there is no winner.

The loser is the Lebanese citizen, the Lebanese economy and Treasury.

And who is responsible, isn't it the Lebanese political class?

When I talk about that, I am not neutral but bias to Lebanon, to its development, growth, security and economic stability.

Hunger constitutes a good background for terrorism, and it is the gate to chaos, it is the right environment for the absence of law... so please, have mercy on Lebanon.

A big part of the Lebanese community is absent or forced to be absent. And I don't know why it does not play a stronger role. They are responsible before history and before the people.

Responsibility is not limited to the officials, for it is a patriotic act that should be carried spontaneously by:

- The intellectuals
- The businessmen
- The economists

Those are the ones that should take the initiative to stand by their companies, so as to stop this continuous breakdown.

It is no secret that nobody would help Lebanon, if it does not help itself.

Are the Lebanese aware that the world is split in the way they see the Lebanese events? Some gloat some just watch, and some rejoice; but few are sad or even frightened and want to help Lebanon.

This is a painful situation, but it is true; and it can be changed only by the Lebanese. Nobody in the world would give a country what its own people refuse to give.

One final time I say: "Have mercy on Lebanon."

I do not regret writing this message, and I do not consider it an intervention in your affairs, because I am not neutral towards what happens in your country.

I am with you, when you bleed, I bleed too. The end of the tunnel is within reach and clear, but it needs a brave decision that's unselfish.

I am sure that Lebanon abound with that quality of leaders and people; but when?

Khalaf Ahmed Al Habtoor

Covering Letter to President Carter

Dubai, July 5th 2012.

To President Jimmy Carter

Dear Mr. President,

I apologise for not being able to see you in Europe during your visits. I hope you and your family are in good shape and health.

I enclose a proposal and its essence and main points I believe warrant further debate. I would very much like to ask your opinion on how we can progress the points I make in some form of dialogue.

My idea is to bring together like minded colleagues from Palestine, Israel, Egypt and the GCC in a conference to be held at a mutually acceptable location and hammer out these points to form a solution to be presented in a cohesive document.

I would value your comments on this idea and your suggestions for participants. I look forward to progressing this very important issue.

Best regards,

Khalaf Ahmad Al Habtoor

Cc: Mr. Curtis Kohlhaas
     Dr. Hrair Balian

Palestinian/Israeli Resolution

With all that's happening in the Arab world, it saddens me greatly that international efforts towards a Palestinian state have been placed on the backburner.

Unfortunately in these days, the idea of a Palestinian state is on the point of being shelved and we must rearrange our priorities to make it on the top of our list.

My aim is not to point fingers at who to blame. The fact is that the tragic situation we are in is primarily due to Israel's unwillingness to compromise and its expansion on Palestinian land in east Jerusalem and the West Bank. The international community is also guilty by default. The majority of UN member countries, including the US, proclaim their backing for a Palestinian state, but shy away from holding any Israeli governments responsible.

The blame game gets us nowhere, so let us put aside the rights and wrongs of the argument and be realistic.

There is one point on which I am confident we can all agree.

Palestinians, whether in Gaza, the West Bank or refugees anywhere in the Arab world, live a life that we wouldn't wish on our worst enemies. Palestinians are abandoned to needless misery and humiliation. In most of their host countries, they are fated to remain stateless and jobless, and they do not have the right to own land or open their own businesses. Sadly they do not even have access to decent health care and education for their children.

As an Arab and a rational human being, I cannot help but feel ashamed that we are abandoning them.

The Camp David Accords may have sounded good at the time but, in practice, for the Palestinians rights and the right to return, it wasn't successful. It's time that we admit that and create a Plan B.

That is why I am suggesting that we meet and work together towards achieving some humble realistic goals for our Palestinian brothers, which I believe should be based on the Arab Peace Initiative proposed by King Abdullah of Saudi Arabia during a 2002 Arab League summit.

However, due to changing circumstances since then, I would suggest a meeting to discuss the following stipulations, keeping in mind that these points will not take away from the fact that they will always consider Palestine as their motherland.

The meeting agenda will discuss;

1. The 'refugee' status must be lifted and Palestinians must be allowed to be true residents in the country in which they presently reside.
2. They must have access to first-class education and training so that they can gain skills that can benefit both their families and their newly-adopted homelands.
3. Creating a Housing Fund, supported internationally, for the construction of homes for Palestinians in the appropriate designated homeland.
4. A reasonable/feasible approach should also be taken with respect to Israel, again for the sake of Palestinians. So rather than battling over this sacred soil beloved by all Abrahamic prophets, Israelis and Arabs must find a way to peacefully coexist.
5. A committee should be appointed made up of respected Palestinians, Israelis and selected representatives from Arab states to negotiate directly with the Israeli government.
6. Talks should be without preconditions on both sides with one exception. Israeli settlement expansion should come to a halt; the reasons for this are obvious.

With hope of success I suggest this, but if all fails or an independent Palestinian state is no longer practical in the light of realities on the ground, Palestinians should be offered the choice to pursue either a 'One-state solution' or an autonomous region within an Israeli/Palestinian federation.

We must work together to try and give our Palestinian brothers a decent life, an existence which we take for granted. Likewise, a good outcome from this will affect Israelis positively and will allow them to live peacefully with the Palestinians instead of living behind isolating high walls.

Khalaf Ahmad Al Habtoor

Dubai, July 5th 2012.

Tribute to Lady Diana

Tragedy has become an inescapable part of our lives. Each time we switch on the television set, listen to the radio, or open a newspaper, we are presented with the latest disaster to have "shocked" the world. Why? Because as far as the international media is concerned, tragedy is sensation, sensation makes news, and news sells. The formula to attract an audience is so predictable, the barrage of bad news so intense, that we are becoming immune to the suffering of other people. Our instinct is to switch off, to ignore, to try and forget.

In view of this, perhaps the biggest "sensation" surrounding the tragic and untimely death of Diana, Princess of Wales, was the overwhelming response of not just the British people but of countless millions the world over. The scenes at the British Consulate here in Dubai, of people leaving flowers to express their heartfelt sympathy, were no different from those at consulates and embassies throughout the world. All of us, regardless of nationality, were distraught at the loss of the "People's Princess", who had touched our lives with her tireless compassion and enchanting beauty .

Princess Diana singlehandedly redefined the British monarchy. Instead of hiding behind veils of royal protocol, she met her challenges head on and her spellbound admirers face to face. A self-styled Queen of Hearts, she made charitable causes her life's work and her commitment to them remained rock solid, even after her traumatic breakaway from the royal family. Only weeks before her death, she visited victims of the war in Bosnia, and, earlier in the year, when others had stayed away, she travelled to Pakistan as part of a fund-raising campaign for cancer patients.

If perhaps Diana's agendas were becoming more controversial towards the end, her one true passion - children - remained constant. Her unique rapport with children from all nations and walks of life was a central part of the public's fascination with her. And although the pressures of being in the public glare were steadily mounting, Diana never lost sight of her duties as a mother, raising her two sons to appreciate their own challenges responsibly and with humility.

The People's Princess was an example to us all: courageous, compassionate and fiercely independent. Whatever the cynical tactics of the media over the years to milk sensation from the tragedies of everyday life, the events of the past month have shown that we haven't lost our ability to feel. Diana, Princess of Wales, shall always remain a part of our lives, an abiding image of the fairy tale she was meant to be but sadly never was.

This is also a time when we are mourning the terrible loss of Mother Teresa, whose lifelong contribution to the cause of love and peace was simply immeasurable. In this edition, we pay her tribute.

Khalaf A. Al Habtoor

This was published as the 'Chairman's Message' in Al Shindagah *magazine, October 1997.*

Woman of Distinction: Mother Teresa

Wherever people needed comfort, Mother Teresa always seemed to be there, whether it was during Ethiopia's famine, Chernobyl's fallout, or Armenia's earthquake disaster.

Mother Teresa's response to being told she had won the Nobel Peace Prize, in many ways sums up her selfless attitude. "I am not worthy," she said.

But for nearly five decades, she worked to ease the suffering of the poor in Calcutta and around the world, and earned more than eighty national and international honours. She was in every sense - worthy.

The Missionaries of Charity Order, which Mother Teresa founded, now comprises at least 4,500 nuns in more than 100 countries. Their mission? To show the poor they are loved.

Mother Teresa was born to Albanian parents, Agnes Goinxha Bejaxhiu in August 1910. She became a nun at the age of 18, and originally travelled to Calcutta to teach geography at one of the city's convent schools.

Her divine calling to work among the poor came in 1946, when she set up her first home for the dying in a Hindu rest home after seeing a poor woman rejected by a hospital.

Mother Teresa went on to create a global network of homes for the poor, everywhere from the shanties of Calcutta to the ghettos of New York. She was also behind one of the first homes for AIDS sufferers.

Her work was financed by public foundations, private donors and many, many awards, including the 1979 Nobel Peace Prize for almost $200,000.

The woman known by so many in India as simply "Mother", took her full name from the French Saint, Theresa of the Child Jesus.

For many Mother Teresa was a living saint, and the description of her as the "Saint of the Gutters" will remain the strongest and most symbolic legacy of her work. There have already been calls for her to be canonised.

We shall remember Mother Teresa as a small, bowed woman, wrinkled by age and work, and yet despite her frailty, she was unquestionably one of the most resilient human beings the world has ever known. Her conviction seemed to give her an unfaltering sense of strength, empowering her to stand tall for the rejected, the poor, the downtrodden, all in the name of human kindness.

Wherever people needed comfort, Mother Teresa always seemed to be there, whether it was during Ethiopia's famine, Chernobyl's fallout, or Armenia's earthquake disaster.

The Pope John Paul knew the respect and power she commanded the world over and was one of her greatest admirers; Mother Teresa is believed to be the only woman with whom he has shared his famous Popemobile!

Mother Teresa's passing away in the same week as Diana, Princess of Wales, has meant the world has lost two if this century's most famous humanitarians. The pair met four times, most recently at the Missionaries of Charity residence in New York, this June.

There appears to be little point in comparing these two truly great women, as some have attempted to do. Neither would have placed their role above the other - surely the motivation behind their work was compassion and selflessness, not competition.

In March of this year, due to Mother Teresa's increasingly failing health, Sister Nirmala was elected to succeed her as the leader of the Missionaries Charity. It is some comfort at least for the thousands of people around the world who have mourned her passing, that Mother Teresa's Order and its work will live on, devoted like she was to doing all that is good.

Julia Wheeler

This article was commissioned as a tribute to Mother Teresa and was published in Al Shindagah *magazine, October 1997.*

Khalaf Ahmad Al Habtoor:
A Biographical Note

Khalaf Ahmad Al Habtoor is a prominent and highly respected citizen of the United Arab Emirates. A self-made man, he's Chairman of the Al Habtoor Group – one of the most successful conglomerates in the Gulf.

Al Habtoor is known not only for his many business achievements but also his extensive knowledge of international political affairs; his philanthropic activity; his efforts to promote peace; and the fact that he has long acted as an unofficial ambassador for his country abroad.Writing extensively on both local and international politics, he publishes regular articles in the media and has released a number of books.

Al Habtoor began his career as an employee of a local UAE construction firm and in 1970 established his own company, Al Habtoor Engineering. The UAE Federation, which united the seven emirates under one flag for the first time, was founded in 1971 and this inspired him to undertake a series of innovative construction projects – all of which proved highly successful.

The company later became the Al Habtoor Group and over the last forty years, it has grown with the United Arab Emirates. Today it's recognised as one of the most prominent business corporations in the region with interests not just throughout the Middle East, but around the world.

While best known for construction, it's also recognised for its luxury hotels, real estate companies, educational establishments, insurance groups, automobile dealerships and publishing sector. Today, it employs thousands of people and continues to grow.

Al Habtoor's long list of awards and achievements reflect not only his business acumen. He believes it is his strength in the face of adversity; his willingness to take calculated risks; and the fact that he's always looking ahead, that has enabled the Al Habtoor Group to grow and diversify.

Known for his optimistic outlook and warm personality, Al Habtoor is well respected by his associates and considered a well-balanced and progressive man. An active member of society, he feels it is his civic duty to contribute to his country in any way that he can. He's also a devoted family man who loves meeting new people, enjoys acquiring knowledge and looks forward with pleasure to each new day.

CURRENT POSITIONS
- Chairman of the Al Habtoor Group
- Chairman of Dubai National Insurance and Reinsurance Company

FORMER POSITIONS
- Member of the Federal National Council
- Member of the Board of Directors of the Dubai Chamber of Commerce and Industry
- Chairman of the Commercial Bank of Dubai
- Member of The John F. Kennedy School of Government, Harvard University
- The only non-US member of The World Board of Governors of the American United Services Organisation (USO) (1994–1997)

AWARDS AND ACHIEVEMENTS
- Knighthood from the President of Lebanon (1995)
- Grand Ambassador of Eminence award from the American Biographical Institute, in recognition of professional achievements and social contribution to the UAE (2004)
- Included in *ABI Leading Intellectuals of the World*, listed amongst an elite group of men and women, dedicated to making improvements in society (2005)
- Genius Laureate of the UAE from the American Biographical Institute, for 'Distinguished progression and mastery in the field of accomplished leadership' as recorded in the *500 Greatest Geniuses of the 21st Century* (2006)
- Gold Laurels Award from ABI, for triumphant deeds based on excellence in numerous achievements in the field of accomplished leadership (2007)
- Honorary Doctorate degree in Humane Letters from the American University College of Science and Technology in Beirut (2005)
- International Peace Prize from the United Cultural Convention of America, recognising achievements in peace and justice across political, religious and ethnic divisions
- Appreciation awards from International Indigent Orphan Relief Organisation, Palestinian Children's Relief Fund, Al Ain Centre for Handicapped Children and Rashid Paediatric Therapy Centre
- Gulf Excellence Award of the United Arab Emirates, presented by His Highness Prime Minister Sheikh Khalifa Bin Salman Al Khalifa, at the Gulf Excellence Forum Bahrain (2005)
- World Forum Award from the British Parliament, for efforts to build bridges between the Arab World and the West (2007)
- Businessman of the Year Award at the 2007 Arabian Business Achievement Awards in Abu Dhabi (2007)
- Sharjah Voluntary Work Award from His Highness Sheikh Dr Sultan Bin Mohammed Al Qasimi, Member of the Supreme Council of the UAE and Ruler of Sharjah (2009)
- The American University of Cairo Honour, as a generous benefactor and in particular for funds donated to build the 'Khalaf Ahmad Al Habtoor Football Stadium and Track' (2010)
- Honorary Doctorate of Humane Letters from Illinois College (2010)
- Honorary Member of the Phi Alpha Literary Society, a sorority which counts amongst its members the sixteenth American President, Abraham Lincoln and US Congressman, Paul Findley (May 2010)
- Outstanding Business Leadership Award from the All-Party Group on Entrepreneurship and the British Institute of Technology and E-commerce at the World High Tech Forum in London, for exceptional leadership qualities, acumen and vision (2010)
- Honour from The American University of Sharjah, in recognition of contribution to the AUS endowment fund (2011)
- Shield of Merit Award from The United Nations, in recognition of support for the Palestinian cause (2011)
- A number of awards and medals over the years from Red Crescent Society of the UAE, in recognition of ongoing financial support, the most recent being the prestigious 'Medal of the Red Crescent for Humanitarian Action' in July 2012

INDEX